International Trade and Investment _____

International Trade and Investment A Managerial Approach

ALEX O. WILLIAMS
University of Virginia

1807 1982

A Wiley-Interscience Publication
JOHN WILEY & SONS
New York • Chichester • Brisbane • Toronto • Singapore

Library of Congress Cataloging in Publication Data

Williams, Alex O., 1934-
   International trade and investment.

   "A Wiley-Interscience publication."
   Bibliography: p.
   Includes index.
   1. Commerce.   2. Investments, Foreign.
   3. International economic relations.
   I. Title.

   HF1411.W56   658.8′48   82-2828
   ISBN 0-471-03293-X   AACR2

Printed in the United States of America

10 9 8 7 6 5 4 3 2 1

To
Eunice, Pierre, and Annetta

Preface _____

In the second half of this century, several developments have fostered a growing realization of the dependence of countries on the resources and production of other countries in the world economy. European regional integration gave birth to the European Economic Community and the European Free Trade Area. The growing dependence of U.S. firms on raw materials and products from foreign markets has increased American involvement in the world economy. Transnational enterprises have developed worldwide export markets and built worldwide distribution systems to serve the foreign markets. These firms have also developed worldwide networks of production systems to manufacture components that are shipped to assembly points in other countries, with the finished products exported to their global markets.

A growing number of U.S. firms participate in world trade and foreign investment in one way or another. Their managers need to know the concepts and methods of international trade and investment. They can use this knowledge to formulate strategies to improve their performance and develop skills to help them compete effectively in international business.

Previous texts on international trade and investment have taken the macroeconomic viewpoint of looking at the effect of foreign trade on the economies of the trading countries and the benefit of international investment to the recipient countries. International business texts have emphasized the political, social, and cultural factors affecting international trade and foreign investment.

This book deals with the microeconomic aspects of international trade and foreign direct investment. It is written specifically for managers and for students in business schools who will be managers. Its primary focus is the trading firm and how its managers can use international economic and business concepts in planning the company's strategy for foreign exports or investment. The growth of the multinational corporation and the emergence of the transnational enterprise as the main channels of international trade and direct foreign investment dictate this microeconomic emphasis.

The book is divided into four parts. The first part includes five chapters dealing with international trade and country risk. Chapter 1 presents an overview of the dimensions of world trade and foreign investment and the competitive position of the United States in world trade. In Chapter 2, the rationale of trade is examined in order to develop some understanding of why countries trade with each other. It is important that the manager understand the nature of the forces that influence the structure and direction of world trade.

Chapter 3 examines the barriers to free trade that governments sometimes impose in order to foster growth and development in their domestic economies. The chapter goes on to discuss specific trade barriers and the efforts made since World War II to reduce them by way of multilateral trade negotiations, which culminated in the Tokyo Round Agreements. Chapter 4 uses the information discussed in the first three chapters to sketch various strategies that a firm can use in export management. A variety of factors contributing to country risk are examined in Chapter 5; alternative approaches to measuring country risk are evaluated and strategies are developed to minimize risk.

Part 2 covers balance of payments and the international payments mechanism. Chapter 6 analyzes the balance of payments in a way that facilitates understanding its components and the remedies available to fix any imbalance. A country's balance-of-payments policies affect its international trade and its foreign investment problems and opportunities, so an understanding of the balance of payments of specific countries can aid a firm in planning its international operations.

The foreign exchange market is examined in Chapter 7, followed by a discussion of how foreign exchange rates are determined. Chapter 8 discusses the kinds of risks to which firms in international trade are exposed because of foreign exchange rate fluctuations and outlines strategies to cope with such risks.

Part 3 treats the international capital markets and the institutions that provide financing and guarantees for international trade and foreign investments. The offshore banking system and the international capital markets are presented in Chapter 9. Chapter 10 deals with private sources of financing, which are provided largely by commercial banks, and Chapter 11 examines the array of guarantee programs provided by the Export-Import Bank in support of private financing, as well as the bank's medium- and long-term direct financing programs. Chapter 12 is a survey of the export credit financing systems of national and regional agencies.

Part 4 deals with the foreign direct investment of transnational and multinational enterprises. Chapter 13 outlines the dynamics of decision-making in foreign investment and the factors influencing decisions. Techniques for evaluating foreign projects and other opportunities for direct foreign investment are developed in Chapter 14. In Chapter 15 the transnational enterprise's role in the internationalization of production processes and technological diffusion is examined, as well as strategies that have been developed for locating industries in foreign countries.

ALEX O. WILLIAMS

Charlottesville, Virginia
April 1982

Acknowledgments _____

In an undertaking of this magnitude, one normally obtains the assistance of a variety of individuals and institutions. I would therefore like to express my gratitude for the useful comments made by my academic colleagues at the University of Virginia and elsewhere who reviewed parts, or the whole draft, of the manuscript. The chapter on country risk has benefited from the many class discussions with banking executives who took my course on country risk while attending the Center for International Banking Studies programs at the University of Virginia.

I am also grateful to my professional colleagues who made special contributions in reviewing parts of the manuscript and suggesting changes that significantly improved its quality. While I cannot mention everyone, I would like to express my appreciation to William T. H. Huxtable, Director, International Lending Division, Robert Morris Associates; Arthur Bardenhagen, Irving Trust Company; R. Alex McCullough, Export-Import Bank of the United States; Felton McL. Johnston, Overseas Private Investment Corporation.

Various members of the staff of the U.S. Department of Commerce, the Treasury Department, the International Monetary Fund, and the World Bank provided invaluable assistance at various times during the development of the manuscript, for which I am very grateful.

My very special thanks to Bette Collins who went through several drafts of the manuscript to make them readable and accurate, and to Nina Hutchinson who typed the entire manuscript.

The editorial staff at John Wiley & Sons did the final editing, making many suggestions for improving the clarity of the text.

Finally, my heartfelt gratitude to my wife, and to my son and daughter, who provided encouragement and support during the preparation of this book.

A. O. W.

Contents _____

Contents   xvii

1

World Trade

1

World Trade
and Investment

World trade affects almost everyone in one way or another. Some countries are more closely tied to cross-border trading than other countries, of course, and world trade has a different impact on the economy of each country. Until the Marshall Plan, following the cessation of hostilities in World War II, the United States' involvement in world trade was minimal in comparison with that of the other world powers. The U.S. economy was partly insulated from world trade because the country had an abundance of raw material resources and a large and rapidly growing domestic market which expanded as the Western frontier was pushed toward the Pacific Ocean.

The massive economic aid under the Marshall Plan brought many U.S. businesses into international trade for the first time, and the high demand for U.S. products during the European reconstruction period maintained the momentum of U.S. exports. Later, some of these exporters established branches, subsidiaries, and affiliates abroad in an effort to maintain their European markets when tariff barriers were installed.

RECENT DEVELOPMENTS IN WORLD TRADE

Some developments in world trade in the last decade have made business firms and consumers in the United States increasingly aware of the importance of world trade and its effect on the economy. These developments include (1) the growing realization of the dependence of countries on the resources and production of other countries in the world economy, (2) European regional integration, (3) the rapid growth of transnational enterprises and their impact on world trade, (4) the General Agreement on Tariffs and Trade (GATT), (5) the effort to promote free trade, and (6) technological advances in transportation and communication, which have significantly reduced real distance, thereby bringing the countries closer together. These developments have changed the structure and development of world trade.

Interdependence and International Trade

Industrial and developing countries are increasingly interdependent in the world economy. Industrial countries are short of raw materials for their production processes and must import them from developing countries that have abundant natural resources. For their part, developing countries lack the technological know-how to manufacture the products they need and must depend on the manufacturing exports from the industrial economies for these requirements. Differences in technology, production techniques, and factor endowments (capital, labor, natural resources) give firms in some countries a competitive advantage over firms in other countries in the production of some goods. Therefore, firms in the industrial economies have come to specialize in the production of items in which they have a competitive advantage, and these firms export some of their output to other countries. This process forms the core of world trade. Concepts underlying the direction and structure of world trade will be discussed in more detail in Chapter 2.

Regional Integration and Direct Foreign Investment

Another development in world trade took place when the European Economic Community (EEC) was formed in 1957 and created a customs union for both industrial and agricultural goods.[1] Cross-border tariffs among members of the community were eliminated, and an external tariff was set up to deter imports from countries outside the EEC. The new trade barriers affected the exports of U.S. firms that had been exporting to the members of the EEC before the community was created; the barriers made exports into the EEC more expensive and, therefore, less competitive. At the same time, the trade barriers made the establishment of production facilities within the community more profitable. To protect their markets, then, some of the U.S. firms established branches, subsidiaries, and affiliates in the EEC, which encouraged direct investment and the growth of the modern-day multinational corporation.

The European Free Trade Association (EFTA) was formed in 1960 when negotiations failed to expand the EEC to include all members of the Organization for Economic Cooperation and Development (OECD).[2]

Growth of Transnational Enterprises

The transnational enterprise (TNE) has become an important factor in world trade. The production and marketing expertise of this kind of firm greatly facilitates the flow of goods and services across national frontiers. The TNEs have developed worldwide markets for their products and created worldwide distribution systems to serve the national markets. In a similar way, TNEs have developed worldwide production processes through which parts manufactured in the United States, Great Britain, France, or West Germany, for example, are purchased for assembly in, say, South Korea, Singapore, Taiwan, or Panama. The assembled products are then exported to the United States, the Western European nations, and other countries of the world. The worldwide production processes of these TNEs transcend international frontiers and make it increasingly difficult to keep track of a product's country of origin.

A Smaller World

Technological advances in both transportation and communication have made it possible and even easy for a businessman to cover great distances in relatively short periods of time and to have fast and reliable communications via satellite with almost any part of the world. Developments in these two areas have made the world seem much smaller and more integrated. The ability to cover great distances by air has diminished the effective distances between countries and permitted fast and efficient delivery systems between producers and their foreign markets. Improved communication has facilitated management planning and coordination on a global basis.

THE DIMENSIONS OF WORLD TRADE

World trade increased at a rapid pace during the 1970s. By the end of 1978, world exports by the market economies (that is, countries whose economies are based primarily on the market forces of supply and demand, as opposed to the centrally planned economies like those of Eastern Europe) totaled $1.17 trillion—a fourfold increase over the 1970 level. During the same period, total imports of the market economies amounted to $1.18 trillion.

The recent history of world trade can be divided into pre-1974 and post-1974 periods for the clearest consideration. The dividing line is based on the October 1973 price increases by the Organization of Petroleum Exporting Countries (OPEC), which had its first full-year impact in 1974. The dollar size of world trade changed then, because the OPEC price increases brought about higher export prices as the developed market economies worked the increases through their economies.

From 1970 to 1974, total exports of the market economies increased 2.7 times to reach $769.2 billion. World exports increased 1.5 times from 1974 to 1978. Some insights into how the market shares of the major economic groups were affected by the rapid growth of world exports from 1970 to 1979 may be gained from Table 1.1. A look at the figures for the developed market economies and the developing market economies shows that the market share of world exports of the developed market economies fell from 80.3 percent in 1970 to 70.6 percent in 1974, but some of the lost market share was regained by 1978 when the developed market economies' share increased to 74.5 percent. On the

Table 1.1   World Export Trade 1970–1978 (Billions of dollars)

Type of Economy	Exports ($)			Percentage Share of World Exports		
	1970	1974	1978	1970	1974	1978
Developed market economies	224.9	543.4	874.2	80.3	70.6	74.5
Developing market economies	55.2	225.8	300.9	19.7	29.4	25.5
Total world market economies	280.1	769.2	1,176.3	100.0	100.0	100.0
OPEC	17.4	125.8	145.3	6.2	16.4	NA
Centrally planned economies	31.0	65.5	113.5			

Source: United Nations, *Monthly Bulletin of Statistics* (May and June 1981).
NA Not available.

other hand, the developing market economies' share of export trade rose from 19.7 percent in 1970 to 29.4 percent in 1974, and then fell again to 25.5 percent in 1978. Further insight can be gained by delineating the exports of OPEC in the export total of the developing market economies. OPEC's share rose from 6.2 percent in 1970 to 16.4 percent in 1974, which was slightly above the increase in the world export share of the developing market economies, and which would appear to indicate that the change in market shares during this period was essentially the result of price increases for energy.

There was only a slight change in the share of world imports between the developed market economies and the developing market economies from 1970 to 1974 (see Table 1.2). The developed market economies' share of world imports fell 1.8 percent between 1970 to 1974, and 2.1 percent between 1974 and 1978, while the developing market economies' share gained correspondingly for the respective period.

The preceding analysis shows that the developed market economies at the end of 1978 had lost only slightly more in export share than in imports. The net deficit of the developed market economies may be attributed to higher energy costs and the rise in their imports of oil from OPEC.

U.S. Exports and World Trade

World exports of the market economies grew at an annual rate of 12.5 percent from 1957 to 1978. In the same period, the exports of the United States grew at an annual rate of 9.9 percent. The growth rate of U.S. exports has trailed the growth rate of world exports since 1957, when the U.S. share reached 19.8 percent—its highest share of the world export trade since World War II. The U.S. share of world export trade has consistently declined from that high in

Table 1.2   World Import Trade 1970–1978 (Billions of dollars)

Type of Economy	Imports ($)			Percentage Share of World Imports		
	1970	1974	1978	1970	1974	1978
Developed market economies	237.8	612.2	921.5	80.9	79.1	77.0
Developing market economies	56.3	162.2	290.1	19.1	20.9	23.0
Total world market economies	294.1	774.4	1,211.6	100.0	100.0	100.0
OPEC	9.9	33.1	93.5	4.2	4.3	NA
Centrally planned economies	31.7	70.9	124.1	10.8	9.2	

Source: United Nations, *Monthly Bulletin of Statistics* (May and June 1981).
NA Not available.

1957 to its 1978 share of 12.1 percent. The fall in the U.S. share of the world export market is reflected in the comparative analysis and breakdown of the respective rates of growth given in Table 1.3.

The United States lost almost a quarter of its share of world export trade between 1960 and 1971 when its share dropped from 17.5 percent to 13.9 percent. During the 1960s the United States was enjoying domestic prosperity owing to demands created by the Vietnam conflict and the space program; U.S. exporters sold less abroad as they attempted to meet the seemingly insatiable domestic demand. Meanwhile, world export trade grew. Competing industrial countries made up for the shortfall in U.S. exports and increased their export trade shares at U.S. expense. From 1957 to 1970, while world export trade grew at an annual rate of 8.4 percent, U.S. exports grew at an annual rate of only 6.2 percent.

From 1970 to 1978 world exports grew at the rapid pace of 19.6 percent annually; in comparison, U.S. exports grew at an annual rate of 16.2 percent.

Table 1.3   Comparative Rates of Trade Growth: United States and World (Current dollars)

Year	Exports (%)		Imports (%)	
	World	United States	World	United States
1957–1978	12.5	9.9	12.1	13.3
1957–1970	8.4	6.2	8.0	8.7
1970–1978	19.6	16.2	19.1	21.0
1973–1978	17.7	15.0	17.6	21.6

Source: United Nations, *Monthly Bulletin of Statistics*, Vol. 33, No. 5 (May 1979).

The growth comparison shows that, through 1978, the United States had not been able to increase its exports as fast as the rapid world rates of growth. From 1973 to 1978, the United States improved its export performance somewhat, although it still lags the world export rate of increase.

The U.S. share of world export trade reached 11.7 percent, its lowest point, in 1977. In 1978 it regained some of the export trade it lost in 1977; its share climbed back to 12.1 percent. The year 1978 was the first year in which the United States has been able to break the steady decline in its market share since 1964. This break may be a promising sign that the country is again starting to look for markets beyond its domestic economy. U.S. exports grew 26.5 percent from 1978 to 1979 and 22.2 percent from 1979 to 1980. The export promotion program of the United States government should help to maintain these improved growth rates and the U.S. share of export trade in the near future.

Regional Integration and World Trade

Regional integration has been a major force in world trade in the last two decades. Two important regional trading blocs were created in the 1960s—the EEC and the EFTA. The importance of the regional trading blocs in world trade can be seen in Table 1.4.

The EEC's export trade increased from 49.7 percent to 51.9 percent of the export market of the developed exporting economies in 1980. The community enjoyed the second highest growth rate in exports (after Japan). The EFTA has a much smaller export market, as reflected in its market share. Together, the EEC and EFTA had a market share of 61.1 percent of the developed market economies' export trade in 1980.

Table 1.4   Growth Rates and Market Shares: Developed Market Economies' Export Trade, 1970–1978 (Current dollars)

Year	Total Developed Market Economies	EEC	EFTA	Canada	Japan	U.S.	Other Countries
	Growth Rate (%)						
1970–1978	18.4	19.1	18.2	14.1	22.5	16.2	21.5
1973–1978	16.4	16.6	15.9	12.7	21.5	15.0	11.0
1977–1978	19.2	19.9	20.9	11.1	21.2	18.7	21.1
1978–1980	20.5	20.2	21.3	18.1	15.1	18.6	24.5
	Market Share (Percentage of developed market economies' export trade)						
1970	100.0	49.7	9.2	7.2	8.5	18.9	6.5
1978	100.0	52.0	9.1	5.2	11.2	16.2	6.5
1980	100.0	51.9	9.2	5.1	10.2	17.2	6.4

Source: United Nations, *Monthly Bulletin of Statistics*, Vol. 33, No. 5 (May 1979).

Japan experienced the highest rate of growth of these countries included in Table 1.4—22.5 percent annually during the period 1970 to 1978. In comparison, U.S. exports grew at an average rate of only 16.2 percent during the same period. Japan's market share increased from 8.5 percent in 1970 to 11.2 percent in 1978, while the United States' export market share dropped from 18.9 percent to 16.2 percent during the same period.

From 1978 to 1980, Japan's rate of growth of exports dropped to 15.1 percent, while all the other countries in Table 1.4 experienced increased rates of growth. Japan's share of export trade among the developed market economies fell from 11.2 percent in 1978 to 10.2 percent in 1980, while the U.S. export market share increased from 16.2 percent in 1978 to 17.2 percent in 1980.

The growth rates were computed for the period 1973 to 1978 to reveal the effect on export trade of higher energy prices. The growth rate of export trade fell for all countries, but it is interesting to note that the United States held up almost as well as Japan, and better than the EEC and the EFTA.

Export Trade with OPEC

OPEC has become an important factor in world trade for several reasons:

1   The significant rise in the cost of oil increased OPEC's market share of world trade by several times, making this bloc an important force in the dynamics of world trade.
2   The rise in OPEC oil revenues significantly increased the cash inflows of OPEC countries and, consequently, their demand for industrial exports from the developed market economies.
3   Countries that import a lot of oil from OPEC must try to export an equivalent amount to OPEC to compensate for the cash outflow for oil. Failure to maintain some equilibrium in the import and export relationship with OPEC can quickly cause destabilization of the balance of payments of the importing countries, particularly in the developed market countries whose industries depend on oil for a significant proportion of their energy needs.[3]

Table 1.5 presents data on exports of selected developed market countries to OPEC. The export data in Table 1.5 indicate that all the countries shown experienced significant growth rates in their exports to the OPEC countries from 1973 to 1978. Japan experienced the highest growth rate from 1973 to 1975, followed by Italy and Canada. From 1975 to 1977, West Germany, Italy, and the United Kingdom experienced the highest rates of growth. Of the group of countries presented, only France has consistently experienced lower rates of growth than the United States in the period 1973 to 1977. The U.S. export growth rate improved between 1977 and 1978, although it was below the growth rates of Italy, the United Kingdom, and Japan. The very high rates of growth experienced by the countries in the period of 1973 to 1975 reflect the rise in the price of oil in those years, and the inflationary response, as the higher oil import

Table 1.5 Exports of Major Market Countries to OPEC (Data based on dollar values of exports)

	Value (in $ billion)		Percentage Change Annual Rates			Exports to OPEC as a Percentage of Total Exports Annual Averages				Share of OPEC Market[a]					
	Annual Average 1972–1973	1978	1973–1975	1975–1977	1977–1978	1972–1973	1974–1975	1976–1977	1978	Annual Average 1972–1973	1974	1975	1976	1977	1978
United States	3.2	16.7	72.0	15.4	17.8	5.3	8.8	10.9	11.6	22.8	23.4	23.0	23.5	21.1	21.1
Canada	0.3	1.3	75.8	20.0	13.3	1.2	2.2	2.7	2.9	1.9	2.0	1.7	1.7	1.8	1.7
Japan	2.3	14.2	86.7	19.1	18.4	7.1	13.1	14.5	14.6	16.4	19.0	18.0	17.2	17.9	17.9
France	1.5	6.3	62.5	10.1	12.3	4.7	7.8	8.6	8.2	10.3	9.8	9.8	8.7	8.8	7.9
West Germany	1.9	12.3	72.9	26.1	14.2	3.3	6.4	8.7	8.6	13.3	14.0	14.4	15.3	16.0	15.5
Italy	1.1	7.0	75.4	25.2	20.3	5.4	9.5	12.3	12.6	7.7	7.8	7.9	7.8	8.7	8.9
United Kingdom	1.6	8.7	60.5	22.1	24.3	6.0	9.3	11.8	12.1	11.6	9.1	9.9	9.7	10.4	10.9
Seven major countries	11.8	66.5	70.6	19.1	17.7	4.7	8.3	10.3	10.5	83.8	85.1	84.8	83.9	84.2	83.8

Source: OECD, Economic Outlook, No. 25 (July 1979).
[a] Percentage of total OECD exports to OPEC.

prices were factored into the cost of production of industrial and commercial goods exported to the OPEC countries. The rates of growth returned to more stable levels in the 1975–1977 period.

The "Share of OPEC Market" presented in Table 1.5 represents the percentage of a country's export share of OECD exports to OPEC. The shares of West Germany, Italy, and the United Kingdom increased from 1974 to 1978, with the United Kingdom experiencing the greatest share increase of 1.8 percentage points, followed by West Germany with 1.5 points, and Italy with 1.1 points. The United States lost the greatest share of the OPEC market, 2.3 percentage points. France lost 1.9 points, and Japan lost 1.1 points.

The loss in the U.S. share of OPEC's market from 1974 to 1978 is important for two reasons. First, U.S. volume imports of oil in 1980 are over 30 percent higher than the 1973 level, which means a higher import bill. Second, the United States is losing its competitive position in the rich OPEC market.

Export Trade with Eastern Europe, the Soviet Union, China, and Selected Other Asian Countries

The share of the USSR and Eastern European countries in world trade increased during the 1970s, as trade between the East and West opened up. Similarly, the opening of China to world trade added a potentially large market for the exports of OECD countries. The China market, although relatively small currently, is expected to grow as the Chinese economy expands. The total dollar value of exports to these markets in 1978 was $40.396 billion, which is approximately 61 percent of the value of trade with OPEC. The dollar figure reflects the importance of this market in world trade. If the political situation between the East and West improves, trade between the two blocs will continue to grow as it has during the 1970s. Similarly, future expansion of the Chinese economy will certainly increase that country's need for imports, which will provide for growth in exports to China. Table 1.6 presents data for selected developed market countries' exports to Eastern Europe, the USSR, China, and selected other Asian countries.

West Germany's exports to the USSR and Eastern Europe in 1978 were more than double the U.S. exports to those countries; in fact, West Germany's exports to Eastern Europe and the USSR were greater than the total exports of the United States, Japan, and Canada. Similarly, Japan dominated the export market to China and selected other Asian countries. Japan's export total to those countries was greater than the combined total of the six other countries.

West Germany has the largest share of the market for exports to the USSR and Eastern Europe—at 24 percent in 1978. The market share of 4 of the 7 countries fell between 1976 and 1978, while the market share of West Germany, Italy, and the United Kingdom increased by 1.6, 0.6, and 1.5 percentage points, respectively. The U.S. market share fell by 1.2 points. Trade between the Eastern and Western blocs is still at relatively low levels; there appears to be room for growth in export business to these countries.

Table 1.6 Exports of Major Market Economies to Eastern Europe, the USSR, China, and Selected Other Asian Countries (Data based on value in U.S. dollars)

	Value in 1978 ($ million)		USSR and Eastern Europe						China and Selected Other Asian Countries					
	USSR and Eastern Europe	China and Selected Other Asian Countries	Exports as a Percentage of Total Exports			Share of Market[a]			Exports as a Percentage of Total Exports			Share of Market[a]		
			1976	1977	1978	1976	1977	1978	1976	1977	1978	1976	1977	1978
United States	3,674	832	3.0	2.1	2.6	12.6	9.1	11.4	0.1	0.1	0.6	3.2	3.6	10.1
Canada	773	463	2.0	1.3	1.7	2.8	2.0	2.4	0.5	0.9	1.0	4.8	7.4	5.6
Japan	3,197	3,456	6.5	3.4	3.3	10.2	9.7	9.9	2.8	2.8	3.5	44.6	46.5	42.1
France	2,916	314	4.9	4.4	3.8	9.9	10.1	9.1	0.7	0.2	0.4	9.1	2.8	3.8
West Germany	7,715	1,096	6.1	5.6	5.4	22.5	24.0	24.1	0.7	0.5	0.8	15.7	11.8	13.4
Italy	2,409	284	5.4	5.1	4.3	7.1	8.3	7.5	0.4	0.2	0.5	3.2	2.2	3.5
United Kingdom	1,873	184	2.6	2.5	2.6	4.3	5.3	5.8	0.3	0.2	0.3	3.0	2.5	2.2
Seven major OECD countries	22,557	6,629	4.2	3.6	3.6	69.4	68.5	70.1	0.8	0.7	1.0	33.6	76.8	80.8
OECD Europe	23,982	2,895	5.0	4.6	4.3	71.6	76.9	74.5	0.4	0.3	0.5	39.2	30.0	35.3
EEC	17,075	2,319	4.3	4.0	3.7	50.0	54.5	53.0	0.4	0.3	0.5	33.8	22.6	28.3

Source: OECD, *Economic Outlook*, No. 25 (July 1980).

[a] Percentage of total OECD exports to indicated country group.

Japan had 42.1 percent of the export market to China and selected other Asian countries in 1978. The market share of the United States to these countries increased threefold between 1976 and 1978: the United States has improved its competitive position in these markets. South Korea, Taiwan, Hong Kong, and Singapore are growing export markets in which United States exports have a competitive advantage.

Export Market Growth and Relative Export Performance of Major OECD Countries

Comparing the growth rate of export markets with the relative performance of the developed market economies gives further insight into how well the latter performed in meeting the demands of the export markets. For example, if an export market is growing faster in total than the exports of one of its suppliers, the exporting country is losing ground in that market. Table 1.7 shows the growth of export markets and the relative export performance of the developed market economies.

The growth of export markets in Table 1.7 is based, as noted, on the growth of the import volume in each exporting country's market; the exporting countries include the 24 OECD countries plus 8 groups of non-OECD countries. Total OECD export volume growth to each of the 8 non-OECD groups is taken as proxy for the non-OECD groups' imports. The imports of OECD countries are adjusted to exclude imports of oil as well as imports from non-OECD

Table 1.7 Export Market Growth and Relative Export Performance of Major OECD Countries (Customs basis; percentage changes at annual rates, seasonally adjusted)

	Growth of Export Markets					Relative Export Performance[a]				
	1976	1977	1978	1979	1980	1976	1977	1978	1979	1980
United States	7	4.5	5.5	7	4.5	(3.5)	(3.5)	4.5	2	5
Canada	16	11	10.5	2.5	2	(3)	(2.5)	(1.5)	0	(7)
Japan	10	8	7.5	3	6.5	12	1.5	(8.5)	(4)	8
France	9.5	5	6	6.5	6.5	(6.5)	2	0.5	3	(1.5)
West Germany	11	5	5	7	7	(1)	1	(4.5)	0	(1.5)
Italy	11	5.5	6	7	7	1	2.5	5	1	(1.5)
United Kingdom	11	6	5.5	6	6	(1)	3	(4.5)	(5)	(8.5)

Source: OECD, *Economic Outlook*, No. 27 (July 1980).
[a] Growth of a country's exports minus growth of its markets.
( ) indicate decline.

countries. The growth in each market is weighted by its share in the country's total exports.

The relative export performance of a country represents the growth of a country's exports minus the growth of its markets. To obtain the relative export performance of the United States for 1980, for example, subtract the growth of the U.S. export markets of 4.5 percent (found in Table 1.7) from the percentage change in U.S. exports for 1980 of 9.75 percent (found in Table 1.9), which results in 5.0 percent (as rounded).

The U.S. relative export performance for 1978 and 1979 compares favorably with that of Japan and Germany. After two big declines in 1978 and 1979, however, Japan turned the situation around in 1980.

EXPORT AND IMPORT PRICE TRENDS

Annual changes in the prices of the exports and imports of a country help explain the competitive trading position of that country. Changes in domestic costs of production and domestic prices are reflected in the changes in the country's exports, and the country's terms of trade (that is, the relationship between its import prices and its export prices). The export and import prices for each of the seven major OECD countries and for other country groups are shown in Table 1.8.

Table 1.8   Foreign Trade Prices (Average Values) of Major OECD Countries and Country Groups (Annual percentage changes; national currency terms)

	Exports					Imports				
	1976	1977	1978	1979	1980	1976	1977	1978	1979	1980
United States	3.4	4.3	7.7	16.1	11.5	3.0	8.0	8.7	17.3	25.5
Canada	2.3	6.6	8.5	20.8	19.5	0.3	11.4	13.6	14.7	18
Japan	(1.5)	(0.6)	(3.9)	9.6	17	3.4	(3.5)	(17.7)	30.0	48.5
France	9.0	10.5	5.7	9.3	14	10.0	12.1	1.8	10.3	20
West Germany	3.9	1.2	0	3.0	7.5	4.9	2.4	(3.6)	9.8	16.5
Italy	20.4	19.8	7.0	17.8	19.5	25.1	17.0	4.5	18.4	27
United Kingdom	19.9	18.3	7.3	11.8	20	22.3	15.6	3.0	7.7	17.5
Seven major countries	6.3	6.0	3.7	11.4	14	7.1	7.0	0.9	15.3	25
Other EEC	6.7	3.5	1.4	9.1	15.5	6.9	4.6	(0.7)	10.6	17
Other North Europe	2.1	6.6	2.4	8.8	14	2.2	8.5	0.7	10.4	16.5
Other OECD	11.6	15.3	12.4	18.3	22.5	13.5	20.0	12.4	19.4	40
Total OECD	6.2	6.2	3.4	11.2	14.5	7.0	7.6	1.3	14.5	24

Source: OECD, *Economic Outlook*, No. 27 (July 1980).

(   ) indicate decline.

Prices were rising at a higher rate for U.S. exports than for the total OECD in 1978 and 1979, and at a lower rate in 1980. On the other hand, prices were rising faster for imports to the United States than for U.S. exports from 1977 to 1980. It is interesting to note that the prices were rising faster for U.S. imports than for the total OECD as a whole for the period 1977 to 1980. The increase in import prices more than doubled the increase in export prices in 1980. This faster rise in import prices might reflect a higher proportion of oil in U.S. imports than in the other countries'.

THE COMPETITIVE POSITION OF THE UNITED STATES IN WORLD TRADE

From the data on the annual rates of change in the volume of exports and imports of the developed market countries presented in Table 1.9, the competitive position of the United States in relation to its major trading partners can be further analyzed. From 1977 to 1980, the United States has been able to achieve increasingly high export growth rates; the rate rose from 1.2 percent in 1977 to 9.75 percent in 1980. In contrast, the growth rate of U.S. imports has been declining in the period. The significant decline in U.S. imports' growth rate from 13.6 percent in 1977 to 3.5 percent in 1979 is in direct contrast to the increasing rates of import growth experienced by the other countries in Table 1.9, except the United Kingdom. This U.S. rate decline shows that the United States is making a concerted effort to slow its imports while trying to expand exports—a trend that should improve its competitive position. All countries experienced a dramatic fall in import growth rates in 1980.

When oil imports are removed from the figures, the growth rate of U.S. imports is seen to have increased in 1978 and then fallen by 0.6 percent in 1979, rising slightly, by 0.75 percent, in 1980. These figures suggest that the growth rate in oil imports was slowed down significantly in 1979 and 1980.

The United States has maintained a favorable net international investment position over the years, reaching a peak in 1976 of $82.6 billion, as shown in Table 1.10. At the end of 1978, the net international investment position was $76.7 billion. A positive net international investment position means that investments abroad are greater than the liabilities to foreigners. Direct investment by U.S. business firms reached $168.1 billion in 1978, while direct investment of foreigners in the United States totaled only $40.8 billion in that year. Direct investment of the United States abroad in 1978 was 2.2 times the 1970 level; in comparison, direct investment of foreigners in the United States tripled during the period.

The item "Nonliquid assets, Private, Other" includes bank loans and other claims on foreigners, which reflect the recycling of petrodollars by U.S. commercial banks through loans to foreign borrowers.

Table 1.9 Volume of Exports and Imports of Major OECD Countries and Country Groups (Customs basis; percentage changes at annual rates, seasonally adjusted)

	Exports (from previous year)					Imports (from previous year)				
	1976	1977	1978	1979	1980	1976	1977	1978	1979	1980
United States[a]	3.6	1.2	9.9	9.1	9.75	21.7	13.6	7.1	2.3	(2.25)
Canada	13.1	8.6	9.3	2.7	(5)	7.8	1.3	3.8	9.6	(2.75)
Japan	21.8	9.7	(1.1)	(0.8)	14.25	8.4	3.1	6.3	11.3	(3.5)
France	3.0	7.0	6.6	9.5	4.75	23.8	1.0	6.1	11.5	5.25
West Germany	10.1	6.1	4.5	7.9	5.5	13.8	3.9	7.9	9.2	3.5
Italy	11.9	8.1	11.0	7.4	2.25	15.6	(0.4)	8.7	13.0	6
United Kingdom	8.8	9.1	4.5	2.3	3	6.4	2.4	7.6	9.9	1.25
Seven major countries	9.1	6.1	5.9	5.9	6.25	14.5	4.8	7.0	8.2	0.75
Other EEC	11.3	2.9	3.7	8.3	3	13.2	4.6	3.7	7.5	1.55
Other North Europe	11.0	3.7	6.8	6.2	5.5	11.3	4.0	(1.6)	10.2	7
Other OECD	15.5	4.6	6.0	8.7	7	9.1	0.4	(4.8)	8.2	3.25
Total OECD	9.9	5.4	5.7	6.3	6	13.7	4.4	5.0	8.3	1.5
Memorandum item Non-oil exports:										
United Kingdom	9.3	6.3	1.3	1.3	(2.25)	6.9	5.7	5.8	14.3	3.5
United States						21.5	10.9	12.1	(0.6)	0.75

Source: OECD, *Economic Outlook*, No. 27 (July 1980).
[a] Derived from values and unit values on a Bureau of the Census basis. A series-break adjustment has been made to the unit value index for 1979.
( ) denote decline.

The liquid liabilities of the U.S. government rose more than sixfold from 1970 to 1978, reaching $153.9 billion in 1978. These liabilities include U.S. Treasury and government agencies' issues of securities. The rapid rise reflects the magnitude of the government's securities transactions in its effort to manage the dollar's foreign exchange position.

SUMMARY

The United States enjoyed a dominant position in world trade from the end of World War II until the mid-1960s. With the aid of the U.S. Marshall Plan, the European countries reconstructed their economies during the 1950s, and the demand for U.S. products during this period resulted in rapid growth in American exports. The recovery of the European economies, however, had the effect of slowing the demand for U.S. products through the 1960s.

Table 1.10   International Investment Position of the United States, 1970-1978 (Billions of dollars)

	1970	1972	1974	1976	1977	1978
Net international investment position of the United States	58.6	37.1	58.8	82.6	72.4	76.7
U.S. assets abroad	165.5	199.0	255.7	347.2	383.0	450.1
Liquid assets						
U.S. government	17.0	15.2	18.0	20.6	21.1	20.6
Private	22.3	32.1	63.2	101.4	114.9	155.7
Nonliquid assets	126.3	151.7	174.6	225.1	247.0	273.8
U.S. government	29.7	34.1	36.3	44.1	47.8	52.3
Private	96.6	117.6	138.3	181.0	199.2	221.5
Direct investments	75.5	89.9	110.1	136.8	149.8	168.1
Other	21.1	27.7	28.2	44.2	49.4	53.4
U.S. liabilities to foreigners	106.8	161.9	196.9	264.6	310.6	373.3
Liquid liabilities	47.1	82.6	118.4	144.7	185.0	230.9
U.S. government	24.4	61.4	76.6	91.2	124.8	153.9
Private	22.7	21.2	41.8	53.5	60.2	77.0
Nonliquid liabilities	59.7	79.3	78.5	119.9	125.6	142.4
U.S. government	1.7	1.8	3.2	14.3	17.1	21.2
Private	58.0	77.5	75.3	105.6	108.5	121.2
Direct	13.3	14.9	25.1	30.8	34.6	40.8
Other	44.7	62.6	50.2	74.8	73.9	80.4

Source: Economic Report of the President (January 1980), p. 321.

The U.S. dominance in world trade has diminished during the past two decades, as other industrial countries have intensified their efforts to increase their share of world trade. Several forces contributed to the decline in U.S. dominance of world trade: European regional integration which gave birth to the EEC and EFTA led to tariff barriers which reduced U.S. exports to the EEC and the EFTA. Meanwhile, increased trade with Eastern Europe and Asia has provided the major industrial countries with opportunities to increase their share of world trade relative to that of the United States.

Growing dependence of American firms on raw materials from abroad and on foreign markets for their products has increased U.S. involvement in the world economy. Because they have fewer resources and smaller economies, the other industrialized countries had long participated actively in the world economy. The developing countries have also become increasingly dependent on the industrialized countries to meet their growing needs for industrial and consumer goods. Thus, since World War II, the countries of the world have experienced a growing interdependence and a corresponding increase in the importance of world trade.

The formation of OPEC in 1973 and the rapid rise in crude oil prices brought into sharp focus the dependence of the United States and other countries on

OPEC's scarce oil resources. Modern technology is based largely on abundant energy supplies. The change from cheap and abundant energy to highly expensive energy virtually overnight destabilized the international economy, resulting in worldwide inflationary and balance-of-payments pressures for the United States and the majority of market-economy countries. The United States imports some 8 to 10 percent of its oil from abroad. The increased cost of energy has significantly contributed to the deterioration of the U.S. balance-of-trade position.

U.S. direct investment has grown significantly in the past 2 decades. Sales by majority-owned foreign affiliates of U.S. companies reached $574 billion in 1976, over one-fifth of which was exported to other foreign countries. The total export sales of U.S. parent firms and their foreign affiliates account for one-quarter of world exports.

NOTES

1 The member countries of the EEC are: Belgium, Luxembourg, Denmark, France, the Federal Republic of Germany, Ireland, Italy, the Netherlands, and the United Kingdom.

2 The member countries of the EFTA are: Australia, Faroe Island, Finland, Iceland, Norway, Portugal, Sweden, and Switzerland. The members of the OECD are Australia, Belgium, Canada, Denmark, Finland, France, the Federal Republic of Germany, Greece, Iceland, Ireland, Italy, Japan, Luxembourg, the Netherlands, New Zealand, Norway, Portugal, Spain, Sweden, Switzerland, Turkey, the United Kingdom, and the United States.

3 Irma Adelman, "Interaction of U.S. and Foreign Economic Growth Rates and Patterns," *U.S. Economic Growth from 1976 to 1986: Prospects, Problems, and Patterns*, Vol. 12, *Economic Growth in the International Context*, Joint Economic Committee, Congress of the United States (Washington, D.C.: GPO, May 23, 1977).

2

Why Countries Trade with Each Other

The fundamental basis of world trade is the difference in cost of goods produced in different countries. In brief, countries trade to take advantage of cheaper prices for goods produced in other countries. Differences in costs of production and prices in the various countries come from different kinds and amounts of resources that are used in the production of goods and services (referred to as "factor endowments"): (1) natural resources, such as land and minerals, (2) capital, including technology, and (3) labor.

An import price is made up of the overseas price, plus the cost of transportation to the United States, plus financing and other contingency fees. Merchants in the United States import a product produced abroad if the imported price is cheaper than the price of the same product produced in the United States, because they can sell the cheaper foreign product in the United States at a price that is competitive with goods produced domestically. In a similar way, merchants in foreign countries import goods produced in the United States if the imported price of the goods, again including costs of transporting the goods from the United States, insurance, and contingency fees, is cheaper than, or at least competitive with, the foreign country's domestic price of the same product.

This chapter examines the factors that influence the prices and volume of imports and exports, and the various models that have been proposed to describe the structure and direction of international trade.

MACROECONOMIC VIEW OF TRADE AMONG COUNTRIES

Each country has sovereignty over its resources. It can either export its natural resources as raw commodities, or use them to manufacture products for sale in domestic or international trade. This section discusses the assumptions underlying the models of international trade, and the factors influencing the actual price and volume of trade among countries. Traditional international economics takes a macroeconomic view of trade among countries. Countries have historically been viewed as economic units of production of the goods and services entering international trade. The "exports of the United States," for example, are made up of the exporting activities of corporations and households in the United States. These exports are added to obtain a total for each country.

Because the currency of one country is not legal tender in another country, payments for goods bought and sold in international trade have to be translated into foreign currencies using the prevailing exchange rates. Each country, therefore, keeps it own accounting of the international transactions of its residents, which are recorded in the balance of payments of the country, providing a macroeconomic picture of the country's international trade. (The balance of payments is discussed in detail in Chapter 6.)

Free Trade

Since the concept of free trade influenced later models of international trade, the assumptions underlying the concept need to be understood. Although international trade has been an integral part of national economic activity for thousands of years, it was not until the eighteenth and nineteenth centuries that the Classical Economists developed the first systematic conceptual tenets of a theory of international trade.[1] The approach of the classical economists to international trade involved the concept of "free trade"—that is, trade not subject to burdens or restrictions such as tariffs. They wanted to show how each trading country would gain from free internatonal trade and how the benefits received would improve the welfare of the participating countries. In classical economics, benefits accruing to the residents of each country from the gains of international trade are maximized when the trade is unencumbered.

In order to develop an understanding of the process of international trade, the classical economists postulated a perfectly competitive market. The conditions they formulated were: (1) there are many firms in the market with no individual firm large enough to dominate the market, (2) entry into or exit from the market must be easy, (3) the product sold in the various markets must be uniform, that is, the product must be perceived in the various markets as identical in quality by the consumers, and (4) the process of decision-making by each firm must not be influenced by other firms operating in the market.

Firms operating under these conditions are usually "price takers"; that is, since no firm is large enough to set the price, the price is set by market forces of demand and supply. A firm would sell all it could produce at the price prevailing in the market. Under these conditions, the firm with the lowest costs will tend to be the most profitable and will outsell the other firms in the market. The firm with the lowest costs will be that firm with access to comparatively cheaper natural resources, more proficient labor, and more efficient technology. Therefore, the perfectly competitive environment ensures that firms with inefficient production processes will become unprofitable and will drop out of the market, or curtail their activities in this product market to minimize their losses. The focus of this theory is the suppliers' costs of production.

In practice, since each country is an autonomous political unit and trade and commerce in each country are governed by the country's individual laws and customs, countries can set up barriers to international trade, such as customs tariffs and exchange controls, which distort the basic tenets of international free trade (see Chapter 3).

Supply/Demand Relationships in Each Country

In each country, firms normally produce to meet domestic demand first; surplus output then becomes available for export. Similarly, demand is normally met first by the supply produced by domestic firms, and any excess demand relative to domestic supply is met from imports. The supply of goods entering international trade, then, represents the excess supply of goods produced over domestic demand in each country. Likewise, the demand for goods in international trade represents the excess demand over the domestic supply. When the total excess supply matches the total excess demand for all countries, the international trade market is cleared, and the market is said to be in equilibrium.

This description assumes that each country is capable of producing all, or at least some, of the products its residents desire. While this situation may be true for some countries, it is definitely not true for a large number of the developing countries. A majority of the smaller countries in the world do not have the resource endowment, the technology, or the capability to produce the variety of products required to meet the needs of their citizens and must therefore import the many products not produced domestically.

Countries that produce a relatively large proportion of the world supply of a given commodity are referred to as "large" countries in the international market for that commodity. Conversely, countries that supply only a small proportion of the world's supply of the commodity are called "small" countries in the international market for that commodity. It is generally true that "large" countries in the international market for a commodity will have an influence on the world market price of that commodity. By the same token, "small" countries are usually price takers in the international market for that commodity. There is a difference, remember, between a geographically large (or small) country and an economically large (or small) one.

Major Determinants of Imports and Exports

Empirical estimates of the supply and demand functions of various countries have shown that income and price are important determinants of the level of imports and exports of goods and services. One study of price and income elasticity was undertaken by Houthakker and Magee.[2] "Elasticity" refers to the extent to which volume will change with a change in price or income. The researchers computed the price elasticities of imports and exports for: (1) a group of countries in the Organization for Economic Cooperation and Development (OECD); (2) U.S. trade with the member countries of the OECD; and (3) certain groups of commodities within the foreign trade of the United States. The results of the first two parts of this study are discussed in the following sections.

Price Elasticities of Imports and Exports

The price elasticities of imports for each country documented in Table 2.1 show to what extent imports will change with a given change in import prices. Similarly, the illustrated price elasticities of exports indicate the extent to which exports will change with a given change in export prices. A negative price elasticity means that the quantity imported, or exported, will increase with a fall in the import, or export, price. An export price elasticity of −1.51, for example, indicates that export price drops will have a significant effect on raising export volume, taking 1.0 as nil effect. As a corollary, changes in price from exchange rate movements or new customs levies would cause only small changes in volume when the price elasticity is low. When the elasticity is unitary (at 1.0),

Table 2.1 Total Imports and Exports of OECD Countries: Income and Price Elasticities (Annual Data, 1951–1960)

Imports			Exports	
Income Elasticity	Price Elasticity	Country	Income Elasticity	Price Elasticity
1.68	−1.03	United States	.99	−1.51
1.20	−1.46	Canada	1.41	−.59
1.45	−.21[a]	United Kingdom	1.00	−1.24
1.23	−.72	Japan	3.55	−.80
1.85	−.24[a]	West Germany	2.08	−1.25
2.19	−.13[a]	Italy	2.68	−1.12
1.89	.23[a]	Netherlands	1.88	−.82[a]
1.66	.17	France	1.53	−2.27
1.94	−1.02	Belgium-Luxembourg	1.87	42[a]
.91	−.52	South Africa	.88	−2.41
1.42	−.79	Sweden	1.75	.67[a]
.90	.83[a]	Australia	1.16	−.17[a]
2.05	−.84[a]	Switzerland	1.47	−.58
1.31	−1.66	Denmark	1.69	−.56[a]
1.40	−.78	Norway	1.59	.20[a]

Source: Houthakker and Magee, *op cit.*

[a] These coefficients not significant at the 95-percent level. Data corrected for autocorrelation have been used where provided.

volume does not change with price, because changes in quantity would just compensate for the price changes, as with the import price elasticity of −1.03 for the United States in Table 2.1. Higher price elasticities mean greater volume changes when prices change. The United States had the third-highest export price elasticity after France and South Africa for the years studied.

An understanding of the import and export price elasticities of a country is useful to U.S. importers and exporters. Knowledge of how volume responds to changes in price of U.S. imports and exports is extremely useful in export planning, in developing pricing policies, and in formulating a firm's marketing mix—all of which are discussed in Chapter 4.

Income Elasticities of Imports and Exports

Knowledge of the income elasticities of imports of various foreign countries is also useful to United States firms in their export market planning and in developing product strategy for their respective export markets. The income elasticities indicate how the volume of imports and exports will change as the incomes of the consumers in each country change. In Table 2.1, income elasticities for both imports and exports are positive, indicating that as incomes rise, imports and exports will grow commensurately. Since both imports and exports carry the same sign, the net effect of changes in income on both import and export volume and on a country's balance of trade is easily computed. For example, for the United States, the income elasticity for imports is 1.68, while the income elasticity for exports is 0.99. Since the income elasticity for imports is greater than the income elasticity for exports, imports will increase by a larger amount than exports for each unit change in income. Under such circumstances, as income grows in the United States, an adverse balance of trade would result.

Income and Price Relationships: United States and Selected Other Countries

The income and price elasticities for U.S. trade with individual OECD countries, presented in Table 2.2, provide even more important information for U.S. firms than does the information on total trade with OECD countries given in Table 2.1. The income elasticity for U.S. imports is an indicator of how imports from each OECD country would change as U.S. consumers' income grew. Japan has the highest elasticity, followed by Australia, West Germany, the United Kingdom, Denmark, and Sweden. The high income elasticities for imports from the various countries contrast with the relatively lower income elasticities for United States exports to these countries. If incomes changed in the United States and in each of the other countries, the volumes of U.S. exports would experience a smaller change than would U.S. imports from almost all the countries listed, resulting in an adverse balance of trade for the United States.

Policymakers in Washington would be concerned if such a trend continued, since it would show that Americans have a greater desire to purchase imports

Table 2.2   U.S. Trade with OECD Countries: Income and Price Elasticities (Annual Data, 1951–1960)

U.S. Imports			U.S. Exports	
Income Elasticity	Price Elasticity	Country	Income Elasticity	Price Elasticity
1.94	.49[a]	Canada	1.13	−1.45[a]
2.39	−4.25	United Kingdom	2.58	−1.69
3.52	−4.96	Japan	2.10	−.41[a]
2.84	−8.48	West Germany	1.21	−2.39
2.05	−3.82	Italy	2.40	−2.04
.75	−2.47	Netherlands	1.92	−35[a]
1.87	4.58	France	2.33	−3.14
1.38	2.08	Belgium-Luxembourg	2.24	−2.38
1.82	−3.10[a]	South Africa	1.05	−2.68[a]
2.25	−2.49	Sweden	1.52	.73[a]
2.93	−4.69	Australia	2.68	−8.10
1.73	.04[a]	Switzerland	1.59	−2.01
2.28	−6.05	Denmark	2.12	−.47[a]
1.48	−1.82	Norway	1.63	−2.26

Source: Houthakker and Magee, *op. cit.*

[a] These coefficients not significant at the 95-percent level. Data corrected for autocorrelation have been used where provided.

from the OECD countries than foreigners have to buy United States exports. Since these countries are the United States' chief trading partners, we would need to develop and promote more programs and incentives to encourage exports to them. Artificially reducing imports would be difficult: the continuing effort to encourage free trade under the General Agreement on Tariffs and Trade (GATT) would make any active campaign to discourage imports counterproductive, since foreign repercussions could be expected from such campaigns (see Chapter 3). Continuation of the tendency shown in Table 2.2 would provide an opportunity for U.S. firms to increase their export role and involvement. Countries cannot continue to enjoy a favorable balance of trade with a trading partner indefinitely; sooner or later the foreign country will take steps to restore the balance. Foreign governments at times encourage imports from their international trading partners to balance their exports and to keep from overloading on certain currencies; such situations usually provide export opportunities for U.S. exporters.

Several factors contributed to the differences in elasticities in Table 2.2: (1) Several OECD countries instituted various types of restrictive barriers against U.S. exports during the period covered by the study. These barriers were set up despite the efforts GATT had made to remove barriers to free trade. (2) During part of this period, the countries of Europe were rebuilding their economies after World War II with vigorous export programs to foster reconstruction.

The data in Tables 2.1 and 2.2 show that actual supply and demand in international trade are dependent on income and price differences between countries. The next section will outline how theories about international trade have evolved.

INTERNATIONAL TRADE MODELS

A conceptual framework to explain the fundamental relationships of factors in international trade was developed over a period of 300 years. The initial analysis of international trade involved only one factor of production, labor. The concept of comparative cost advantage was based on the labor theory of value, a prevalent view in the nineteenth century.[3] The conceptual framework was expanded at a later date by Haberler to include other factors of production, such as natural resources (generally considered to be land) and capital (which incorporates technology). The inclusion of technology and natural resource endowment led to the concept of "opportunity costs," which is much broader than the labor theory of value. The conceptual framework of international trade was further developed in the Heckscher-Ohlin model, which describes the emergence of the structure of international trade. The Heckscher-Ohlin model has gained wide acceptance as an explanation of the basis of international trade in the modern world. However, tests of the Heckscher-Ohlin model carried out by Leontief produced results contrary to the postulates of the model. Additional tests by other researchers have substantiated the findings of Leontief.

Continuing efforts to find an explanation of the basis for international trade have resulted in newer conceptual models. These include: (1) the product life cycle model, (2) a technology and trade model, and (3) the human skills model of trade.

The basic objective in developing the various concepts is to arrive at a logical explanation of the forces and processes at work in international trade. Such an explanation would help businessmen and government policymakers in formulating plans, strategy, and policies. The various concepts of international trade that have been developed since the theory of free trade will be explained in the following subsections.

The Concept of Comparative Cost Advantage

Countries have different kinds and amounts of factor endowments that are used in the production of goods and services. The more abundant factor endowments will be relatively cheap to use in that country; use of the cheap factors in production lowers production costs and creates a "comparative costs advantage." The concept of comparative cost advantage attempts to explain the pattern of production for international trade in each country and the direction of trade between countries. It holds that countries export those goods which they can produce relatively cheaply and which, therefore, have a cost advantage over the same goods produced elsewhere. Likewise, countries import those goods that would cost them more to produce than to import.

The assumptions underlying the comparative cost advantage model are that:

1   International trade takes place in a perfectly competitive environment. (This assumption also implies that there is a free flow of information between countries which enables all trading nations to acquire full information about foreign markets and the goods traded in those markets.).

2   Each trading nation possesses the same level of technology, and new technology is universally and readily available.

3   The pattern of international trade is determined by the production (supply) conditions as opposed to the market demand.

4   Consumers in the various trading nations have similar tastes.

In the theory of comparative cost advantage, each country designs policies to maximize its economic welfare by concentrating on the production of those goods and services in which it has a cost advantage. This effort enables all countries to utilize their factor endowments most efficiently and, in the process, develop greater specialization and expertise than competing countries. This specialization generally leads to the development of technology and expertise in more efficient ways of production, resulting in a higher yield for each unit of the factors used in production, and, therefore, greater total national product output per unit of factor endowment.

Under the comparative cost advantage framework, firms in each country restrict production to those items for which the country has an abundance of factor endowments and, therefore, competitive cost advantage. In this ideal world, with firms in each country producing only what they do best with their available resources, each country would develop the technology to maximize production output of its line of products and would get the highest possible output from its factor endowment at its level of technological development. The total world output would therefore be maximized.

With each country specializing in a line of production, countries would be willing to exchange output beyond their domestic needs for products from other countries. Through this exchange, each country would obtain all the products needed for its citizens. International trade thus provides a mechanism to facilitate this exchange of goods and services between countries.

There are several exceptions to this general principle of international trade. An extreme case, for example, is a country that is not endowed with a specific raw material to produce a particular commodity but nevertheless needs or desires to produce that commodity. In this case the country must either (1) import the raw material to make the product, (2) import the finished product, or (3) do without the product. Usually, the country imports either the raw material or the manufactured product. In most such situations, firms prefer to import the product until the cost advantage of importing is lost as a result of price increases abroad. A vivid illustration of a raw-materials import is oil.

Countries that do not have oil but need it for their production processes must either import crude oil or import the petrochemical form of the distillate. With the aid of expensive technological processes countries can, in many cases, overcome the lack of natural resources to produce a particular product, but at comparatively greater cost than importing the product.

Relative Cost as a Basis for International Trade

Discovery of the significance of relative cost to international trade is generally credited to Ricardo. In Ricardo's model of international trade, a country or region produces the commodity that it can produce more cheaply than any other country. Ricardo's following example compared the physical output of wheat and cloth in a given unit of time in the United States and the United Kingdom:

	Wheat	Cloth
United States	90 tons	120 bales
United Kingdom	30 tons	60 bales

In the example, the United States produced more of each commodity and, therefore, had an absolute advantage. The physical exchange ratios of wheat for cloth within each country, which represented the real price per unit of physical quantity, would be:

United States	1 ton of wheat	= 1.33 bales of cloth
	0.75 ton of wheat	= 1 bale of cloth
United Kingdom	1 ton of wheat	= 2 bales of cloth
	0.5 ton of wheat	= 1 bale of cloth

Ricardo's analysis was based on the labor theory of value; the physical exchange ratio indicated that labor in the United Kingdom was relatively more efficient in the production of cloth than was labor in the United States. Although the United States had an absolute advantage in the production of both wheat and cloth, it was relatively inefficient in the production of cloth, as compared to the production of wheat. The United States produced only 1.33 bales of cloth for each ton of wheat, whereas the United Kingdom produced 2 bales of cloth for every ton of wheat. Therefore, it was to the United States' advantage to trade some wheat for cloth from the United Kingdom. The United Kingdom would also benefit from the exchange, since it was relatively inefficient in producing wheat. The United States would gain if it could sell each ton of wheat for more than 1.33 bales of cloth, and the United Kingdom would gain if it could get more than 0.5 ton of wheat in exchange for each bale of cloth.

The terms of trade, or the international exchange ratio, would range between the pre-trade limits established by the domestic physical exchange ratios given above. That is, for 0.75 ton of wheat exported from the United States to the United Kingdom, the United States would expect to purchase between 1 and

1.5 bales of cloth. Based on the example, the United States would export wheat in exchange for cloth imports, and the United Kingdom would export cloth in exchange for wheat imports. This establishes the direction of trade.

Production Possibilities with Different Factor Intensities and Endowments

The concept of comparative cost advantage, as first postulated, based the decision to produce or to import on the use of only one factor endowment, labor. Since production with only one factor was not representative of the majority of production processes, the relevant factors of production were later expanded to include natural resources such as land, and capital in the form of technology. The use of several factors of production permitted different output possibilities depending on (1) the scale of operations and (2) the intensity with which the factors were being used in the production process.

In the illustration of wheat and cloth, the domestic exchange ratio of wheat for cloth in the United States was 1:1.33, and in the United Kingdom it was 1:2. The difference between the two domestic cost ratios indicates that there is a basis for international trade, since the United States has a comparative advantage in producing wheat, and the United Kingdom a comparative advantage in producing cloth. One significant reason for the difference in the domestic price ratios of the two countries is the different production possibilities facing the firms in each country as a result of differences in their production processes.

The production processes used by firms in each country reflect the level of technology and the intensity of use of the country's productive factors. Using a two-factor (labor and capital) illustration for the sake of clarity, it is usually the case that a high-technology production process uses more capital than labor, and is therefore more capital intensive. On the other hand, a relatively low-technology production process uses more labor than capital and is therefore labor intensive.

Opportunity Costs as a Basis for International Trade

In 1936 Haberler modernized the comparative cost approach as the "opportunity cost theory" of international trade.[4] Haberler pointed out that cost differentials determine the relative prices of commodities. Costs can also be considered as the index of the amount of alternative production that must be forgone in order to produce a given commodity. The costs of the alternatives that are given up represent the *opportunity costs* of producing for international trade.

In the illustration of wheat and cloth, for example, the United States would choose to produce wheat, in which it has a comparative cost advantage, and give up the production of cloth. The real cost of the wheat includes the lost opportunity to produce cloth, which was given up. In terms of the domestic exchange ratios, then, the opportunity cost of each ton of wheat produced in the United States is the 1.33 bales of cloth that would be forgone if the United States should give up the production of cloth when it enters international trade.

Some of Haberler's possibilities of output combinations of cloth and wheat are presented in Table 2.3. It is assumed in the table for purposes of illustration that the total factor endowment of the United States when fully employed can produce either 120 bales of cloth or 90 tons of wheat. Likewise, the United Kingdom's total available resources when fully employed can produce either 60 bales of cloth or 30 tons of wheat. To produce both cloth and wheat in each country, a lower amount than the maximum output of either commodity will be produced. For example, for each bale of cloth produced in the United States, 0.75 ton of wheat must be given up. In the United Kingdom 0.5 ton of wheat must be given up for each unit of cloth produced. The maximum combinations of cloth and wheat that can be produced in each country are shown in the columns of Table 2.3 (the numbers represent constant returns to scale[5]).

Heckscher-Ohlin Model of the Structure of International Trade

Countries have different levels of factor endowments. In addition to different natural resources, some countries have an abundance of labor and very little capital resources, some countries have an abundance of capital resources with a shortage of labor, and the rest of the countries fall somewhere in between the two extremes. The price of a unit of labor would be relatively cheap in a country with an abundance of labor, while the price of a unit of labor would be relatively expensive in a country with a shortage of labor. Similarly, the price of capital would be relatively cheap in a country with an abundance of capital resources, and relatively expensive in a country with a scarcity of capital.

Firms would tend to utilize the abundant factor intensively because of relatively cheaper costs, which would then be reflected in the domestic cost ratios. The domestic price ratios of commodities produced in each country would, therefore, reflect the extent to which the country is endowed with abundant resources and the intensity with which firms utilize the factor endowments in their production processes. Given that each country has different combinations and amounts of factor endowments, firms in different countries would experience different costs of production for a given amount of output of a given

Table 2.3 Production Possibilities of Wheat and Cloth, United States and United Kingdom

United States		United Kingdom	
Cloth	Wheat	Cloth	Wheat
120	0		
60	45	60	0
40	60	40	10
20	75	20	20
0	90	0	30

commodity. Firms in a country with an abundant supply of the most significant factor in production of a commodity would enjoy a competitive advantage in the cost of production of the commodity and would tend to export their products to countries with relatively higher costs of production. Firms in other countries would have similar competitive cost advantages in the manufacture of products that depended on factors in abundance in their countries.

Heckscher[6] first outlined the foregoing process; it was later developed by Ohlin[7] and became known as the Heckscher-Ohlin model of the basis of international trade. The Heckscher-Ohlin model postulates that a country will export the commodities that firms in the country produce from intensive use of its most abundant resources. The model is essentially a reformulation of the comparative cost advantage concept to describe the structure of international trade.

According to the model, if we know that wheat is a relatively capital-intensive product and that the United States has abundant (relatively cheap) capital, then firms that produce wheat in the United States will have a comparative cost advantage over firms in the United Kingdom (if the United Kingdom does not have an abundance of capital). The Heckscher-Ohlin theory, therefore, dictates that the United States export wheat, which is the commodity that firms in the United States produce through intensive use of the abundant capital factor. Both the intensity of use and the factor abundance are stated in terms of comparison with their use in the production of alternative commodities. The Heckscher-Ohlin model can therefore be used as a basis for determining what commodities a country will export.

Empirical Tests of the Heckscher-Ohlin Model   Several studies have been carried out to test the validity of the Heckscher-Ohlin model. The first such test was made by Leontief, who published the results in 1963.[8] Leontief compared the labor and capital input to produce the various commodities of the United States in 1947. Leontief's input-output table (Table 2.4) contradicted the assumptions of the Heckscher-Ohlin model.

On the basis of the Heckscher-Ohlin model of the structure of international trade, the United States would be expected to export more capital-intensive products than other products because it has greater capital abundance than, say, labor resources. But the results of the study, as presented in Table 2.4, indicate that in 1947 products exported by the United States were less capital

Table 2.4   Domestic Capital and Labor Requirements to Produce $1 Million of U.S. Exports and Competitive Imports

	Column 1 ÷	Column 2 =	Column 3
	Capital (1947 prices, $)	Labor (Man-years)	Capital/Labor ($/man-year)
Exports	2,550,780	182	14,015
Imports	3,091,339	170	18,184

Source: Leontief, *op. cit.*

intensive (or, more labor intensive), requiring $14,015 of capital per man-year, than the products imported by the United States, with $18,184 capital per man-year. This apparent disproof of the theory by Leontief had not been anticipated by students of economics, almost all of whom accepted the Heckscher-Ohlin model. Leontief's findings were therefore called "a paradox."

In a follow-up study, Leontief repeated his analysis, using U.S. input-output data for 1951, and obtained the same results, which confirmed his earlier findings.[9] In the first study the capital per man-year ratio of imports to exports was 1.3 ($18,184/$14,015); in the follow-up study the ratio was 1.06.

A later test of the Heckscher-Ohlin hypothesis reported by Tatemoto and Ichimura on Japanese exports and imports in 1959 had mixed results.[10] Their study showed that Japan exported capital-intensive commodities to the rest of the world and imported labor-intensive products. Japan had excess population, however, and a labor abundance. On the basis of the Heckscher-Ohlin model Japan was supposed to export labor-intensive goods and import capital-intensive goods. Tatemoto and Ichimura's findings confirmed the Leontief paradox, but indicated that not all the so-called capital-intensive exports from Japan were in fact produced there with the intensive use of capital. Although production of automobiles, for example, was indeed capital intensive in Japan (as elsewhere), television production, which is capital intensive in the West, was labor intensive in Japan.

When the relative costs of factors change to the point of reversing the price advantage of one factor, firms will change their factor input combination to reflect the change, switching the factor used intensively in the production process.

Factor-intensity use may be reversed as we move from country to country: a product that is capital intensive in the United States may be labor intensive in Taiwan or South Korea, where there is an abundance of labor that is comparatively cheaper to use than capital investment in labor-saving machinery. The advantage of using labor also applies, in varying degrees, to the production processes of firms in OECD countries. The commodities imported by the United States from OECD countries could well be labor intensive in their production process, but would be capital intensive if produced in the United States. A basis for error would therefore develop if one assumes, as Leontief did in his test of the model, that the production processes of U.S. firms are applicable worldwide.

Hirsch[11] introduced factors in the Heckscher-Ohlin model in addition to labor, capital, and technology, such as scientific and technological know-how and management skills. The expanded number of factor inputs creates a dynamic version of the Heckscher-Ohlin model that permits the cost advantage to pass from one country to another over time. The Hirsch model recognizes monopoly profits, which produce a clear incentive to business firms and industries to assume the risks of investing in research and development. The model also allows for technology transfers and the evolution of foreign trade to foreign direct investment (which is discussed in Chapter 15).

A further investigation of the Leontief paradox was carried out by Vanek, who enlarged the relevant factors of production to include the natural resources content of the commodities imported by the United States.[12] Vanek reasoned that some of the commodities imported by the United States involved natural resources that were abundant in the foreign exporting countries but relatively scarce in the United States. Commodities containing imported natural resources are usually capital intensive to produce. Vanek discovered that by excluding natural resources industries from the tabulation of U.S. imports he overcame Leontief's seeming paradox.

In a more recent study, Hillman and Bullard applied the Heckscher-Ohlin theory to U.S. trade between 1963 and 1967, using energy as a reference factor of production.[13] Energy was treated as a nonproduced input, equivalent to labor and capital as a third factor of production. Hillman and Bullard argued that energy and capital exhibited technological complementarity.

The complementary relationship of energy and capital was confirmed in a study of an energy-inclusive cost function for the United States by Berndt and Wood.[14] The results of the study indicated that the United States exhibited a comparative advantage in labor-intensive output when traded goods *sectors* are defined in the Leontief manner inclusive of intra-industry trade, and when sectors are identified on a directional trade basis by the net trade balances. Conversely, the United States had a disadvantage in output that was intensive in composite energy-capital input. The results were consistent for both 1963 and 1967. The deletion of the natural resources sectors had the effect of diminishing the factor-intensity demarcation between domestic import-competing production and export production. The Hillman and Bullard study provided further confirmation of the Leontief paradox by demonstrating the comparative advantage of the United States in labor-intensive production.

Energy and the Structure of World Trade

The theory of comparative cost advantage tells us that firms in countries with relatively abundant resources will engage in the production of those commodities in which they have a competitive cost advantage. This process, in turn, will establish the direction as well as the structure of world trade. The structure of world trade as postulated by the comparative cost advantage model works in a world of free trade and perfect competition, in which all countries have attained essentially the same level of technological progress. The model assumes that there are no trade barriers and that countries use the same technological processes in production. When we consider the difference in levels of technological development, we see that countries do have real differences in capabilities. Industralized countries with sophisticated technology and a relative abundance of capital find it more sensible to import the raw material in which they are deficient than to import the finished products. Importing the raw material minimizes their costs, since technology, capital, and skilled manpower are readily available in the industrialized countries.

Transportation cost, however, is a significant factor in importing raw materials. Until 1974, cheap energy kept transportation costs low, so it was cost-efficient to import raw materials from developing countries that lacked technology and capital to develop their natural resources effectively. Energy costs have, of course, risen dramatically since 1974, and it seems that they will continue to do so until suitable abundant alternative sources of energy can be found to reduce our dependence on hydrocarbons. As transportation costs have risen, importing raw material no longer appears as attractive as it once was. If transportation costs continue to rise at the pace of the last several years, an increasing number of companies in the industrialized countries will find it more cost-effective to establish manufacturing subsidiaries or affiliates overseas where the raw materials are located than to import them. The raw materials would be typically transformed into an intermediate product, with less bulk and more value per unit of weight, for shipment to home plants in the industrialized countries and completion of the production process. (It should be noted that the relative importance of transportation costs to total manufacturing costs depends in part on the bulk and weight of the raw materials.) For production of low-technology products, firms in the industrialized countries sometimes find it more cost-effective to transfer their whole manufacturing process to a subsidiary or affiliate located at the source of the raw materials.

What this discussion shows is that changes in the cost of a key ingredient, such as energy, can affect the location of manufacturing activity and, in the process, change the pattern and structure of world trade.

Relevance of the Concept of Comparative Cost Advantage to Business Firms

To gain a better understanding of the usefulness of the concepts we have just discussed, let us first attempt to illustrate how comparative cost advantages operate in the domestic economy. Once we have gained an understanding of this process in the domestic environment, we can easily transfer the insight to international trade (while remembering the differences between the domestic and international market environments).

The continental United States is a good place to illustrate how the concept of comparative cost advantage works in a domestic market, because of its vast size—spanning roughly half the North American continent, from the Atlantic Ocean to the Pacific Ocean, and from temperate regions in the North to the subtropical regions in the South. (We exclude Hawaii from the illustration because of its distance from the rest of the states.) Each of the 49 continental states has some natural resources endowment, and trade among the states generally follows the pattern of these natural resources endowments.

Texas, Louisiana, and Alaska have abundant oil resources, which makes oil a relatively cheap resource for firms in these states. These firms have a comparative cost advantage in the production of various petrochemical products derived from oil, and will therefore export their petrochemical products to the other states. Because the United States has an integrated national economy, certain petrochemical products, such as petrochemical feedstocks, will be exported to other states, particualrly in the Northeast, to form inputs for the production of plastic fibers and other plastic products.

The South has an abundance of labor, which makes labor relatively cheap in that area. Companies located in Southern states have a comparative cost advantage in the production of labor-intensive commodities such as textiles and agriculture (for example, tobacco).

These examples of the concept of comparative cost advantage at work in the domestic economy illustrate that states specialize in the production of those commodities for which they have an abundance of resources inputs and exchange them for goods produced in other states. In this way, total output is maximized and welfare is increased universally. One clear difference between the U.S. domestic market and international trade is that the domestic laws affecting commerce are uniform among the states. There are no tariffs on goods crossing state lines, and there is a common currency.

Comparative cost advantage works pretty much the same way in international trade. Firms will utilize the relatively cheap, abundant resource endowment in their country to produce commodities that give them a comparative cost advantage. This advantage enables them to price their output competitively and gain an advantage in pricing. The cheaper product will outsell the output of firms located in other countries with a lesser resource endowment, if the import price of the commodity, including transportation and insurance costs, is lower than the price charged by competing domestic firms.

On reflection, the sense of this narrative seems rather plain. What lesson can business draw from the concept of comparative cost advantage? In the absence of protectionism, firms should strive to produce at the least possible cost by using the relatively abundant resources available in their own environment. If firms produce above their domestic demand level, then some of their output will be available for export. The process by which firms with a comparative cost advantage in the production of a commodity become exporters of that commodity determines the direction of trade. How can business firms use these concepts in their strategic planning process? The concept reveals that three important factors in export planning are (1) the location of industry, (2) the pattern of world production, and (3) the direction of international trade.

Location of Industry

One of the key factors in strategic planning by business firms is the location of industry. This factor involves two related questions: (1) Given the available resources of a country, what commodities should be produced? and (2) Where should the plants be located? The concept of comparative cost advantage and its extensions provide us with the basis for decision-making. Firms should use those resources that are abundant in the country—and therefore cheap in comparison with other resources—to produce commodities for the domestic and international markets. Plants should be located near the resource in order to minimize transportation and other costs and to permit intensive use of the resource. This location guideline should be useful to companies considering establishing a subsidiary or an affiliate in a foreign country for direct foreign investment.

Pattern of World Production

The pattern of world production derives from the concept of country specialization. Firms in each country will tend to specialize in the production of those commodities that they can produce cheaply from the abundant resources within the country. A pattern of world production then emerges. Businessmen should be able to examine the distribution of resources and analyze the pattern of world and regional production. The ability to predict the pattern of world and regional production is important to businessmen developing an export marketing strategy or planning for direct foreign investment.

International Trade Flows

Firms entering international trade should know the direction, or flow, of international trade—who's exporting to and importing from whom. Gathering information on the direction of trade helps a firm determine where to distribute its product in the international export markets. Likewise, importers need to learn the direction of trade in their search for foreign producers with competitive prices. Changes in the direction of international trade normally signal changes in the pattern of world production and in the structure of world trade.

The Product Life Cycle Model of International Trade

The product life cycle model examines international trade as it occurs in today's world; it considers both the demand and supply side of the market. In contrast to the comparative cost advantage model, the product life cycle model recognizes that there are different levels of technology among countries and that each new technology originates in an individual country. Firms in the other countries either buy licensing rights to manufacture the product or develop imitation products by copying the technological process. Multinational firms may spread the technology by setting up wholly owned subsidiaries or affiliates in foreign countries to manufacture the product abroad.

The product life cycle model explains the basis of international trade in terms of three stages: the new product introduction phase, the growth phase, and the mature phase of the product. In the first stage, a firm invents a totally new product or modifies an existing product to meet a need. Normally, the firm then introduces the new product in its domestic market, at which stage it enjoys a monopoly, which may or may not be protected by a patent. Patent protection creates barriers to entry by competing products.

A large proportion of new products originate in the United States. One reason may be that, although firms and individuals in every country undertake research and have ideas for new products, the size of their domestic markets and the effective buying power of their consumers limit the amount that can be spent on research and the return that can be expected from new products. The continental span of the U.S. domestic market, and the affluence and the great diversity of the tastes of consumers in the United States, create a substantial demand for a wide variety of new products. Consumers in the United States are known for their willingness to try new products. Producers in the United States, therefore, are willing to undertake research and development of new products, because the likelihood of their success in the dynamic U.S. domestic market is so much greater than in other countries' markets.

Linder[15] has drawn attention to the fact that it is the nature of the demand in the home market of the principal industrial countries that determines what manufactured goods they produce. These goods may be subsequently exported to other countries, but, he contends, firms will not invest in research and development for new products unless demand for them exists in the domestic market. Or, in those cases where a firm has undertaken exploratory research and developed a prototype, the firm will not manufacture the product unless there is a discernible demand for it.

As noted earlier, a major determinant of demand is consumer income. Consumers in high-income countries tend to demand high-technology producer goods and luxury-type consumer goods. Comparing the per capita income of each country, the United States has one of the highest consumer incomes in the world, and with the size of its population, it has the largest total income—an ideal setting for the introduction of new technology and new consumer goods.[16]

Products marketed successfully in the United States sooner or later reach export markets as foreign demand for the products is felt. Importers in these foreign markets import increasing quantities of the product as the local demand increases; then, imitation products are introduced by local firms to compete with the imports. Initially, the imitation products may not offer much competition, because the imported products will have been refined for the U.S. domestic market. Over time, however, the local product is improved. By this time, the product may even have become standardized, lacking differentiation from its substitutes. As foreign firms continue to improve their product and manufacturing process, they also become cost-competitive with the U.S. firms, which are usually saddled with comparatively higher wage and other costs of production. The foreign firms then begin exporting their products to the United States. This process has been described by Vernon[17] as a four-stage process in which (1) the United States has an export monopoly on a new product, (2) foreign production begins, (3) foreign production becomes competitive in export markets, and (4) the product is exported to the United States.

Among the many examples of the product life cycle at work in international trade is television. Television was introduced in the U.S. market because of the market's affluence and size and the consumers' willingness to try new things. Firms in other countries were leery of how their local market would respond to television, which was viewed at the time as a luxury item. The successful introduction of television in the United States led to U.S. television exports. Then

Japan and other countries started producing imitation products for their domestic markets under licensing arrangements. Japan subsequently developed an export market, which eventually included the U.S. domestic market. Television sets manufactured in Japan have gained a significant market share in the United States. Other examples of the product life cycle concept are the automobile, textiles, electronics, and steel industries.[18]

The product life cycle model includes the marketing concept of the factors that generate international trade, and it also embraces the operations concept of technological differences among nations. Coupled with the marketing and the operations concepts on the supply side is the factor of consumer demand. Together, the supply and demand factors determine the growth path of the product over its life cycle. The product life cycle model, then, allows for a dynamic interrelationship of factors in the international trade process, in contrast to the static concept of the comparative cost advantage model. The product life cycle model incorporates the concept of comparative cost advantage contained in the Heckscher-Ohlin model, but also explicity recognizes the role of technological innovation in an imperfect world.

The product life cycle model provides for changes in the factors required for production over the lifetime of the product. From the research and development phase through the initial export of the product, the production process will be in an experimental phase during which changes in production techniques abound as management searches for cost-saving ways to improve on the manufacturing process. Manufacturing develops into mass production during the growth stage and maturity of the product.

Technology and Trade Theory

The production processes used by companies to produce goods and services embody a wide range of technology from the least sophisticated, naive methods to the most sophisticated approaches, which use complex engineering and chemical processes. The technology and trade model takes into account this wide range of technological capabilities and the technological lag among countries. The level of technology used by firms is directly related to the nature of the product and the kinds and amounts of resources needed for its production. Firms will endeavor to use the technology that utilizes the cheapest, most abundant resources in order to hold down costs.

Technological change stems from inventions and innovations flowing from research. Firms invest in research and development that has a favorable risk-reward ratio. New products may, in turn, be developed from the technological inventions and innovations. Since firms in different countries invent new products at different rates, the introduction of new products in foreign markets provides a dynamic basis for international exchange.

New technology also produces new and better ways of producing existing products, generally, by reducing either (1) one or more of the factor inputs for a unit of output or (2) the amount of time required to produce the same volume.

If an improved production process is more cost efficient, the producer can be more competitive at home and abroad. Improved technology may also result in improved quality, which usually raises the demand for the product.

New technology often tends to raise the level of labor skills and increase labor productivity, thereby increasing labor income (see the subsection on Human Skills Theory). Different rates of technological progress therefore result in different rates of income growth among countries. Countries enjoying higher rates of per capita growth in income have a higher effective growth in demand for new products, which in turn sparks more research and development to produce new products for the domestic market, and later for export markets.[19]

This circular pattern reinforces the advantage held by the industrialized countries in modern international trade. The technological advances made by industrialized countries (the major countries in the West and Japan) result in (1) increased per capita income, which increases domestic demand, and (2) increased corporate income as a result of the competitive advantage in cost or quality; greater demand plus cash flow for research and development in turn fuel further technological advances.[20]

Since technology develops at different rates in different places, some countries become leaders in technology while other countries are followers. The production processes used by firms in the various countries reflect these differences in technology, which result in differences in costs and in competitive edge. Firms can take advantage of their technological advantage by exporting to markets with a less efficient production process.[21] Differences in the rates of technological change will always stimulate trade between countries.

The United States had the distinction of being the world leader in technology for several decades.[22] Although in some areas the United States has lost this leadership, many products exported by the United States still reflect its technological superiority in productivity and new product development. Agricultural exports are a prime example of higher productivity from technology: the United States is the world's largest exporter of wheat and soybeans. In the production of airplanes for commercial purposes, as well as for military use, the United States has maintained much of its world leadership. Technology developed for space exploration and research has resulted in many electronics products and miniaturization techniques.[23]

Rates of growth in productivity have fallen for many industries in several major industrial countries since 1973. As shown in Table 2.5, the average annual rates of growth in productivity in 13 manufacturing industries for the United States, Japan, West Germany, and the United Kingdom fell for most industries. West Germany experienced the least number of industries in which productivity fell during the period 1973 to 1977, followed by Japan. West Germany also experienced relatively lower rates of decline in the industries in which productivity fell.

Analysis of Table 2.5 shows that the United States is losing its leadership edge in technology, as reflected in the productivity figures, to West Germany and Japan. This lag is reflected also in the U.S. balance-of-trade figures for the

Table 2.5 Productivity in 13 Manufacturing Industries (Average annual rates of growth, in percent)

Industry	United States			Japan			West Germany			Great Britain		
	1963–1973	1973–1977	Change	1963–1973	1973–1977	Change	1963–1973	1973–1977	Change	1963–1973	1973–1977	Decline
Food and tobacco[a]	2.5	3.3	0.8	5.8	(0.4)	(6.2)	5.3	6.1	0.8	3.2	1.6	1.6
Textiles	3.4	2.7	(0.7)	8.0	8.3	(0.3)	6.3	7.2	0.9	6.0	(0.1)	6.1
Pulp, paper, and paper products[b]	4.6	(1.0)	(5.6)	9.8	2.9	(6.9)	6.1	5.3	(0.8)	3.9	(0.8)	4.7
Chemicals	4.6	0.6	(4.0)	11.3	5.4	5.9	9.0	3.0	(6.0)	6.9	2.1	4.8
Petroleum and coal products	3.7	0.4	(3.3)	9.5	(0.9)	10.4	4.0	3.0	(1.0)	6.9	(2.2)	9.1
Nonmetallic mineral products	1.5	0.5	(1.0)	7.0	(2.2)	(9.2)	6.0	7.1	1.1	5.3	(0.8)	6.1
Basic metal	1.7	(3.6)	(5.3)	13.2	1.0	14.2	6.4	(0.5)	(6.9)	2.9	(3.3)	6.2
Processed metal products	1.9	0.2	(1.7)	10.4	(1.4)	11.8	4.7	5.2	0.5	1.8	0.1	1.7
Machinery	2.2	(0.7)	(2.9)	9.0	6.3	(2.7)	3.9	2.8	(1.1)	4.2	(1.4)	5.6
Electrical machinery, equipment, and supplies	4.8	1.4	(3.4)	12.5	11.1	(1.4)	6.5	7.3	0.8	5.3	0.3	5.0
Transport equipment[c]	2.9	3.6	0.7	9.2	10.8	1.6	3.5	2.7	(0.8)	2.3	(2.4)	4.7
Precision instruments	2.6	1.3	(1.3)	6.0	14.9	8.9	4.8	3.7	(1.1)	6.5	2.8	3.7
Others	2.5	0.9	(1.6)	9.1	3.3	(5.8)	5.5	4.7	(0.8)	4.3	1.0	3.3
Total manufacturing	2.8	1.2	(1.6)	9.4	4.9	(4.5)	5.6	4.5	(1.1)	4.1	(0.1)	4.2
Variance	1.1	1.8	0.7	2.2	5.4	3.2	1.4	2.2	0.8	1.7	1.7	—

Source: OECD, op. cit.
[a] Excluding tobacco for Japan.
[b] Including printing and publishing for Great Britain.
[c] ( ) denote decline.

period since 1973 (see Chapter 6). This loss suggests a need for a program to rekindle research efforts to enable the United States to regain its role as world leader.

Human Skills Theory

As noted previously, the basis of trade was originally thought to lie in the value added by labor. Labor was treated as a homogeneous factor of production, and no attempt was made to differentiate labor skills. All labor was considered to have the same proficiency in producing any type of product traded between countries. While this assumption may have been true in the days of Ricardo, it is certainly not true in the modern world of high-technology production processes. The labor skills in the advanced industrial countries are comparatively more proficient than labor skills in the developing countries. Furthermore, the proficiency of labor in some industries and in certain commercial and management areas varies among the industrial countries themselves.

Labor skills can be considered to be human capital in much the same way as physical capital is considered to be a factor of production. If a farmer in the United States can produce four times as much of the same crop as a farmer in another country, then the U.S. farmer is more proficient, and his proficiency is a capital investment which requires less investment in time and money.

Opportunities for training in various fields abound in the United States and to a varying extent in the other industrial countries. The skills acquired through education and training are the equivalent of capital invested in each worker and, therefore, the equivalent of human capital.

The U.S. farmer who can produce four times as much as a foreign farmer is equivalent to four foreign farmers. Multiplying the number of U.S. farmers by four to equal the foreign farmers would significantly increase the number of U.S. farmers needed to produce the same amount of goods. U.S. exports of agricultural products would then be considered labor-intensive products as opposed to capital-intensive products. Using this approach in other industries, if we assume that the workers in all U.S. industries are equally proficient relative to foreign workers, then the number of workers in the United States would be significantly increased—making the United States a labor-abundant country. If we use this larger number of workers to compute the capital/labor ratio for the United States, a much smaller ratio would result, which explains why U.S. export industries generally pay higher wages than U.S. import-competing industries; U.S. exports are comparatively more skills-intensive than the exports of its trading partners.[24]

Several studies have been carried out to test the empirical validity of the hypothesis that the content of human skills in U.S. exports is higher than in the exports of its trading partners. Keesing used the 1960 Census data to develop human skills coefficients and applied them to an analysis of trade between the United States and 13 foreign countries for the year 1962.[25] There were 11 industrial countries and 2 developing countries in the group of foreign countries. The results of Keesing's study confirmed the hypothesis that the skills content of U.S. exports was higher than that of the exports of the 13 other countries that offered import-competing goods in the United States.

Similar studies were carried out by Kenen,[26] Baldwin,[27] Mitchell,[28] and Bransom.[29] These studies confirmed the fact that the United States has a comparative advantage in manufacturing requiring a high level of skills. The findings of these four studies have provided some insights into the nature of the labor content of U.S. exports which help to explain the apparent paradox that Leontief observed when the Heckscher-Ohlin concept of factor intensity as the basis for trade was applied to U.S. trade.

SUMMARY

This chapter has examined the factors that influence the prices of imports and exports, and the various models that have been proposed to describe the structure and direction of international trade.

The concept of free trade implies perfectly competitive markets in which the firms with the lowest costs would tend to be the most profitable and would outsell the other firms. The firms with the lowest costs would be those firms with access to comparatively cheaper natural resources, more proficient labor, and more efficient technology than the others. The perfectly competitive environment, therefore, ensures that firms with inefficient production processes will become unprofitable and drop out of the market.

In practice, since each country is an autonomous political unit and trade and commerce in each country are governed by the country's laws and customs, barriers, such as custom tariffs and exchange controls, can be erected which distort the movement of trade.

Empirical estimates of the supply and demand functions of various countries have shown that prices and income are important determinants of the level of imports and exports of goods and services. An understanding of the import and export price and income elasticities of a country is useful to U.S. firms, particularly in export planning, in developing pricing policies, and in formulating a firm's marketing mix.

The theories about international trade have been developed in an effort to explain the forces and processes at work in international trade, in order to help businessmen and government policymakers formulate plans, strategy, and policies.

The concept of comparative cost advantage explains the pattern of production for international trade in each country and the direction of trade between countries. Within the comparative cost advantage framework, firms in each country restrict production to those goods for which the country has an abundance of factor endowments and, therefore, a competitive cost advantage. Countries then export those goods which they can produce more cheaply than their trading partners can. Several exceptions to this general principle of international trade have been noted, however; for example, a country may, for a variety of reasons other than relative costs, produce a commodity for which it has to import the raw material. Nevertheless, the concept of comparative cost advantage provides some guidance to businessmen on where to locate industries and how the structure of worldwide production operates.

The Heckscher-Ohlin model states that a country will export the commodities that firms in the country produce from intensive use of its abundant resources. It is essentially a reformulation of the comparative cost advantage concept to describe the structure of international trade.

The Leontief paradox deals with the inability of the Heckscher-Ohlin model to predict the direction of international trade on the basis of the abundance of capital relative to labor in the United States. From recent studies on the determinants of comparative advantage, the general conclusion suggests that the explanatory variables in the Heckscher-Ohlin model may be too restrictive.

The product life cycle model explains the basis of international trade in terms of the stages in the life cycle of a product and includes (1) the marketing concept of what factors generate international trade and (2) the operations concept of technological change and its impact on trade.

The technology theory goes further in explaining the basis of international trade, in holding it dependent on the different rates of technological change in various countries. These differences make some countries technology leaders and other countries followers. Firms utilize their competitive advantage to export to foreign markets where the technology of the production process is not as efficient as their own.

The human skills theory recognizes the differences in the quality of labor available in the various countries. New technology tends to raise the level of labor skills and increase labor productivity. Labor skills can be considered to be human capital in much the same way as physical capital is considered to be a factor of production.

NOTES

1   Fathers of Classical Economics were Adam Smith, David Ricardo, John Stuart Mill, and Frank Taussig.

2   Hendrick S. Houthakker and Stephen P. Magee, "Income and Price Elasticities in World Trade," *Review of Economics and Statistics*, Vol. 51, No. 2 (May 1969), pp. 111–125.

3   The labor theory of value holds that all value comes from labor, which is considered the only factor of production; see, for example, David Ricardo, *Principles of Political Economy and Taxation* (New York: E. P. Dutton and Co., 1912).

4   Gottfried Haberler, *The Theory of International Trade* (London: William Hodge and Co., 1936).

5   According to Haberler, there are three types of returns to scale in production: (1) constant returns—the most common type, (2) increasing returns, and (3) decreasing

returns. For most types of production processes, output increases at a constant rate for each unit increase in factor input. In an increasing-return situation, output rises at an increasing rate as factor input is increased; in contrast, output decreases as factor input is increased in the situation of decreasing returns to scale.

6   Eli Heckscher, "The Effects of Foreign Trade on the Distribution of Income," in *Readings in the Theory of International Trade* (Philadelphia: The Bolakistan Co., 1950).

7   Bertie Ohlin, *Interregional and International Trade* (Cambridge, Mass.: Harvard University Press, 1933).

8   W. W. Leontief, "Domestic Production and Foreign Trade: The American Position Re-examined," *Proceedings of the American Philosophical Society* (September 1953); reprinted in *Readings in International Economics*, R. E. Caves and Harry C. Johnson, eds. (Homewood, Ill.: Richard D. Irwin, 1968), pp. 503–527.

9   W. W. Leontief, "Factor Proportions and the Structure of American Trade: Further Theoretical and Empirical Analysis," *Review of Economics and Statistics*, Vol. 38, No. 4 (November 1956), pp. 386–407.

10 M. Tatemoto and S. Ichimura, "Factor Proportions and Foreign Trade: The Case of Japan," *Review of Economics and Statistics*, Vol. 41, No. 4 (November 1959), pp. 442–446.

11 Seev Hirsch, *Location of Industry and International Competitiveness* (Oxford: Clarendon Press, 1967).

12 Jaroslav Vanek, "The Natural Resource Content of Foreign Trade, 1870-1955, and the Relative Abundance of Natural Resources in the United States," *Review of Economics and Statistics*, Vol. 41, No. 2 (May 1959), Part I, pp. 146–153.

13 Arye L. Hillman and Clark W. Bullard, III, "Energy, the Heckscher-Ohlin Theorem, and U.S. International Trade," *American Economic Review*, Vol. 68, No. 1 (March 1978), pp. 96–106.

14 E. R. Berndt and D. O. Wood, "Technology, Prices and the Derived Demand for Energy," *Review of Economics and Statistics*, Vol. 57, No. 3 (August 1975), pp. 259–268.

15 Staffan B. Linder, *An Essay on Trade and Transportation* (New York: John Wiley & Sons, 1961).

16 Louis T. Wells, Jr., "A Product Life Cycle for International Trade," *Journal of Marketing*, Vol. 32, No. 3 (July 1968), pp. 1–6.

17 Raymond Vernon, "International Investment and International Trade in the Product Cycle," *Quarterly Journal of Economics*, Vol. 80, No. 2 (May 1966), pp. 190–207.

18 Peter S. Heller, "Factor Eondowment Change and Comparative Advantage: The Case of Japan, 1956-1969," *Review of Economics and Statistics*, Vol. 58, No. 3 (August 1976), pp 283–292.

19 William H. Gruber, Dileep Mehta, and Raymond Vernon, "The R&D Factor in International Trade and International Investment of United States Industries," *Journal of Political Economy*, Vol. 81, No. 1 (February 1967), pp. 20–37.

20 Robert Gilpin, "Technology, Economic Growth, and International Competitiveness," a report prepared for the use of the Subcommittee on Economic Growth of the Joint Committee of Congress of the United States (Washington, D.C.: GPO, July 1975).

21 Steven Globerman, "A Critical Summary and Analysis of Industrial Diffusion Research," unpublished paper, York University, Canada (1977).

22 Donald B. Keesing, "The Impact of Research and Development on United States Trade," *Journal of Political Economy*, Vol. 75, No. 1 (February 1967), pp. 38–48.

23 Regina Kelly, *The Impact of Technological Innovation on International Trade Patterns*, U.S. Department of Commerce, Bureau of International Policy and Research, Office of Economic Research, Staff Report OER/ER-24 (Washington, D.C.: GPO, December 1977).

24 Irving B. Kravis, "Wages and Foreign Trade," *Review of Economics and Statistics*, Vol. 38, No. 1 (February 1956), pp. 14–30.

25 Donald Keesing, "Labor Skills and Comparative Advantage," *American Economic Review*, Vol. 56, No. 2 (May 1966), pp. 249–258.

26 Peter B. Kenen, "Native Capital and Trade," *Journal of Political Economy*, Vol. 73, No. 5 (October 1965), pp. 437–460.

27 Robert E. Baldwin, "Determinants of the Commodity Structure of U.S. Trade," *American Economic Review*, Vol. 61, No. 1 (March 1971), pp. 126–146.

28 Daniel J. B. Mitchell, *Essays on Labor and International Trade*, Monograph No. 15 (Los Angeles: Institute for Industrial Relations, UCLA, 1970); and "Recent Changes in the Labor Content of U.S. International Trade," *Industrial and Labor Relations Review*, Vol. 28, No. 3 (April 1975), pp. 355–375.

29 Jack Branson, "Technology Transfer: Effects on U.S. Competitiveness and Employment," paper delivered at the Conference on the Impact of International Trade and Investment on Employment, Washington, D.C. (1976).

3

Free Multilateral Trade and International Commercial Policy

The preceding chapter showed that, when international trade is conducted on the basis of comparative cost advantage, each country derives increased benefits from the gains of trade. The benefits of free trade are derived from the relatively cheaper prices of the goods produced by firms with a competitive advantage. Free trade tends to eliminate inefficient productive processes that result in higher costs. While resource allocation in a competitive pricing system has some drawbacks, it is far superior to any alternative system of allocation. A competitive pricing system presupposes free multilateral trade.

The benefits of free trade were discussed by David Ricardo in the eighteenth century in a debate on trade protection in the British Parliament, where he espoused the principle of comparative advantage in international trade. Over the centuries governments have nevertheless erected tariff and other nontariff barriers that interfere with the smooth flow of commodities in multilateral trade. The next section will discuss why countries do, from time to time, feel justified in building trade barriers.

TARIFF BARRIERS

Several plausible reasons have been advanced for the imposition of trade barriers.[1] These include: the revenue effect of tariffs, the infant industry argument, and the need to attract foreign investment.

The Revenue Effect of Tariffs

A tariff is a tax imposed by a government or its agency on goods entering or leaving the country. The most common type of tariff is the customs duty. The basic purpose of a tariff is to provide revenue for the government. The revenue collected could be for general revenue purposes or for specific revenue objectives such as to defray the cost of customs administration or the cost of meeting health-control requirements in the supervision of a product.[2]

Tariff levies on goods crossing national boundaries have been used since the earliest times as a major revenue source by developing countries, by countries with few or no income taxes, and by small countries. The effect of tariffs, when used for revenue purposes, is to increase the cost of the imported good by the amount of the tariff. If consumer income in a country is constant over time, demand will decrease as the amount of the tariff levy increases, thereby reducing consumption of the good. Tariffs on imports, therefore, tend to reduce the quantity of the good imported, which restricts the smooth flow of international trade.

The Infant Industry Argument

Countries have also used tariff and nontariff barriers to protect domestic industries at various times. Developing countries in particular will use tariff barriers to protect their industries and the process of development in their countries. These countries feel that their industries cannot compete effectively with imports from the industrialized countries under conditions of free trade. They argue that their industries must be protected if their development is to continue.[3]

Other countries use tariff and nontariff barriers to protect a domestic industry in its initial phase of growth. They argue that protection is needed in the early stage to allow the industry to develop, to provide the country with a comparative advantage in the industry, and to encourage needed labor skills in the country. Since trade restrictions usually result in higher costs, the protected industry is being subsidized by the consumers. The cost of the subsidy and the distortion in trade must be weighed against the benefits to be derived from the establishment of the industry.

Attracting Foreign Investment

Countries erect protective tariff walls also to raise the price of imports and force foreign firms either to lose sales to domestic producers or begin production within the country's market. Tariffs levied for this purpose have to be raised high enough to make the imported products less competitive, in order for market share to be lost. The EEC, for example, created a customs union among its members and built a tariff wall against imports in a variety of areas. United States firms then established production facilities in the EEC countries to protect their shares in EEC markets. Brazil used tariffs to encourage the development of an automobile and an electronics industry by inducing European and U.S. multinational corporations to invest in Brazil.

NONTARIFF BARRIERS

Countries use an array of nontariff barriers to restrict international trade for many of the same reasons that tariffs are imposed. Nontariff trade barriers include both quantitative measures, such as quotas, and nonquantitative measures, such as standards and classifications, subsidies, government procurement policies, import licensing, and customs valuation. The various nontariff trade barriers are used individually or in combination as economic measures to meet national policy objectives—for example, to redress balance-of-payments problems or to provide protection to domestic firms in certain industries.

Import Quotas

Import quotas are used to limit directly the quantity or value of a good imported into a country. Three types of import quotas are widely used: a unilateral quota, a bilateral or multilateral quota, and a tariff quota.

Countries generally take the idea of reciprocity into account in formulating economic policy measures like the imposition of a quota. Countries will enter into prior consultation or will negotiate the measures they intend to adopt before they implement them because they generally expect reciprocal contracts by foreign governments when those governments intend to adopt international economic policies that would affect them.

At times countries ignore international protocol and apply quotas unilaterally, without prior consultation or negotiation. The unilateral action may be done intentionally or may arise from problems in prior contact. Consultations or negotiations may follow the unilateral quotas. The quota may apply uniformly to all foreign exporters to the country—a global quota—or it may have a different effect among the foreign exporters—an allocated quota. Countries usually find quotas difficult and expensive to administer because foreign exporters or domestic importers try to circumvent the restrictive provisions of the quota.

Bilateral and multilateral quotas are generally negotiated before implementation. In these cases, an agreement is reached by all parties concerned regarding the extent and duration of the restriction to be imposed. Negotiated quotas avoid much of the difficulty of administration since foreign exporters and domestic importers freely comply with the measures. There is usually either no retaliatory action by the affected nations or the retaliatory measures constituted part of the negotiated agreement.

Tariff quotas combine the revenue features of a tariff with the quantitative restriction of a quota. The tariff quota allows a predetermined quantity of a product to enter the country at a given level of tariff. At times the quota will permit a certain amount of goods to enter the country duty free. Under tariff quotas, additional imports are permitted, but at higher tariff levels. The additional tariff is usually sufficiently high to keep the flow of imports within the tariff's intended limitation.

Export Quotas

Export quotas may be used to restrict the type or amount of certain strategic items exported to specified countries that are considered unfriendly or potential enemies. The United States, for example, uses export quotas in this way. Another purpose of export quotas is to limit the quantity of exports of a particular product that may be in short supply domestically. Export quotas are used also to control national and international surpluses of a product. For example, the Organization of Petroleum Exporting Countries has export quotas on the amount of oil allocated to international markets.

Nonquantitative Trade Barriers

Nonquantitative, nontariff trade barriers are frequently used measures of government policy. Most of these trade measures are a normal part of economic or social policy, but they can also be used to restrict international trade.[4]

Standards and classification systems, for example, can be used to ensure that imported products meet the same health and safety standards as domestic products. Or, government expenditures for procurement, which now account for a significant proportion of national income, can frequently provide preference to domestic suppliers and limit the degree of participation by foreign suppliers. Import licensing is intended to control the flow of imports, and in developing countries, it can also help generate revenues for the government. The administrative practices connected with import licensing can in themselves create enough delays and extra costs to limit the quantity of imports. Customs valuation determines the value of the imported goods as a base for levying duties. Numerous methods of valuation are used, some of which can be capricious or discriminatory enough to erect a barrier to international trade.

PROTECTIONISM AND THE CRUSADE FOR FREE TRADE

Pressure for protectionism increases during periods of economic recession within a country. Government policymakers who are charged with the responsibility for fostering economic growth and economic well-being may resort to protectionist policies at these times.[5] Other countries then retaliate by setting up their own protectionist measures. The growth of trading blocs in the past three decades has given further impetus to protectionist forces by erecting a series of invisible barriers to trade. And so the process of protection continues until it seems to be the natural economic order. Worse, once instituted, protectionist measures tend to stay in place even when their rationale has been eliminated.

Periods of free trade can be interspersed with periods of protectionism. Historically, protectionist measures have increased during economic slumps while free trade pressure mounts during periods of prosperity. Too often free trade, instead of the natural type of trade, is an ideal which countries only periodically try to achieve.

The Great Depression of the 1930s weakened the economies of the major trading countries. The experience of the major trading nations during the interwar years of 1920 to 1939, when economic antagonism was generated by the Fordney-McCumber tariff of 1922 and the Hawley-Smoot tariff of 1930 in the United States, spurred efforts following World War II to avoid a return to protectionism. The United States had been a leader in the protectionist movement during the interwar years but in the postwar years became a free trade champion and often led the campaign to eliminate trade barriers.

World War II had destroyed the basic infrastructure of international trade. When trade negotiations reopened at the end of hostilities, the United States and other leading nations sought to avoid a return to the prewar policies of protectionism. The United States laid plans for a free, multilateral system of world trade unencumbered by protectionism. Free trade was considered essential for the reconstruction and redevelopment of Europe, in order to stave off the threat of the Communist Eastern European countries.

The General Agreement on Tariffs and Trade

GATT was established in 1947 following 6 months of negotiations at an international conference in Geneva, Switzerland. Some 22 nations signed the original GATT pact, which covered about 45,000 tariff rates. The objectives of GATT include nondiscrimination in trade among the signatories, observance of the tariff concessions negotiated in the agreement, protocols prohibiting the use of quotas and other quantitative restrictions on exports and imports, and special provisions encouraging increased trade with the developing countries. GATT was the culmination of the efforts by the major trading nations, particularly the United States, to promote free trade.[6]

Liberalization of Trade under GATT

GATT has achieved a degree of success in instituting mechanisms that promote liberalized trade. The mechanisms were set up under the agreements reached in six conferences on Multilateral Trade Negotiations (MTN) held under the auspices of GATT. The seventh conference, known as the Tokyo Round, reached a series of agreements on a wide range of subjects. In the discussion below, the agreements of the first six MTNs will be outlined and the final agreements reached at the seventh MTN explained.

The prime objective of GATT is the liberalization of international agreements that set up mechanisms to regulate tariffs and trade. The liberalization of international trade is necessary to minimize, and where possible eliminate, practices and procedures that result in barriers to free trade, through tariffs or nontariff systems.

Tariff Reductions   The first six MTN agreements on tariffs achieved significant across-the-board tariff reductions, but at the sixth, the Kennedy Round, the United States and the EEC were unable to agree on a formula that would permit a fair and equitable reduction in the tariff barriers between them. The terms of GATT mandated nondiscriminatory treatment by all signatories in levying customs duties on exports and imports, customs regulations, domestic taxes, and tax regulations. Some special protective relationships, like those within the British Commonwealth, were exempted.

GATT prohibited the creation of new tariff preferences or the increase in existing tariff preferences. The signatories committed themselves to adhere to the negotiated tariff concessions drawn up in the schedules included in the protocols to the agreement. A signatory was allowed to take action to have a tariff modified or withdrawn if its continued imposition would result in injury to domestic producers of like or directly competitive products.

The agreement on tariff reductions in the Tokyo Round affected 90 percent of industrial trade between the developed countries (as of 1976). When the agreement is fully implemented by 1987, there will be a substantially liberalized world trade structure. The tariff reductions under the agreement are to be put in place at 1-year intervals over a 7-year period. The first round of reductions in tariffs took effect on January 1, 1980; the second round took effect on January 1, 1981, and so on. Table 3.1 compares the average tariffs between the major trading groups prior to and after the MTN agreements.

Protocols Formalizing the MTN Tariff Reductions   Thirty-two countries and the EEC signed the two protocols which formalized the MTN tariff reductions

Table 3.1   Effect of Tokyo Round: Comparison of Average Tariff Rates before and after MTN (Tokyo) Reductions

	Industrial Imports from					
	All GATT Nations (%)			United States (%)		
Importing Nation	Before	After	Reduction	Before	After	Reduction
United States	6.1	4.2	32	—	—	—
EEC	6.3	4.6	27	7.2	4.7	34
Canada	12.0	7.4	38	11.0	6.4	42
Japan	5.0	2.5	50	6.2	2.3	62

Source: U.S. Department of Commerce, International Trade Administration, *Tokyo Round Tariff Reductions: A Descriptive Summary* (Washington, D.C.: June 1980).

made in the Tokyo Round under GATT. The two protocols are: (1) the Geneva (1979) Protocol to the General Agreement on Tariffs and Trade, and (2) a supplementary protocol to the Geneva (1979) Protocol. Table 3.2 shows the countries accepting the codes as of March 1980.

In order to make the MTN tariff reductions workable, signatories to the MTN agreement contained in the protocols are restricted in their ability to raise the tariffs covered in the agreement. Individual tariffs, therefore, are "bound" in the protocols. Changes to "bound" tariffs can be made by a signatory, but only under very specific provisions of GATT, which are intended to maintain a balance of concessions among the signatories and are, therefore, very exacting in their requirements. A signatory must offset any raise intended for a "bound" tariff in the future by an equivalent lowering of a tariff on other trade items.

Substantial cuts in tariffs were made across the board; the average cut ranged from 27 percent for the EEC on a multilateral basis to 62 percent for Japan in its bilateral trade with the United States. The so-called Swiss formula was used by the majority of the developed countries to determine the tariff reductions on industrial goods. The Swiss formula made proportionately greater cuts in the higher tariffs.

Bilateral Tariff Reductions   Bilateral negotiations were carried out on a product-by-product basis, and countries did not adhere strictly to the Swiss formula. Some cuts were greater, and others were less than the cuts provided for in the formulas. Tariff reductions for agricultural products were negotiated for each product. Several countries involved in the negotiations for reductions in agricultural product tariffs were not involved in the other negotiations.

The United States was unable to adhere to the Swiss formula in cases where Congress had mandated exceptions or national security was involved. But the United States did allow larger cuts in some areas, up to the U.S. statutory limit of 60 percent, and eliminated duties to under 5 percent in other areas. Bilateral tariff reductions between the United States and its trading partners are described below.

United States and Canada   The United States was successful in negotiating significant reductions in high Canadian duties. Tariff cuts averaged 42 percent across the board for U.S. exports of industrial goods to Canada. The previous average Canadian tariff on United States industrial exports was 11 percent, with some tariffs reaching 15 percent and above. The new average tariff would be 6.4 percent.

Canada had a 15-percent duty on nearly all forms of industrial machinery not made in Canada, which increased the cost and cut the competitiveness of imported industrial machinery. Under the bilateral agreement, Canada agreed to remove the duty from a wide range of foreign industrial machines. Canada also agreed to reduce its current duties by 50 percent on computers, scientific and control instruments, nonelectrical industrial machinery, photographic equipment, and paper and wood products.

The United States made significant tariff reductions in certain categories of U.S. imports of Canadian goods and major reductions in tariffs on nonferrous

Table 3.2 Country Acceptance of Codes in the Tokyo Round Trade Agreement (as of March 19, 1980)

Country	Tariff Protocol	Customs Valuation	Subsidies/ Countervailing Duties	Standards	Licensing	Government Procurement	Aircraft	Anti-dumping
Argentina	a			s	s			
Australia								
Austria	a	s	s	s	s	s		s
Brazil			a					c
Bulgaria								
Canada	s	c	a	a	a		c	a
Chile			s	s	s			
EEC	a	a	a	a	a	c	a	a
Finland	s	s	s	s	s	s		s
Hungary	a				a			
Iceland	s							
India					s			
Israel	s							
Jamaica	a							
Japan	s	s	s	s	s	s	s	s
New Zealand	a			a	a			
Norway	a	s	a	a	a	s	a	a
South Africa	a			a	a			
Sweden	a	s	a	s	a	s	a	a
Switzerland	a	a	a	a	a	a	s	a
United States	a	s	a	a	a	s	a	a
Uruguay			a					

Source: U.S. Department of Commerce.

a = Accepted.

s = Subject to ratification.

c = Accepted with reservations or conditions.

metals, and eliminated some import duties on paper products and all duties on aluminum imports. Agricultural and horticultural machinery and related equipment, implements, and parts imported for use in the United States were exempted from import duties.

United States and the EEC   The United States and the EEC negotiated a bilateral agreement to reduce tariffs on each side by an average of 35 percent. Significant reductions in tariffs were made by the EEC on several U.S. products, including machine tools and electrical machinery, certain chemical items, scientific and control instruments, photographic equipment, and printing machinery. The EEC also increased its quota on duty-free imports of plywood from 400,000 cubic meters to 600,000 cubic meters. The United States made significant reductions on some textile items, watch and bicycle parts, leather gloves, and on future products in the chemical sector.

United States and Japan   Japan reduced its tariffs on imports of U.S. industrial goods by an average of 62 percent, a significant reduction which should open many opportunities for U.S. exports to Japan. Japanese tariff cuts were on U.S. automotive products (reduced by 83 percent), office and computer equipment (71 percent), electrical machinery and nonconsumer electronics equipment (65 percent), and some others.

In exchange, the United States agreed to cut tariffs on imports of Japanese electrical machinery and power equipment by 45 percent, scientific instruments by 48 percent, construction and mining equipment by 47 percent, office and computer equipment by 38 percent, and photographic equipment by 44 percent.

United States and Other European Countries   The United States made significant tariff reductions on the following imports from European countries not covered by the agreement with the EEC: nonelectrical machinery from Finland and Sweden, chemicals from Switzerland, alcoholic beverages from Finland, and watches from Switzerland.

United States and Developing Countries   Tariff reductions were negotiated between the United States and 27 developing countries in bilateral agreements which recognized each country's stage of development and its capacity to make reciprocal concessions.

Nontariff Agreements   Quantitative restrictions on trade were prohibited by the first six agreements of GATT, but developing countries could make four important exceptions: infant industries, agricultural products, imports that would threaten the balance of payments, and trade that would weaken national security.

The developing countries were allowed to use import quotas to promote infant industries. Prior approval of GATT had to be obtained by a developing country before it imposed a new import restriction, however. The agreement also permitted the use of import duties when necessary to achieve government objectives in agricultural programs. Developing countries were allowed to use import tariffs to control or rectify serious problems in the balance of payments which could result in the complete depletion of monetary reserves. Signatories were required to consult with each other and with the International Monetary Fund before imposing a tariff, and to design the tariff in ways that would not defeat the intent of GATT. Restrictions were allowed also for national security or health reasons—for example, restrictions on the export of strategic goods, or import restrictions of certain plants or food items.

Special provisions to promote the trade of developing countries were incorporated into GATT, under Section IV Trade and Development, in which the developed countries committed themselves to take positive action, to the fullest extent possible, in these areas: High priority would be given to reducing or eliminating barriers to products currently or potentially of particular interest for export to less-developed signatory countries; barriers on these products would not be introduced or increased. The developed countries agreed not to impose new internal taxes that would significantly hamper the consumption of primary products produced in the developing countries, and accorded high priority to the goal of reducing or eliminating these taxes.

Section IV of the agreement also required the developing countries to give commensurate consideration in their trade to the less-developed countries. Supervision of the provisions of this section was assigned to a new Committee on Trade and Development.

The Tokyo Round agreements were more comprehensive and far-reaching than those of the six prior MTNs in GATT's 30-year history. The Tokyo Round agreements included not only the large tariff reductions over the succeeding 8 years (discussed above) but also the elimination of nontariff barriers, which have severely restricted international trade. International machinery to settle disputes among the signatory nations and handle infractions was also set up. An important agreement on international trade in civil aircraft and a framework for the conduct of international trade in general were established in the Tokyo Round.

Separate agreements or "codes" were prepared for each of the following nontariff barriers: subsidies and countervailing measures, customs valuation, import licensing procedures, technical barriers to trade, and government procurement restrictions.

Subsidies   Governments often provide subsidies in various forms to help firms achieve specific national economic and social objectives and to give a competitive edge to exported goods and services. Subsidies distort a free trade market and can restrict market efficiency by inhibiting free competition.

Subsidies take such forms as tax credits, low-interest loans, building a needed infrastructure, and direct grants. In general, subsidies provide a financial incentive to help a firm achieve certain national or international objectives. For example, a subsidy could encourage a firm to locate its plants in regions in need of industry. Subsidies could also be used to encourage exploration for a scarce commodity.

In international trade, subsidies can be used to stimulate exports of goods and services. These export subsidies tend to distort international trade by creating an artificial competitive advantage for the subsidized goods. In extreme cases, subsidies can wreak severe economic dislocation in the market place; unsubsidized foreign competitors can suffer serious economic problems as a result of an overgenerous subsidy program established in another country.

The MTN addressed the problem of subsidies and countermeasures during the Tokyo Round of negotiations and drew up some new rules to govern the actions of the governments in the major trading nations in the use of subsidies to meet domestic and international policy objectives. These rules are codified under the Agreement on Interpretation and Application of Articles VI, XVI, and XXIII of GATT, also known as the "Subsidies Code," which came into force on January 1, 1980. The Subsidies Code set broad guidelines and established a mechanism to enforce them, as discussed and illustrated in the next sections.

Export Subsidies Governments were permitted to continue to use export subsidies on primary products—that is, any product of farm, forest, or fishery that is in its natural form or that has undergone only the processing customarily required to prepare it for marketing in substantial volume in international trade. (Frozen meat and cured meat were examples. Other forms of preserving meat generally used for volume shipping in international trade would meet the classification requirements of the code as primary products.) Export subsidies on primary products are permissible under the following conditions: (1) The subsidized product does not result in the displacement of the exports of another country that adheres to the code; and (2) the subsidized primary goods do not undercut the price charged by other suppliers to the same market.

All forms of export subsidies on nonprimary products and primary mineral products were expressly prohibited by the Subsidies Code. Three examples of prohibited subsidies are presented here:

Case 1 Maputo Chrome Company The government-owned Maputo Chrome Company, which is the only chrome mining company in the Maputo Republic, had a uniform pricing system for its chrome in both the domestic and international markets prior to 1978. A dual pricing system was introduced in 1978 under Administrative Decree No. 15, which allowed a 20-percent price discount on chrome purchased by domestic firms in Maputo that used chrome in their products and would make a 10-year commitment to export half of their manufactured goods incorporating chrome.

The 20-percent discount allowed under Administrative Decree No. 15 is an export subsidy of the type now prohibited by the Subsidies Code, which in part forbids "the delivery by governments or their agencies of imported or domestic products or services for use in the production of exported goods, on terms or conditions more favorable than for delivery of like or directly competitive products or services for use in the production of goods for domestic consumption, if (in the case of products) such terms or conditions are more favorable than those commercially available on world markets to its exporters."

Case 2 Kingdom of Kurine Recent tax legislation enacted in the kingdom of Kurine provided tax credits to companies engaged in export trade. The credits would exactly offset the firm's tax liability, which is normally 40 percent of profits from export activities—the same rate applicable to nonexporters.

A remission of the normal tax liabilities of export companies represents an export subsidy to these firms. The Subsidies Code now prohibits "the full or partial exemption, remission, or deferral specifically related to exports, of direct taxes or social welfare charges paid or payable by industrial or commercial enterprises."

Note that if the export is of primary products, such as farm, forest, or fishery products in their natural form, the exporter may not necessarily be in violation of the Subsidies Code if he receives a tax-credit subsidy.

Case 3   Kumar Company   The Bramilian government, under its Export Trade Development Act for Electronics Products, makes direct grants to companies of 8 percent of the annual increase in the company's earnings attributable to electronics products exports.

The Kumar Company is engaged in the manufacture and export of electronics products. The company's earnings directly attributable to the export of electronics products rose from $5 million in 1980 to $7 million in 1981. The Bramilian government grant to the Kumar Company amounted to $160,000 for 1981.

The grants made by the Bramilian government under the Export Trade Development Act for Electronics Products are now classified as a prohibited export subsidy by the Subsidies Code list, which in part forbids "the provision by governments of direct subsidies to a firm or an industry contingent upon export performance."

Domestic Subsidies   Governments sometimes subsidize domestic industry to achieve certain economic and social objectives. These subsidies ordinarily have no direct connection with international trade, but they may have an adverse indirect effect. Thus the Subsidies Code does not prohibit domestic subsidies, but it does prescribe basic ground rules that recognize the potential adverse effect of domestic subsidies, and it provides a mechanism for an affected country to impose countervailing duties.

Domestic subsidies may have adverse effects on (1) the competitive ability of imports in the domestic market, and (2) local competition when subsidized foreign products are imported into the local market. In the first case, a domestic subsidy to an industry may enhance the competitive ability of the companies in that industry to the point where they overshadow imports, thereby injuring the interests of the foreign exporters to the domestic market. An example will illustrate the second case. Japanese automobiles are sold at relatively cheaper prices in the United States than in Japan because, it may be argued, of domestic subsidies awarded by the Japanese government. The lower prices give the Japanese autos a competitive edge over United States cars, and cut into the market share of United States autos, thereby injuring the interests of United States automobile manufacturers.

Subsidies Code Dispute Settlement   A Committee of Signatories to the Subsidies Code has ultimate responsibility to adjudicate disputes that may arise in the implementation of the code. The Committee of Signatories is made up of representatives from each of the countries participating in the MTN Agreement, with each country having an equal vote in the decisions of the committee. The committee is scheduled to meet on regular business twice yearly in Geneva, but parties to the code may request a special meeting of the committee at any time if necessary.

The dispute settlement process is designed to provide an opportunity for a country found in violation of the code's restrictions to correct the situation, by the removal or termination of any subsidies that may be considered to contravene the restrictions of the code, before countermeasures or retaliatory actions are instituted. The provisions for settlement of disputes contain procedures that allow the parties to go through the process in stages. The initial stage requires that the two parties involved in the dispute enter into consultation at the earliest possible time to work out a mutually acceptable solution. The code allows a period of 30 days for the consultation process; when satisfactory progress is being made by the parties, the 30-day period may be extended by agreement between the parties.

In the next stage, the dispute is referred to the Committee of Signatories by either party if a mutually agreeable solution has not been reached. The facts of the dispute are reviewed by the committee, which can terminate the proceedings if it finds no justifiable grounds to review the case. Negotiation between the parties in the dispute would continue, under the auspices of the Committee for Conciliation, for a 30-day period. If no resolution is achieved in that period, the country claiming injury from export subsidies inconsistent with the provisions of the agreement may ask the committee to appoint a panel of experts to conduct a factual review and report its findings to the committee. The rules require the committee to set up the panel within 30 days of the request.

The panel of experts has 60 days to make its findings in the case and submit a report to the committee. The panel's report would contain its conclusion on whether the subsidy contravened the provisions of the Subsidies Code. The parties would be provided with a copy of the report and would have further opportunity to negotiate a bilateral settlement prior to the committee's consideration of the report.

Within 30 days of the receipt of the panel's report, the committee is required to make a recommendation for retaliatory countermeasures if it finds that subsidies have been granted that contravene the restrictions of the code.

Countervailing Duties Governments have generally protected their domestic industries from the damaging effects of export subsidies on goods imported from abroad by levying countervailing duties on the imported products. The countervailing duties offset the competitive advantage provided by the subsidies.

The Subsidies Code authorizes countermeasures when foreign export subsidies cause injuries to the international or domestic trade of a signatory country to the agreement. The code authorizes the injured country to institute countervailing duties against export subsidies that are inconsistent with the code (the countervailing duty would be imposed on the subsidized product).

Countervailing duties are authorized under specific conditions. The injured government is required to begin investigation of the existence of a subsidy when there is sufficient evidence to indicate that (1) a subsidy exists, and (2) that there is a causal link between the alleged subsidy and the injury to the domestic industry. The offending government must be provided a consultation opportunity to clarify the situation before the government of the injured party proceeds with the investigation.

The code requires the following steps be taken once the investigative process begins: (1) a public notice should be made of the investigation, (2) the evidence of the subsidy and of the injury caused by the subsidized import should be considered simultaneously, (3) the results of the investigation must be released in public notices as the investigation progresses, and (4) a time limit of one year is allowed for the investigation.

Provisional Countervailing Duties   The code authorizes the injured country to impose provisional countervailing measures against the imported goods if there is sufficient preliminary evidence to show positively that a subsidy exists and that it is causing injury. The provisional measure could be a provisional countervailing duty, or the imposition of a penalty award in the form of cash deposits or bonds in an amount equal to the estimated net subsidy on the imported product. The code permits levying retroactive countervailing duties on subsidized imports but not more than 90 days before the investigation opens.

Definitive Countervailing Duties   Definitive countervailing duties can be imposed only after the investigations are completed and it has been determined that the import is indeed being subsidized, with material injury to a domestic industry. The definitive countervailing duty cannot exceed the amount of the subsidy on each unit of the imported good. The duty can remain in effect only as long as the export subsidy on the imported goods continues; when the export subsidy ceases, the countervailing duty must be removed.

Undertakings   The Subsidies Code provides for some flexibility in the investigative process: the investigative proceedings can be suspended if the government of the exporting country is aware of evidence that supports a positive determination of the existence of a subsidy and voluntarily removes or limits the export subsidy or decides to take other measures that would eliminate the possibility of injury to the affected industry in the importing country. This government-to-government agreement between the importing country and the exporting country, known as an "undertaking," can be negotiated under the rules of the code. Once countervailing import duties are lifted, the agreement to undertake correction would no longer need to be in effect.

Determination of Injury   Under the Subsidies Code, "injury from subsidized imports" applies to a domestic industry producing a like product in the importing country. The entire industry must be found to be injured or threatened with injury. Furthermore, the injury to the industry must be a direct result of the subsidized imports and not of all imports taken together. Nor could the injury result from other factors such as changes in the pattern of consumption within a market.

When an examination of actual or threatened injury to an industry is conducted, the code requires that both the volume and price effects of the subsidized imports and the impact the imports have on the industry in question must be considered by the investigating authorities in the importing country. The investigating authorities must also determine (1) whether there has been either an absolute or relative increase in the volume of subsidized imports and whether the price of the subsidized imports has the effect of significantly undercutting or depressing the price of like products in the market; (2) the impact of relevant economic factors on the industry; (3) the actual or potential decline in sales, market share, and profits; and (4) the actual or potential negative effects on cash flow or employment. In the case of agriculture, the impact on government support programs must be determined. All these factors must be evaluated and their various influences and effects considered in determining whether a subsidized import causes or threatens to cause injury in the importing country.

Countervailing Duty Investigation: An Illustration   Figure 3.1 presents a flow chart of the procedures to be followed and the time schedule in a countervailing duty investigation by the U.S. Department of Commerce and the International Trade Commission (ITC) as set up by Section 301 of the Trade Act of 1974, and amended by Section 901 of the Trade Agreement Act of 1979. The procedure outlined in the countervailing duty investigation conforms to the requirements of the Subsidies Code.

Customs Valuation   Common practice among countries in restricting international trade is to boost import duties by using valuation methods that inflate the value of the dutiable goods; the valuation formula is arbitrarily adjusted to obtain the desired degree of restriction.

The Agreement on the Implementation of Article VII of the General Agreement, known as the "Customs Valuation Agreement," eliminates the use of arbitrary valuation methods to restrict international trade. The Customs Valuation Agreement had been signed by eight countries and the EEC as of March 1, 1980. The effective date of the agreement was January 1, 1981, but the United States and the EEC put the terms of the Customs Valuation Agreement into force earlier, on July 1, 1980.

The Customs Valuation Agreement prescribes a primary method and several alternative methods for valuation of imported goods. The rules are intended to provide for a uniform, neutral, and fair system of valuation of goods traded internationally. In using one of the prescribed valuation methods of the agreement, the dutiable value can be determined on the basis of either (1) free on board (f.o.b.) value, or (2) cost, insurance, and freight (c.i.f.) value.

Primary Method of Valuation   The primary method of valuation in the agreement uses the "transactions value" to determine the dutiable value of goods and is intended for general use. The transactions value is essentially the price

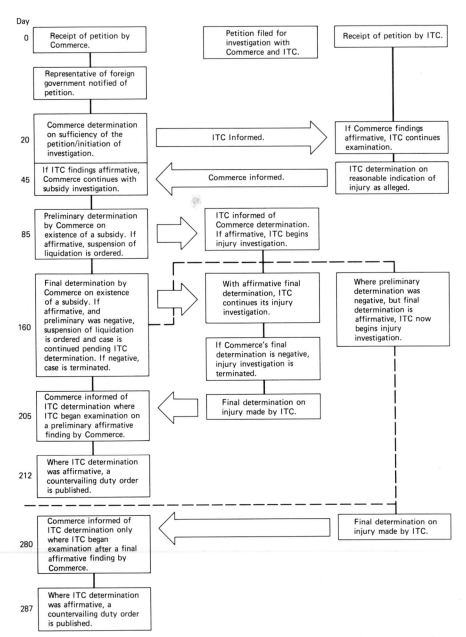

Figure 3.1 Flow chart of procedures in a typical countervailing-duty investigation. (Source: *Subsidies and Countervailing Measures*, Vol. 1, U.S. Department of Commerce, Washington, D.C.: GPO, 1980).

actually paid for the goods plus other costs not included in the price that are normally added to the price to arrive at the purchase cost. These additional items include selling commissions, packing costs, and certain production costs for materials and service borne by the buyer but not directly included in the price paid or payable for the goods.

The transactions value method may not be applicable when the price is not determined by market forces, such as in a transaction between family members, in which part of the price reflects the special relationship of the parties. The actual price paid in these special transactions cannot be summarily ignored, however, unless the price is determined not to reflect the transaction value, as defined by the agreement.

Alternative Methods of Valuation   The Customs Valuation Agreement provides other methods to determine dutiable value when the primary transactions value method cannot be used. One example would be an unknown price. The alternative methods must be applied in a prescribed sequence when valuing a product. This process is intended to set a dutiable value closely related to the valuation under the primary transactions value method, if it could have been used. The three recommended alternative valuation methods are: (1) the transactions value of identical or similar goods, (2) deducted value, and (3) a computed value. These three methods and the provision for other alternatives are discussed briefly below.

The first alternative method is closely akin to the primary transactions value method. If the price of a good is not indicated, the dutiable value of the good must be determined by first establishing the transactions value of *identical* goods sold for export to the country of importation. When there are no identical goods imported into the country, the next step is to ascertain the transactions value of *similar* goods sold for export to the country of importation.

When the dutiable value of the imported good cannot be determined by the transactions value of either identical or similar import goods, two other methods are used, the deducted and the computed value methods. Ordinarily the deducted method is used first, but the importer can request that the computed value method be used first, reversing the order.

In the deducted method, the dutiable value is figured from the price of the first sale following import of either the good itself or an identical or similar product. The costs and charges incurred after import that were included in the sale price are subtracted to arrive at the dutiable value. The deducted value method can be applied to cases in which an imported good is no longer being manufactured, for example. Or, the importer can request that the deducted value method be used to determine the dutiable value of goods processed after importation (when goods are so valued, an allowance is made for value added in processing).

The computed method calculates the dutiable value on the basis of the total cost of materials, manufacture, and general expenses, plus profits of the imported goods.

The Customs Valuation Agreement provides for other valuation methods to be used in determining the dutiable value of imported goods, if the prescribed methods listed in the protocols fail. Other methods used must be reasonable and consistent with the principles of the agreement and of Article VII of GATT on customs valuation. The agreement lists the methods used in determining dutiable values that are considered arbitrary and unreasonable and are, therefore, prohibited.

Implementation of the Customs Valuation Agreement Responsibility for implementation of the Customs Valuation Agreement rests with the Committee on Customs Valuation, which was established in the protocols formalizing the agreement. The duties of the committee include: (1) supervision of the implementation of the provisions of the agreement, (2) consultation with signatories on matters involving the management of the agreement, and (3) resolution of disputes arising from the implementation or the management of the agreement.

When a dispute arises between signatories, the Customs Valuation Agreement prescribes procedures for consultation between the parties concerned to resolve the dispute. Either party can refer the dispute to the Committee on Customs Valuation if the dispute cannot be resolved during the consultation process. The committee is provided with expertise on the technical aspects of the agreement by the Technical Committee, set up through the protocols of the agreement under the auspices of the Customs Cooperation Council.

Import Licensing Procedures Import licensing procedures can be restrictive devices in international trade. Cumbersome import licensing systems, for example, can lead to unnecessary bureaucratic delays, increased import costs, red tape, complications, and delays, as well as arbitrary decisions, such as denying a license without explaining how the decision was reached.

The MTN Agreement on Import Licensing Procedures, also known as the "Licensing Code," deals with the administration of import licensing procedures. The purpose of the code is to set up rules governing import licensing procedures in an effort to eliminate procedures and practices that impede the free flow of international trade, and to simplify the procedures that importers must follow to obtain import licenses. The Licensing Code became effective on January 1, 1980, and 14 countries and the EEC had signed the code by March of that year (see Table 3.2).

The Licensing Code attempts to simplify and unify the procedures that importers must follow in obtaining an import license, so as to prevent any unnecessary obstacles to international trade. Two key aspects of import restrictions—embargoes and quotas—are covered by GATT rules, and therefore are not covered by the Licensing Code. The code has three main features: (1) the general provisions, (2) rules for automatic import licensing, and (3) rules for nonautomatic import licensing.

General Provisions The general provisions deal with a variety of subjects affecting all types of import licensing:

1 The Fairness Doctrine requires that the regulations importers follow to obtain import licensing must be applied fairly and equitably to each signatory to the code.

2 Open publication of regulations is required. Any other information about the licensing system that could aid in the application process should also be made public.

3 The code recommends simplification of the application and renewal process. Wherever possible, one administrative body should handle all the applications. When consolidation of all the procedures into one administrative body is impossible, the code requires that the number of administrative bodies that an importer would have to apply to be kept to the minimum.

4 Reasonable time periods should be allowed to importers for application of licenses.

5 Minor errors in documenting an application should not be used as the basis for refusal to grant an import license.

6 Minor variations in value, quantity, or weight of the product under license should not be used as the basis to refuse a license.

7 Foreign exchange should be provided, without discrimination, to pay for goods imported under license and for goods not subject to licensing.

Automatic Import Licensing   An automatic import license is defined as import licensing for which approval is freely granted. Statistical data and general trade information on imported goods are routinely collected as a part of the automatic import licensing process. The procedures normally do not interfere with or impede international trade, although they may have restrictive effects if improperly designed or administered.

The Licensing Code specifies that automatic licensing systems that cause unnecessary delays should be maintained only as long as necessary for their purpose. Licenses required under this kind of system should be made available to anyone fulfilling prescribed and published criteria. Automatic import licenses should be granted immediately upon request, to the extent administratively feasible—but in any case within 10 working days.

Nonautomatic Import Licensing   The Licensing Code attempts to simplify the procedures used by countries to administer nonautomatic import licensing. Approval for these licenses is not granted freely or automatically. The code requires that signatories (1) publish information on the amount and value of licensed goods and names of persons granted licenses, (2) publish information on the administration of quotas, as required under the general provisions, and (3) permit any person, firm, or institution to apply for a license.

The code also requires that the period for processing a license application should be as short as possible. The length of time the license is valid should not be so short as to become an import barrier itself. Signatories should take into account the utilization of previously issued licenses when granting new licenses. Signatories are required to ensure that new exporters receive a reasonable distribution of licenses. Signatory countries cannot restrict license-holders' choices of import sources when allocating quotas if there were no previous quota allocations on imports from the supplying countries.

Technical Barriers to Trade   One type of nontariff barrier that countries erect is a technical barrier, such as product standards, certification systems, and procedures designed to test whether certain classes of imported goods conform to technical standards.

The Agreement on Technical Barriers to Trade, also known as the "Standards Code," was the first attempt to establish international rules for standards and certification systems. Rules were established also for the proper adoption and application of these standards and certification systems.

The Standards Code requires signatories to refrain from using standards and certification systems as impediments to trade. Systems designed for legitimate domestic reasons must not be manipulated to inhibit trade. Adherence to the rules of the code by all the signatories is designed to facilitate free trade among countries.

The code requires national and regional certification systems to be nondiscriminatory and accord most-favored nation treatment to all signatories of the agreement. Foreign suppliers or suppliers outside a group such as the EEC are to be subject to the same certification rules and procedures as apply to domestic or group suppliers. The code encourages signatories to simplify product testing and certification processes by accepting the results of tests conducted by a technically competent body using appropriate testing methods in the country of export. The time required for testing and certification should be significantly reduced as signatories move towards greater acceptance of foreign test results.

It is important for all members of the international trading community to know what changes are being considered by other members in their standards and procedures for testing. The code therefore requires signatories to publish information on any domestic standards or technical regulations they are drafting or revising or any new certification system they have introduced.

Problems of interpretation arise in using design or descriptive characteristics in specification of standards. To minimize this problem, the code recommends that performance characteristics be used as the basis for specification of standards in preference to design and descriptive characteristics. International standards developed under the auspices of GATT are available for use by signatories. The code suggests that relevant existing international standards be used by signatories when available. The use of international standards has several advantages. It facilitates the process of testing and compliance. Both parties have full prior knowledge of the appropriate methods and level of technical competence involved in the international standard. The foreign manufacturer is in a position to produce the goods to meet the specification of the international standard. General use of international standards would significantly reduce the cost of compliance for exporters, because they would have to satisfy just one set of standards instead of different standards in each country.

Importers and exporters frequently have difficulty in obtaining exact information on specific rules and procedures covering standards and certification systems. They have even more difficulty locating the person or persons in the position to give authoritative answers to specific questions on standards and certification systems. The code requires signatories to publish, and make publicly available, all information on the rules and procedures of their standards and certification systems. Easily accessible facilities are also to be made available in one department to handle all inquiries and questions about the systems.

All published information on technical regulations and rules of certification and copies of notices regarding new or revised regulations are now to be transmitted to the GATT Secretariat, which serves as the distribution center for such information. Distribution by the GATT Secretariat is designed to ensure that the governments of all the signatories are duly informed about standards and certification systems.

Many developing countries lack the technical competence necessary to develop adequate rules and procedures for their standards and certification systems. Other signatories are required to provide the necessary technical assistance when they are asked to do so by developing countries. The technical assistance is to be provided on terms and conditions agreed upon between the developing country and the assisting nation.

The procedures for resolving differences between signatories under the Standards Code require informal, bilateral consultations between the parties involved as the first step. If these bilateral consultations fail to resolve the dispute, either party can refer the dispute to the Committee on Technical Barriers to Trade, set up to administer the provisions of the code. A working group of technical experts advises the committee. This group of experts reviews the dispute and submits recommendations to the committee for resolving the dispute. The code provides for withdrawal of code benefits from a signatory found guilty of an infraction of the code by the committee.

Government Procurement   Government procurement policies often give preference to domestic goods. Some countries promote "buy national" campaigns, and goods produced domestically are given preference in government procurement procedures. These policies set up barriers that tend to discriminate against foreign producers.

The objectives of the Agreement on Government Procurement are twofold: fair treatment of foreign goods in government procurement programs and nondiscrimination in purchases by government entities. The effective date of the agreement was January 1, 1981. As of March 1, 1980, the following countries had signed the Government Procurement Agreement: Australia, Finland, Japan, Norway, Sweden, and Switzerland. The EEC and the United States signed the agreement subject to the completion of satisfactory negotiations with the various procurement agencies in their governments. The following four countries have expressed their intention to sign the agreement: Canada, Jamaica, Korea, and Singapore.

Signatories to the agreement are obligated not to discriminate against, or among, the products of other signatories in the purchases subject to the provisions of the agreement. Government entities that normally carry out the functions of government, including procurement, are listed in the agreement and are bound by its protocols not to discriminate in contracts involving purchases of goods valued at Special Drawing Rights (SDR) 150,000 (see Chapter 7) and more. The government entities listed include ministries, departments, and most of the various agencies and other government entities of the signatory countries. State and local government purchases, including purchases funded by central governments, are not covered by the agreement.

It should be noted that there are situations in which governments legitimately restrict procurement to purchase of domestic products. These situations relate to national security, efforts to develop a natural resource, or special programs to help develop minority-owned businesses. For example, the U.S. programs to favor small or minority-owned businesses in government procurement are not affected by the agreement.

Government procurement in the following types of transactions also are not covered by the agreement: purchase of national security items, construction contracts, and service contracts (except when a purchase contract requires after-purchase service on covered goods).

As explained below, the protocols of the agreement promulgate rules to govern the conduct of government purchasing, ensure compliance, and promote the exchange of data on purchases covered by the agreement.

Conduct of Government Purchasing The Government Procurement Agreement requires that all signatories follow certain procurement procedures, strict adherence to which would eliminate discrimination against foreign goods. Invitations to bid on all contracts for government procurement must be openly published. Documents required to bid on contracts must be furnished by the government entity that extended the invitation to bid. Likewise, all information and explanation at every stage of the procurement process must be published and communicated to all parties involved. To eliminate discrimination against foreign products, both domestic and foreign firms must be subject to the same qualification and selection criteria.

Government purchasing is usually done through two types of tendering—open or selective. The provisions of the agreement stipulate the procedure that signatories must follow in tendering. Any firm, domestic or foreign, must be allowed to bid under open tendering. When selective tendering is used, the government entity invites selected qualified suppliers to bid on the tender. The agreement requires that the list for selective tendering include, upon request, all qualified bidders from signatory countries. Furthermore, foreign bidders must be given full opportunity to compete in the selection process.

Compliance There are enforcement provisions in the agreement that deal with contract violations on individual contracts and with systematic violations on a larger scale. The provisions of the agreement uphold the right of a supplier who fails in his bid on a contract to inquire how the winner was selected and why his own bid did not win. Signatories are required to provide an appeals procedure that can be used by suppliers who feel that the selection process violated the agreement. A signatory may request bilateral negotiations if there is any indication of a pattern of violation by another party to the agreement. If the bilateral negotiations fail to resolve the dispute, the dispute can be referred to a committee of signatories. The agreement provides sanctions that can be authorized by the committee if an international panel of experts finds the subject country to be in violation of the agreement.

The Agreement on Trade in Civil Aircraft   The governments of various industrial countries have been providing increasing support for their national aerospace industries. Government support takes such forms as (1) procurement practices that favor airplanes built domestically or have subassemblies built by local firms; (2) subsidies for aerospace research and development; (3) tariffs or other duties that increase the cost of an imported airplane; and (4) other practices such as requiring domestic subcontracts.

An agreement was negotiated between the United States and other major aircraft-producing countries during the MTN to deal with the problem of increasing government interference in aerospace industries and the attendant drift toward restrictive trade policies for civil aircraft. The Agreement on Trade in Civil Aircraft, known as the "Aircraft Agreement," deals with aircraft trade policy issues. The Aircraft Agreement is directed toward the (1) establishment of a comprehensive basis for free and fair trade in the aircraft sector, and (2) creation of an international forum to settle disputes and monitor developments in the civil aircraft industry.

The Aircraft Agreement seeks to promote competition in the commercial trade in civil aircraft and, to that end, sets up a framework to regulate trade in the civil aircraft sector. Much stronger tariff prohibitions were adopted in the Aircraft Agreement than in the other MTN agreements.

Aircraft Procurements   The Aircraft Agreement sets forth four basic principles of procurement, mandatory subcontracts, and sales inducement transactions for the signatories to the agreement:

1   Airline companies, aircraft manufacturing companies, other corporations, and government agencies must not be required, or be subject to unreasonable pressures, to buy civil aircraft from any particular source.
2   In the awarding of civil aircraft contracts, any arrangements requiring particular subcontracted production or support contracts are strictly forbidden. In inviting bids for a contract for civil aircraft procurement, a signatory may stipulate only that qualified firms have access to bidding opportunities.
3   The offer or denial of privileges, such as landing rights, intended to influence procurement decisions in civil aircraft contravene the provisions of the agreement.
4   The selection of suppliers should be based on commercial and technological factors.

Subsidies and Standards   The provisions of the Aircraft Agreement encourage the elimination of subsidies by requiring that pricing of civil aircraft be based on a reasonable expectation of recovery of all costs, including nonrecurring program costs. A framework for upgrading and maintaining standards in the operation and maintenance of civil aircraft is contained in the specifications on operating and maintenance procedures drawn up in the Standards Agreement.

Customs Duties   All customs duties and similar charges of any kind levied on, or in connection with, the import of civil aircraft and engines, and of ground flight simulators for civil aircraft, are eliminated under the Aircraft Agreement.

Subassemblies, components, or parts intended for use in civil aircraft are classified under one of the specific customs tariff headings listed in the annex to the agreement and should be allowed to be imported duty free. The agreement further provides for the elimination of all duties on foreign repair of civil aircraft.

Implementation of the Aircraft Agreement   The reductions in customs duties and similar charges went into effect on January 1, 1980. These reductions were estimated to affect close to 95 percent of the value of trade in civil aircraft and parts. The agreement required that implementation of its protocols according duty-free treatment to civil aircraft, engines, and specified parts involve ways to minimize administrative processing. In general, exemption from customs duty was granted for civil aircraft on the importer's declaration and subsequent customs approval of the aircraft. Engines and parts classified in accordance with the list of specified tariff headings, and intended for use in civil aircraft, were granted exemption from duty.

Value added taxes and excise taxes that affect both domestic and imported products were not covered by the provisions of the Aircraft Agreement, nor were fees charged for the cost of import processing.

The reduction in duties by the signatories under the Aircraft Agreement were "bound in GATT," which means that the provisions of GATT, Article XXVIII, govern any future plan by a signatory to raise a tariff on items included in this agreement, and that such a tariff must be matched by a compensatory reduction in another tariff. As a further deterrent, a penalty would be exacted from the party that intends to contravene the provisions of the agreement.

Supervision of the Agreement   A Committee on Trade in Civil Aircraft, known as the Aircraft Committee, was established by the protocols of the agreement to supervise operation of the agreement's provisions and to settle any disputes that might arise between the signatories. The committee was to be made up of a representative from each signatory, who were required to meet once a year. It could meet as often as necessary for consultation on matters arising from the operation of the agreement, or ensure the continuance of free and undistorted trade.

The committee was authorized to establish subsidiary bodies as its working arm. Their responsibilities would include regular review of the implementation of the agreement's provisions relating to product coverage, end-use systems, customs duties, and other charges.

A signatory could request a review by the Aircraft Committee if it knew of any contravention of the rules of the agremeent by another signatory. The committee would then undertake the review and make its recommendations. Formal procedures for settlement of disputes were provided under the Framework Agreements (discussed below). The Aircraft Committee would then proceed under the "Understanding Regarding Notification, Consultation, Dispute Settlement and Surveillance" procedure of GATT.

The rules of the agreement provide for retaliatory action to be taken by a party that wins a case in a dispute settlement procedure. The accused party may offer prior conciliatory action to accommodate the injured party before the latter takes retaliatory action. After retaliatory action has been sanctioned in the settlement of a dispute, the action is accorded international recognition.

Framework for the Conduct of International Trade

An agreement on the framework for the conduct of international trade was reached in the Tokyo Round of MTN. There are five separate agreements included in the package making up what is generally called the Framework Agreements. The objective of these agreements was to reform various sections of the GATT framework to accommodate the special needs of the developing countries in light of the six major international codes on nontariff measures adopted during the Tokyo Round. The package of agreements in the Framework Agreement was approved by the contracting parties at the thirty-fifth session of GATT and went into force on November 29, 1979.

The subject areas covered by the five Framework Agreements were: (1) an enabling clause, which set up the legal basis for preferential treatment of developing countries within the GATT framework and the principles of reciprocity and graduation; (2) safeguard action for balance-of-payments purposes; (3) safeguard action for development purposes (that is, infant industry measures); (4) settlement of disputes, consultation, and surveillance procedures under GATT; and (5) GATT rules governing the use of trade restrictions affecting exports.[7] The first four of these areas are described below.

Enabling Clause The GATT provisions established a legal basis for different (more-favored) treatment for developing countries. The enabling clause was the mechanism for providing the legal basis for the preferential treatment and contained guidelines to ensure that the preferential treatment accorded developing countries met their objectives but, at the same time, did not produce any adverse effects on the trade of developed countries. To this end, the enabling clause provided some guidance for the implementation of the agreement: (1) The special treatment was to be provided so as to respond to a country's development needs and not to hinder trade flows—in other words, the special treatment should avoid erecting barriers to trade with a third party; (2) the special treatment accorded to a developing country could not impede the effort to reduce tariffs and other trade restrictions required under the general provisions of GATT.

The enabling clause listed four types of special arrangements covered by the Framework Agreement: (1) the Generalized System of Preferences (GSP) between the developed countries and the developing countries (this refers to the set of preferences that provides for preferential treatment for developing countries by the developed countries.); (2) the provision for preferential treatment of developing countries applicable to nontariff measures prescribed under the MTN Agreements of the Tokyo Round, (3) the mutual reduction or elimination of tariffs among developing countries, in regional or global arrangements, and (4) the provision of special treatment for the least-developed countries within the general framework for preferential treatment to developing countries.

All members of GATT, called the contract parties, had to be notified of any actions taken to provide special treatment to a developing country. The contracting parties also had to be provided opportunity to make consultations with the parties involved. To ensure that the special treatment was tailored to the needs of the developing country, all measures for preferential treatment had to be modified as those needs changed.

Reciprocity   The development needs of developing countries do not generally permit them to extend full reciprocity to the trade and tariff concessions made by developed countries. The reciprocity clause recognized that the goal of full reciprocity might be inconsistent with the needs of these countries. A developed country was not prohibited by the reciprocity clause from asking for reciprocal concessions or contributions, however, when they were consistent with the development objectives of a developing country.

Graduation   The special treatment accorded developing countries was not intended by GATT to be a blanket open commitment. For example, a developing country no longer in need of special treatment could not expect to continue receiving benefits from such treatment. Provisions were included in the agreement for scaling the amount of special treatment accorded developing countries, and for these countries correspondingly to assume greater responsibilities under GATT as their economic situations improved.

Safeguard Action for Balance-of-Payments Purposes   The second agreement under the framework package of agreements dealt with safeguards for balance-of-payments purposes. This agreement provided a more effective mechanism than the prior one for notification and consultation when member countries take trade measures to correct balance-of-payments problems. The objective of the safeguard action was to limit the restrictive effect of the measures. In this regard, the agreement on safeguard actions enumerated the following points: (1) the need to recognize that trade measures taken to rectify balance-of-payments problems generally prove to be inefficient; (2) full consultations should be carried out when any trade measures, other than quantitative restrictions, have been used to rectify balance-of-payments problems; (3) an industry or economic sector must not be protected by trade measures used ostensibly for balance-of-payments purposes; and (4) trade measures should not be used by developed countries to rectify balance-of-payments problems. If trade measures must be used, the agreement stressed that countries give preference to measures that would have the least disruptive effects.

Safeguard Action for Development Purposes   The third agreement within the framework package explicitly permitted a developing country to restrict its imports when necessary to promote domestic economic growth by protecting an infant industry. The provisions of Article XVIII in GATT were, therefore, broadened by this agreement to protect infant industries in the developing countries.

Developing countries were accorded the right to take immediate protective measures in emergency situations, on a provisional basis, after other GATT members had been duly notified. All trade actions taken by developing countries under the provisions of Article XVIII would have to avoid the disruption of trade as much as possible.

Dispute Settlement   The dispute settlement agreement provides a mechanism for resolving trade disputes between GATT member countries. The two key elements of the mechanism are communication and consultation. GATT required that member countries publish announcements and notify other GATT members when trade measures were being instituted. The objective was to make GATT member countries that might be affected aware of the actions and give them the opportunity to initiate consultation with the parties involved to head off any resultant problems or injuries to trade. The country contemplating a new trade measure was obligated to notify other GATT members in advance of, or if that was not possible immediately after, implementation of the measure.

The dispute settlement agreement provided for the establishment of a panel of experts, on request of one of the disputing parties, should consultations fail to resolve a dispute. The panel is required to review the facts of the case and present its findings to the contracting parties within three to nine months. The contracting parties, the representatives of member countries of GATT, would use the panel's findings as the basis for their decision.

United States Enforcement of Trade Agreement Rights

The eight major international agreements concluded during the Tokyo Round of the MTN under GATT provided rules to achieve the objectives of each agreement and procedures to ensure compliance by the signatories to the provisions of each of the agreements. The compliance provisions put teeth into the agreements through the enforcement procedures laid down in the protocols of the enabling articles to the agreements. The compliance provisions made it possible for an aggrieved party to initiate action against an offending party to cease and desist from practices that contravene the provisions of any of the agreements.

The United States, as a signatory to the agreements and a leading proponent of free trade, has had a major role to play in monitoring the activities of the other signatories to ensure compliance. The United States can use the enforcement provisions itself when it needs to initiate action against any country breaking the agreements. The articles of each of the eight agreements form a legal basis for enforcement and function as international law. The Committee of Signatories constitutes the world's highest tribunal for the enforcement of the international obligations of signatories under each agreement.

The United States' vehicle for the enforcement of any international trade agreement is Section 301 of the U.S. Trade Act of 1974. Under Section 301 the President is authorized to take appropriate action (1) to enforce United States export rights under any trade agreement, (2) to respond to a policy or practice by a foreign nation that is inconsistent with, or denies the United States benefits under, a trade agreement, or (3) to respond to a foreign country's policy or practice that is unjustifiable, unreasonable, or discriminatory and restricts or burdens United States commerce. Section 301 gives the President the authority to suspend or withdraw benefits of trade agreements or to impose retaliatory import restrictions.

The U.S. Trade Agreements Act of 1979 approved U.S. acceptance of the eight major MTN Agreements—two tariff and six nontariff agreements. The 1979 Act authorized the President to implement the agreements in the United States. Section 901 of the Trade Agreements Act of 1979 amended Section 301 of the Trade Act of 1974 specifically to provide an effective mechanism for the enforcement of U.S. rights under the Tokyo Round Trade Agreements of GATT, Section 301 provided protection for U.S. exporters, but did not provide protection for U.S. producers from import competition. The procedures set up in Section 901 for the President to use in enforcing U.S. rights under the Tokyo Round MTN Agreements include these basic steps: (1) the initiation of a case, (2) post-initiation procedures, and (3) presidential action. The Office of the U.S. Trade Representative (USTR) was assigned the responsibility for implementing the provisions of the Tokyo Round MTN Agreements on behalf of the President.

Initiating a Case under Section 301

Action on a case usually begins when a private party makes a formal or informal petition to the U.S. government. Under the informal process, the first step is for the private party to file an informal complaint (petition) to the USTR. The complaint alleges that an act or a practice of a foreign signatory is inconsistent with the provisions of an agreement, and results in the United States being denied benefits in accordance with the agreement. The informal complaint would be reviewed by the USTR, which would pursue the matter if its assessment indicated a problem.

In filing a formal petition with the USTR, a private party specifies what practice, policy, or act of the foreign signatory contravenes the provisions of an agreement, and how the complainant sees the rights of the U.S. government being impaired. The USTR is obligated to determine within 45 days after the receipt of the formal petition whether it merits a formal review. If it does, the USTR would then initiate an investigation, and the text of the complaint is then published in the *Federal Register*. The USTR is required to report its action (or its reasons for rejecting the complaint) in the *Federal Register*.

Petition Review Process

Following a decision by the USTR that the practice, policy, or act of the foreign signatory is indeed inconsistent with the provisions of a specific U.S. trade agreement, the petitioner can request that a public hearing be held within 30 days after the date the petition was filed. The USTR would then proceed to obtain all pertinent information and advice from the petitioner and from all U.S. government and other private sources.

In the meanwhile, the USTR would proceed to request bilateral consultations with the foreign government or other foreign entity responsible for the offending practice, policy, or act. This request for bilateral consultation takes place the same date the petition is filed. In the bilateral consultation process, the USTR and the foreign entity seek to resolve the problem in a mutually satisfactory manner.

As described previously, each of the trade agreements provides a mechanism for settlement of international disputes about agreement infractions. The bilateral consultation process initiated by the USTR is part of the dispute settlement procedure. If the bilateral consultation between the USTR and the foreign government or foreign entity fails to reach a mutually acceptable resolution of the dispute, the USTR would then proceed to make a formal complaint to GATT's Committee of Signatories.

USTR Recommendation

The USTR is required under Section 301 to report on the development of the case and make recommendations on possible courses of action by the President. The USTR is required to make its recommendations within the following prescribed time limits:

In the case of a violation of a trade agreement, the recommendations must be made no later than 30 days after the completion of the dispute settlement process. In a case involving an export subsidy under the international Subsidies Code, the USTR must make its recommendation no later than 7 months after the case is initiated; in disputes involving other areas of the Subsidies Code, the recommendations must be made no later than 8 months. In all other areas not covered by the trade agreements, the USTR is required to submit its recommendations no later than 12 months following initiation of the case.

The time limits set by Section 301 for the USTR to make its recommendations to the President were made long enough to cover the period required for
the completion of the dispute settlement procedures under the MTN agreements. The USTR is expected to take into account the recommendations of the
International Committee of Signatories in its recommendations to the President. Figure 3.2 presents a flow chart showing the domestic and international
procedures and the time schedules involved in cases on subsidies provided in
Section 301 of the U.S. Trade Act of 1974, as amended by Section 901 of the
U.S. Trade Agreement Act of 1979.

Action by the President

The President is required to make a final determination of what action will be
taken no later than 21 days after receipt of the recommendations of the USTR.
The President must publish the decision and the reasons supporting the decision in the *Federal Register*.

SUMMARY

The commercial policies of the major trading nations set the general climate for
international trade. Tariff and nontariff measures are commonly used as instruments of national policies to achieve domestic objectives, and these same
measures can be manipulated in various ways to form barriers to trade. The
governments of the industrialized countries have become heavily involved in
the process of domestic economic growth and development. The governments
may use nontariff measures to set up trade barriers to provide incentives for
private business in an effort to redirect production and consumption patterns
between domestic and foreign markets. When tariff and nontariff measures are
used as barriers to trade, they distort trading patterns and result in inefficiencies
in the patterns of trade.

Following World War II, a movement for trade liberalization arose, led by
the United States, that brought about the creation of GATT in 1947 and a
subsequent series of multilateral trade negotiations under the auspices of GATT.
The latest multilateral trade negotiations under GATT, the Tokyo Round, which
lasted the six years from 1973 to 1979, reduced both tariff and nontariff barriers
to international commercial policies. The scope of areas covered made the
Tokyo Round one of the most comprehensive multilateral trade negotiations
undertaken since the inception of GATT.

The agreements reached in the Tokyo Round are far-reaching, and the enforcement machinery promotes adherence by the signatories to the terms of the
agreements. When the agreements are fully implemented, by the mid-1980s,
they should provide for freer trade, greater competition, and a more efficient
trade structure. The world's major trading nations indicated their commitment
to an open trade system in the seven major agreements on nontariff measures.
The new sector agreement on commercial aircraft reaffirms the objective of a
fair international trading system.

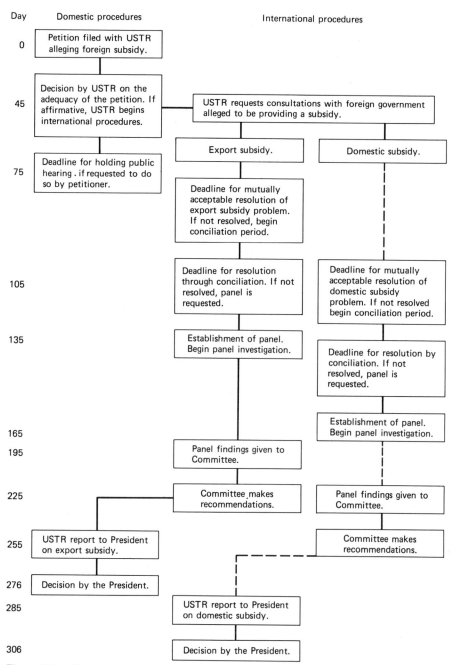

Figure 3.2 Flow chart of procedures in Section 301 cases concerning subsidies. (Source: U.S. Department of Commerce, *op. cit.*).

To sum up, the MTN agreements established large tariff reductions over the next eight years, and they limited nontariff barriers, many of which have a significant restrictive impact on international trade. The following nontariff barriers were covered:

Subsidies and countervailing measures that prejudice imports

Duties used to counter predatory pricing

Discriminatory government procurement

Technical barriers to trade (standards)

Unfair or discriminatory customs valuation

Import licensing complexities

Special favor in civil aircraft trade (which is a tariff and nontariff issue)

The agreements also included several codes dealing specifically with trade in agriculture, and established a much-needed international trading framework to take into account the particular needs of developing countries.

NOTES

1 Tibor Scitovsky, "A Reconsideration of the Theory of Tariffs," *Review of Economic Studies*, Vol. 9 (1947), reprinted in the American Economic Association's *Readings in the Theory of International Trade,* Howard S. Ellis and Lloyd A. Metzler, eds. (Homewood, Ill: Richard D. Irwin, 1949), pp. 358 ff.

2 S. P. Magee, "The Welfare Effects of Restrictions on U.S. Trade," *Brookings Papers on Economic Activity*, No. 3 (1972), pp. 645–701.

3 Samuel Morley and G. W. Smith, "Import Substitution and Foreign Investment in Brazil," *Oxford Economic Papers*, Vol. 23, No. 1 (March 1974), p. 133.

4 William B. Kelly, Jr., "Nontariff Barriers," in *Studies in Trade Liberalization*, Bela Balassa *et al.*, eds. (Baltimore: Johns Hopkins University Press, 1967).

5 Merle Holden and Paul Holden, "Effective Tariff Protection and Resource Allocation: A Non-Parametric Approach," *The Review of Economics and Statistics*, Vol. 60, No. 2. (May 1978), pp. 294–300; Jagdish N. Bhagwati and T. N. Srinivasan, "The General Equilibrium Theory of Effective Protection and Resource Allocation," *Journal of International Economics*, Vol. 3, No. 3 (August 1973), pp. 259–281; William M. Carden, *The Theory of Effective Protection* (Oxford: Oxford University Press, 1971); V. K. Ramaswami and T. N. Srinivasan, "Tariff Structure and Resource Allocation in the Presence of Factor Substitution," in *Trade, Balance of Payments and Growth: Papers in International Economics in Honor of Charles P. Kindleberger*, J. N. Bhagwati *et al.*, eds. (Amsterdam: North-Holland Publishing Co., 1971); Ray J. Ruffin, "Tariffs, Intermediate Goods and Domestic Production," *American Economic Review*, Vol. 70, No. 3 (June 1969), pp. 261–269; Augustin Tan, "Differential Tariffs, Negative Value Added and the Theory of Effective Protection," *American Economic Review*, Vol. 60, No. 1 (March 1970), pp. 107–116.

6 R. F. Baldwin, J. H. Mutti, and J. David Richardson, "Welfare Effects on the United States of a Significant Multilateral Tariff Reduction," paper presented to a Conference on General Equilibrium Modelling for International Trade Policy Analysis at the University of Western Ontario, Canada, February 23–24, 1979.

7 Complete information on GATT rules can be obtained from the Office of Trade Policy, International Trade Administration, U.S. Department of Commerce.

4

Export Management and International Trade

From 1965 to 1980, exports of the United States rose eightfold—from $27.5 billion to $220.7 billion. Since World War II, U.S. companies have significantly increased their international role and market share in world trade. The rise in international trade is expected to continue through the 1980s and 1990s as a result of the growing interdependence in the world economy, and, as the world market expands, the demand for U.S. products will also grow. Opportunities for export trade and export marketing will increase.

Selling abroad has many similarities to selling in U.S. markets, and U.S. businesses design strategies for their markets abroad in much the same way as they do for the domestic market. But there are many differences in the overseas markets that make them distinct from the U.S. market and that necessitate special handling and tailored treatment of these markets. The various export markets have different types of geographic, climatic, and cultural environments that may require redesign or adaptation of the product or product line to meet the needs of the markets. Special attention must be given also to the differences in the commercial policies of each foreign country to assess their potential impact on the marketing activities of the company. Companies should be aware that the differences in the foreign marketing environment will affect each firm's objectives and marketing strategy in a different way.

WHY UNITED STATES COMPANIES ENTER THE EXPORT MARKET

U.S. companies enter the export market for several reasons. Some companies have always viewed their markets in international terms because their domestic market was too small to justify production for domestic sales alone (for example, airplane manufacturers). In this view, the whole world is essentially one global market which is becoming increasingly interdependent and integrated through transportation and communications advances.

One group of businesses sees a company's entry into international marketing as basically a way of extending a product's life cycle. A new product is introduced in the U.S. domestic market, where the product enjoys high rates of growth during the earlier part of its life cycle. Then, as the product approaches maturity and its rate of sales growth slows, the firm becomes interested in expanding the market for the product to sustain the faster growth of the earlier stages of the cycle and to extend the product's economic life and profitability. Companies enter international trade at this point in a product's life, usually by export marketing. As the product's export market develops over time, the company may want to establish greater control over its distribution channels abroad by establishing subsidiaries or foreign affiliates.

A company may decide to enter the export market for strategic reasons, after a review of the major business and economic trends in its industry indicates that there may be potential problems for the firm in meeting its future performance objectives by restricting itself to the domestic market. The firm's move into the export market may be designed to permit the full use of its production capacity, for example, to avoid the necessity of closing plants.

The export market can provide a firm with the opportunity to stabilize its market—when the seasonal or cyclical pattern of sales in the foreign export market counterbalances the firm's domestic sales pattern. The benefits of this low correlation between the peaks and valleys in the company's foreign sales and those of its U.S. sales are that the sales in the domestic market and the foreign market will not move down at the same time. With this type of counter-cyclical sales, the firm will not experience slumps in each market at the same time. For example, countries in the Northern and Southern hemispheres tend to have reverse sales patterns because their seasons are opposite. In foreign markets with a low correlation in sales seasons to domestic markets, a slowdown in one market's sales will tend to lag behind a slowdown in the other market's sales. During a world economic slowdown, for example, timing of the effect on sales differs from one country to another. Markets that have a negative correlation experience reverse sales cycles; that is, when a company's domestic sales are up, the company's foreign sales will be down, and vice versa. In summary, a company tends to benefit when it diversifies into overseas markets.

Companies with untapped resources or surplus capacity that are operating at a low margin can also benefit from the expanded opportunities that marketing abroad provides.

PLANNING FOR EXPORT MARKETING

Every company does some planning, on either a regular or an *ad hoc* basis. Planning is an integral part of business management. A good plan lays out a strategy and tactics to meet management's objective. The process of developing a plan includes a thorough examination and evaluation of past performance as well as a chart for the future. A plan is a must in any situation where there is some degree of uncertainty.

Selling abroad needs careful planning to judge the potential of the export market. Careful planning pays handsome dividends; it is necessary for success. This point cannot be overemphasized. We live in a dynamic world economic environment that is subject to continual change; careful planning helps management to anticipate changes that could be inimical to their company's interests. Planning thereby reduces the risk of possible loss. Planning also helps management to optimize the company's profits.

The planning process begins as management decides (1) what product(s) it wants to produce for export, (2) what export market(s) are most suitable, (3) its target growth rate in export sales over a predetermined period of time (given the strengths and weaknesses of the company), and (4) what level of profitability is desired from the company's export operations. The formulation of the company's export policies will stem from these decisions.

The next step of the planning process is the development of strategies to achieve the company's export sales objective, such as, reaching a certain target. This sales target may be expressed in aggregate dollars or in unit volume terms. A sales target stipulated in volume terms is designed to measure real physical growth and would not be distorted by inflationary changes. Another export objective might be to maximize the company's market-penetration ratio. The market penetration ratio measures the company's share of the export market sales. A third objective might be to achieve the maximum market coverage, then to focus on optimization of profits from export sales.

The export planning process requires management to project a product's foreign sales potential from a determination of the demand for its product, the extent of product acceptance, and the size of the export market. Another important facet of export planning is a decision about the mode of distribution: does the company want to be actively involved in the export market or only passively committed to international selling? The degree to which the company wishes to be involved in international trade will determine which channels of distribution should be selected (the various channels of distribution will be discussed later in this chapter).

Export planning is important for all types and sizes of companies. In a series of decisions, the planning process produces a choice about the future course of action for the company in export markets from possible alternatives as well as a choice of means to achieve the objectives set by the company. Systematic evaluation of the alternative courses of action involved in planning, if done properly, will help minimize the risk exposure of the company in the export market and enable the company to capitalize on opportunities.

The Planning Process

Following the company's decision to market its product abroad, the planning process begins with the selection of the best markets for the company's products. This process begins with a preliminary screening of various foreign markets to determine their suitability and capacity to serve as export markets for the company's products. The screening should, for example, consider such factors as: the foreign country's political stability, whether it is on friendly relations with the United States, and whether coverage by the Export/Import Bank's export credit, guarantee, and insurance programs is available. Since some products are designed to meet certain climatic needs or may be affected by climatic conditions, it may be necessary to determine which regions and geographic areas are most suitable for the product. Another factor to be considered is the existing pattern of imports in the contemplated export markets. Do current product demand and acceptability make success likely for this type of product?[1] Data on the types of any tariffs or quotas in each market should also be evaluated to determine how they may affect imports in general and the company's products in particular.

The preliminary screening process resulted in a selected group of export markets that meet certain criteria. These markets are then analyzed to determine their specific potential for the company's products. This analysis of market potential involves a sales and demand analysis. Knowing the sales potential is the first step in setting sales targets for production and for financial planning.

There are several approaches that can be used in estimating the sales potential of each market. One approach is to undertake a survey of consumers' buying habits, income, and spending rates. Surveys can be very expensive, however, especially in a large, faraway market. An alternative approach is to use published historical data to project the likely future sales potential. Historical data can be analyzed by computing historical growth rates of export sales in the market and adjusting the past growth rates in light of expectations for the market. Sophisticated quantitative techniques for analyzing historical export sales data involve the use of trend analysis and correlation analysis to extrapolate future export sales levels. If a product similar to the company's product is produced locally in the foreign market, it is important to ascertain its current output level and growth potential in determining probable demand and in deciding on a distribution channel.

The marketing environment in each country is affected in varying degrees by different combinations of laws and regulations. It is important to know these laws and administrative regulations, which might affect the company's sales to the market. Important local codes might include government regulations of patents and trademarks, labeling requirements, countervailing duties, antimonopoly laws, and antidumping and other trade restrictions. Customs duties and excise taxes (tariffs) should be examined to determine their impact on sales. Similarly, it is important to determine the impact of government regulations on product pricing and marketing costs within each foreign market.

An examination of the structure of each export market is essential to determine its competitive structure, the market leader, the degree of monopoly, and ease of entry and exit. These dynamics provide insight into the export sales potential for the company's products in each market and the share of the export market the company could anticipate.

When the data are gathered for the export marketing planning process, the company will have enough information to choose the export markets that have the ideal export sales capacity and a desirable legal and regulatory environment. The company will have obtained sufficient information to enable it to decide on its "mix" of export products for each of its foreign markets.

Selection of Overseas Markets

Companies entering export trade for the first time may find the principle of "similitude" helpful in selecting foreign markets. The principle of similitude states that the best foreign market for a company is the country that is the most like, or the least unlike, the markets currently served by the firm.[2] In other words, companies should seek to identify those foreign markets whose characteristics are very similar to those of their U.S. domestic markets. Making the right product policy decision is greatly simplified when the company sells in similar markets. For example, the company would not have to worry about product acceptance in the prospective market. Furthermore, the product can be sold in the new market with little or no change in the core product, which helps the company control costs.

Examples of products for which the principle of similitude works best include industrial products and equipment that use a basic technological process to produce a product, or a service. Cosmetics products also sell in most cultures that use them with little or no need for modification. Companies selling cosmetics usually carry a large number of varieties to suit different tastes and needs; in selling to overseas markets, the companies would simply have to select within the range of cosmetics products suitable for the tastes of the specific market. Pharmaceutical products generally sell in all markets without need for any adjustment, since the medical needs of consumers in all markets are pretty much the same.

Determining which overseas markets a company will sell to and how well its product will be accepted is very important in formulating product strategy, because different countries often have very different needs and tastes based on their income, level of development, culture, geographical location, climate, and so on. The company has a choice of three product strategy options: (1) selling a standardized, uniform product in several countries, (2) modifying or adapting the product to fit distinctive local needs, or (3) inventing a unique product in the cases where alternatives (1) or (2) are not possible.[3]

Management can use a "market segmentation" strategy to group countries that have common characteristics relevant to the marketing of its product line. The process of grouping allows management to sell one product, perhaps with some modifications, in several foreign countries with similar characteristics as if they were one fairly homogeneous market.

The identification of an appropriate market segment involves grouping by four criteria (see Table 4.1): (1) socioeconomic characteristics, like demographic, economic, geographic, and climatic characteristics, (2) political and legal variables, (3) consumer or marketing variables, such as culture, taste, style, and (4) financial variables. Market segmentation on the basis of these categories can be carried out step-by-step. First, countries are grouped by socioeconomic variables; that is, the international market is segmented along macroeconomic lines, indicating levels of economic development and industrialization and focusing on the overall market's capacity to buy. These socioeconomic groups are then subdivided on the basis of the political and legal variables, and these subgroupings are further divided on the basis of consumer and marketing variables and, last, by the financial variables. In this way, management can successfully segment the international market into homogeneous market groups for the four elements of its marketing mix: product, price, channels, and promotion.

Market segmentation using groupings can also be done with the aid of multivariate statistical techniques of factor analysis and cluster analysis.[4] Through factor analysis, a large number of variables can be reduced to a manageable number of underlying "factors."[5]

The four groups of variables are listed in Table 4.1. This list is not intended to be exhaustive, and all the variables in each group need not be used for every purpose in connection with doing market segmentation. For example, a company entering export marketing with a limited number of target countries in prospect and with no desire of establishing its own marketing channels in the export countries may not need to examine many of the variables in this analysis. Some companies, on the other hand, may need variables in addition to those included in the table. A determination of the number and types of products the company will offer should be made prior to the choice of product strategy for each grouping.

While grouping is an efficient approach to market segmentation, it would be time-consuming and expensive to collect all the data needed for every country on each variable. Fortunately, much of the data is being collected by international agencies that regularly publish statistics useful for grouping analysis. The World Bank publishes the annual *World Development Report*, which is a rich compilation of economic and demographic data, as well as various computed statistics. The *World Development Report* groups countries by level of economic development and by operating principle: centrally planned versus market economies (we are using the term "market" economies for those countries, primarily in the West, in which the market is still determined largely by the forces of supply and demand). This macroeconomic grouping can be used by smaller companies or new companies whose international activities and resources may prevent the more extensive grouping analysis. It can also be used as a first, general screening by companies who later refine their groupings based on other criteria. The *World Development Report* uses four groups: (1) industrialized countries, (2) middle-income countries, (3) low-income countries, and (4) cen-

Table 4.1 Variables for Grouping of Countries

Socioeconomic variables

    Economic growth indicators
    Inflation
    Import-export restrictions
    Labor availability and skills
    Size of managerial class and number of managers
    Capital sources and costs
    Raw material availability
    Infrastructure
    Religious-racial-language
    Literacy rate
    Population composition

Political-legal variables

    Government attitude toward foreign investment
    Government stability
    Strength and philosophy of labor unions
    Capital repatriation restrictions
    Exchange controls

Political-legal variables (cont.)

    Foreign policy and relations
    Tax laws
    Ownership restrictions
    Nationalism

Marketing variables

    Distribution channels and costs
    Market potential and size
    Projected market share
    Competition
    Promotional resources and costs
    Socioeconomic and cultural characteristics of consumers

Financial variables

    Return on investment
    Length of payback period
    Credit availability

Source: Eugene D. Jaffe, *Grouping: A Strategy for International Marketing* (New York: AMACOM, 1974).

trally planned economies. The World Bank adds a fifth group of countries called the "Capital Surplus Oil Exporters."

Another grouping of countries on the basis of their economic development can be effected by refining the first two World Bank groups, for example: (1) major industrial countries (like Canada, Japan, Germany, France, the United Kingdom, and Italy), (2) large advanced countries (Sweden, Switzerland, Australia, Belgium, Austria, and the Netherlands), (3) large developing countries (Brazil, Argentina, Mexico, India, and Spain), (4) smaller advanced countries (Norway, Denmark, Finland, Israel, and South Africa), and (5) smaller developing countries (the Philippines, Peru, Colombia, and Chile). The *World Development Report* contains many computed indicators that can be combined in various ways to obtain other groupings.

In addition, United Nations agencies produce a series of statistical abstracts each year covering economic, demographic, political, and social characteristics that are very useful for grouping analysis. Data on international trade and finance are published quarterly and annually by the International Monetary Fund (IMF). Both the Organization for Economic Cooperation and Development (OECD) and the European Economic Community (EEC) publish a variety of statistical reports and studies on their respective member countries.

Market segmentation though grouping provides management with a basis for delineating the international export market into various segments. Management can examine those segments that meet its basic criteria in order to narrow the field to those countries that meet its final screening tests. The next step is to develop strategies for the various elements of the marketing mix, namely, as noted previously: product, price, promotion, and channels of distribution. The marketing mix is important because the success of the strategy as a whole depends to some extent on the effectiveness of each of the strategy's components.

Product Strategy

The grouping technique enables the firm to link various countries into one homogeneous market which meets the company's marketing objectives. The next task is to develop a product strategy for the selected export market. The export market clusters obtained by using the grouping approach fall into three categories.

The first category would be countries with the same basic characteristics as those of the U.S. market. In these nations, the firm can market the same core product it markets in the domestic market without any change, and with little or no change in promotional and auxiliary services—such as after-sales servicing. Here, the company is selling a standardized, uniform product to a group of countries. A ready example of this kind of consumer product is soft drinks. The Coca-Cola Company markets essentially one "Coke" worldwide. Every country has the same demand-marketing characteristics for "Coke," thus no change is needed. Another consumer product that has gained worldwide market acceptance in its classic form is "blue jeans." Levi Strauss & Company and other manufacturers export and market jeans worldwide without any basic change. In point of fact, some products are demanded by foreign consumers just because of their "foreign" characteristics: this type of product must be marketed abroad just as it is sold in the domestic market in order to maintain its strong appeal. Coca-Cola and jeans carry this type of appeal. Calculators and portable stereos are good examples of U.S. products that carry the special "foreign" appeal abroad. These products are enormously popular abroad. Conversely, examples of foreign products sold in the United States with a "foreign" appeal are Scotch whiskey, French cognac and wines, English woolens, and Swiss watches.

Products that can be standardized may satisfy basic consumer needs that do not vary with climate, economic conditions, or culture. Some examples of consumer products that can be marketed from one country to the next without change are food, cosmetics and toiletries, pharmaceuticals, and certain electronics products. A standardized product is the cheapest to sell abroad, since the firm does not incur any additional manufacutirng costs to adapt the product to the needs of foreign markets. Industrial products tend to be standardized to a greater extent than consumer products. Industrial products are manufactured to be operated at certain levels of technology with specific material inputs; particular equipment is designed for a specific production process. In many cases, the technology is bought as is. There are, of course, cases in which the equipment may have to be slightly modified to meet local needs. A slightly different example of the standardized, universal product line for export marketing is the product that requires minor or superficial changes (such as brighter or duller colors, different sizes, or new packaging). The modified product can then be marketed in a group of countries in basically the same form as in the domestic market. Climate, topography, culture, or government regulations may require some minor change, which leaves the core of the product essentially unchanged. Standardized product marketing abroad usually requires a greater amount of promotional effort than in domestic markets to inform consumers of the product's attributes and how well it meets their needs.

A second group of countries might be suitable for a product strategy in which the product (for example, cars) must be modified or adapted to fit a unique set of needs or uses in the new markets or countries. This kind of domestic product either does not meet the needs of the foreign consumers or it does nto satisfy administrative regulations of the foreign countries. Market segmentation through the grouping technique would produce a cluster of homogeneous countries for which product modification would be worthwhile.

A third group of countries would require a brand-new product because neither the standardized product nor the modified product would be salable. This third alternative is the most expensive, since it entails costs of research, development, and new marketing techniques to promote a product the firm has no domestic experience with.

In terms of the firm's risk and probable return on its investment, the standaidized product presents the least risk and often offers the most profitable return, since the firm does not incur additional start-up or retooling costs in manufacturing the product for the export market. Most U.S. exports fit into this general category. In the second alternative, the modified product, if the company cannot price the product high enough to cover the cost of modification, it will have to absorb the extra cost and accept less return on investment. The risk exposure of the firm also increases when the product is altered to meet the needs of distinctive markets. The demand for the modified product may be limited to the specific country for which it was modified. If the modification or adaptation can be reversed, the risk will be commensurately reduced. On the other hand, the cost of restoring the product to its original form for another market will increase costs and correspondingly impair profitability, unless this cost can be passed on to the customers.

The product strategy decided on by the firm will determine the nature of the auxiliary services the firm will have to provide. The usually enormous distance between buyers and sellers increases the need for auxiliary service in the foreign markets in which the firm's products are used. Auxiliary services are always required if the product is consumer durable and, in many cases, if the product is an industrial product. Provision of auxiliary services is a must when the firm's brand name is not well established. To be successful, a firm must pay close attention to assisting consumers to achieve maximum use of the product by providing efficient auxiliary services.

Export Pricing

The second key element in the export marketing mix is the pricing policy—a marketing tool that could enable a firm to attain the planned sales objectives and other goals in its target export markets. Pricing policy plays a key role in the firm's competitive position in its export markets. More often than not, U.S. firms are competing with their European industrial counterparts. These European competitors have become very keen pricing tacticians, because of their need to sell in export markets within the EEC, in the Eastern European countries, and in the Third World countries. Pricing, therefore, is a major determining factor for the U.S. firm in achieving its export sales targets in overseas markets.

Pricing decisions always involve a consideration of complex factors, since pricing strategies can affect the firm's promotion and distribution efforts. Pricing decisions in the export market are especially complex because they have to interrelate also with consideration of the foreign cultural, political, and social environment. There are special factors that affect export pricing that are not normally part of domestic pricing, import duties for example. As part of its pricing policy, the firm has to decide who pays for the local import duties on the firm's products. The firm may decide to pass all of the duties on to the consumer, or it may absorb all of the duties into its profit margin—or it may split the duties between the consumer and the firm. The decision on how the firm treats import duties should also take into account the firm's competitive position and its competitors' prices, as well as the firm's price level in relation to its sales objective.

Other special considerations in export pricing include nontariff barriers such as local taxes on imported goods, and national preference laws or campaigns, such as "buy Canadian" or "buy British." Foreign governments may impose special regulations on imports such as labeling requirements, "unfair" pricing laws, and price controls that could have an impact on the pricing decisions of the firm.

In developing the firm's export pricing policy, management should take into consideration not only the explicit cost of the product but also implicit costs— that is, indirect costs that affect the firm's marketing mix, its goals and objectives, and its available resources. For example, an export product may have to be subsidized if it is to meet a firm's market-penetration goals. The price impact on the company's activities includes a range of questions related to overall marketing policy and strategy.

Management should ascertain the life cycle of the firm's product in the target market and identify the current stage in the cycle of the product, since timing factors influence its pricing decisions. The pricing policy of a firm can be either passive or active. Pricing a product in its mature stage is called "passive" pricing because the commodity or product by then is in a market in which the firm cannot set a price for it. Such situations arise when the product is a standardized commodity such as an agricultural product, like grains such as wheat or corn, or coffee. Other types of standardized commodities include natural resources such as iron ore or copper. These commodities lack product differentiation such as a brand name that would tie the product to the firm. There are other situations in which the market structure dictates a passive pricing policy. Firms in "perfect competition" with each other have no control over the price of the product. Generally, perfect competition occurs when the product traded is standardized; therefore, the buyer has no preference for any one seller's product. For most manufactured goods, however, the firm can differentiate its product, so that consumers cannot accurately compare prices of the different brands. In summary, the firm controls its prices to varying degrees, depending on the product's stage in its life cycle, and the type of market, competition, and government regulation.

In an active pricing policy, the firm integrates its pricing decision into the market mix and develops pricing strategies to achieve the firm's planned objectives. An exporter can enjoy a considerable amount of pricing flexibility when the demand already exists for its product in the export market and foreign consumers show a preference for that product. This consumer preference may reflect the product's performance, its styling, or its general quality. When a firm enjoys a high level of consumer preference for its products, it can adopt a most profitable pricing strategy. The problem that still faces the firm is integrating its pricing policy into its marketing mix; that is, achieving the optimal pricing strategy while meeting the firm's other objectives.

Pricing policy has a lot to do with the type of distribution channel selected by the company. For example, companies selling products directed at a mass market, or companies that wish to adopt mass-marketing techniques, usually price their product at relatively low markups and use mass-merchandising channels of distribution.

An active pricing strategy should be synchronized with the product's stage in its life cycle. In many cases, when a firm enters an export market, its product is new, differentiated, and enjoys a special status in the market. In such situations, the firm has a choice between two basic pricing strategies.

Under the first strategy the firm's policy is to "skim the cream" of the demand by charging the highest price it determines the market will bear. The degree to which the firm has the leverage to use this strategy would, of course, be related to the extent of the product's differentiation from its competitors in the export market, except that sometimes a high price has "snob appeal," which in itself is a promotional factor. The skimming price strategy gives the firm comparatively high profit margins, which then attract competitors, who introduce similar products which appeal to the same consumers. As competition multiplies, the original firm will be forced to reduce its price to increase—or even maintain—sales. The skimming price strategy is most effective over the long run, therefore, when the firm has a monopoly on the basic ingredients in the product or is the sole owner of the patent on the technology involved. Skimming price strategy was used effectively in the case of Polaroid instant film. Polaroid had a monopoly on its film technology, with patent protection. In the absence of competition, the Polaroid Company enjoyed a very high price for its camera for a long time. With the entry of Kodak into instant film technology, the price of Polaroid's cameras has dropped significantly.

The other pricing strategy for a differentiated product is "penetration" pricing, which attempts to penetrate the market as quickly as possible and gain the largest possible market share. To this end, the price of the product is set comparatively low. This low price appeals to consumers, who switch their brand preference or develop a new-found demand for this kind of product and so enter the market. Penetration-pricing strategy is particularly effective in the developing countries, where income levels are lower than in industrialized countries. Penetration pricing produces low margins per unit, but in total it can be just as profitable as skimming, if the lower price stimulates the demand for the product and significantly increases sales volume.

An ideal way to determine the best export price of a firm's product is to survey consumers about their differential demand over a range of prices. On the basis of the demand schedule, matched with a cost-supply schedule, the price would be computed at the level where marginal revenue just equals the marginal cost. This is the textbook approach of economists. In practice, information on consumers in export markets is not readily available and details of their buying history are scarce.

In addition, as we shall see, while companies use "marginal-cost" pricing to some extent for production, "average cost-plus margin" markup is the more widely used method for determining the selling price. Companies use three general approaches in setting the price of their products for the export market. In the first approach, firms determine the price on the basis of their cost for a unit, plus a margin of profit. This approach is known as the "cost-plus" method. It is widely used because of its relative simplicity. Export companies usually start with their domestic price as the equivalent of their cost basis and add to it a markup for profit. This practice of using the firm's domestic price as the cost analog has been criticized for various reasons, including: (1) the company's promotional and sales costs already included in the domestic price are not relevant to the export market; (2) on the other hand, packaging and documentation costs connected with overseas shipping may not be fully accounted for; and (3) research costs may not be properly allocated among the markets. The ideal cost-plus pricing formula would be materials and labor cost, plus manufacturing overhead, plus selling expense, plus general overhead expenses equals Cost, plus a given profit margin equals Price. To counter some of this criticism, a modified form of the pure cost-plus pricing formula could forsake an arbitrary profit add-on for one which took account of demand and competitive conditions in the target market, resulting in a profit margin markup that changed from market to market and from product to product.

The second pricing approach—"marginal-cost" pricing—simply takes the prevailing price in the target export market as the firm's selling price, working backward to compute the theoretical residual profit margin after all costs had been incurred. Management would decide whether the prevailing price was appropriate based on the size of the estimated residual profit margin. If the residual profit margin met the firm's profit objective, management would approve sales to the export market; if the profit margin was smaller than the firm's profit objective, management would have to decide whether it was adequate in terms of the firm's other marketing policy objectives. If the margin was too low and if the other policy objectives could not be met, management might decide not to sell in that particular export market.

A third approach to pricing is a hybrid of this marginal-cost pricing approach. It is called the "profit-contribution" approach.[6] In this approach, the final buyer's price is used as the "base" price for the pricing strategy and discount structure. The use of the final buyer's price as the base presupposes that the exporter has control of its distribution channels, but not all exporters would be in this position. In the profit-contribution approach, the profit contribution is computed at various prices on various levels of unit volume. From the total revenue the incremental costs of selling are subtracted to arrive at the estimated profit component. The figure with the highest profit contribution would offer the optimal price level. However, management would then have to determine whether its other policy objectives are best satisfied at the optimal profit-contribution level. This profit-contribution approach can be used to analyze various price levels and their corollary sales volume and profit contribution, in deciding whether to use a skimming or a penetration pricing policy.

Export Marketing Channels

The export marketing channel serves as the connecting link between the manufacturer and the consumer. It represents an organization of channel members who move the product from the producer to the ultimate consumer in the export market. An export channel may be a direct link between the United States producer and the foreign user, as in the exports of high-technology industrial equipment, or it may involve numerous intermediate agents, as in the case of a typical consumer item. The type and configuration of the channel depend on such factors as the nature of the product and the firm's marketing objectives. The export marketing channel provides the U.S. producer with the distribution facilities to move the firm's product to the consumer. Channel members, therefore, represent an important link in the export marketing process. An efficient export strategy requires careful selection of the marketing channel that fits best with other elements in the marketing mix, such as pricing, packaging, advertising, and inventory management.

The choice of channel usually follows a study of the various target markets to identify potential consumers and the marketing process in those markets. This study provides the firm with information to evaluate the types of distribution channels currently available in the market and their effectiveness.

The choice of distribution channel depends also on the type of product policy the firm has adopted for its product strategy. A product differentiation strategy, for example, involves significant promotional effort to develop brand preference and loyalty in the target market. A firm with a product differentiation strategy would select the type of marketing channel that is most efficient in promoting brand preference and loyalty. In contrast, a firm with a market segmentation strategy would choose the type of marketing channel that would focus on those attributes of the product that would appeal to each market segment. Or, a firm with a skimming price policy would select a channel serving specialty shops. The channel also provides the auxiliary services that would support the product after its sale.

There are other types of agents involved in the marketing process that are not considered to be members of the export channel of distribution. These agents provide various services to exporters but they do not control the physical flow of the merchandise at any stage of the distribution process. These agents are generally considered to be facilitating agencies. Examples include banks, advertising agencies, transportation companies, forwarders, and public warehouses. It is important to distinguish these facilitating agencies from the export channel members.

Indirect Export Channels of Distribution

Indirect exporting involves the use of independent U.S. middlemen to market the firm's products overseas. These middlemen, known as export representatives, assume responsibility for marketing the firm's product through their network of foreign distributors and their own sales force. It is common for a U.S. producer who is new to export marketing to begin its export operation by selling through an export representative. Some other U.S. firms' export activities may be too limited to warrant setting up their own export department. In these cases, the U.S. middlemen play a significant role, especially for the smaller company that is interested in only a few foreign markets. Such a company can initiate its export operations through U.S. export representatives who know the markets and have experience in selling in them. The middlemen can save the company the cost of starting up its own export department and allow it to gain time and experience in the market.

There are several types of U.S. export representatives. The most common are (1) the combination export manager, (2) the export merchant, (3) the export broker, (4) the export commission house, (5) the trading company with U.S. offices, and (6) the "piggyback" exporter.

The Combination Export Manager

The CEM is the most important of the independent export representatives, but there are only a few good CEMs in the United States. The CEM acts as an export department to a small manufacturer or to a large producer with relatively small export sales. In either case, the scale of export activities does not warrant the setting up of a special export department to sell to the target export markets. The CEM often uses in correspondence the letterhead of the company he represents. The CEM has extensive experience in selling abroad and expertise in the mechanics of export shipment. The CEM usually has a network of overseas distribution channels with thorough knowledge of and direct access to the foreign markets.

A CEM carries the accounts of several export clients, with similar but not competing products, on a commission basis. The CEM operates in many foreign markets and cannot concentrate his efforts on marketing any individual client's product in a particular market.

CEMs are most effective when they deal with clients with businesses in related lines, but until their reputation is established, they usually have to accept all clients to achieve enough sales volume to survive. Later, when the agent is in a position to be selective, he may have difficulty in winnowing out old clientele. The more reputable CEMs tend to limit their number of clients to around 10 accounts to give the CEMs greater specialization in the product lines they handle and the foreign markets in which they operate. Other CEMs sometimes handle up to 40 or 50 accounts, thereby spreading themselves thin across many different countries.

The income of the CEM depends in part on the export activities of the client exporting firms. Naturally, when a CEM loses a major account, its business suffers until that account can be replaced. Because of the vulnerability of the CEM that comes from its dependence on clients, there has been a shift from the CEM who is a representative of export companies on a commission basis to the CEM middleman who buys from producers for export on his own account. This shift has been reinforced by the reluctance of the export clients to extend credit to foreign buyers. Since credit plays an increasingly important role in export sales, CEMs have found it increasingly difficult to consummate export sales on behalf of clients without their credit support. When they are buyers and exporters of products on their own account, CEMs can extend the necessary credit themselves. A number of good and reputable CEMs still operate on a commission basis, although they may be a vanishing breed.[7]

The Export Merchant The export merchant sells products bought from U.S. producers through a large, worldwide marketing organization. Since the export merchant buys and sells on his own account, he assumes all responsibilities for the exporting of the products. In this situation the manufacturers do not control the sales activities for their product in the export market and are entirely dependent on the export merchant for the foreign sales performance of the product. Some export merchants even repack and relabel products bought from U.S. manufacturers before selling them abroad.

One major drawback of using the export merchant as a middleman for export marketing is this total loss of control over the marketing effort. If a manufacturer who starts exporting by using middlemen some day wishes to develop more direct marketing channels, then the producer will have little knowledge of the export markets and just as little expertise in managing the marketing mix to operate in those markets.

The Export Broker The activities of the export broker are implied in the name: a broker who brings together a foreign buyer and a U.S. manufacturer for the purpose of completing an export sale. The export broker earns a commission for establishing a contact which results in a sale. A broker develops a specialty in dealing with certain foreign markets and kinds of products—often staple or standardized manufactured goods. The role of the export broker was highlighted in an article in *Business Week* of October 27, 1973, called "Bartering to beat the chemical shortage," which showed how brokers stepped in during a U.S. chemical shortage by arranging barter deals.

Export Commission Houses Foreign buyers of U.S. goods usually contract for the services of a U.S. representative to act on their behalf. This resident representative in the United States is usually an export commission house. The house places orders for its foreign clients with U.S. manufacturers and acts as finder of U.S. goods to get the best buy for its clients. The export commission house acts only on behalf of its clients and does not buy on its own account.

Trading Companies with Offices in the United States These trading companies are large foreign organizations engaged in importing and exporting. They buy on their own account in the United States and export the purchases back to their country of origin. These large trading companies handle a wide range of commodities and products, and can also be used by U.S. companies to market their products overseas.

Most of the well-known trading companies are Japanese or Western European. Japanese trading companies like Mitsui and Mitsubishi operate worldwide and handle around 90 percent of Japanese foreign trade. The reputable United Africa Company (UAC), a subsidiary of Unilever, operates extensively throughout West Africa and other parts of Africa. UAC handles everything from manufacturing activity to retail outlets. Another European trading company is Jardine Matheson in Hong Kong, a major trading force in Southeast Asia. The Danish East Asiatic Company also operates in Southeast Asia. The European trading companies in Southeast Asia, Jardine Atheson and the East Asiatic Company, and the UAC in West Africa operate with the consent of the host countries; they are perceived as multinational giants.

Their widespread channels of distribution can be used by U.S. manufacturers who wish to enter the export market. One drawback is that these trading companies carry great varieties of products, some of which may compete with a given U.S. product. Furthermore, this diversity of product line means that there is little or no promotion for several individual products, some of which may have to sell themselves.

The Piggyback Exporter   Some U.S. manufacturing firms that have an established in-house export department do assume, under cooperative arrangement, the responsibility for export marketing the products of other U.S. companies that are new to export trade, lack their own export department, or prefer not to invest the resources to establish an export department. In these cases, a "carrier" with a functioning export department and an established overseas distribution network will accept compatible, noncompeting product lines from the cooperating firms, called the "riders," for exporting piggyback style (in the sense of a shared responsibility for transportation and selling). Both cooperating firms benefit from the arrangement. The carrier benefits from adding a compatible product line and thereby broadening its own line of product offerings. The rider benefits from the carrier's established international marketing network and experience in selling in foreign markets.

The carrier usually buys the rider's products and markets them independently. The rider plays a passive role in the marketing effort overseas. For companies that do not want to commit their firm's resources to establishing an export department, piggybacking may be a desirable path to reach the export market. But as in the arrangement with the export merchant, the company loses control over its product sales overseas and may lose close contact with market information that could help it increase its export marketing role in those markets in the future.

Direct Export Marketing

In the previous section we considered several ways of using middlemen in the United States to conduct an export business. As the product becomes well known to consumers abroad with the passage of time, sales volume will rise. As sales volume abroad becomes a higher percentage of the company's total sales, the company may find the use of middlemen to be cumbersome. At this point, the establishment of an in-house unit to handle the company's sales abroad will be desirable.

There are two ways the company can set up its in-house entity: (1) by creating an export department or (2) by establishing a company-owned export subsidiary.

In-House Export Department   In establishing an in-house export department, the first step is to assign a full-time export officer to manage export activities. Companies will commonly assign the executive who had been the *de facto* supervisor, on a part-time basis, of the company's export activity via its middleman. The total manpower resources committed to the company's new export unit will depend on the volume of sales at the time the need is identified. If the need is identified early, then a single manager may be adequate, with more manpower needed as sales volume rises. Since credit plays a significant role in foreign sales, a foreign credit manager may be the next one to be hired, followed perhaps by a foreign distribution manager. The organization of the export department will depend on company policy and the organization of the company's domestic activities. The export department can be organized along product, functional, or geographical lines. How to run a direct exporting operation will be explained later in this chapter.

The Subsidiary Export Company   Another vehicle available to a U.S. manufacturer for its exporting business is the wholly owned export subsidiary. This subsidiary export company is located in the United States and takes care of all the export activities of the parent company. The subsidiary provides many advantages to the parent manufacturing company over other export arrangements. The subsidiary export company is frequently organized to take advantage of some law that applies to export companies. The subsidiary formed under such laws usually enjoys certain tax advantages designed by Congress to encourage export by U.S. corporations. Such legal entities must meet certain prescribed requirements that qualify them as: (1) a Western Hemisphere Trade Corporation (WHTC), (2) a United States Possessions Corporation (USPC), or (3) a Webb-Pomerene Association.

The wholly owned export subsidiary has the primary responsibility for managing the exports of the parent company. In some cases, the subsidiary has the full responsibility for all overseas activities, including overseas branches and manufacturing facilities abroad. When the export subsidiary assumes full control of all overseas operations, it assumes the responsibility for financial and tax obligations of overseas operations. This insulates the parent company from any foreign financial problems or tax complications arising from operations abroad.

The Western Hemisphere Trade Corporation   To qualify as a WHTC, a firm must do all its business in the Western Hemisphere, derive at least 90 percent of its gross income from the active conduct of business (as opposed to investments), and derive at least 95 percent of its gross income from sales outside the United States. A WHTC can establish branches abroad, but it cannot establish subsidiaries abroad where the dividend income from the subsidiaries is less than

10 percent of the corporation's gross income. Subsidiaries that qualify as a WHTC are subject to a lower corporate income tax rate—36 percent—and 85 percent of the dividends paid by the WHTC to its U.S. parent company are exempt from parent-company income taxes.

The WHTC is essentially the export sales arm of the parent. It functions somewhat as the export merchant. It buys from its U.S. parent and sells to non-U.S. Western Hemisphere customers at a markup. The WHTC may solicit orders and carry out after-sales service and technical assistance on the products it sells, on a fee-reimbursement basis, for the parent.

The United States Possessions Corporation   This type of subsidiary is designed to encourage U.S. businesses to increase their activities in the U.S. possessions, such as Puerto Rico, by offering attractive incentives like tax relief and tax exemptions. A USPC can be incorporated in either the United States or a U.S. possession, except that the Virgin Islands are not considered a possession for this purpose.

The income of the USPC that is incorporated in the United States is generally exempt from U.S. corporate income taxes if: (1) at least 80 percent of its gross income is derived from within qualified U.S. possessions, and (2) at least 50 percent of its gross income is from the active conduct of trade or business.

When, on the other hand, a USPC is organized and operating in a U.S. possession, it is not subject to any U.S. corporate income taxes. Then, to encourage U.S. industry to locate in these U.S. possessions, the local government offers tax exemptions or tax holidays to U.S. companies. A USPC organized and operating in a qualified U.S. possession can thereby manufacture goods in the possession and export worldwide without being subject to taxation from either government.

The Webb-Pomerene Association   To enable U.S. exporters to compete effectively with foreign businesses, Congress enacted the Webb-Pomerene Act in 1918, which permits U.S. exporters to form "associations" for the sole purpose of promoting exports through cooperative efforts. These Webb-Pomerene Associations are exempt from antitrust laws only for export trade activities and cannot participate in domestic trade. Webb-Pomerene Associations provide their members with counseling and promotional information on related products.

Distribution in Overseas Direct Exporting   The U.S. exporter may distribute its products through distribution channels located overseas in the foreign country where the export markets are, just as the firm would use a domestic distributor in the United States. When an exporter uses a foreign business intermediary to distribute its products in the export market, the exporter is engaged in a form of indirect exporting, but since the company deals directly with the foreign intermediary, it is, to some extent, involved in direct exporting activities. It may have its own in-house export department to manage the foreign distribution channels. In contrast to the use of domestic middlemen or agents, the use of foreign representatives increases the company's involvement in its export activities.

Companies involved in direct exporting can use several different types of marketing channels in overseas markets to reach the target consumers. Direct marketing involves the shipment of the goods by the manufacturer to the export market. When the goods arrive in the foreign country, the manufacturer has a choice of (1) using foreign middlemen or sales representatives or (2) setting up a branch or an affiliate to handle the product. The choice between middlemen and the company's own facilities depends on the extent of control the manufacturer desires over its channel of distribution. New entrants into a foreign market may find it convenient to use foreign middlemen at least initially to take advantage of the middleman's experience and knowledge of the target market. As the sales volume increases, the manufacturer may desire to increase its involvement in the marketing of the product in the overseas market. The logical step then would be to set up a branch or an affiliate that would permit the manufacturer to retain control of overseas distribution.

The type of product sometimes dictates the type of channel used in a foreign market. Standardized products, for example, can normally be sold through foreign wholesalers and foreign retailers. Determination of the best distribution channel to use in each foreign country would involve consideration of the company's policy objectives and marketing mix.

The firm would, of course, also have to consider the kind of distribution system available in the target markets. The industrialized countries usually have distribution channels similar to those of the United States. But they may also have other types of marketing channels. Distribution channels in developing countries may differ to a greater or lesser degree from those in the United States. It is important, therefore, that the firm investigate the types of distribution channel available in each country and their relative efficiency before a choice is made.

There are four general approaches to the form of organization a firm could use in overseas distribution. They are: (1) the foreign distributor, (2) the commission representative, (3) an overseas corporate branch of the firm, and (4) a wholly owned foreign subsidiary.

The Foreign Distributor   The foreign distributor is usually an independent business representative who buys and sells on his own account. A good foreign distributor knows the target market well and is familiar with all the nuances of doing business in that market. The distributor has his own facilities, thereby freeing the exporting firm from the need to commit its own resources for physical facilities and financial support.

The U.S. firm benefits from the distributor's knowledge of and expertise in the local market. A new entrant in a foreign market lacks information about the market and has to learn how the market works, which takes time and experience. The services of the foreign distributor allow the company time to gain knowledge of the market while its products are penetrating the market.

As an independent businessman, the foreign distributor will be handling a variety of products, in addition to the company's. It is important that the company select a distributor with a marketing philosophy similar to that of the company. The type of product to be handled will dictate the best kind of distributor. Of course, it is in the company's best interest that the distributor not handle competing products. Other factors to be considered by the firm in the choice of distributor are: marketing capacity, the lines of products handled, financial status, sales policy, reputation within the trade, trade-group affiliations, political influence, and nationality.

The exporter should find out whether the distributor will maintain inventory or simply relay orders from his customers. The possibility of lost sales between orders and shipment may affect the firm's ability to attain maximum potential sales. Sometimes the exporter provides credit to help finance the distributor's inventory if credit is a constraining factor for an otherwise attractive candidate.

The process of selecting a foreign distributor may be divided into three major steps: (1) identifying a possible distributor, (2) screening, and (3) contact. Information on distributor candidates can be obtained from several sources, including trade lists available from the U.S. Department of Commerce field offices; the World Trade Directory, which gives reports on firms, is also available from the field offices of the Department of Commerce. Dun and Bradstreet Guides are also a useful source of information on foreign distributors. A list of potential distributors can be easily extracted from the various sources. The firm should draw up a list of attributes it desires in a distributor in order to have the best match with its product and marketing strategy. From the list of potential distributors the firm can screen out its selection. The next step is to make contact.

The Commission Representative   The commission representative is an agent who seeks out buyers for the company's products and takes orders for the company. He forwards the orders to the company and the company prepares the consignment and ships the products directly to the buyers. The commission representative earns his commission when the sale is consummated.

The commission representative plays an important role in the distribution of U.S. exports in overseas markets. The representative normally represents several manufacturers of noncompeting products and possesses an expert knowledge of the market with a proven track record in marketing products of his principals.

Unless the commission representative takes title to the consignment, the exporter is responsible for the goods until they reach the buyer. In addition, the exporter, rather than the commission representative, usually assumes responsibility for credit risks. The representative does, however, provide assistance to the exporter's collection procedures.

The commission representative is ideal for distribution of highly valued equipment where special sales effort and handling are required.

The Overseas Corporate Branch   Companies retain full control of their export marketing channels when they have an overseas corporate branch under the direct control of the headquarters export marketing department or an international division responsible in part for export marketing. The overseas branch can be expected to coordinate its activities with those of the U.S. corporate headquarters and to execute the plans faithfully to achieve the company's overall goals. Because the marketing channel in exporting is a continuous chain linking the producer to the ultimate consumers, with the producer ultimately responsible for the distribution of its products to the consumer, the producer must ensure that the consumer receives the best sales service for its products in order to increase consumer awareness of and satisfaction with the products, thereby increasing demand for the products. Thus an overseas corporate sales branch can increase the effectiveness of its company's export sales by providing the consumer with this service before and after the sale.

A local overseas branch affords the parent company several other advantages, which can be grouped into the categories of (1) management and control, and (2) tax benefits.

There are several benefits to manufacturers in the form of management and control from the establishment of overseas branches. Control over the branch comes from staffing: as the company's own employees, they are part of the corporate team and can be expected to give maximum cooperation in achieving the company's marketing objectives. The foreign branch is convenient: it can be easily set up and, if necessary, can be just as easily dissolved. The physical makeup of the local branch can be tailored to meet the company's needs, from a simple one-room office to an elaborate suite. In fact, maintaining a local branch may have cost advantages over other forms of distribution, when all factors are considered. The local branch benefits from the creditworthiness of the parent when it borrows locally. And the U.S. parent company can deduct losses from foreign exchange transactions from its taxable income.

The Wholly Owned Foreign Subsidiary The wholly owned foreign subsidiary provides the U.S. parent company with advantages in respect to control of the export marketing channel that are similar to those of the overseas branch. The foreign subsidiary is incorporated in the country in which it operates and is, therefore, a foreign (that is, non-U.S.) corporation, but it remains under the direct control of the U.S. parent corporation. The foreign subsidiary may have branches in the foreign country, which could be needed if demand for the product increases or if the company wishes to expand its market penetration. The foreign subsidiary's liability is limited to the extent of its own assets; therefore, the parent company is insulated from risk exposure from the subsidiary's activities. (Of course, the parent company's investment in the subsidiary may be exposed to some risk, including the risk of expropriation.) Locally incorporated companies enjoy a much more favorable acceptance in foreign countries than do branches of U.S. companies and may, for that reason, generate better sales than a branch setup.

Host foreign countries often offer a variety of tax incentives to locally incorported subsidiaries of U.S. companies. For example, developing countries may have tax holiday plans and other incentives to encourage the local incorporation of subsidiaries. Another tax advantage of a locally incorporated subsidiary is that, since it is a foreign company although wholly owned by a U.S. parent, its profits are not treated as part of the parent's U.S. corporate taxable income. Its dividends to its U.S. parent company are not taxed until they are remitted to the U.S. parent. (Note that under subparagraph F of the Revenue Act of 1962, this postponement of the tax is not allowed to corporations nominally located outside the United States but in fact incorporated in the United States and wholly controlled by the U.S. parent.)

SUMMARY

The rapid growth of world trade during the past two decades has provided U.S. firms with increased opportunities to enter the export market or to expand their present activities abroad. U.S. companies enter export markets for several reasons. Some companies view the world as a global market which enables them to take advantage of economies of scale in their operations. Other companies see the international market as basically a way of extending the life cycle of their product. Still other companies enter the export market to take up the slack in domestic demand for their product.

It is important for a company that is considering either entering or expanding its activities in the export market to develop a good plan to provide management with tactical and strategic designs to fulfill the company's objectives. A clear definition of objectives is essential in effectively planning product development, export marketing, target growth rate in export sales, and desired level of profitability.

Once management has decided to market its product abroad, it sets in motion an export marketing planning process to: (1) select attractive markets for further, detailed analysis, (2) evaluate each market's potential, and (3) design the best marketing mix. The marketing mix includes the development of product strategy, export pricing policy, and the design and selection of marketing channels.

A careful analysis and assessment of the foreign market is important to future success. Companies use a variety of approaches in selecting overseas markets. Many firms entering export marketing find the principle of "similitude" useful in minimizing start-up costs and thus improving chances of success: choice of a familiar market environment can be an important factor in determining good product strategy. A second approach for market selection is market segmentation through grouping techniques, which enable the firm to categorize various countries into homogeneous markets that can then be supplied with the most appropriate products.

Following the choice of export market, the next task is the development of the firm's product strategy. Three basic product strategies are generally used: (1) exporting the same product sold in the domestic market, (2) modifying or adapting the export product to fit local needs or applications, and (3) tailoring a new product to an export market where a standardized or slightly customized product cannot be sold.

The firm's export pricing policy can be an effective marketing tool in enabling the firm to attain its planned sales objectives and other goals. In formulating its pricing policies, the firm must take into consideration complex factors such as the cultural, political, and social environment, in addition to the usual supply/demand factors. An active pricing policy should also reflect the stage of the life cycle the product is in at the time.

Companies use one of three general approaches to price their products for export markets: (1) cost plus, (2) prevailing price for similar products in the export market, and (3) profit-contribution. The pricing approach selected would depend on the forces then prevailing in the export market and on management's objectives.

Selecting the best export marketing channels is critical, because the marketing channel serves as the connecting link between the manufacturer and the consumer. The choice of channel depends on the foreign market's consumer characteristics, type of product, and pricing policy of the firm. The firm can use either a direct or indirect channel of distribution, depending on the firm's marketing mix.

NOTES

1 Data for previous years can be obtained from publications of the OECD, EEC, the United Nations, and the U.S. Department of Commerce.

2 Eudel J. Kolde, *International Business Enterprise* (Englewood Cliffs, N.J.: Prentice-Hall, 1968), p. 309.

3 Warren J. Keegan, "Multinational Product Planning, Strategic Alternatives," *Journal of Marketing* (January 1969), pp. 58–62.

4 With the aid of the minicomputers now readily available at reasonable prices, factor analysis and cluster analysis can be done by almost anyone. There are some canned programs available for the minicomputer. For discussion of the various techniques see Michael R. Anderberg, *Cluster Analysis for Applications* (New York: Academic Press, 1973).

5 For an example of market segmentation based on groupings with the application of factor analysis see Eugene D. Joffe, *Grouping: A Strategy for International Marketing* (New York: AMACOM, 1974).

6 See Franklin R. Root, *Strategic Planning for Export Marketing* (Denmark: Bianco Lunos Bogtrykkeri, A.S., 1964), pp. 75–78.

7 CEMs are listed in the *American Register of Exporters and Importers* and the Yellow Pages of the telephone directory.

5

Managing Country Risk

Because companies engaged in international commerce carry out part of their business activities within the national boundaries of foreign countries, the operations of these companies are affected by forces and events in the foreign environment that are controlled directly or indirectly by the foreign government. The effect of the foreign environment on the business activities of the international company may thus result in economic and financial gains or losses. Country risk embodies the total risk that arises from the economic, social, and political environment peculiar to a given foreign country (including government policies instituted in response to trends in the environment) that may have favorable or adverse consequences for the profitability and/or recovery of debt or equity investments made in that country. Consideration of country risk must include an assessment of the probability of its occurrence and its impact on the investment, whether it is an equity or debt investment. Country risk does not include normal casualty or business risks routinely encountered in the course of business in any country.

In this chapter we identify and examine various factors and events that underlie country risk, how to assess risk, and how to control exposure to country risk.

CLASSIFICATIONS OF COUNTRY RISK

Some of the determinants of country risk that must be considered in deciding whether to invest in a given country include: nature of the transaction or type of loan taken by the borrower (or purchaser), type of borrower or purchaser, geographical location, and kinds of events or situations. These considerations are not mutually exclusive; they tend to overlap and are usually used in combination. Table 5.1 gives four of the various considerations that are relevant to country risk for each major type of international investment. Considerations of geographical location are relevant to all types of lenders or investors. Interna-

Table 5.1   Determinants of Investment

Type of Lender	Consideration			
	Nature of Transaction or of Loan	Action Taken by Borrower or Purchaser that May Cause a Loss	Type of Borrower or Purchaser	Situations or Events that May Result in Country Risk
Commercial bank or other lending institution	√	√	√	√
Portfolio investment	NR	NR	√	√
Company involved in international trade	√	√	√	√
Direct investment	NR	NR	NR	√

NR = Not relevant.

tional Lending and International Trade involve all classes, while Portfolio Investment and Direct Investment involve only certain classes. A discussion of each class follows.

Nature of Transaction or Purpose of Loan

The most common kinds of investment transactions are export financing, project financing, establishment of a line of credit, and development, balance-of-payments, and other types of loans. The type of loan indicates whether the activity is self-liquidating (most private-sector loans) or not self-liquidating, as in the case of balance-of-payments loans, which are usually taken out by a country's authorities. A self-liquidating loan generates sufficient cash flow to repay the loan and interest on the loan. The borrower in this case does not have to use funds from elsewhere to service the loan, which is the case for non-self-liquidating loans. In assessing risk, the purpose of the loan, or investment, is considered for each type of event or borrower.

Action Taken by Borrower (or Purchaser)

The foreign borrower (or purchaser) may take certain action that causes a loss to the investor, such as default, repudiation, renegotiation, or rescheduling. Default and repudiation have similar effects on the lender (or seller). The creditor is notified that the debtor cannot, or will not, make any further payment to service the outstanding balance. In the case of default, the borrower (or purchaser) lacks the financial or economic capacity to continue to reduce the outstanding balance as a result of one or more economic, political, or social events. In repudiating a debt or a purchase transaction, the debtor (or buyer) nullifies the debt (or purchase) for economic, political, or legal reasons. In either case the creditor loses all or part of the outstanding balance.

In renegotiation, the creditor generally agrees to a reduction of the interest terms of a loan or, in a purchase transaction, a reduction in the price. In either case, the creditor settles for less than they originally agreed, which results in a loss. Rescheduling means that the creditor agrees to lengthen the original repayment schedule of a loan or, for a purchase, of installment payments. The total obligation remains the same, but the creditor in effect suffers an "opportunity" loss because lengthening the time for repayment reduces the cash inflow over that period which would have been available to the creditor for relending, or reinvestment, to earn further income.

Type of Borrower or Purchaser

The Type of Borrower (or purchaser) classifies risk in terms of the public sector (government or sovereign) or the private sector (corporate or individual). The Type of Borrower classification is used in conjunction with other classifications for assessing the degree of country risk. As a general rule, the risk involved in dealing with the government or one of its entities is less than the risk involved in investing in or lending to the private sector because, as country risk specifically is defined, the government itself controls the events that give rise to a possible loss. Somewhat different sets of criteria are used for assessing risk in each sector.

Geographical Location

The country of jurisdiction must be determined in the assessment of country risk, since the events and factors that can cause the realization of a loss are within the control of the governments of each country. Geographical location is the term used to classify country risk by country of jurisdiction.

Determination of which country's jurisdiction the risk is located in may be complex and difficult because the borrower's country of domicile is not always obvious, as in the case of loans guaranteed by a third party that is not domiciled in the same country as the borrower. When a parent company guarantees a loan made to a foreign subsidiary, country risk is attributed, as a rule, to the country where the main responsibility for repayment of the loan belongs.

The assignment of the geographical location of country risk for a given loan involves careful consideration of two related questions concerning the principal safeguard against a loss: (1) identification of who has the ultimate responsibility for repayment of the loan and (2) location of country jurisdiction. Export financing loans guaranteed by the Export-Import Bank can be ready examples of the difficulty of determining whether the guarantor or the borrower provides the principal protection for the lending bank. Another example is the guarantee provided by Comecon, the Communist Eastern European bloc, for Poland's debt to Western creditors, who did not receive the necessary protection from the group's leader, the Soviet Union, when Poland's ability to service the debt deteriorated during 1980 and 1981.

When the guarantor of a loan has its head office located in country A but the bulk of its assets in country B, it is sometimes difficult to determine where the principal safeguard for the loan is located. Many companies, for example, have their head office in Belgium but most of their assets in France: is the country risk in Belgium or in France? In structuring a loan, the country of jurisdiction for attribution of country risk should be agreed on and clearly stated.

In shipping loans, the borrower's head office is often located in Panama but the shipping company is registered in the Netherlands. The principal safeguard of a shipping loan is the mortgage on the ship. Is the risk attributable to the Netherlands, where the company is registered, or to Panama, whose flag the ship is flying and where its headquarters are? The question is further complicated by the fact that the ship, which forms the principal safeguard, sails from country to country. Which is the country of jurisdiction? Can this type of risk, in fact, be assigned to any one country? The creditor is constrained from attempts to seize the ship in a third country (that is, other than the Netherlands or Panama) because of restrictions on the lender's legal ability to enforce the seizure, under the provisions of Article VIII, Section 2(b) of the Articles of Agreement of the IMF, which reads: "Exchange Contracts which involve the currency of any member, and which are contrary to the exchange control regulations of that member maintained or imposed consistently with this agreement shall be unenforceable in the territories of any member. . . ."[1]

Situations

Country risk may arise from economic, political, or social causes, or some combination of the three. Some of the destabilizing economic factors in country risk include a decline in export earnings over a period of time, a sharp increase in imports of energy or consumer goods, inflationary pressures causing rapid increases in costs of production, strikes resulting in production losses, and a persistent dropoff in the rate of growth in Gross National Product (GNP). (These factors are discussed in detail in the next section of this chapter.) Destabilizing political factors include a conflict of economic interests, riots, political polarization, ideological splits, disorder caused by conflicting territorial claims, war, and occupation by a foreign power. Destabilizing social factors include antagonism between social classes, tribal strife, riots, civil war, religious divisions, union militancy, and disorder stemming from unequal income distribution.

The effects of economic recession or war can be regional or worldwide, of course, rather than limited to one country. In such cases, the risk would not be classified as country risk as long as the government takes remedial action, for example, by instituting an appropriate countercyclical antidote to recession.

ECONOMIC FACTORS

National economic problems can create a large number of country-risk situations. These problems can arise from one source or from a chain of events.

Balance-of-Payments Prospects

A country's responsibility for debt service, repatriation of capital, and remittance of profits and dividends must be met from its foreign exchange available after payment for imported goods and services. Inadequate foreign exchange to meet these needs creates balance-of-payments problems and the concomitant likelihood that foreign lenders and investors will not be able to collect the income and principal they expect. A chronic deficit in the balance of payments can very well develop into a serious problem.

Decline of Export Earnings

The main source of foreign exchange is export earnings. When export earnings decline, the amount of foreign exchange available to pay for imports, debt service, and remittance of foreign profits and dividends is reduced. The shortfall can at first be made up for by borrowing abroad or drawing down external reserves (including foreign exchange in foreign central banks, gold tranche, and SDR facilities of the IMF), but a continued decline in export earnings would eventually impair the country's ability to meet any foreign exchange needs and would necessitate restrictions on the use of available foreign exchange.[2] How soon exchange controls would be imposed would depend on the extent and the duration of the decline in export revenues and the amount of external reserves.

The pattern of a country's exports can provide some indication of the potential for possible export decline. Countries with exports heavily concentrated in a few commodities are adversely affected when world demand for these commodities falls. Export revenues will also fall when world prices of these commodities fall. Thus the probability of decline in export earnings increases if world demand and price of the commodities are elastic, which makes earnings subject to wide fluctuations.

A country whose exports are concentrated in a few geographical markets is likely to experience a decline in export earnings if the demand for its exports is affected by an unstable rate of growth in the economies of those markets, or in an economic slow down, if the exports constitute only a small portion of the market's total imports. Imports from marginal sources are the most affected if buyers' economies slow down: those that supply only a small part of buyers' purchases are the first to be dropped when buyers reduce purchases.

Table 5.2 presents some important ratios for assessing the outlook for the balance of payments. As shown, the degree of commodity concentration of a country's exports can be measured by dividing the value of the country's five main commodity exports by the value of the country's total merchandise exports. The higher the concentration ratio, the greater the concentration of exports in the five main export commodities measured. The commodity concentration index uses the five main commodity exports to increase the degree of concentration in the ratio. Beyond the five commodities, the degree of diversification is felt to increase significantly, reducing the probability of a decline in

Table 5.2   Ratio Analysis of the Balance of Payments: A Four-Country Comparison

		Brazil (%)	Mexico (%)	Spain (%)	Belgium (%)
Five main commodity exports as a percentage of total merchandise exports	1970	49.2	29.1	29.0[d]	28.0
	1979	38.5[c]	58.5	20.9[c]	19.2
Merchandise exports to main customers[a] as a percentage of total merchandise exports	1970	26.2	57.8	15.4	25.4
	1979	18.9	69.2	61.1	22.5
"Nonessential"[b] imports as a percentage of total imports of goods and services	1971	4.8	2.0	8.0	5.4
	1979	3.0	6.3	7.6	10.9
Imports of goods and services as a percentage of gross domestic product	1970	6.9	10.2	14.4	41.9
	1979	8.3	11.5	21.9	52.1
External reserves as a percentage of imports of goods and services	1970	41.7	38.3	30.2	24.9
	1978	60.7	44.2	18.4	9.4

Sources: IMF, *International Financal Statistics Yearbook* (1979); *International Financial Statistics* (September 1980); United Nations, *Yearbook of International Trade Statistics* (1974 and 1979).

[a] The United States for Brazil, Mexico, and Spain; Germany for Belgium.

[b] The arbitrary definitions used here include (with Standard International Trade Classification reference numbers in parentheses): beverages and tobacco (1), perfumes (551 and 553), passenger road motor vehicles (7321), television and radio receivers (7241 and 7242), miscellaneous manufactured goods (8), and foreign travel expenditure.

[c] Four commodities.

[d] 1971.

export revenues from fluctuations in world demand, prices, or economic growth in the foreign markets.

Table 5.2 shows that the degree of concentration was significantly lower in 1979 than in 1970 for three of the four countries represented—Brazil, Spain, and Belgium—which reflects these countries' efforts to diversify their exports. ("Belgium" here applies to Belgium and Luxembourg.) The commodity concentration index for Mexico more than doubled between 1970 and 1979 as a result of Mexico's dependence on exports of oil for foreign exchange revenue. Note the similarity between the ratios of Brazil and Mexico, on the one hand, and Spain and Belgium, on the other. Both Brazil and Mexico had high commodity concentration ratios (although Brazil's has decreased) because of their reliance on a single commodity to make up a significant percentage of exports— coffee, in the case of Brazil. Spain and Belgium, on the other hand, have had lower (and decreasing) ratios, which indicate that their export revenues would be less affected by declines in their main export commodities than would Brazil's and Mexico's and are therefore more stable.

To estimate geographical concentration, the value of the country's merchandise exports to its main customers is divided by the value of the country's total merchandise exports. The higher the geographical concentration index, the greater the concentration and thus the greater the probability that a fall in world demand, a drop in the prices of the commodities, or an economic slump in the main export markets would cause a decline in the country's exports.

The export customer concentration ratio decreased for Brazil and Belgium from 1970 to 1979, increased slightly in the case of Spain, and increased significantly in the case of Mexico. These concentration indexes are more useful for assessing the creditworthiness of developing countries and Eastern European nations than of Western, industrialized countries because the latter have fairly well-diversified economies and export markets.

Compressibility of Imports

A country's ability to weather a balance-of-payments problem depends to some extent its capacity to "compress" its import bill in order to reduce the outflow of foreign exchange. A compressibility index can be constructed by dividing the value of the country's "nonessential" imports by the value of its total imports of goods and services. This index measures the amount of imports that are nonessential to the survival of a country's economy in the total import bill. If the index is high, the country has a greater degree of latitude in curtailing imports to release foreign exchange for other, more pressing needs (if necessary) than if the compressibility index is low. On the other hand, a high index can indicate that too much foreign exchange is being spent on nonessential imports. Therefore, countries will try to reduce this index to a minimum.

The compressibility index for both Brazil and Spain declined from 1970 to 1979—Brazil's by 38 percent, Spain's only slightly. In contrast, the compressibility index for Mexico more than doubled. The sizable decline in Brazil's index reflects that country's effort to conserve foreign exchange to meet its increased debt-service burden (see the discussion of Table 5.4).

Essential imported goods, by contrast, are the least compressible. Sharp increases in imports of these goods can eventually result in a shortfall in the foreign exchange balances available to meet foreign debt service and foreign remittance requirements. Examples of two essential import goods are energy and staple foodstuffs.

Payments for imported energy supplies use a significant part of the foreign exchange of a large number of countries. The price of imported oil is controlled by the Organization of Petroleum Exporting Countries (OPEC) cartel, which raises the price of oil periodically. A sharp increase in the consumption of oil by a country that has few or no alternative domestic sources of energy will result in a sharp jump in its import bill, which could create a balance-of-payments crisis. The impact of a sharp rise in oil imports on the flow of cash out of a country and its capacity to meet its payment obligations abroad depends on how much of the imported oil comes from the OPEC cartel and how high the world price of oil is. If the country is totally dependent on OPEC sources for its energy, and if oil prices are very high, a sharp rise in oil imports could have an adverse effect on the country's net cash flow position.

Many developing countries import a portion of their staple foods, partly because their domestic production fluctuates with weather conditions. Bad weather results in poor harvests and a sharp rise in the need for imports of staples, which significantly increases the import bill and the amount of foreign exchange used. The extent of the rise in imports depends on how much of the supply can be met domestically and how severe the weather problems are.

Coverage of the Import Bill

The size of a country's import bill relative to its gross domestic product (GDP), as shown in Table 5.2, can be measured by dividing the value of the country's imports of goods and services by its GDP in the same period. As the proportion of imports to GDP increases, the amount of foreign exchange needed to pay the import bill increases, and a sharp rise in the import bill can sharply reduce the amount of foreign exchange available for debt service and foreign remittance.

The import ratio increased for all four countries in Table 5.2 between 1970 and 1979, indicating that imports have been increasing in proportion to the countries' GDPs. The increase in the import ratio was modest for Brazil and Mexico and higher for Spain and Belgium, which reflects the greater dependence of the latter two countries on imports.

Note Belgium's relatively great dependence on imports, reflected in the size of its ratios. The high import bill may be attributed to the high energy import bill.

Because of the relatively low commodity and customer concentration indexes for Belgium, revenues from exports would not be affected enough to increase the problem of debt servicing as a result of the high import ratio. Belgium does not have the same constraint on debt service as the other countries do because it has access to the credit facilities of the EEC and OECD.

By dividing the country's external reserves by its total import bill, a coverage ratio is derived that correlates with the probability of balance-of-payments problems. Sharp increases in the import bill over a period of time without commensurate increases in export revenues would sharply reduce the foreign exchange reserved for coverage of import bills and could even wipe it out, thereby creating a need for external borrowing and/or exchange controls.

The figures in Table 5.2 indicate that the ratio of external reserves to imports of goods and services from 1970 to 1978 rose by 33 percent for Brazil and by 15 percent for Mexico, while it declined significantly for Spain and Belgium. Belgium's reserves declined to 9.4 percent of its import bill, which represents about 1 month or less of imports. Again, as a member of the EEC and OECD, Belgium has access to more flexible credit facilities than Brazil and Mexico do; they must maintain much higher levels of reserves in order to maintain liquidity.

Prospects for Long-Term Growth

The prospects for long-term growth in the economy of a country are important in assessing country risk for two reasons. First, they are an indication of how well the economy is being managed. Mismanagement, or the potential for mismanagement, can be identified and assessed, and the impact on the future prospects of the economy can be determined. Second, problems in the long-term growth of the economy will be reflected in the balance of payments, resulting in future debt-service and foreign-remittance problems.

The prospects for long-term growth can be determined by the rate of increment in capital goods investment, which expands the country's capacity to produce goods and services in the future. A ratio measuring the rate of investment is a useful guide to the direction of long-term growth.

Table 5.3 shows the proportion of GNP that is invested in plant and machinery ("gross domestic fixed investment") for the same four countries depicted in Table 5.2. Higher ratios indicate that a high proportion of output is invested to expand productive capacity, which, in turn, permits greater production output in the future. The reciprocal of this ratio would measure output per unit of capital invested, a rough indication of the efficiency of the productive process.

Brazil, Belgium, and Mexico invested similar proportions of GNP in fixed capital formation in 1970 and 1978. Belgium's investment declined from 23.1

Table 5.3 Growth Rate and Ratio Analysis: Assessing Long-Term Growth Prospects—A Four-Country Comparison

		Brazil (%)	Mexico (%)	Spain (%)	Belgium (%)
Average annual real rate of growth in GNP	1960–1970	5.3	7.2	7.3	4.8
	1970–1978	9.2	5.0	4.4	3.3
Average annual growth in GNP per capita	1960–1978	4.9	2.7	5.0	4.1
Gross domestic fixed investment as a percentage of GNP	1970	22.3	20.8	13.5	23.1
	1978	24.7	21.2	21.4[a]	21.3
Net capital imports as a percentage of gross domestic investment	1970	5.4	12.6	NA	NA
	1978	14.1	11.2	8.2	7.7
Gross domestic savings as a percentage of gross domestic investment	1970	77.6	53.2	57.1	75.9
	1978	64.1	57.9	56.9[a]	51.5
Gross domestic savings as a percentage of GNP	1970	17.3	12.7	15.5	17.0
	1978	14.4	13.0	9.4	10.9

Source: Same as for Table 5.2.
[a] 1977.

percent to 21.3 percent during this time, while that of Brazil and Mexico increased. Spain's investment of 13.5 percent in 1970 indicates that it had a lower potential rate of growth at that time than the other countries did, but by 1978 Spain's investment in fixed capital formation had increased to Mexico's and Belgium's level.

Another ratio (not shown in Table 5.3) can be computed to give an indication of the rate of growth in capacity investment relative to the growth in GNP per period. By dividing the increase in gross domestic fixed investment during one period by the increase in the GNP during the next period, an idea is obtained of the marginal capital output. The higher this ratio, the faster the rate of capacity expansion relative to the increase in output, thus the higher the long-term rate of growth in the economy.

Part of a nation's outlays for capacity expansion may go for imported plant and machinery. A useful measure of the contribution of imported plant and machinery to total capacity expansion is the ratio in Table 5.3 of net capital imports to gross domestic fixed investment. This ratio is an important measure of long-term growth prospects for developing countries, since they must import a considerable portion of their plant and machinery. Accordingly, they must either generate adequate foreign exchange revenues through exports to pay for the capital imports or attract foreign investment to supplement their foreign exchange earnings. Their country risk would increase with a decline in export revenues, which would necessitate compressing imports and hence cutbacks in imported capital equipment. The cutback in imports of capital equipment in turn would reduce investment in new productive capacity, curtailing future economic growth. Then, if part of the imported capital goods is paid for through foreign investment, a risk arises that this outside financing could be discontinued, which would also cut the rate of economic growth. In short, the lower the country's ratio of capital imports to total capital investment, the more control the country has over its investment policy.

Table 5.3 shows that in 1970 Mexico imported a much higher proportion of investment in fixed capital formation than Brazil did. By 1978, however, Brazil's net capital imports had exceeded those of Mexico. Brazil's two-and-a-half-fold increase indicates the growing reliance of that country on imported plant and machinery for capital formation. This significant increase in net capital imports increased Brazil's external debt during the period, which, in turn, increased its debt-servicing requirements (as reflected in the increase in its debt-service ratio in Table 5.4 and the ratio of gross long-term external borrowing to exports of goods and services in Table 5.4).

Mexico's ratio of net capital imports to gross domestic investment declined slightly during the period, from 12.6 to 11.2 percent—an indication of decreasing dependence on imported capital goods for capital formation. Spain's and Belgium's comparatively lower ratios reflect less reliance on imported capital goods for investment purposes than was the case for Mexico and Brazil in 1978.

The ratio of gross domestic savings (GDS) to gross domestic investment (GDI) indicates to what extent domestic investment is financed from domestic savings versus foreign investment and borrowing abroad. The higher the ratio, the greater the prospects for self-generating long-term growth. An increase in this ratio over a period of time could indicate that savings are rising because of a postponement of current consumption. Of course, the more investment is financed from domestic savings, the less the country relies on foreign borrowing and foreign investment and, other factors being equal, the lower the risk of balance-of-payments problems in generating foreign exchange revenues to meet requirements for debt service and remittance of income and dividends.

Conversely, as the GDS/GDI ratio falls, the shortfall between savings and investment requirements must be met from foreign capital, through either direct investment or borrowing. Thus, the likelihood of balance-of-payments problems increases as this ratio falls, since the reliance on foreign capital increases. A persistent decline in this ratio—that is, a low GDS/GDI ratio over a long period of time—would mean a steady absorption of foreign capital and the foreign exchange revenues needed to service the mounting foreign debt. Foreign capital investment could become substantial, necessitating the use of part of the foreign capital inflow to augment foreign exchange balances for debt service. When this point is reached country risk increases significantly as the need for external financing is built into the debt-servicing problem. The likelihood of foreign exchange controls also increases considerably. Another element of risk is the increased likelihood of interruptions in the flow of foreign financing, which would cause serious problems to the continued financing of the level of investment necessary to sustain a desirable long-run rate of growth.

As can be seen in Table 5.3, slightly more than 75 percent of gross domestic investment was financed from domestic savings in 1970 in Brazil and Belgium, while Mexico and Spain financed slightly more than half of their domestic investment from domestic savings. The ratios fell significantly for both Brazil and Belgium during the period—an indication of their increased reliance on foreign capital and the increasing debt-servicing burdens on their balance of payments. In the case of Brazil, the increased debt-service burden is reflected in the increase from 0.9 to 2.2 in the ratio of external debt-service payments to GNP shown in Table 5.4.

The decline in the savings-to-income ratio relative to the investment-to-income ratio can be discerned from a comparison of the ratio of gross domestic savings to GNP with the ratio of gross domestic fixed investment to GNP in Table 5.3, since the denominator of the ratios is the same. In the case of Brazil, for example, savings represented 17.3 percent of GNP in 1970 and investment represented 22.3 percent—a shortfall of 5 percent which was covered by imported capital. By 1978 savings had declined to 14.4 percent while investment had increased to 24.7 percent, thus widening the shortfall to 10.3 percent.

It is important to note that, when an economy is experiencing very high rates of growth, the GDS/GDI ratio can safely by relatively low. While debt-servicing may still be a problem in this case, the risks for long-term investment in that country may be either negligible or nonexistent.

The ratio of gross domestic savings to GNP in Table 5.3 reveals how much of total output is being saved. The higher the GDS/GNP ratio, the more favorable the long-run outlook, since this ratio indicates that a relatively high proportion of income is being saved (rather than spent) and is, therefore, available to finance domestic investment. The GDS/GNP ratio supplements the information gained from the GDS/GDI ratio and may help explain some cases of a low GDS/GDI. It is possible for the GDS/GNP to be high while the GDS/GDI is relatively low. This situation arises when the growth rate of gross domestic product is very high, and domestic savings, although high, are still not adequate to finance the high rate of growth.

Country risk increases when the consumption rate is high and the savings rate is low while, at the same time, the rate of investment remains high, so that the resultant shortfall between savings and investment must be met from foreign capital inflow. The degree of risk will diminish if exports are increasing at a rate sufficient to generate adequate export revenues to meet the needs of importing, debt servicing, and remittances. On the other hand, if export concentration ratios are low, the likelihood of a fall in export revenues increases, and this situation would have the effect of increasing the risk of problems in debt servicing and the imposition of exchange controls.

The GDS/GNP ratio declined significantly from 1970 to 1978 for all four countries indicated on Table 5.3; all experienced increasing reliance on external financing for domestic investment. An increase in external financing increases the external debt commensurately. In the case of Brazil, the ratio of external

Table 5.4 Ratio Analysis: Assessing the Prospects for Debt Servicing[a]—A Three-Country Comparison

		Brazil (%)	Mexico (%)	Spain (%)
Available liquid foreign exchange as a percentage of external debt[b] (CFI)	1970	48.32	24.14	71.75
	1978	15.76	7.43[c]	49.11
Debt-service ratio	1970	13.5	23.6	3.6
	1978	28.4	59.6	11.0
External debt-service payments as a percentage of gross long-term external borrowing	1970	12.8	27.3	26.9
	1978	17.2	41.3	30.0
Gross long-term external borrowing as a percentage of exports of goods and services	1970	38.8	56.8	11.2
	1978	79.4	144.2	15.2
External debt-service payments as a percentage of GNP	1970	0.9	2.1	0.5
	1978	2.2	6.9	1.8
External debt as a percentage of GNP	1970	8.0	9.8	3.3
	1978	15.6	28.7	5.5

Sources: The World Bank, *World Development Report*, 1980; *World Bank Annual Report*, 1980; IMF, *International Financial Statistics Yearbook*, 1979.
[a] External debt and debt servicing cover public and publicly guaranteed debt.
[b] External debt here refers to projected debt-service payments during the coming year.
[c] Did not show foreign assets of commercial banks.

debt to GNP (see Table 5.4) increased by 7.6 percent, in contrast to the shortfall of 10.3 percent between GDI/GNP and GDS/GNP in 1978. The difference of 2.7 percent was met from short-term financing and grants.

Capacity to Service External Debt

In the preceding discussions on balance of payments and the prospects for long-term growth, we examined the sources and uses of foreign exchange and the effects of some principal economic variables on the balance of payments. The capacity to service external debt will now be considered; it is important because debt is a contractual obligation and must be paid when due or the borrower will be in default. Balance-of-payments problems frequently arise when a country's capacity to service its external debt is diminished by causes such as those discussed previously or by other causes.

When a country has external debt-service problems, the risk of loss increases for all the country's creditors in one way or another. Lenders may not receive the interest and/or principal repayment punctually, which results in a loss of income for the period and an opportunity loss to reinvest the cash flow. Exchange controls may be imposed, which could restrict all remittances abroad, as well as interrupt the normal course of business. External debt-service problems affect the creditworthiness of the country, so that its ability to attract foreign capital for investment may be impaired. If the country is dependent on foreign capital inflows to augment its domestic savings to fund investment, then any interdiction of the foreign capital inflow would affect the long-run growth rate of the country.

An assessment of the likelihood of debt-service problems can be made by examining the ratios presented in Table 5.4.

The Cash Flow Indicator (CFI) shown at the top of Table 5.4 is derived from the available liquid foreign exchange divided by the service payments on external debt.

The CFI was developed by Duff and Peacock[4] to measure the likelihood of debt-servicing problems. The component, total liquid foreign exchange available to the country from which service payments on external debt can be made, includes:

1 The export balance on the current account before debt service for the coming year.
2 The balance of external loans not yet used, including interbank credit lines.
3 The net foreign assets of commercial banks.
4 The gross foreign exchange reserves of the central bank.

The other component, projected debt-service payments during the coming year, forms the denominator of the CFI. When the total available liquid foreign exchange is greater than the expected service payments on external debt, the CFI ratio is greater than 100 percent—an indication that the total foreign exchange available to the country is greater than its total external debt obligations and that the country has the resources to meet its expected debt-service obligations during the coming year. If the CFI ratio is less than 100 percent, the available liquid foreign exchange is less than the country's total external debt obligations. Countries with a CFI less than 100 percent may run into debt-service difficulties if export revenues fall while imports remain the same or increase.

The CFI ratio is less than 100 percent for the majority of developing countries, with the exception of the oil-exporting countries, because items 1 and 3 above are usually negative for these countries. Developing countries normally have negative current account balances because their imports are usually greater than exports and factor payments abroad increase the deficit; for countries with exports greater than imports, the factor payments usually exceed the export surplus. The net foreign assets of commercial banks of developing countries are usually negative.

The CFI declined drastically between 1970 and 1978 for all three countries shown in Table 5.4. The decline was sharpest for Brazil (32.56 percent), followed by Spain (22.64 percent) and Mexico (16.71 percent). The increase in the size of these countries' external debt contributed significantly to the decline of the CFI.

The debt-service ratio (DSR) in Table 5.4 measures external debt-service payments as a proportion of the liquid foreign exchange available from export revenues for goods and services. The DSR index would appear to be more restrictive than the CFI (above) because it measures debt-service requirements against just the foreign exchange derived from trade revenues, as opposed to total foreign exchange reserves (including those of the central bank and the commercial banks) in the CFI. Because the DSR focuses on the cash flow available from domestically generated foreign currency receipts, it can be used as a first line of screening. A low DSR implies that debt-service payments take up a small part of the foreign exchange receipts from exports, leaving a greater share for imports. A high DSR indicates a strong possibility of debt-servicing problems, since the higher debt service is in relation to export revenues, the less foreign exchange is available to meet the country's import bill.

The DSR has been criticized as a measurement on several grounds. By using gross export revenues as a denominator, it fails to take into consideration the import bill, which is always a significant factor in the balance of payments of developing countries. The compressibility of imports is another factor that needs to be considered. Non-oil-producing developing countries have high energy-import bills, and those that import staple food have difficulty in cutting imports of these items when they have balance-of-payments problems. Another criticism of the DSR is its failure to consider the quality of export earnings. When the source of export earnings is concentrated in one or two commodities or only a few customers, the revenues can fluctuate with changes in world demand.

The DSR increased significantly for the three countries in Table 5.4 between 1970 and 1978. Debt service for Mexico, for example, represented 59.6 percent of export revenue in 1978. With such a high DSR, a country would have to use portions of any new external borrowing each year to meet debt service if the country were to pay for its imports from export revenues. External debt-service payments represented 41.3 percent of gross long-term external borrowing for Mexico in 1978. Since such a significant portion of the gross long-term external borrowing must be used for debt-service payments, the external debt will grow ever faster. Indeed, gross long-term external borrowing for Mexico in 1978 was 144.2 percent of total exports of goods and services.

One suggested reformulation of the DSR is to net out imports from exports. Thus, external debt-service payments would be measured against the country's total export revenues less total import expenditures. Since this net trade balance (total exports less total imports) is negative for a great many developing countries, a negative denominator will result, rendering the DSR meaningless. Further refinement to consider the concentration factor would only result in a more negative net trade balance for most developing countries.

Another way of examining the DSR is to relate it to the country's total long-term debt. The third ratio in Table 5.4 expresses payments on external debt as a proportion of gross long-term external borrowing. When the service payments make up a substantial part of external borrowing, one can infer that part of any new borrowing will be used to meet service payments—a situation that may lead to a snowball effect and could indicate problems down the road, other things being equal. The fourth ratio in Table 5.4 expresses gross long-term external borrowing as a proportion of revenues from exports of goods and services. A high ratio indicates that debt makes up a substantial part of the available cash flow from foreign exchange—a situation that may increase the risk of future balance-of-payments problems. When these two ratios are multiplied together, we obtain the DSR: external debt-service payments times exports of goods and services. The denominator of the third ratio in Table 5.4 is the same as the numerator of the fourth ratio in Table 5.4, so that the two can be crossed out, and we are left with the DSR. The criticisms of the DSR also apply to this modified ratio; nevertheless, the ratios provide some insight into probable risk prospects in connection with debt service.

From the relationship of the two ratios above, one can see that the DSR would be low if external debt-service payments make up a small portion of gross long-term external borrowing and if, at the same time, gross long-term external borrowing is low in relation to the foreign-exchange earnings of exports.

Taking external debt-service payments in relation to GNP shows what proportion of the country's output of goods and services goes to service its debt. The smaller the proportion of GNP that is going to service external debt, the greater the national resources available for domestic consumption and investment. On the other hand, as the proportion of GNP used for debt service rises, domestic investment may be impaired, which in turn would affect the economy's long-term growth rate.

A high percentage for this ratio would also imply a high DSR, which requires increasing export revenues to meet the debt-service requirements if further borrowing is to be avoided. If domestic investment falls because external debt-service payments are high in relation to GNP, then the investment in agriculture or industry that is needed to increase exports might be lacking, thereby compounding the problem.

The external debt-service payments for Mexico represented 6.9 percent of its GNP in 1978—a threefold increase over 1970 and a figure that is very significant when compared with the 2.2 and 1.8 percent, respectively, for Brazil and Spain. Such high debt service is an overburden on the whole economy and especially on the balance of payments, particularly since the CFI is only 7.43 percent. Since 1978, Mexico has joined the oil-exporting club of countries, however, and future oil exports are expected to generate adequate foreign-exchange earnings to meet the heavy debt-service payments. A significant part of the large increase in Mexico's external debt was incurred, in fact, to import oil and gas machinery, equipment, and pipelines.

The sixth ratio in Table 5.4 measures basically the magnitude of the country's external debt in relation to its GNP. Since GNP provides the resources to repay the external debt, knowing the size of the debt relative to GNP helps determine the capacity of the country to assume more debt. A low ratio of external debt to GNP would indicate that the country could take on more debt in the short term, if circumstances warrant it. It is a good ratio for monitoring the trend in debt financing, as well as providing insight into how much of the country's wealth is being tied up in debt.

A further ratio (not shown in Table 5.4) can be devised to discount the future debt-service payments on external public debt and express the present value of these future payments in relation to the external public debt. The ratio shows what the future commitment means in today's dollars. The higher the ratio, the greater the future burden; the lower the ratio, the more favorable the debt structure.[5]

External debt as a proportion of GNP increased significantly for both Brazil and Mexico from 1970 to 1978; the ratio nearly doubled for Brazil and nearly tripled for Mexico. Both countries have been undertaking rapid industrialization, which has necessitated large infusions of capital to meet the shortfall in domestic savings and to assist in the rapidly rising debt-service burden discussed above. Both Brazil and Mexico have experienced debt-servicing problems, although Mexico's oil and gas exports should help alleviate its problems.

The problem is somewhat different in the case of Brazil, since its main export commodity at the present time is coffee—an agricultural product that is affected by adverse weather conditions from time to time. As noted previously, Brazil has been trying to diversify its exports and is now increasing its exports of industrial products, which may help to increase its foreign-exchange earnings.

Brazil and Mexico have been enjoying relatively high economic growth rates from the investments made there that were financed partly by the increased external debt, as shown by the growth rates in Table 5.3. All the countries except Mexico have enjoyed relatively high per capita growth rates over the same period. The somewhat low per capita growth rate for Mexico reflects its higher (relative to the other countries) population growth rate during the period.

The high debt-service payments and high outstanding external debt of the countries signal a probability of debt-service payment problems in the future and, therefore, some degree of risk to foreign lenders of encountering delinquent or slow repayment of loans. On the other hand, the relatively high growth rates enjoyed by these countries indicate that their economies are basically healthy, which suggests good opportunities for long-term investment. The current foreign-exchange bottlenecks that cause short-run problems in debt servicing are likely to be removed in the future as the investments financed by foreign loans generate growth in the economy. A key consideration is the extent to which investments financed with external funds generate exports, directly or indirectly. If the investments go directly into export-generating activities and industries or indirectly stimulate exports, then the resulting increase in export revenues will provide foreign exchange for servicing the debt. On the other hand, if the proceeds of the external loans are used for nonexport-generating activities, such as building infrastructure or meeting deficits in the government's budget, then a question arises as to how foreign exchange can be generated to meet the higher debt service in the future.

Ratio analysis presents useful insights for analyzing and assessing country risk. Ratios should not be interpreted in absolute terms, however, since the components of a ratio are related to other factors, and their values are a function of what happens to these other components. The ratios, for the most part, measure economic relationships that are interdependent. A ratio must therefore be interpreted with care and in relation to the other factors (such as the size of the economy, the level of economic development, the economic structure, the type of exports, and the world demand for the country's exports).

As mentioned in Chapter 4, the World Bank has developed five categories of countries based on the countries' level of development, income, and other criteria that are useful in making comparisons among countries. The categories are stated as low-income, middle-income, and industrialized countries, capital-surplus oil exporters, and centrally planned economies.[6]

COUNTRY-RISK RATING SYSTEMS

So far, we have analyzed some of the economic variables that figure in country risk. A large number of other variables, including political and social factors, also need to be considered in the analysis and assessment of country risk.

The best kind of rating system is one that enables international creditors to compare borrowing countries on the basis of potential risk. With such a ranking system, the creditor can more accurately assess the amount of risk each international loan involves and how to allocate its lending capacity among countries to minimize its loan portfolio risk. A total country-rating system is useful not only for lenders, but also for investors: it is a helpful decision-making tool for a corporation in determining where to place its international investment portfolio and where to locate new plants.

Various country-risk rating systems have been developed which fall into several broad categories. Four main methods discussed below are: (1) the checklist approach, (2) the survey approach, (3) the market-return-spread index, and (4) the probability approach.

The Checklist Approach

The checklist approach assumes that, in order to quantify country risk, the probability of risk can be assessed. Risk, in this view, is presaged by certain types of economic, political, or social forces that have to be taken into consideration in some rational way to assess the likelihood of the events' occurring.

The checklist contains all the indicators considered relevant to assessing the likelihood of an occurrence that would precipitate risk. A well-constructed checklist would use the indicators systematically to track the types of risks that the creditor would be exposed to back to the institutional and structural framework within the country. This line of causation would then show how the occurrence of certain events could increase the likelihood of a loss.

An extensive checklist of some of the most relevant factors is given in a system developed by Nagy.[7] The checklist divides risk into four categories— political, policy, balance of payments, and economic. Each category is made up of several indicators. For example, political risk includes war, occupation by a foreign power, civil war, revolution, riot, disorder, and takeover by an extremist government.

The Survey Approach

The magazine *Institutional Investor* uses a survey approach to develop country credit ratings. The ratings are based on the responses of 75 to 100 of the leading international banks. The bankers grade each country on a scale of 0 to 100, with 0 representing the least creditworthy countries—those with the greatest chance of default—and 100 representing the most creditworthy countries—the ones with the least chance of default. The banks do not rate their home countries. *Institutional Investor* uses a formula to weight the individual responses. The formula gives most weight to the responses from banks with the largest worldwide exposure and the most sophisticated country-analysis systems.

The *Institutional Investor* country credit rating is a global rating system. Table 5.5 presents the March 1981 ratings of 100 countries and the global average. New ratings are published every 6 months, with the changes in ratings and rankings from the levels of the prior 6 months and 12 months. This system provides useful information for monitoring the change in a country's rating over the 6-month period, as well as information on how the country is performing in relation to other countries. Table 5.6 presents the "winners" and "losers" for the past 6 months and the past year. The winners are the countries whose ratings went up the most, and losers are the countries whose ratings went down the most over the 6-month and 12-month periods.

Table 5.5 *Institutional Investor*'s **March 1981 Country Credit Ratings**

Rank March 1981	September 1980	Country	Credit Rating March 1981	Six-Month Change	One-Year Change
1	1	United States	98.1	−0.5	−0.1
2	2	Switzerland	97.0	−0.7	−1.4
3	3	West Germany	96.3	−1.4	−2.1
4	4	Japan	95.2	0.1	−0.2
5	5	Canada	92.0	−1.0	−1.1
6	6	France	90.2	−1.5	−2.2
7	9	Australia	90.0	0.6	1.8
8	8	United Kingdom	89.9	−0.3	−1.4
9	7	Netherlands	89.6	−1.0	−0.3
10	10	Norway	89.5	0.5	1.3
11	11	Austria	85.9	−1.7	−0.5
12	12	Belgium	84.4	−2.4	−2.9
13	13	Sweden	83.5	−1.7	−1.5
14	16	Singapore	78.6	1.1	0.0
15	15	New Zealand	78.0	0.2	0.8
16	14	Hong Kong	77.6	−0.3	−0.1
17	17	Finland	77.5	0.9	3.1
18	18	Italy	74.7	−1.1	0.0
19	19	Saudi Arabia	73.6	−1.8	−5.0
20	21	Ireland	73.4	0.1	1.1
21	20	Denmark	73.0	−1.4	−0.2
22	23	Malaysia	72.7	−0.3	0.9
23	22	Mexico	71.4	−1.6	−0.3
24	24	China	71.2	−0.9	−2.4
25	25	Kuwait	70.4	−1.6	−2.7
26	26	Spain	70.2	−0.1	−0.3
27	27	U.S.S.R.	69.6	−0.1	−1.9
28	28	Venezuela	69.3	−0.1	−1.9
29	29	Taiwan	68.7	2.1	2.0
30	30	Argentina	63.4	−0.9	0.8
31	31	Greece	62.5	0.4	1.0
32	34	South Africa	61.7	1.9	−0.7
33	33	United Arab Emirates	59.8	−0.5	−1.3
34	37	Colombia	59.1	0.1	−0.8
35	38	Iceland	58.7	0.0	1.9
36	32	East Germany	58.4	−1.9	−3.0
37	38	Bahrain	58.2	−0.6	−0.5
38	35	Czechoslovakia	57.6	−2.2	−3.1
39[a]	41	Hungary	57.4	−0.9	−1.9
40[a]	44	Algeria	57.4	0.8	1.1
41	45	Indonesia	57.1	2.0	2.6
42	36	Qatar	56.9	−2.4	−2.2
43	47	Portugal	56.6	1.7	2.0

Table 5.5 (*continued*)

Rank					
March 1981	September 1980	Country	Credit Rating March 1981	Six-Month Change	One-Year Change
44	40	Trinidad & Tobago	56.5	−1.8	−2.0
45	49	Nigeria	55.8	1.9	1.6
46	43	South Korea	55.4	−1.5	−9.5
47	46	Chile	54.4	−0.5	1.6
48	52	Ecuador	52.3	0.1	0.0
49	51	Thailand	52.2	−0.4	−1.9
50	48	Libya	51.8	−2.1	−6.3
51	54	Rumania	51.2	−0.7	−1.4
52	53	Yugoslavia	50.3	−1.7	−3.1
53	55	India	50.0	0.2	−2.4
54	50	Brazil	49.7	−3.0	−8.3
55	56	Tunisia	48.3	−0.7	−0.9
56	57	Bulgaria	47.4	−0.3	—
57	58	Oman	46.7	−0.2	−0.4
58	65	Papua New Guinea	46.3	3.5	—
59	61	Paraguay	46.0	0.4	1.5
60	42	Iraq	44.5	−13.2	−12.2
61	59	Philippines	44.4	−2.5	−4.1
62	60	Ivory Coast	44.2	−1.9	−3.5
63	69	Peru	43.4	3.0	8.2
64	62	Panama	42.7	−1.1	−2.6
65	64	Kenya	42.5	−0.8	−2.5
66	66	Jordan	41.9	−0.3	−0.9
67	63	Israel	41.4	−2.0	−6.3
68	67	Uruguay	41.1	0.2	−1.1
69	68	Morocco	39.7	−1.0	−3.8
70	69	Costa Rica	38.7	−1.7	−2.4
71	72	Cyprus	36.8	0.2	0.1
72	75	Egypt	36.0	1.1	2.7
73	74	Republic of Gabon	35.3	0.2	1.0
74	71	Poland	32.9	−4.2	−8.8
75	73	Syrian Arab Republic	32.2	−3.4	−4.1
76	76	Dominican Republic	29.9	−0.6	−2.6
77	77	Cuba	28.6	−1.8	−3.7
78	79	Zimbabwe	26.2	−0.7	2.7
79	78	Senegal	25.4	−3.1	−3.5
80	—	Malawi	25.1	—	—
81	84	Pakistan	22.1	1.8	0.7
82	81	Bolivia	21.9	−3.3	−5.9
83	82	Lebanon	21.8	−1.5	−3.0
84[a]	83	Seychelles	21.0	−1.3	−0.8
85[a]	80	Liberia	21.0	−4.6	−18.7

(*continued on p. 122*)

Table 5.5 (*continued*)

Rank					
March 1981	September 1980	Country	Credit Rating March 1981	Six-Month Change	One-Year Change
86	85	Angola	19.7	−0.6	0.7
87	86	Tanzania	16.8	−1.3	−5.0
88	87	Zambia	16.3	−1.4	−2.1
89	—	El Salvador	15.8	—	—
90	88	Jamaica	15.5	−1.1	−4.4
91	91	Congo	15.3	−0.7	1.3
92	90	Sierra Leone	15.1	−1.2	−3.8
93[a]	93	Turkey	13.7	1.0	2.3
94	89	Iran	13.7	−2.7	−2.2
95	92	Sudan	12.3	−0.8	−1.8
96	94	Ethiopia	11.3	−1.2	−0.8
97	95	Nicaragua	11.1	1.3	1.4
98	96	North Korea	7.0	−1.5	−3.9
99	98	Zaire	6.8	−1.2	−0.7
100	97	Uganda	6.3	−1.8	−2.0
	Global average rating		50.7	−1.6	−2.8

Source: Institutional Investor, Vol. 15, No. 3 (March 1981).
[a] Order determined by the actual results before rounding.

The *Institutional Investor* country credit rating is practical in that it represents the best thinking of all the leading banks in the world actually involved in country-risk analysis and rating systems, and it covers the 100 most important countries. The IMF calls *Institutional Investor*'s country credit ratings "the best creditworthiness indicator." The World Bank feels that the rankings are "a reasonable measure of the market's perceived default probabilities."[8]

These ratings prove useful to the thousands of small companies that cannot afford to do their own country-risk ratings because of a lack of resources or because their activities abroad are not extensive enough to warrant the cost of setting up their own systems. The ratings also provide a comparison with any in-house country-risk rating, since they reflect the combined judgment of the leading international banks which collectively provide the greatest share of the world's international and domestic financing.

Companies that do not have in-house capability would have to obtain the analysis of the causes for the change in a country's ratings from one of the leading world bankers or from *Institutional Investor* itself for use in determining how such a change affects its operation in that country. The six-month interval between ratings seems a reasonable span of time.

Table 5.6 *Institutional Investor*'s Winners and Losers:
The Six-Month Record (September 1980 to March 1981)

Who's Up the Most		Who's Down the Most	
Country	Change in Credit Rating[a]	Country	Change in Credit Rating[a]
Papua New Guinea	3.5	Iraq	−13.2
Peru	3.0	Liberia	−4.6
Taiwan	2.1	Poland	−4.2
Indonesia	2.0	Syrian Arab Republic	−3.4
Nigeria	1.9	Bolivia	−3.3
South Africa	1.9	Senegal	−3.1
Pakistan	1.8	Brazil	−3.0
Portugal	1.7	Iran	−2.7
Nicaragua	1.3	Philippines	−2.5
Egypt	1.1	Qatar	−2.4
Singapore	1.1	Belgium	−2.4
Turkey	1.0	Czechoslovakia	−2.2
Finland	0.9	Libya	−2.1
Algeria	0.8	Israel	−2.0
Australia	0.6	Ivory Coast	−1.9
Norway	0.5	East Germany	−1.9
Paraguay	0.4	Uganda	−1.8
Greece	0.4	Cuba	−1.8
Republic of Gabon	0.2	Trinidad & Tobago	−1.8
Cyprus	0.2	Saudi Arabia	−1.8
Uruguay	0.2	Costa Rica	−1.7
India	0.2	Yugoslavia	−1.7
New Zealand	0.2	Sweden	−1.7
Ecuador	0.1	Austria	−1.7
Colombia	0.1	Kuwait	−1.6
Ireland	0.1	Mexico	−1.6
Japan	0.1		

The One-Year Record (March 1980–March 1981)

Country	Change in Credit Rating[a]	Country	Change in Credit Rating[a]
Peru	8.2	Liberia	−18.7
Finland	3.1	Iraq	−12.2
Egypt	2.7	South Korea	−9.5
Zimbabwe	2.7	Poland	−8.8
Indonesia	2.6	Brazil	−8.3
Turkey	2.3	Israel	−6.3
Portugal	2.0	Libya	−6.3
Taiwan	2.0	Bolivia	−5.9
Iceland	1.9	Saudi Arabia	−5.0
Australia	1.8	Tanzania	−5.0
Chile	1.6	Jamaica	−4.4
Nigeria	1.6	Philippines	−4.1
Paraguay	1.5	Syrian Arab Republic	−4.1
		North Korea	−3.9

Table 5.6 (*continued*)

Who's Up the Most		Who's Down the Most	
Country	Change in Credit Rating[a]	Country	Change in Credit Rating[a]
Nicaragua	1.4	Morocco	−3.8
Congo	1.3	Sierra Leone	−3.8
Norway	1.3	Cuba	−3.7
Algeria	1.1	Ivory Coast	−3.5
Ireland	1.1	Senegal	−3.5
Republic of Gabon	1.0	Czechoslovakia	−3.1
Greece	1.0	Yugoslavia	−3.1
Malaysia	0.9	East Germany	−3.0
Argentina	0.8	Lebanon	−3.0
New Zealand	0.8	Belgium	−2.9
Angola	0.7	Kuwait	−2.7
Pakistan	0.7		

Source: Institutional Investor, loc. cit.
[a] Change in points on a scale of 1 to 100. See Table 5.5.

The Market-Return-Spread Index

The magazine *Euromoney*'s country-risk rating system uses the market's definition of country risk as reflected in the premium over Libor (London Interbank rate) that the borrower has to pay in interest. The premium is measured by the spread between the rate of interest on the loan and the Libor rate. The Libor rate is the rate of interest charged for loans between banks and is considered to be practically risk free. Lenders use the Libor rate as the base rate to which premiums are added. Borrowers with low country risks are assessed low premiums. The premium spreads above the Libor rate are intended to reflect partly the lender's assessment of the country risk of the borrower and partly the country's record on a number of other factors, including the number of times the borrower has tapped the market in any one year, the skill of its negotiators, the country's record of servicing its debt, and the level of its existing debt. To prevent the spread from reflecting also the state of demand and supply conditions in the overall market, the *Euromoney* index of overall trends has been incorporated in the numerator of the formula (see below). The leading international banks undertake country risk analyses and country rating systems that are reflected in the kinds of premiums that they demand for their participation in loan syndicates.

The *Euromoney* country-risk ratings are based on the value of each country's "spread index." The formula for computing the country's spread index is:

$$[(\text{Volume} \times \text{Spread}) / \textit{Euromoney} \text{ Index}] \div (\text{Volume} \times \text{Maturity})$$

(Volume here means volume of loans that year.) The spread is calculated in U.S. dollar and deutsche mark syndicated loan rates over the Libor rate; all fixed-rate, tax-sparing, acceptance facilities and loans above the U.S. prime rate, or rates other than Libor, are excluded from the analysis. By restricting the index to loans priced at Libor, biases from pricing differences are removed from the index. The rating system is based on public-sector loans.

In the formula, each loan to the country is weighted by the *Euromoney* index for the month that the loan was signed, which corrects for general market conditions operating at the time the loan was consummated. The *Euromoney* index which is used to weight the spread of each loan is:

$$\text{Weighted Average Spread} \div \text{Weighted Average Maturity}$$

To ensure that each loan is weighted appropriately and to avoid distortion, fixed weights for each country grouping and the size of loan within each country grouping are used for weighting the spreads and maturities in the formula. The index uses the 1979 average value as the base value of 100.

The World Bank's classification of economies is the basis for dividing the borrowing countries into five groups that are used as weights for the index.[9] Each group's share of borrowing in the syndicated loan market over the five years 1975 to 1979 is used to determine the fixed weight for the group. The weighting is fixed at: 32.7 percent share of total loans for Group 1 (prime industrialized borrowers), 28.5 percent for Group 2, 27.0 percent for Group 3, 3.1 percent for Group 4, and 8.7 percent for Group 5.

The *Euromoney* index is designed to reflect general market conditions. The index rises when borrowings, on average, become more expensive—when spreads have risen or maturities shortened, or both. The index falls when borrowing becomes cheaper.

The *Euromoney* country-risk ratings for 1980 are presented in Table 5.7. The United States and West Germany are excluded in the ratings, because dollar and deutsche mark syndicated loans form the basis of the analysis for the ratings. Some of the change in ratings between 1979 and 1980 was caused by two changes in the country rating table to incorporate two changes in the way the rankings are calculated: (1) each loan is now weighted by the *Euromoney* index for the month that the loan was signed in order to eliminate the effect of changes in overall lending conditions during the period, and (2) the weighted spread is now adjusted to take greater account of maturities. Table 5.8 shows the seven risk classes used in the *Euromoney* rating.

The rating has certain characteristics that may limit its usefulness and may also affect the way the ratings are computed. First, the league table covers only those countries that enter the Eurocurrency loan syndication market to borrow during the year. The league ratings thus are unaffected by year-to-year changes for countries that do not borrow in the Eurocurrency syndicated loan market every year. Second, by covering only public loans, the country-risk rating covers only one of the two types of borrowers involved in country risk. Furthermore, as will be discussed in the next section, the risk associated with a public loan is lower than with a loan to a private borrower in that country. How much

Table 5.7 *Euromoney* Country-Risk League Table 1980

Country	Number of Public-Sector Loans in Sample	Total Number of Public and Private Loans	Total Volume of all Loans ($ millions)	*Euromoney* Rating	Ranking 1979[a]	Ranking 1980
Australia	2	18	1,623.6	EM-I	17	1
United Kingdom	1	29	1,541.5	EM-I	5	2
France	7	13	1,668.4	EM-I	3	3
Finland	5	7	1,110.6	EM-I	18	4
Sweden	6	16	1,831.0	EM-I	4	5
Canada	5	9	6,448.3	EM-I	33	6
Belgium	2	4	2,881.1	EM-I	—	7
New Zealand	3	4	690.0	EM-I	1	8
India	3	3	112.0	EM-I	13	9
Denmark	8	18	1,095.8	EM-I	14	10
Malaysia	3	4	1,060.8	EM-I	10	11
Hungary	2	2	550.0	EM-I	16	12
Mexico	21	41	5,315.2	EM-II	34	13
Singapore	1	2	280.0	EM-II	—	14
Norway	4	16	777.1	EM-II	12	15
Italy	36	59	6,480.7	EM-II	19	16
Ireland	1	3	254.4	EM-II	8	17
Cyprus	1	5	141.1	EM-III	—	18
Iceland	2	2	35.0	EM-III	21	19
Colombia	8	9	649.9	EM-III	40	20
Spain	59	92	4,977.2	EM-III	38	21
Greece	10	16	1,498.6	EM-III	7	22
Argentina	16	23	2,544.0	EM-III	37	23
Algeria	1	2	300.0	EM-III	59	24
Philippines	13	20	1,270.4	EM-III	45	25
Jordan	2	3	251.9	EM-III	—	26
Thailand	6	10	844.3	EM-III	28	27
Portugal	11	15	723.2	EM-III	44	28
Romania	3	4	469.1	EM-IV	36	29
East Germany	5	8	373.1	EM-IV	20	30
Czechoslovakia	3	5	485.0	EM-IV	15	31
Trinidad	3	3	301.0	EM-IV	30	32
Papua New Guinea	2	3	103.5	EM-IV	31	33
Taiwan	1	3	143.5	EM-IV	26	34
Uruguay	4	4	116.0	EM-V	53	35
China	2	2	325.0	EM-V	6	36

Table 5.7 (*continued*)

Country	Number of Public-Sector Loans in Sample	Total Number of Public and Private Loans	Total Volume of all Loans ($ millions)	*Euromoney* Rating	Ranking 1979[a]	1980
Chile	10	28	964.7	EM-V	41	37
Sri Lanka	3	3	63.3	EM-V	51	38
Sharjah	1	1	55.0	EM-V	—	39
Nigeria	13	16	849.8	EM-V	55	40
Ecuador	13	14	1,023.5	EM-V	50	41
Morocco	3	3	450.0	EM-V	52	42
Egypt	1	8	243.2	EM-V	—	43
South Korea	5	23	1,942.0	EM-V	27	44
Abu Dhabi	3	5	37.4	EM-V	29	45
South Africa	3	4	469.0	EM-V	61	46
Tunisia	1	1	35.2	EM-V	39	47
Yugoslavia	15	20	2,013.1	EM-V	46	48
Niger	1	3	27.1	EM-V	72	49
Venezuela	27	38	6,575.4	EM-VI	22	50
Panama	2	2	225.0	EM-VI	43	51
Brazil	27	44	5,548.7	EM-VI	47	52
Ivory Coast	5	7	565.2	EM-VI	67	53
Peru	5	11	392.0	EM-VI	64	54
Costa Rica	6	6	167.5	EM-VI	48	55
Poland	4	9	1,088.6	EM-VI	56	56
Dominican Republic	3	3	220.0	EM-VI	60	57
Zimbabwe	2	2	27.6	EM-VI	—	58
Malawi	1	1	12.0	EM-VI	63	59
Malagasy Republic	1	1	5.5	EM-VII	75	60
Mozambique	1	1	20.0	EM-VII	—	61
Lesotho	1	1	10.0	EM-VII	—	62
Kenya	1	1	10.0	EM-VII	53	63
Burma	2	4	66.5	EM-VII	—	64
Ghana	1	1	27.7	EM-VII	—	65
Pakistan	5	6	534.8	EM-VII	73	66
Guatemala	1	1	50.0	EM-VII	—	67
Total	429	744	72,992.0			

Source: "The Country Risk League Table," *Euromoney* (February 1981), pp. 66–79.
[a] The 1979 ranking method excluded overall market weighting by *Euromoney* index.

Table 5.8   How the *Euromoney* Rating Works

Country Rating	Value of Country Index	Number of Countries
EM-I	Under 0.065	11
EM-II	0.065 to 0.074	5
EM-III	0.075 to 0.089	11
EM-IV	0.090 to 0.099	7
EM-V	0.100 to 0.129	15
EM-VI	0.130 to 0.249	10
EM-VII	0.250 and over	8

Source: Euromoney, loc. cit.

weight should be given to the other factors that affect country risk but are not taken into consideration in the formula?

The Probability Approach

Risk can be defined as a potential loss plus the probability of its occurrence. "Loss" is the difference between expected net income and actual net income (if any) received. The net income for a creditor would be interest received for the loan minus interest payments on the funds needed to finance the loan, less any unrecovered principal. "Expected" net income is always positive, since it represents the income that will be received if the loan is repaid without any problem. The actual net income could be negative if the interest received is less than the cost of the money plus any unrecovered principal.

To standardize the definition of loss for purposes of comparison, loss is expressed as a ratio of present values. Loss then means the difference between the discounted present value of expected net income and the discounted present value of actual net income in a given period, expressed as a proportion of the discounted present value of expected cash inflows during the same period. "Expected cash inflow" is expected net income plus the principal of the loan.

The following example should clarify the definition of loss: The Bank of Nova makes a $1,000 loan to the Rokel Company at a rate of interest of 12 percent per year with a maturity of 5 years. The principal is to be repaid in five equal annual installments. The Bank of Nova is paying interest of 10 percent per year on the funds it used to make the loan. The Rokel Company defaults on the loan in the third year.

The bank is fortunate to recover the balance of principal outstanding at the end of 5 years, but loses the interest income for part of the third year and all interest income for the fourth and fifth years. Table 5.9a shows the computation of the present value of expected net income, and Table 5.9b presents the computation of the present value of actual net income.

Table 5.9

(a) Calculating the Present Value of Expected Net Interest Income

(1) Year	(2) Loan Outstanding during Year ($)	(3) Expected Interest Income @ 12% ($)	(4) Interest Expense @ 10% ($)	(5) Expected Net Interest Income (3) − (4) ($)	(6) Present Value Factor @ 12%	(7) Present Value of Expected Net Interest Income (5) × (6) ($)
1	1,000	120	100	20	.893	17.86
2	800	96	80	16	.797	12.75
3	600	72	60	12	.712	8.54
4	400	48	40	8	.636	5.09
5	200	24	20	4	.567	2.29
						46.53

(b) Calculating the Present Value of Actual Net Income

(1) Year	(2) Loan Outstanding during Year ($)	(3) Interest Income @ 12% ($)	(4) Actual Interest Income Received ($)	(5) Interest Payments @ 10% ($)	(6) Actual Net Interest (4) − (5) ($)	(7) Present Value Factor @ 12%	(8) Present Value of Actual Net Interest Income (6) × (7) ($)
1	1,000	120	120	100	20	.893	17.86
2	800	96	96	80	16	.797	12.75
3	600	72	30	60	(30)	.712	(21.36)
4	600	72	—	60	(60)	.636	(38.16)
5	600	72	—	60	(60)	.567	(34.02)
							(62.93)

129

The realized loss on the loan will be:

Realized loss = Present value of expected net interest income −
present value of actual net income/present value
of expected cash inflows
= \$46.53 − (−\$62.93/\$767.51)
= .1426 or 14.26

Developing Estimates for Maximum Loss Possible (MLP)

The size of the loss that a lender could experience in a country can be calculated
by tabulating, where possible, the past loan loss experiences of all lenders from
available loan records. Such tabulation will provide information about the size
of loss and the frequency of loss for each type of risk. The dollar amounts of loss
experiences in a particular country provide a range of losses, from which a
range of possible future losses, including high, medium, and low loss values,
can be extrapolated.

However, sufficient historical data—perhaps any data at all—on the loss
experiences for a particular country may not exist because few loans have been
made to that country. In such cases, the loss experience of similar countries in
the same geographical region, or countries with the same level of economic
development or some other common characteristic may give some indication of
a country's potential loss experience.

The actual loss that a lender would experience also depends on the assumptions made about the political, sociocultural, and economic factors that influence the environment within the country. Changes due to economic development and growth, as well as changes in political and social stability, could make
future loss experience different from past loss experience. If past loss experience
is used, therefore, the data should be adjusted to reflect the changes.

In the absence of historical data for a particular or a comparable country, a
hypothetical assessment must be made about the size and the likelihood of
potential loss. In this case, statistical decision theory can be used to develop
estimates of exposure to loss. One approach is to begin by assuming that the
worst possible situation will occur, in which case the maximum losses possible
will occur. It is assumed that, if a risk index is constructed using the maximum
losses possible and the risk is found to be acceptable, then any actual loss would
be acceptable.

The possible loss for each type of risk is based on assumptions about the
conditions that will prevail following the occurrence of certain events, and how
these conditions affect a borrower's ability to pay back a loan. The maximum
loss possible would result from the greatest constraints on a borrower's ability
to service a loan.

The four types of risk the lender faces are shown in Table 5.10: blocked funds
because of foreign exchange control, in which case no transfers or remittances
out of the country can be made; technical default, in which the borrower cannot

Table 5.10   Maximum Percentage Loss Possible Each Year during the Life of the Loan by Type of Risk[a]

Year	Blocked Funds	Moratorium and Rescheduling	Renegotiation	Default
1	41	31	57	147
2	34	26	39	101
3	30	22	30	68
4	16	20	22	41
5	8	19	5	18

[a] 3 percent added for average administrative costs after risk has materialized.

meet the terms of the loan for some reason and may have to request a moratorium on payment of interest or principal or both, or reschedule of the loan; renegotation, in which the borrower finds the terms of the loan unduly burdensome because of changed conditions and desires to have the terms reduced; and default, when the borrower (who may have gone out of business) does not have the economic resources to service or pay off the loan.

The loss tabulations shown in Table 5.10 were computed on the basis of a $1,000 loan made at 12 percent interest for 5 years. The lender is paying interest of 10 percent for the funds used to make the loan, which allows a spread of 2 percent. It is assumed that the loan is amortized over the 5 years in equal annual installments, which reduces the lender's risk exposure. (If the principal were to be repaid in one lump sum at the end of the fifth year, the lender's risk during the 5 years would increase significantly.)

The assumptions made in computing the maximum loss possible for each type of risk were as follows: For blocked funds it was assumed that the funds were blocked for 3 years, during which the principal and interest on the loan were reinvested locally at 12 percent and transfer of the funds was resumed during the fourth year. The currency had depreciated 20 percent during the 3 years of exchange control, and the funds were transferred at the depreciated exchange rates.

In the second type of risk, the borrower went into technical default, which resulted in a moratorium on repayment of the principal for 5 years. The loan was rescheduled for repayment in 6 to 10 years.

Under renegotiation it was assumed that a 4-year grace period was given on repayment of the principal. Repayment was resumed in the fifth year. The interest rate on the loan was reduced by 50 percent to 6 percent, resulting in a negative 4 percent return.

Under default it is assumed that the principal and interest income would be lost for the balance of the loan if default occurred in any year.

In Table 5.10, the maximum loss possible represents the present value of the net interest income, including principal not repaid, expressed as a percentage of the present value of the net cash inflow (over the life of the loan) that the lender

Table 5.11 Calculating Country-Risk Probabilities for The Republic of Rokel Government and Government-Guaranteed Private Loans

Factors that May Pre-cipitate Country Risk	(1) Prob. from Table A	(2) Year	(3) Pr(3/1) Conditional Probability of Country Risk Resulting	Transfer Block			Technical Default Moratorium, or Rescheduling			Renegotiation			Default		
				(4) Prob. from Col (3)	(5) Joint Prob. Col (1) × Col (4)	(6) Year	(7) Prob. from Col (3)	(8) Joint Prob. Col (1) × Col (7)	(9) Year	(10) Prob. from Col (3)	(11) Joint Prob. Col (1) × Col (10)	(12) Year	(13) Prob. from Col (3)	(14) Joint Prob. Col (1) × Col (13)	(15) Year
Political															
Disorders, riots	.6	2	.1	0	0		.1	.06	3	0	0		0	0	
Revolution, civil war	.3	4	.4	0	0		.3	.09	5	.1	.03	4	0	0	
Foreign conflict	.1	5	.2	0	0		0	0		0	0		.1	.01	5
Occupation by foreign power	0														

132

Economic

Slowdown in GNP growth

.1	4	.3	0	0	.2	.02	4	.1	1.01	4	0	0

Rapid rise in producer costs

.3	1	.3	0	0	.2	.06	3	.3	.09	2	0	0

Labor unrest, strikes

.2	3	.1	0	0	.1	.02	4	0	0	0	0	0

Credit squeeze

.2	1	.4	0	0	.4	.08	2	0	0	0	0	0

Recession, depression[a]

.1	3	.4	0	0	.2	.02	4	.2	.2	3	0	0

Natural disasters[a]

.1	1	.3	.1	.01	0	0		0	0	.2	.02	1

Balance of payments

Sharp drop in export revenue

.3	3	.3	.2	.06	.1	.03	4	0	0	0	0

Rapid rise in imports

.4	2	.2	.2	.08	.1	.04	3	0	0	0	0

Excessive external borrowing

.1	4	.7	0	0	.4	.04	5	.3	.03	3	0

Currency depreciation, devaluation

.1	1	.7	.2	.02	.4	.04	3	.1	.01	2	0

[a] Natural disasters include floods, storms, famine, etc.

expected at the time the loan was made. The cash inflow includes expected net interest income plus the principal repayment. A flat 3 percent was added to represent the average cost of additional expenses such as travel or communications, incurred by the lender.

Calculating the Probability of Loss

The probability of loss for each type of risk can be obtained by tabulating the frequency of loss for each type of risk. As noted previously, if loan records produce enough incidence of loss experience to use in tabulating the frequencies, this method of computing the probabilities is useful.

Another approach that provides useful estimates of likely frequency is a two-step method of computing the probabilities of the occurrence of each type of risk. First, probabilities are assigned to various political, social, economic, and balance-of-payments factors that, when changed, can precipitate one or more types of risk. The probability of a change in each factor may be estimated by asking: How likely is the event to occur, and in what year is the event most likely to occur?

The second step is to obtain the probability that at least one of the four types of risk will occur, as well as the probability of occurrence for each specific type of risk. The subjective probabilities can be obtained in answer to three questions: What is the probability that at least one type of risk will occur? What is the probability that a specific risk will result (for example, blocked funds, rescheduling, renegotation, or default)? In what year will the specific type of risk occur? (Assigning probabilities is discussed in more detail in the appendix to this chapter.)

In Table 5.11 probabilities obtained from the appendix and assigned to the factors are entered in Column 1. An indication of the year of their likely occurrence is entered in Column 2. Column 3 contains the probability that country risk will result following the occurrence of one of the factors. The probabilities in Columns 1 and 3 are then used to calculate the probability of occurrence of each type of risk. It is assumed that each of the four risks are independent of each other; the sum of their probabilities must therefore equal the probability of country risk. The value in Column 3 for each factor is assigned to one or more type of risk.

The first item under economic—slowdown in GNP growth—will be used to illustrate the process. The probability that there will be a slowdown in GNP growth is thought to be very low and is assigned a .1. From evaluation of the economy, the analyst decides that such a slowdown would take place around the fourth year, as indicated in Column 2. The likelihood of country risk resulting when GNP growth slows is assessed at .3. Although the probability of a slowdown of GNP growth is felt to be low, if it does occur, the chance of country risk resulting is higher. Country risk will probably take the form of technical default, moratorium, or rescheduling (TMR), and renegotiation. The probability in Column 3 is split between TMR and renegotiation, with a .2 entered in Column 7 and .1 entered in Column 10.

The next step is to calculate the probability of TMR and renegotiation occurring. The product of Columns 1 and 7, in this case .02, is entered in Column 8. Similarly, the product of Columns 1 and 10 is entered in Column 11. Note that the probabilities of .01 in Column 11 and .02 in Column 8 are the joint probabilities of the probability of a slowdown in GNP growth and the probability of country risk resulting when the slowdown in GNP growth has occurred. It is assumed that TMR and renegotiation would take place in year 4, the year following the slowdown. The year is entered in Columns 9 and 12. The other entries are made on the same basis.

Computation of a Country-Risk Index

The computation of a country-risk index is illustrated in Table 5.12 showing the country-risk rankings. The hypothetical maximum loss possible (MLP) has been transferred from Table 5.10 to the column for maximum loss possible under each type of risk in Table 5.12. The next step is to sum the joint probabilities in Table 5.11 for each type of risk by year of occurrence and enter each total in the probability of risk column under each type of risk for each year. The following example illustrates the summing up process.

Under transfer block in Table 5.11, there are two entries in Column 5 for the first year:

Event	Probability of Occurring in Year 1
Natural disaster	.01
Currency depreciation or devaluation	.02
Total	.03

The total of .03 is entered in Table 5.12 in the probability of loss column (2) in the first-year row. The entries for the second and third years under transfer block in Table 5.12 are .08 and .06, respectively. The probability of loss for the other types of risk are totaled for each year in Table 5.11 and entered in the appropriate column in Table 5.12.

The entries for maximum loss possible and probability of risk under each type of risk for each year are multiplied and the product entered in the adjacent column for risk factor. Under transfer block for first year, for example, multiply 41 by .03 to get 1.23, which is entered in the risk-factor column. This process is repeated for all types of risk and for each year that has entries for maximum loss possible and probability of risk, and the products are entered in the proper risk-factor column. All the risk-factor entries under each type of risk should then be totaled and entered in the total column. The grand total country-risk index is obtained by summing across the total row; in this case the total is 25.9.

Then to ascertain what the 25.9 country-risk index means ("Is this high, medium, or low risk?") a rating system such as that presented in Table 5.13 can be constructed. In this table, a risk index of 25.9, for example, carries a Ba risk

Table 5.12 Computation of Country Risk Index for the Republic of Rokel for Government or Government-Guaranteed Private Loans

	Type of Risk											
	Transfer Block			Moratorium or Rescheduling			Renegotiation			Default		
Year of Loan	(1) Maximum Loss Possible[a]	(2) Probability of Risk[b]	(3) Risk Factor[c] (1) × (2)	(4) Maximum Loss Possible	(5) Probability of Risk	(6) Risk Factor (4) × (5)	(7) Maximum Loss Possible	(8) Probability of Risk	(9) Risk Factor (7) × (8)	(10) Maximum Loss Possible	(11) Probability of Risk	(12) Risk Factor (10) × (11)
First	41	.03	1.23	31	.08	2.08	57	.10	3.9	147	.02	2.94
Second	34	.08	2.72	26	.20	4.4	39	.05	1.5	101		
Third	30	.06	1.80	22	.20	1.8	30	.04	0.88	68		
Fourth	16			20	.09	1.8	22			41		
Fifth	8			19	.13	2.47	5			18	.01	0.18
Total			5.75			10.75			6.28			3.12

Index of country risk = 5.75 + 10.75 + 6.28 + 3.12 = 25.9

Source: Tables 5.10 and 5.11.

[a] Maximum loss possible obtained from Table 5.10.
[b] Probability of risk obtained from Table 5.11.
[c] Risk factor is the expected value of maximum loss possible.

rating, which is described as "average." The ratings in Table 5.13 are designed to rank countries in order of the probability of default, that is, the inability to meet interest payment or repayment of principal.

Like all systems, this rating system has technical shortcomings. The method of estimating probabilities needs a certain degree of refinement; the assessment of probabilities is always a difficult task. Augmentation by historical loss experience can be helfpul. Probabilities can be computed objectively if data are available, but probabilities developed from historical data need adjustment to reflect later changes and anticipated developments. In the absence of historical data, subjective measurements have to be substituted.

The country risk of a multinational corporation with direct investment in a branch, subsidiary, or affiliate in a foreign country is different from that of a lender to a government or private citizen in a foreign country. First, direct investment usually takes the form of equity. Second, there are usually no host government guarantees as there are in the case of loans. Third, the parent company normally has assets in the foreign country, in the form of buildings, land improvements, mineral rights, or raw material and finished goods inventories, that are subject to expropriation. The direct investor is exposed to risks that can affect its ability to continue operations, such as loss of the right to continue to do business or a forfeiture of its assets or other investments in the foreign country.

Four types of country risk for the direct investor have been identified: transfer block, restriction on import of raw material or component parts used in production, indigenization or creeping indigenization, and nationalization or expropriation. Transfer block makes remittances to the parent company impossible for the branch, subsidiary, or affiliate as a result of exchange control or other government restrictions. When there is a transfer block, the parent company is temporarily denied the use of the cash from repatriation of profits, dividends, or principal. If a profitable opportunity exists to reinvest the cash in the local economy, the effect of the transfer block may be reduced.

Restrictions on the import of raw material or component parts used in production may result in reduced output or other types of production problems that can cause a fall in profits. Import restrictions on raw material and compo-

Table 5.13   Country-Risk Rating

Risk Factor (Range)[a]	Description	Rating
0 − 1.00	No risk	Aaa
1.01 − 3.00	Negligible risk	Aa
3.01 − 10.00	Below average risk	Baa
10.01 − 30.00	Average risk	Ba
30.01 − 50.00	Above average risk	B
50.01 − 80.00	High risk	Bcc
80.00 <	Very high risk	c

[a] Risk factor is derived from Table 5.12.

Table 5.14 Calculating Country-Risk Probabilities for The Republic of Rokel—Direct Investment

Risk	Factor Occurring		Conditional Probability of Country Risk Resulting	Transfer Block			Restriction on Import of Raw Material and Component Parts			Indigenization or Creeping Indigenization			Nationalization or Expropriation		
	(1) Prob.	(2) Year	(3) Pr(3/1)	(4) Prob. from Col (3)	(5) Joint Prob. Col (1) × Col (4)	(6) Year	(7) Prob. from Col (3)	(8) Joint Prob. Col (1) × Col (7)	(9) Year	(10) Prob. from Col (3)	(11) Joint Prob. Col (1) × Col (10)	(12) Year	(13) Prob. from Col (3)	(14) Joint Prob. Col (1) × Col (13)	(15) Year
Factors that may Precipitate Country Risk															
Political															
Disorders, riots															
Revolution, civil war															
Foreign conflict															
Occupation by foreign power															
Takeover by an extremist government															
Other															

138

Economic

Long-run slowdown
in GNP growth
Rapid rise in pro-
ducer costs
Labor unrest, strikes
Capital squeeze
Recession, depression
Natural disasters
Gross capital
formation
Domestic savings
Consumer prices
Unemployment rate
Other

Balance of Payments

Exports
Imports
Terms of trade
Currency deprecia-
tion, devaluation

nents are imposed when balance-of-payments problems result from falling exports or rising imports that persist over a number of years and cannot be corrected by other means. Governments usually impose restrictions on these types of imports when they want to encourage domestic production of the raw material or manufacture of the imported component.

Indigenization occurs when, through government legislation or edict, foreign owners are compelled to relinquish control of their business enterprises to the nationals of a country—for example, Nigerianization or Mexicanization. Creeping indigenization is a subtler means to achieve indigenization over a longer period of time: a government uses various types of pressure to induce foreign owners to relinquish control to nationals.

Nationalization, or expropriation, occurs when a state takes over the enterprise. The take-over may be for economic or political reasons, or for reasons of national interest. Adequate compensation may or may not be paid, and payment may be made promptly or after a prolonged delay.

In both indigenization and nationalization, the foreign owner loses the business or the right to continue business in the host country. It is important to distinguish between indigenization, when ownership is relinquished to private entities, and nationalization, when the state takes over ownership of the business. Another important difference is that indigenization usually takes place under rightist governments, whereas nationalization usually takes place under leftist governments.

Table 5.14 presents a grid for calculating country-risk probabilities for the Republic of Rokel for a direct investment by a foreign owner. More economic than other factors may precipitate country risk, which increases the significance and therefore the relative weight of the economic category in calculating country-risk probabilities. Political factors carry the next greatest weight because of the importance of indigenization and nationalization risks. (It should be noted that political problems frequently develop as a result of underlying economic problems such as mismanagement of the economy, slow economic growth, recession, or so on.)

The process for calculating country-risk probabilities in direct investment is the same as that used in calculating the probabilities for Table 5.10. The probabilities of the factors' occurring, Column 1, would be the same, or approximately the same, even if the number of factors in a category increased (see the appendix and Table A for assigning probabilities to factors). The conditional probability for transfer block, Column 3, may also be the same as in Table 5.10. Since the conditional probabilities for the three other risks and the year of occurrence will be different from the risks in Table 5.10, the country-risk probabilities calculated in Table 5.14 will be different. Similarly, a different maximum possible loss (Table 5.9) would have to be calculated for the risks of direct investment. A different value for the country-risk index (Table 5.13) will be obtained and a different country-risk rating result. It is obvious that two different country-risk ratings can be obtained for the same country, depending on whether a loan or a direct investment is involved.

Country-risk assessment for a lender emphasizes liquidity and the ability to transfer funds through foreign exchange in the short to medium term. Country-risk assessment for the direct investor normally focuses on economic growth and political stability in the medium to long term.

Monitoring Country Risk

Country-risk ratings project a perception of the future on the basis of present information. Their accuracy depends on the ability to assess the likelihood of future events. The conditions prevailing at the time of the risk-rating process and the accuracy of extrapolating change, of course, over time. In fact, in some cases, changes occur overnight. Therefore, periodic monitoring of country risk to update the ratings is necessary in order to keep abreast of developments that may affect exposure to risk.

Since the process of monitoring involves lender costs, the frequency and extent of updating undertaken by a bank or a corporation will depend on the magnitude of the lender's risk or the corporation's investment exposure as measured by its maximum possible loss, the level of the country's risk factor, how that factor translates into a credit rating, the emergence of any high-risk event that needs close observation, and the cost-benefit ratio of frequent monitoring. Management would have to decide the trade-off between costs and benefits before authorizing frequent monitoring for each country the company invests in. A minimum amount of updating is necessary in all cases.

Monitoring also helps catch incipient change that can damage a country's rating over a period of time. Imperceptible developments can take place that become significant shifts during a hiatus in monitoring. Monitoring can be an early warning signal that provides a bank or company with the notice to evaluate the situation and take necessary action to protect its interests.

Monitoring tests the accuracy of the probability assumptions factored into the rating system. The key premises should be rechecked frequently to see how well they are holding up. Some will hold up, others will perform fairly well, and others will do poorly. The credit rating should be reassessed in light of the performance of the assumptions, and assumptions should be changed when necessary. If necessary, the risk rating should be adjusted to reflect the new information and new assumptions. Changes in the risk rating should be taken into consideration for policy and strategy review by the company. A monitoring sheet should be constructed with a list of key assumptions and a record of the dates on which they were most recently evaluated.

As an aid in monitoring economic, political, and social trends, the IMF publishes a quarterly statistical review called *International Financial Statistics*, which gives historical statistics and estimates of important economic and financial indicators for every member country for the four succeeding quarters. Graphs of the key indicators are plotted on semi-logarithmic scales, permitting the growth trend of the indicator to be observed. These graphs are useful aids in monitoring the indicators. The United Nations also publishes a monthly bulle-

Table 5.15 (*continued*)

	(1) Weights	June 1980	December 1980	June 1981	December 1981	June 1982
		Date of Assessment				
Determinants[b]						
Net change (%)		9	−8	11		
Country-risk monitor index		109	100	111		

[a] Country-risk monitor index for Spain.
[b] Data for calculating changes in the determinants may be obtained from *International Financial Statistics* (IMF); *U.N. Monthly Bulletin of Statistics*; *World Financial Markets* (Morgan Guaranty Trust Company, N.Y.), and the London *Financial Times*.

Politics	25
Economy	25
Fiscal management	15
Money management	15
Balance of payments	10
External debt	10
	100

The weights in each category are distributed to the determinants in the category. The points assigned to each determinant also reflect an assessment of its relative significance in contributing to country risk within the category, as well as in relation to determinants in other categories since the last country-risk evaluation was done. If the analyst feels that the situation has changed enough to warrant a change in the weights, another comprehensive evaluation of the country may be warranted. The weights of the items in a category add up to the weight for that category. The weights are assigned for either a positive or negative change in the determinant. For example, a range of −5 to +5 can be given to the determinant, money, under money management during each assessment, which would make the total weight assigned equal to 10 points. Negative points are assigned to a variable when it changes in the negative direction; that is, its change would increase the realization of country risk. Positive weights are given when a change is considered favorable, or would lead to a decrease in country risk. The weight for each variable is therefore from − to + and is therefore equal to 2 times the number assigned.

Two factors have to be taken into consideration when determining how many points to give a variable during an assessment: First, the amount of positive or negative change in the variable and, second, the persistence in the same direction of change. Persistence of change in the same direction is viewed as reinforcing the trend. Ordinarily, up to two-thirds of the allotted points are awarded for the amount of change and the remaining third for the persistence of the change.

An example will illustrate the award of weights. One graph in Figure 5.1 shows the unemployment rate increasing at about a constant rate but persisting in the same direction, which indicates a worsening unemployment situation. A negative 2 points has been assigned here for June 1980 and December 1980 and a negative 1 for June 1982 in expectation that a smaller actual change may result from the new government's policies instituted at the beginning of 1981.

The graph on the Spanish peseta shows a decline persisting since the first quarter 1980 although the rate of decline is decreasing. A minus 4 was therefore

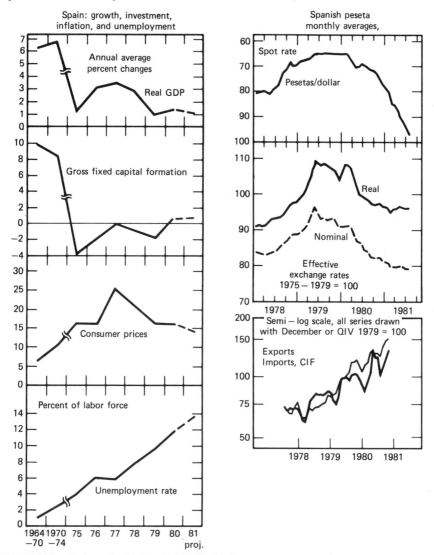

Figure 5.1 Charts Showing: Real GDP Growth, Gross Fixed Capital Formation, Inflation, Unemployment, Pesata Exchange Rate, and Exports and Imports for Spain. Source: Morgan Guaranty Trust Company of New York, *World Financial Markets*, April 1981; IMF, *International Financial Statistics*, Nov. 1981, Vol. 34, No. 11.

assigned to this variable for December 1980 and June 1981 to reflect the likelihood of a devaluation if this trend continues and the situation worsens.

The maximum weights should not be automatically assigned during each assessment unless the change is sufficiently large and persistent to warrant it. It should be remembered that the objective is to monitor relative change, and assignment of maximum weights all the time would fail to show the relative magnitude or to distinguish crisis situations from less serious occurrences.

The plus and minus sign at the top of Column 1 is intended to indicate that the values assigned as weights have a range from minus (value) to plus (value). The values in Column 1 are therefore the absolute numbers.

The weights assigned are summed up to obtain the subtotal for each category, and the subtotals summed up to get the net change for the assessment period. The net change is then expressed as the country-risk monitor index. The assessment period ending December 1979 has an index of 100 to begin the computation. The net change for the assessment period ending June 1980 is +9 percent, which makes the CRMI 109 (100 + 9). The net change for the period ending December 1980 is −8. Recall that the weights in Column 1 total 100. A net change of −8 indicates a minus 8 percent change, or a fall in the index by 8 percent from the last index value of 109 (that is, .92 × 109 = 100.28 or 100).

The CRMI improved slightly in June 1980 but slipped back in December 1980 because of the poor economic performance, which resulted in a change of government in early 1981. The new government improved the political situation and instituted some needed economic reforms. However, the rate of economic recovery is expected to be slow and the full effects of the economic recovery program are expected to be slow in taking effect. The CRMI improved by 11 percentage points in June 1981 to reflect the new economic program and political environments.

CONSTRAINTS IMPOSED IN HOST COUNTRIES

Corporations doing business abroad usually find that the financial goals and policies they develop for their foreign affiliates are in conflict, to varying extents, with the policy objectives and goals of the host countries in which they operate. Foreign affiliates have to operate within economic and political restrictions imposed by the host governments. These restrictions usually have the effect of constraining the ability of the foreign affiliate to achieve profit maximization, or to earn the highest return possible for the parent company's investment in the affiliate. One of a corporation's financial goals is the maximization of its shareholders' return on their investment. If the foreign affiliate cannot earn the return expected because of restrictions imposed by the affiliate's host government, then the parent company suffers a financial loss, measured by the difference between the income expected and the actual income from its investment in the affiliate. A parent company, therefore, can be exposed to possible financial losses from the operations of its foreign affiliate as a result of the restrictions that are sometimes imposed to meet economic or political policy objectives. These restrictions may not necessarily be imposed in response to the risk-provoking events dicussed previously.

The restrictions discussed below were identified by a group of international executives of U.S. multinational companies in response to a survey question-naire as those most commonly imposed in host countries.[10] The restrictions are mainly economic, political, and legal. The next sections of this chapter will briefly note aspects of the restrictions that affect country-risk assessment.

Economic Restrictions

The economic restrictions are tariffs and duties, import quotas, export com-mitments, export restrictions, licensing restrictions, local sourcing requirements, local manufacturing requirements, price controls, dividend remittance restric-tions, capital repatriation restrictions, and financing restrictions.

Tariffs and Duties

Tariffs and duties are two of the oldest types of customs that countries impose on goods and services coming into or leaving the country. These levies serve a dual purpose as a source of revenue as well as a means of controlling trade. When they are imposed simply as a source of revenue to cover the cost of operating the port of entry and to provide additional income for the govern-ment, tariffs and duties may be considered as passive instruments of policy that are not intended to restrict trade.

Tariffs may be used as active instruments of government policy by restricting imports. Countries use tariffs to protect their domestic industry against foreign competition. The tariffs are set at a level that brings the importer's selling price up to the domestic price, eliminating any price advantage of foreign goods over their domestic counterparts. Although the use of tariffs to protect domestic industries is a common practice worldwide, the General Agreement on Tariffs and Trade (GATT) has been successful to a certain extent in reducing tariffs and other trade barriers, as discussed in Chapter 3. Developing countries still use tariffs to protect their infant industries from what they sometimes perceive as predatory foreign competition.

Import Quotas

Import quotas are another form of trade restriction that are used as instruments of government policy. Such a policy may have two objectives. First, it may protect domestic industry by limiting foreign competition. Countries experienc-ing high domestic unemployment in industries that cannot compete successfully against imported goods may impose import quotas to limit the inflow of the foreign goods. Import quotas are used frequently by developing countries that wish to limit domestic consumption of imported goods that are of better quality and, thus, more desirable than locally produced goods. Import quotas are used in this way to ration outgoing scarce foreign exchange for essential imports.

Export Commitments

Countries sometimes desire to generate foreign exchange earnings or to replenish their foreign exchange reserves, which are used to purchase goods from overseas. For this purpose, they request affiliates and subsidiaries of foreign corporations to make export commitments. An export commitment is a pledge or an agreement by the domiciled affiliate or subsidiary to take affirmative steps to market a certain proportion of its output outside the host country. The objective is to draw foreign exchange into the host country. The majority of developing countries, for example, experience shortages of foreign exchange. Foreign exchange reserves must be carefully managed. Companies that undertake foreign production operations usually have to import parts of the input for their manufacturing, and they use foreign exchange (for example, U.S. dollars for an American company) to pay for the imports. Their host countries may stipulate that they replenish the foreign exchange used in this way by making commitments to export part of their output. The Communist Eastern European countries, for instance, have used export commitments as a basis for negotiation with multinational companies bidding for contracts there.

A multinational company usually has an established or growing worldwide network of marketing channels to which its affiliates and subsidiaries can export part of their production output. A company that is a newcomer to overseas production operations will have a more difficult time meeting an export commitment.

Export Restrictions

Export restrictions are imposed by countries for a variety of reasons: (1) to increase the world price of a commodity, (2) to restrain domestic prices, (3) for foreign policy, (4) in connection with trade warfare, or (5) to promote national security. Export restrictions are generally imposed in the form of licensing procedures which require exporters to obtain a license that permits the goods to be exported. The licensing process is a mechanism for the government to exercise control over the rate at which the restricted commodity is exported.

A classic example of export restrictions to increase the world price of a commodity was the move by OPEC in 1973 and 1974 that successfully raised oil prices by restricting the output and export of oil. The success of OPEC in raising the world price of oil and in maintaining the higher world price has increased the chance of other cartels being formed by producers of natural resources.

Many countries impose export restrictions to restrain local prices in situations where unrestricted exporting could create domestic shortages and higher domestic prices, which would result in inflationary pressures.

The United States has imposed export restrictions from time to time for domestic or foreign strategic reasons. The Export Administration Act of 1969, amended in 1974, for example, provided authority for the imposition of controls for (1) protection against scarcity and inflation, (2) foreign policy efforts, and (3) security reasons. A provision of the act imposed an embargo on all exports to Cuba, North Vietnam, North Korea, and Southern Rhodesia.

The United States has imposed export restrictions on agricultural commodities at certain times. In 1973 and 1974, for example, public pressure forced the United States to place an embargo on grain exports to the Soviet Union when it appeared that such shipments might increase inflationary pressure in the United States. Similar restrictions on the export of huge consignments of wheat to China were imposed by the denial of export licenses.

The United States has used export restrictions to advance its foreign policy objectives. In July 1978 President Carter imposed an embargo on the sale of an advanced-technology computer to the Soviet Union's news agency, Tass, and limited sales of oil equipment to the Soviet Union by requiring license approval for each transaction. The President's action was in retaliation for the harassment of Soviet dissidents, which was contrary to the Helsinki Convention on Human Rights. The export of nuclear weapons and high-technology products to certain nations has been restricted from time to time for security reasons.

Licensing Restrictions

Governments of developing countries may impose licensing restrictions on multinational corporations or other foreign companies to achieve certain policy objectives. Licensing policies may favor technology, for example, that uses certain abundant resources in the country. Licensing by developing countries may favor labor-intensive technology, for instance, which uses their abundant labor supply, while restricting the use of relatively scarce capital resources. Another objective may be to ensure that imported technology is obtained at the lowest possible price in order to reduce the strain on the country's financial assets. The government may also want to ensure that imported technology is compatible with the country's needs and development program and that the technological transfer is of optimum benefit to the country's economy. In these cases, licensing contracts must be registered through an application process administered under some type of technology-transfer legislation; licensing agreements that do not meet the requirements of the law are rejected. Contracts that are not registered under the law are invalid and unenforceable.

Local Sourcing Requirements

For economic and political reasons, countries increasingly require that local industry use as many local components as possible in their products. The objective is to help the domestic economy by stimulating demand for domestic output. In addition, local sourcing helps save foreign exchange, which can then be used to procure non-competing components from abroad.

The drawback to local sourcing is that in many countries, especially in the developing countries, the local components may be inferior in quality to imported components. From the perspective of these countries, however, the economic and political benefits to be derived from local sourcing requirements far outweigh the temporary drawbacks of inferior quality.

Local Manufacturing Requirements

The economic benefits that accrue to a nation from local manufacturing by a foreign company vary widely depending on the nature of the product and how extensive the manufacturing process is. Local manufacturing creates employment and income for the workers. Combined with local sourcing, it can also create demand for local goods and services which, in turn, creates further employment and income. Local manufacturing tends to save foreign exchange reserves, and if the product is a high-technology item, the benefits from technological transfer can be impressive. Because of all of these economic benefits, host countries may provide tax breaks and other economic incentives to foreign companies that undertake local manufacturing.

Price Controls

Price controls are imposed by many countries to restrain inflationary pressures that already exist or are building up within their economies. Price controls may be used to encourage, or even force, companies to do more local sourcing by effectively making local products cheaper than imports. For the foreign company, the effect of price controls is to limit its ability to set its own prices. A mandated lower price may result in lower return and, perhaps, a longer period of time to recover the company's investment. In many cases, companies plan to charge higher prices on their offshore production in order to earn high returns to cover perceived risks in doing business abroad. Price controls limit their ability to earn those higher returns. Thus, companies need to know the impact of price controls on their profitability.

Dividend Remittance Restrictions

Host countries may impose limits on the amount of capital that foreign companies can repatriate within a given accounting period or calendar year for a variety of reasons. The host country's economic growth is achieved through increases in capital formation and greater productivity. Countries seeking to increase their rate of economic growth must increase investment in capital goods. One way of increasing investment is to plow back some of the profits generated by businesses. If profits are not plowed back into the economy by way of investment to expand production capacity, the resulting low rate of capital formation will retard the rate of economic growth. One of the main reasons why host countries seek to impose limits on the amount of dividend repatriation is to channel investment to the host country's economy.

Another reason is that dividend remittance may use up scarce foreign exchange that is needed to pay for imported goods and to build up reserves to support the foreign exchange rate. The less adequate foreign exchange income from exports is, the more likely the country is to curb the remittance of dividends. In general, developing countries tend to restrict repatriation of dividends more than developed countries do.

Restricting dividend remittance limits the amount of profit that companies can repatriate in any given period of time. This constraint extends the time required to achieve income objectives from foreign operations. On the other hand, the company will eventually be able to repatriate additional dividends stemming from incremental reinvested earnings.

Capital Repatriation Restrictions

When a host country wants to encourage foreign companies to commit their capital as long as possible, it may restrict the repatriation of capital. The experience of many countries has been that foreign companies try to recover their invested capital as soon as possible by setting pricing policies and generating high profit margins that will produce sufficient cash flows to permit fast payback. After they recover their capital, the companies may even cease operations and return home. The cessation of production results in economic destabilization, which can cause serious problems for the economy and the government of the host country.

Other companies continue to earn substantial profits long after their initial capital investment has been fully recovered, but they continue to repatriate their profits. As discussed earlier, however, long-term capital formation and the growth in the capital base are major ingredients in the formula for economic growth. Host countries therefore seek to encourage foreign companies to make longer-term investments and to maintain their investments at levels that enhance local economic growth.

Restrictions on repatriation of capital are generally imposed by capital-poor developing countries where disinvestment by foreign companies would result in severe economic destabilization and hardship. Management should assess the extent of risk exposure that capital repatriation restrictions may impose on the safety of the capital and the prospects for the continued viability of their business activities abroad. This risk/return tradeoff must be carefully evaluated.

Financing Restrictions

Countries experiencing balance-of-payments problems may restrict outflows of capital through exchange controls or taxation policy. In 1964 the United States levied an interest-equalization tax on income from portfolio investments overseas in foreign securities issued in the United States.

Labor unions have objected to the investment in plants overseas in industries beset my domestic unemployment. The United States, for example, tried to curb the outflow of capital for direct investment overseas during the 1960s through moral suasion. Later, laws were enacted to control this outflow.

Political Restrictions

The most frequent political/legal restrictions imposed by host countries include limitations on geographical expansion, nationality restrictions on management and directors, abrogation of rights to royalties, foreign ownership limitations, nationalization, and expropriation.

Limitations on Geographical Expansion

Many foreign companies, particularly multinational companies, have a monopoly position or a dominant position in their industry in certain areas of a host country. Sometimes these companies seek to expand their activities geographically in order to head off potential competition. In such a case, the host country may impose limitations on the geographical expansion of the monopoly company.

These geographical limitations are imposed most frequently when a host government fears that the foreign monopoly would crush any emerging local competition if its expansion went unchecked. In order to foster the growth and development of local industrial and commercial firms, host governments may restrict foreign firms to specific geographical markets. Such restrictions permit local firms to grow without the pressure of foreign competition. Developing countries usually resort to geographical limitations on expansion to encourage the growth of firms in infant industries.

Nationality Representation

The growth of nationalism has resulted in grassroots demands to domiciled foreign companies to employ more natives in management positions, where they can influence the companies' decision-making processes. This pressure is worldwide. In Europe and elsewhere, host countries have sought to restrict the representation of foreign nationals in the ranks of management of foreign companies. Some countries try to encourage the foreign companies to set up programs to train local managers in order to replace the foreign managers within a reasonable, negotiated time limit. In the developing countries, this process is called "indigenization"—the replacement of foreigners by the indigenous population.

Foreign companies can benefit greatly from replacing their expatriate employees with qualified indigenous personnel—or by employing the maximum number of indigenous people from the start. Companies that rapidly indigenize generally enjoy relatively abundant goodwill in host countries because these companies are seen as providing employment opportunities for the host population. The host countries are readier to cooperate with such companies than with all-foreign companies, and a feeling of cordiality develops that can ameliorate the impact of other restrictions that could hinder the company's activities. Also, the opportunity given to local managers exposes them to foreign management techniques which help to develop their skills and increase the pool of talent available to the company. Another benefit to foreign companies of indigenization is that native staff can serve as a conduit between the company and the government. From a pragmatic point of view, it is usually much cheaper to employ qualified local managers than to bring in foreign managers, who generally receive much higher pay.

One problem arises for the foreign company: these nationality restrictions can dilute management quality if there is an inadequate supply of qualified, trained, and experienced local personnel. Another problem can stem from pressure on foreign companies from host countries to replace foreigners with local management personnel at a faster pace than consistent with sound, effective management principles. Companies must consider the tradeoffs between management's need to maintain effective control, on the one hand, and the pressure for accelerated replacement of foreign managers on the other hand.

Abrogation of Rights to Royalties

Multinational corporations are increasingly using licensing agreements instead of exports. These agreements permit their products to enter the overseas markets without the commitment of capital or inventory funds, without the risks connected with direct investment, and without any of the drawbacks of exporting. Licensing allows multinational corporations to gain some tactical or strategic advantages in marketing its products overseas. The royalties represent income for the licensor without any further commitment of funds beyond the initial investment in the research and development of the process. The income from royalties augments the corporation's revenue and thereby increases the profitability of the company.

The patenting process used in the industrialized countries permits an orderly flow of technology across national boundaries. The patent system provides the inventor of a new technology protection through ownership rights to the exclusive use of the new technology for a number of years, during which period the owner can recover the investment in research and development and earn a fair return. Laws exist in each country against restrictive licensing practices that would give unfair advantage to the owner.

The licensing process helps foreign businesses because it permits them to acquire another nation's technology, which can be used to foster economic growth and development. As buyers of technology, developing countries are usually at a disadvantage, however, when negotiating licensing agreements with foreign companies. The developing countries complain that the foreign companies use their monopoly or quasi-monopoloy positions to exact restrictive and unfair provisions in their licensing agreements. As a result, developing countries have in some cases abrogated their licensing contracts or refused to register contracts for patents in cases where they judge the contracts too restrictive. Countries usually develop guidelines to determine whether licensing agreements are overly restrictive.

Some licensing contracts are abrogated or patents refused registration when (1) technology is already available in the country, (2) it could be obtained through a more favorable contractual arrangement, (3) the royalty would be an excessive burden on the economy, or (4) the validity period for the licensing agreement is deemed excessive.

Creeping Indigenization

Governments of foreign countries frequently harbor some degree of apprehension about foreign companies, especially multinational corporations, controlling and dominating the local economy. They fear that control of the economy will pass to foreigners whose interests and objectives are different from those of the host country. To minimize the degree to which their respective economies may be subject to foreign control, foreign governments have in some cases instituted rules and regulations to limit foreign ownership of local business. The limitations usually restrict foreign ownership to a given percentage of total capitalization of a company or forbid total foreign ownership of a company, or forbid all foreign ownership of local companies, or exclude certain types of business activities from foreign participation.

In the first case, foreign companies are limited to stipulated percentages of ownership in a company. The percentage may be the same or different for each industry. The prevalent practice in the developing countries is to vary the limit by industry. Companies in high-technology and capital-intensive industries generally have fewer restrictions on foreign ownership than do companies in low-technology, less capital-intensive industries.

In many countries, total foreign ownership of local corporations is forbidden. The objective here is to foster indigenous participation in the ownership of companies operating within the economy. One approach used is to legislate that the only foreign companies eligible for registration and operation within the country are joint local-foreign ventures. The proportion of foreign-to-local participation is usually stipulated and varies among different industries.

Another widespread practice is to ban foreign companies from all activity in certain industries. The service industry is a common example. Countries usually feel that foreign companies, with their superior financial resources and better management and marketing techniques, could easily destroy local competition in the service area. The development of a middle class of local entrepreneurs in the service industries is considered a desirable objective in the continued growth and development of the local economies.

Nationalization and Expropriation

Nationalization takes place when a company, an industry, or field of economic activity is taken over by the government through a policy decree. It is a blanket form of takeover which may cover one or more firms in an industry. Firms in the industry or field of economic activity are then wholly owned by the government and run as quasi-public corporations.

Governments may resort to nationalization for various reasons. In the industrialized countries, an industry is nationalized usually as a last resort to preserve an ailing economic sphere that is considered vital to the nation. Several British companies have been nationalized for this reason (among others). Part of the U.S. rail passenger service was taken over by regional and national government authorities following the bankruptcy of the Penn Central Corporation in 1970.

In developing countries, vital industries may be partially or wholly owned by multinational corporations that are beyond the reach of the host government. The power of the local government to control the business policies and activities of the foreign-based multinational companies is usually minimal. The local affiliate may not be able to cooperate in a satisfactory manner with the host government's economic policies, which may be at variance with the parent's global business policies. Growing frustration by local governments with their inability to influence and control the activities of vital segments of their economy has caused these governments to attempt various measures to return these areas of their economy into their sphere. One such approach is the nationalization of the industry.

Several forms of nationalization are now practiced by the developing countries. The traditional form of nationalization is the outright takeover of the industry by the government, followed by the establishment of a quasi-governmental corporation to run the industry. A newer form of nationalization is an indigenization process similar to the replacement of foreign managers with local personnel. "Indigenization" can also mean letting foreign companies continue under private ownership, but replacing some or all of the foreign shareholders or owners of the local corporations with indigenous owners. The government's objective in this case is to foster indigenous businesses in areas where there has been almost complete foreign domination in ownership and control. A notable example was the Nigerian "indigenization" program, which decreed that by 1978, 17 categories of business had to be wholly transferred from foreign ownership to Nigerian ownership and 19 other categories had to be 60-percent Nigerian-owned. The 17 categories of business that had to be wholly transferred were largely in the service industries, construction trades, retail trade, and transportation.

A selective form of takeover of a business is expropriation, in which the assets of a business are seized by the government through an expropriation decree. Seizure may occur "on the grounds or reasons of public utility, security or the National interest which are recognized as overridingly purely individual or private interests, both domestic and foreign," as expressed in U.N. Resolution 1803 (XVII).[11] An increasingly popular defense by foreign companies is the use of joint ventures with indigenous business interests.

In both nationalization and expropriation, U.N. Resolution 1803 stipulates that adequate compensation be paid to the former owner of the nationalized or expropriated property under the rules of the host country and in accordance with international law. Fair compensation should be prompt and adequate, but how "adequacy" is defined is always a thorny problem. Businessmen want to include some potential income, but in some cases this can defeat the purpose of the takeover.

CONTROLLING COUNTRY RISK

The preceding sections have identified a variety of factors that cause the materialization of country risk and have examined several techniques to assess the degree of exposure as well as the probability of events occurring. This section discusses ways of controlling country-risk exposure, such as through insurance and guarantee programs. The insurance and guarantee programs can provide a mechanism for transferring the bulk of risk from the private company to the insurer.

Government-sponsored insurance and guarantee programs can mitigate country risk for companies doing business either with residents of a foreign country or directly in a foreign country. The first group of companies includes lenders, such as financial institutions that extend credit to units of the foreign country, and companies involved in international trade. The second group comprises companies engaged in business within a foreign country; these companies are ordinarily domiciled within the country. Country risk involves somewhat different consequences for each group. For the first group, the risk can involve default, renegotiation, or rescheduling, among others, while the second group would be more likely to be exposed to expropriation, controls, or other constraints that interfere with the normal course of business and could result in financial loss.

Two U.S.-government-sponsored insurance and guarantee programs are designed to treat these kinds of risks. The Export-Import Bank of the United States (Eximbank) provides insurance and guarantee programs for creditors and companies engaged in international trade, and the Overseas Private Investment Corporation (OPIC) provides insurance and guarantee programs for companies engaged in private business activities in foreign countries. (Further descriptions of worldwide insurance, guarantee, and direct financing programs are found in Chapters 11 and 12.)

The Eximbank

The Eximbank is an agency set up by the U.S. government to foster international trade by providing export credit financing cooperatively with private financial institutions, and insurance and guarantee programs for private export credit financing. The Eximbank covers commercial and credit risk and political risk. Commercial and credit risks include insolvency of the buyer or protracted delay in reaching settlement in the case of default. Political risk coverage includes war, revolution, insurrection, expropriation, and currency inconvertibility (see Chapter 11).

OPIC

The U.S. government provides direct investment insurance and guarantees through OPIC. These programs allow multinational corporations and other companies involved in making foreign investments to transfer their political risk exposure, in whole or in part, to OPIC.

OPIC was established as an agency of the U.S. government by the Foreign Assistance Act of 1969. The agency was formally organized in 1971 with the purpose of mobilizing and facilitating the participation of U.S. private capital and skills in the economic and social development of less-developed, friendly countries and areas in order to complement the development-assistance objectives of U.S. foreign policy. OPIC fosters economic development in Latin America, Asia, Africa, and Europe by providing qualified U.S. investors (including financial institutions) in some 90 countries with political risk insurance, financial assistance, and investment counseling.

OPIC is required by law to manage its financing, insurance, and reinsurance operations on a self-sustaining basis, and its insurance operations must be conducted with due regard to the principles of risk management. Preference is given to projects in countries with per capita income below $520, and to undertakings by U.S. small businesses, usually below the *Fortune* 1,000 in size.

Types of Risks Covered

The operations of OPIC involve two main programs areas: (1) insurance for U.S. private investments in less-developed countries against political risks of expropriation, inconvertibility of local currency, war, revolution, and insurrection; and (2) a credit financing program for projects sponsored by U.S. investors in less-developed countries.

Inconvertibility   Insurance against the risk of inconvertibility covers situations in which a U.S. company or investor is unable to transfer earnings, capital, principal and interest, or certain other defined remittances from the local currency into dollars. The risk of inconvertibility from local currency into dollars is considered "active" if the blockage of funds results from the direct actions of exchange-control authorities in the foreign country as they institute new, more restrictive regulations that prevent the transfer of funds. The risk is considered "passive" if the blockage of funds results from the failure of authorities to act within a specified period (usually 60 days) on an application for foreign exchange, thereby creating a protracted delay in the transfer of funds. Protection is also provided against the risks of adverse discriminatory exchange rates being imposed on the insured. Inconvertibility coverage does not include foreign exchange risks resulting from normal currency appreciation or depreciation, or local currency that the investor has held for over 18 months.

Expropriation   Expropriation risk coverage includes the risk of outright take-over of the property or the nationalization of an enterprise of a foreign investor by action that is either taken, authorized, ratified, or condoned by the government of the country in which the project is located. Expropriation risk coverage also protects against creeping indigenization or creeping expropriatory action. An action of this type must persist for more than 12 months to be considered under the purview of the expropriation insurance (3 months or less for claims involving bank loans).

Expropriation insurance does not cover legitimate regulatory or revenue actions, which are considered proper actions by the host country government, nor does it cover situations in which actions by the investor or foreign enterprise invited the expropriatory reaction by the host government.

The amount of compensation under the expropriation insurance coverage is based on the original insured value of the asset or property. Adjustments are made for retained earnings (or losses) or accrued interest, and prior recoveries of the investment, as of the date of expropriation. OPIC requires that the proper documentation for the assets and property expropriated be sent to the agency before any compensation is paid to the insured.

War, Revolution, and Insurrection   The risk of losses resulting from war, revolution, or insurrection in the host country can be covered by OPIC. The coverage does not cover civil strife of a lesser degree than revolution or insurrection. The types of assets covered under this policy include equity investment and certain kinds of debt investment.

Basic compensation under this policy is for the original cost of the covered property and is limited to the extent of the insured interest in the assets involved. The policy also covers loss arising from default on a scheduled payment of principal or interest for a period of three months for institutional lenders or six months for parent company lenders. For subsequent consecutive defaults, the period is reduced to one month.

Levels and Cost of Coverage

The investor is allowed to specify, within given limits, a "maximum" and a "current" amount of insurance coverage required. The current insured amount specifies the insurance actually in force in the contract year. The maximum insured amount gives the total insurance coverage permitted, and the difference between the maximum and current insured amounts is the "standby amount" of insurance coverage. The premium cost is the product of the prescribed rate and the amount of coverage. As shown in the premium rates given in Table 5.16, the rates for current insurance are higher than for standby insurance.

The base rates can vary by up to one-third to reflect the risk profile of the specific project and can vary more for natural resource and hydrocarbon projects or large projects ($50 million of total project costs or $25 million of insured investment). All OPIC insurance contracts (except those for institutional lenders) carry provisions that allow for premium rates to be increased up to 50

Table 5.16   Basic OPIC Rates (Percentage of insured amount per year)

Industry	Inconvertibility		Expropriation		War, Revolution, Insurrection	
	Current	Standby	Current	Standby	Current	Standby
Manufacturing/service	.30	.25	.60	.25	.60	.25
Natural resource projects						
(other than oil and gas)	.30	.25	.90	.25	.60	.25
Service contractors	.30	.25	.60	.25	.60	.25
Institutional loans	.25	.20	.30	.20	.60	.20

Source: Investment Insurance Handbook (Washington, D.C.: Overseas Private Investment Corporation, December 1979).

percent within the first 10 years, with a further increase up to 50 percent in the second 10 years of the contract life. OPIC has never exercised such a provision, however.

OPIC also insures against loss due to the "arbitrary" (not justified by failure to meet contract terms) drawing down of bid, performance, or advance-payment guarantees that contractors and exporters are required to post when doing business in many countries, particularly in the Middle East.

Special Programs for Mineral and Energy Projects

Special insurance coverage for mineral and energy projects (exploration and development) are provided by OPIC to meet the needs of this industry. For mineral projects, OPIC's insured coverage ranges from 50 to 90 percent of the initial investment plus an amount equal to retained earnings. OPIC provides coverage for intangible and tangible assets against inconvertibility, expropriation, and war, revolution, and insurrection during the exploration phase. Additional coverage is available for the risk of losses resulting from the closing of operations as a result of war, revolution, or insurrection for a period of up to 6 months. OPIC provides further coverage for the breach of certain specified contractual obligations by the host government.

Up to 90 percent of net unrecovered costs is covered by OPIC for oil and gas projects. The net unrecovered cost represents (1) the value of covered tangible property, plus (2) operating costs, made up of direct costs plus a 6-percent allowance for U.S. overhead, less (3) the value of recoveries, such as the cost of oil received under a production-sharing contract or a portion of the receipts attributable to such purposes and any return of capital. The duration of coverage for oil and gas projects is 12 years. OPIC may extend coverage for another 8 years at its discretion.

While insurance provides protection and allows the lender or investor to control country risk, when spreads are thin, the premium cost of the insurance sometimes takes up much of the spread between the lender's lending rate (or the return on the investment) and the cost of funds. The lender is left a small unattractive margin, which can render the loan or investment unprofitable.

Portfolio Diversification

An alternative method of controlling country risk is to diversify loans or investments among different countries in order to spread the risk in a manner similar to diversifying foreign exchange risk using a portfolio of different currencies. (The various approaches to diversifying currency risks are discussed in Chapters 7 and 8). The approach of controlling foreign direct investment risks by diversifying investments among different countries is presented in Chapter 14.

SUMMARY

The effect of forces and events in the foreign environment that are controlled directly or indirectly by the government authorities on the operations of international companies may result in economic and financial losses. Country risk is the term used to define the likelihood of the realization of losses from the occurrence of events under the control of a foreign government.

Country risk may be classified by the nature of the transaction or purpose of the loan, the action taken by the borrower or purchaser, the type of borrower or purchaser, geographical location, and nature of the event. Since these classifications overlap, they are usually used in combination to define country risk. International lending and international trade involve all classes, while portfolio investment and direct investment involve only certain classes.

Country risk may reflect economic, political, or social factors, or a combination of the three. Economic problems within a country are responsible for a large number of situations that give rise to country risk. These problems can arise from one event or a chain of events.

Country-risk rating systems enable international creditors to make comparisons among borrowing countries and rank them by degree of assessed risk. A country-rating system is a useful decision-making tool for a corporation in its determination of how best to allocate its investments in developing an international portfolio and where to locate its plants. With such a system, a creditor is in a better position to determine the amount of risk involved in each international loan and how to distribute lending among countries to minimize loan-portfolio risk.

The four primary types of country-risk rating approach are a checklist, survey, market-return spread, and probability. The checklist is made up of all the indicators considered relevant to assessing the likelihood of an event occurring in a country. The *Institutional Investor* survey approach uses a formula to weight the responses of leading international bankers in developing its global credit rating system. The *Euromoney* country-risk ratings are based on the variation or spread between the country's costs for borrowing money and the costs assessed similar borrowers at the same time. The probability approach treats country risk as the combination of the size of the potential loss and the probability of its materialization, with loss defined as the difference between expected net income and the actual net income received.

Since country-risk ratings reflect an assessment of the future risk profile of a country on the basis of the information available at a particular time, monitoring country risk periodically is necessary in order to keep abreast of developments that may affect exposure to risk. Management can use a country-risk indicator systematically to assess changes in the riskiness of a country over time.

Foreign affiliates of international corporations have to operate within economic, political, and social restrictions that can be imposed by host governments to achieve national economic and political objectives. Such restrictions have the effect of constraining the affiliates' ability to meet their profit objectives.

Various approaches to controlling country-risk exposure are available to management. The U.S. government provides insurance and guarantee programs through two agencies—the Eximbank and OPIC. Eximbank programs cover exports and imports; OPIC programs cover direct investments abroad.

APPENDIX

ASSIGNING PROBABILITIES

When historical frequencies are not available, other methods of assigning probabilities, although basically subjective, can produce fairly reliable probabilities if done carefully. One such method is illustrated in Table A, in which the likelihood of an event occurring is P. Probabilities are assigned in the following way: Starting with the event that is considered least likely to occur, assign P to that event. In Table A, for example, under Political, P is assigned to foreign conflict. If the likelihood of revolution and civil war (RCW) is felt to be twice as likely as foreign conflict, assign $2P$ to RCW. Continuing the assessment of likelihood, the combination of disorders and riots (DR) has been considered to be twice as likely as RCW, thus is assigned $4P$ ($2 \times 2P$). Summing up the Ps and expressing the number of Ps assigned to each event as a proportion of the total Ps gives the subjective probabilities in Column 4.

Table A   Assigning Probabilities to Events That May Result in Country Risk

(1) Events	(2)	(3) Ratio	=	(4) Probability
Political				
Disorders, riots	4P	4/7		.57
Revolution, civil war	2P	2/7		.29
Foreign conflict	P	1/7		.14
Occupation by foreign power (very unlikely)	—	—		—
	7P			1.00

(*continued on p. 162*)

Table A (*continued*)

(1) Events	(2)	(3) Ratio	=	(4) Probability
Economic				
Slowdown in GNP growth	2P	2/14		.14
Rapid rise in producer costs	4P	4/14		.29
Labor unrest, strikes	2P	2/14		.14
Credit squeeze	3P	3/14		.21
Recession, depression	2P	2/14		.14
Natural disaster (weather, floods, poor harvest, famine)	P	1/14		.08
	14P			1.00
Balance of payments				
Sustained fall in export revenues	3P	3/10		.3
Rapid increase in imports	4P	4/10		.4
Excessive external borrowing	2P	2/10		.2
Currency depreciation, devaluation	P	1/10		.1
	10P			1.00

NOTES

1 Joseph Gold, "The Fund Agreement in the Courts," *IMF Staff Papers* (March 1977), pp. 193–231.

2 Exchange control is discussed in detail in Chapter 7.

3 See discussion of import and export elasticities in Chapter 1.

4 Deelan Duff and Ian Peacock, "A Cash Flow Approach to Sovereign Risk Analysis," *The Banker* (January 1977), pp 55–61.

5 Pierre Dhonte, "Describing External Debt Situations: A Roll-Over Approach," *IMF Staff Papers* (March 1975), pp. 165–166.

6 *World Development Report* (Washington, D.C.: World Bank, annual publication).

7 Pancras J. Nagy, *Country Risk: How to Assess, Quantify and Monitor It* (London: Euromoney Publications, 1979).

8 *Institutional Investor*, Vol. 15, No. 3 (March 1981), p. 233.

9 *World Development Report, op. cit.*

10 Michael G. Duerr, *The Problems Facing International Management* (New York: The Conference Board, 1974).

11 United Nations General Assembly Resolution 1803 (XVII) on "Permanent Sovereignty Over National Resources" (December 14, 1962), Section 4.

2

The International Payments System

6

Understanding the Balance of Payments

The balance of payments presents a summary report of the trade, investments, and payments between the residents of one country and the residents of another country for the period of time during which the international transactions took place. Residents of a country are defined as all individuals ordinarily living in the country, government agencies, and corporations organized under local laws of the country. All foreign branches and subsidiaries of U.S. corporations are, therefore, residents of the countries in which they were incorporated. Similarly, all branches and subsidiaries of foreign concerns incorporated in the United States are residents of the United States.

The balance of payments, as its name implies, is a system of accounting that seeks to measure the difference between payments to a country by all other countries and the payments made by that country to all other countries. The principle underlying the balance of payments is that the international transactions of a country should balance at the end of each accounting period; that is, the aggregate inflow of funds from the sale of goods and services to foreigners, factor receipts (primarily receipts from investments) from foreigners, and short- and long-term capital from private and public foreign sources should equal the aggregate outflow of funds for the purchase of goods and services from foreigners, factor payments to foreigners, and short- and long-term capital from private and public domestic sources. The balance of payments is a flow concept; it measures the flow of funds into and out of the country during each accounting period.[1] It is different from a balance sheet, which measures the level of the assets and liabilities of a company at a particular point in time. The accounts in the balance of payments represent changes in the levels of assets and liabilities of a country. In essence, the balance of payments is a combination of an income statement and changes in the accounts of a balance sheet, which gives us a sources and uses of funds statement, or a change in working capital position.

The principle of balancing the payments to and from a country originated in the days of the barter system when residents in one country produced those goods that used the country's natural resource endowments, labor, and capital, and exchanged them for goods produced by residents of other countries. In the barter system, the exchange process provided an automatic balancing mechanism. Under the "gold standard," trade between countries developed to the point where goods were shipped "on account." At the end of each accounting year, countries with a net payments position were required to balance their international accounts position by shipping out gold to the countries they owed. Since gold formed the monetary base, shipment of gold reduced the country's monetary base and, as a result, reduced the money supply as well. The lower money supply reduced the country's ability to import, and reduced imports restored the balance of payments.

BALANCE-OF-PAYMENTS ACCOUNTING

Each transaction is entered in the balance of payments on a double entry basis. For example, when the United States sells abroad, an export item is entered as credit in the balance of payments. The export gives rise to a claim for payment upon the foreign buyer. Therefore, a corresponding debit entry is entered in the balance of payments under "claims against foreigners," which completes the double entry and balances the transaction.[2] When the foreigner pays for the goods, the "claims against foreigners" account is credited and the "short-term capital movement" account is debited. The double entry recording system for the balance of payments is akin to double entry accounting for corporate accounts. Instead of the cash account, the balance of payments uses the short-term capital movement account, since the currency of one country is not legal tender in another country. Like all double entry systems, every debit entry must have a corresponding credit entry, and every credit entry must have its corresponding debit entry.

The general form of the balance of payments is given in the schematic outline in Table 6.1. As shown in the table, it is grouped into four general classes. Items 1 through 8 in Sections A, B, and C of Table 6.1 are commonly referred to as "autonomous" items since they arise in direct response to economic and commercial activity. Items 9 and 10 are termed "accommodating" items because they are essentially balancing items.

The exports and imports are netted to obtain the balance of trade. This balance of trade is positive when exports exceed imports, and is known as a balance of trade *surplus*. On the other hand, if imports exceed exports, there is a balance of trade *deficit*. When a country has a balance-of-trade surplus, it has excess revenues available to meet other needs. With a balance-of-trade deficit, financing from other activities must be obtained to meet the balance-of-trade

Table 6.1   Schematic Balance of Payments

		Debits (−)	Credits (+)
A.	Current account		
	1. Merchandise	(−)	(+)
	2. Transportation	(−)	(+)
	3. Tourist expenditures	(−)	(+)
	4. Investment income; fees and royalties; other services	(−)	(+)
	5. Military and other government expenditures	(−)	(+)
	Total, 1–5	(−)	(+)
B.	Unilateral transfers		
	6. Private remittances	(−)	(+)
	7. Government transfers	(−)	(+)
	Total, 1–7	(−)	(+)
C.	Capital account [increase in assets or reduction in liabilities (−)]		
	8. Foreign investment; direct and portfolio	(−)	(+)
	Total, 1–8[a]	(−)	(+)
D.	Balancing items [increase in assets or reduction in liabilities (−)]		
	9. Short-term official capital movements		
	10. Gold and other international reserve movements		
	Total, 1–10	____ =	____
		(−)	(+)

Source: Robert M. Stern, *The Balance of Payments: Theory and Economic Policy* (Chicago: Aldine Publishing Co., 1973).

[a] The difference in totals (+) or (−) of items 1–8 "above the line" measures the balance of payments surplus or deficit, which will be reflected in the balancing items recorded "below the line" in items 9 and 10.

deficit. Table 6.2 presents a *pro forma* balance of payments showing a breakdown between the trade items and the transfer items. The transfer items provide financing to meet trade deficits.

The major component of the Current account in Table 6.1 is Merchandise trade. This account is composed of the export and import of all merchandise goods. Since most international commercial activity involves the sale and purchase of merchandise goods, this account is very important. For the majority of countries, merchandise trade provides the main source of foreign income. It is even more significant in the balance of payments of developing countries than it is in more developed economies.

Transportation includes airline and shipping services provided by common carriers of a country. For the United States and other industrialized countries,

Table 6.2 *Pro Forma* **Balance of Payments**

Debits	Credits

| *Trade Items* | |

| 1. Visible imports (i.e., imports of goods) | 6. Visible exports (i.e., exports of goods) |
| 2. Invisible imports (i.e., payments by the home country for services rendered by foreigners) | 7. Invisible exports (i.e., payments to the home country for services rendered to foreigners) |

| *Transfer Items* | |

3. Gold imports (i.e., physical imports of the metal, or increases in the amount of gold held on earmark abroad)	8. Gold exports (i.e., physical export of the metal or reduction of the amount of gold held on earmark abroad)
4. Unrequited payments (gifts, etc., paid to foreigners)	9. Unrequited receipts (gifts, etc., received from foreigners)
5. Capital payments (i.e., loans to, capital repaid to, or assets purchased from foreign nationals)	10. Capital receipts (i.e., loans from, capital repaid by, or assets sold to foreign nationals)
Total payments	Total receipts

4+9 Does not give rise to a claim or debt or take place in settlement of a claim or debt. Not matched by simultaneous flow of goods and services in the other direction.

5+10 Long-term capital movements: bonds, securities, or tangible assets intended to earn future income.

Short-term capital movements: relatively quick movements from country to country to take advantage of interest rate differentials; speculative; trade credit to balance.

transportation is an important source of export service revenues. Greece has a large shipping fleet, which makes transportation an important source of export revenues for that country. Panama and Liberia have many ships registered under their flags of convenience, so the shipping account under Transportation would be of particular significance for those countries.

Investment income includes dividends and interest income. For many countries, the dividends and income owed to foreigners have grown to be an important source of outflow.

The capital account represents increases in assets, or reductions in liabilities, of foreign direct investment or foreign portfolio investment. Direct investment refers to the direct ownership of tangible assets used to produce goods or services, or of a natural resource that is a depletable asset (such as oil). Portfolio investment includes investment in intangible financial assets, such as bonds. In general, only long-term assets are included in capital accounts, but short-term assets with maturities of less than a year are sometimes included.

THE U.S. BALANCE OF PAYMENTS

The U.S. balance of payments presents data on the flow of goods, services, and capital between the United States and other countries as well as changes in official gold reserves of the United States, international investments, and foreign assistance programs.

The responsibility for compiling export data rests with the Bureau of the Census in the U.S. Department of Commerce. The data on exports are collected mainly from shippers' export declarations filed with U.S. Customs. The value of exports is defined as the free alongside ship (f.a.s.) value at the U.S. port from which the commodity is shipped. The export data on certain low-value shipments include estimates based on selected samples of such shipments.

The import data are collected on Census forms filled in by Customs officials. Import values since 1974 have been presented on one of three bases: (1) the transaction values f.a.s. at the foreign port of export; (2) the cost, insurance, and freight (c.i.f.) value; and (3) the customs import value based on Customs' appraisal in accordance with Sections 402 and 402a of the Tariff Act of 1930, as amended. Computations of customs duties are based on (3), which may not reflect the transaction value. The "country of origin" is the country in which the merchandise was grown, mined, or manufactured.

The United States is the leading market economy in the world, and the U.S. dollar has been the international numeraire (major international currency) since the end of World War II and the creation of the IMF. The dollar is the chief currency in which other countries hold reserves for foreign debt payment and forms the basis of the Eurodollar and Eurocurrency markets (see Chapter 9). Since the U.S. dollar is used as the chief international currency, the U.S. balance of payments is affected by significant changes in capital and monetary flows among all the major trading countries. The United States cannot take unilateral action affecting its balance of payments without affecting the international monetary system. In order to have dollars in reserve, foreigners must have claims against the United States; thus, there must be deficits in the U.S. balance of payments. (Further problems arising from use of the U.S. dollar as the international numeraire are discussed in the next chapter.)

The U.S. balance-of-trade (the Trade Items in Table 6.2) position has recently shifted from one of surplus to one of deficit (see Balance on goods and services under Item 5 in Table 6.3), and this shift has created added pressure on the U.S. balance-of-payments position.[3]

MEASURING THE OVERALL BALANCE

As noted earlier, when a country's total receipts from its exports of goods and services to the rest of the world exceed its total payments for goods and services imported from the rest of the world, the country is said to have a surplus in its balance of trade or a favorable balance of trade. In addition to trade, a country

Table 6.3 U.S. Balance of Payments 1976–1978 (billions of dollars)
(Data seasonally adjusted, except as noted)

	1976 ($)		(1977) ($)		(1978) ($)	
Merchandise trade	(9.3)		(30.9)		(33.8)	
Investment income	16.0		18.0		21.6	
Net military transactions	0.7		1.7		0.5	
Net travel and transportation	(2.5)		(3.2)		(3.0)	
Other sources	4.7		5.0		6.2	
Balance on goods and services	9.6		(9.4)		(8.4)	
Remittance, pensions, and other unilateral transfers	(5.0)		(4.6)		(5.1)	
Balance on current account		4.6		(14.1)		(13.5)
U.S. assets abroad, net [increase/capital outflow]		(51.3)		(35.8)		(60.9)
U.S. official reserve assets	(2.6)		(0.4)		0.7	
Other U.S. government assets	(4.2)		(4.0)		(4.7)	
U.S. private assets	(44.5)		(31.7)		(57.0)	
Foreign assets in the U.S., net [increase/capital inflow]		36.4		50.8		63.7
Foreign official assests	17.6		36.7		33.7	
Other foreign assets	18.8		14.2		30.0	
Allocations of Special Drawing Rights (SDRs)	—		—		—	
Statistical discrepancy		10.3		(0.9)		10.7

Source: International Monetary Fund, *Balance of Payments Yearbook*, Vol. 31 (Washington, D.C.: December 1980).

engages in movements of short- and long-term capital, both private and government. One-to-one transfers take place to and from the citizens of a country with the rest of the world. To determine the country's total receipts and payments position vis-à-vis the rest of the world, the capital flows, unrequited transfers, and changes in the monetary authority's international reserves are added to the net balance of trade to obtain the overall balance-of-payments position. As in the case of the balance of trade, a country with an excess of receipts over payments is said to have a surplus, or favorable balance-of-payments position. A country with payments in excess of receipts is said to have a deficit or unfavorable balance-of-payments position.

Countries prefer a surplus to a deficit in their balance of payments because they are then in a position to increase their international reserves with the surplus foreign exchange balances. Rising international reserves create strong underpinnings for a country's foreign exchange rate. The reverse is true for the country with a deficit in its balance of payments. Countries with a deficit balance of payments have to draw down their international reserves or undertake short-term borrowing abroad to obtain the foreign exchange needed to make up for the deficit. When a country's international reserves are drawn down to meet these deficit claims, the reserves supporting its currency diminish, which, in turn, weakens its currency. Short-term borrowing abroad is necessary when international reserves have been diminished. Increased borrowing also results in a weakened international currency. From these facts we can see that a country experiencing persistent deficits in its balance of payments will have diminished international reserves, and will have to accumulate substantial short-term debt to finance its deficit. The country's international exchange rate will depreciate as the deficits continue and its international reserves dwindle, and foreign borrowings will increase the more.

Deficits in the Balance of Payments

Balance-of-payments problems are usually symptomatic of problems in a country's economy as a whole. A persistent unfavorable balance of trade or chronic deficits in the current account and long-term capital account are considered undesirable because they require compensating adjustments in the short-term sector of the balance of payments. If the deficits persist long enough, foreigners become concerned about the accumulation of short-term debt obligations and start disposing of their short-term claims on the country. The increase in the international supply of the country's short-term claims without a corresponding increase in demand causes the foreign price of the country's currency to decline. Persistent depreciation often results in devaluation of the currency.

What are the underlying economic causes of balance-of-payments problems? A country's currency is legal tender usually only within its national boundaries.[4] The currencies of other countries are acquired through trading, or by borrowing—which must be repaid with the currency acquired through trade. Therefore, basically, a country must sell as much as it buys over a period of time—say, several years. A country's exports plus long-term capital investment inflows must cover its imports; otherwise a deficit arises, which must be covered by short-term borrowing. If this situation continues for a number of years, short-term debts will accumulate and foreigners will no longer be willing to provide additional short-term loans.

Inflation and the Balance of Payments

Another problem occurs when a country is experiencing a higher rate of inflation than the rate experienced by its international trading partners. In this situation, the prices of the country's exports rise faster than those of its trading partners—making its exports relatively more expensive than its partners' and, therefore, less competitive. The country will sell less abroad as foreigners cut their purchases of the country's (expensive) exports. Meanwhile, imports become cheaper because foreign prices are rising at a slower rate than domestic prices. The cheaper imports become more attractive buys, and demand for imported goods increases. Imports then are increased at the same time exports are decreasing, which results in a current account deficit.

Such a situation cannot continue indefinitely without bringing the country's international trade to a halt. The country must combat the inflationary pressures and bring inflation under control. To be effective, the domestic policy prescription must be made after careful diagnosis of the underlying causes of the inflation.

Among the causes of inflation are: (1) a growth rate in the money supply higher than the growth rate of output, resulting in too much money chasing too few goods; (2) persistent high deficits in the govenment budget combined with a policy of easy government borrowing or printing money to finance the deficits; (3) wage increases in excess of gains in labor productivity; and (4) rapid increases in raw material costs. Each of these factors causes prices to rise and can prompt inflationary pressure. Measures to counteract these factors should vary depending on the factor or factors being attacked.

Policies that increase the money supply (easy monetary policies) are considered desirable for stimulating growth in an economy by increasing liquidity, which makes money cheaper by lowering interest rates. Low interest rates stimulate business investment and fixed-capital formation in, for example, housing and construction, which then stimulates growth. If the easy money policy results in a higher output of goods, inflation will not rise. (Most economists feel that a small level of inflation is tolerable in order to stimulate growth.) When the rate of output is less than the rate of increase in the money supply, inflationary pressures build. The necessary corrective action is to reduce the money supply through tighter monetary policy.

Deficit spending by government became a tool of fiscal policy with the acceptance of Keynesian macroeconomic theory during the Depression of the 1930s. Deficit spending is used to stimulate the economy during periods when it is sluggish and demand is slack. Deficit spending has also resulted from politically inspired additions to government spending. These programs create the need for ever-rising government expenditures.

Deficit spending is of particular concern in many developing countries where the government controls much of the private sector through ownership of major industries. A "government deficit" in a developing country refers to both normal government excess expenditures and what are generally considered private expenditures.

Worse, in a developing country, because there is usually a low level of internal savings, government deficits are covered by borrowing overseas, which directly ties its economy to external financing. The inflow of external capital alleviates the balance-of-payments liquidity problems for the time being, but the problem quickly resurfaces if the country does not generate sufficient foreign exchange to meet its import needs as well as its foreign debt-service requirements. It is clear, then, that developing countries should, as a general rule, borrow externally only to finance productive economic activity that directly or which makes payment to the relief fund by drawing down its local currency balance in Thailand.

11   The Canadian Central Bank buys $20 million worth of gold from the U.S. Treasury and pays by drawing down its dollar deposits held in New York.

12   Mr. Jack Wainwright buys 2,000 shares of common stock in BL (British Leyland Corporation) at the equivalent of $30 a share on the London Stock Exchange and pays $60,000 for the stock by check drawn on his New York bank account.

13   The Texas Petroleum Company of Spain (Texpertco) pays a $2.5-million dividend into its U.S. parent account in a Spanish bank, increasing the company's Spanish balances.

14   U.S. Goodpast Rubber Company makes a long-term loan of $3.5 million to its Liberian affiliate through a time draft (payable at a future time, such as, 30, 60, or 90 days later) drawn on its New York bank account.

15   An Italian businessman repays a $1.5-million installment of a loan from the First National Bank of Manhattan with a check on his account at an Italian bank.

16   The IMF receives an allocation of $15 million from the United States.

17   The Bank of England decreases its official reserve holdings with New York banks by transferring $4.5 million to London banks.

In Example 1, the U.S. manufacturing corporation exports the equipment bought by the Brazilian company for $2 million. The export account is credited at the time the equipment is shipped 1(a). Although the Brazilian company has deposited the $2 million into the Brazilian bank and the U.S. manufacturing corporation may have received payment from the Chase-Brooklyn Bank in the United States, the $2 million had not yet been transferred to the United States when the shipment was made. Therefore, it becomes an accounts receivable to the United States and appears as a debit in the short-term capital movements account 1(b).

Looking at Example 2, when the U.S. ships grain for foreign aid, the United States buys the grain from a domestic farmer, who exports the grain to the recipient overseas. The export account is credited and the U.S. official Unilateral transfer is debited in this case, since Thailand is not expected to pay for the grain, and consequently, no short-term capital transfer takes place in return.

In Examples 3, 4, and 5 the U.S. wholesale importer imports the $5 million worth of cobalt; therefore, the import account is debited for the $5 million, plus the cost of freight and insurance. The short-term capital account is credited with the respective amounts.

For Example 6, the transfer of $1 million by the Japanese bank from New York to Tokyo and the exchange of yen at the Japanese Central Bank reduces U.S. liabilities to foreigners. Therefore a debit is recorded against the amount

indirectly increases the country's capacity to export. Attacking the problem of government deficits in developing countries usually takes cuts in government spending, but such a task is not easy because of the numerous political demands for public spending in these countries.

Developing countries do not usually produce their own capital plant and machinery, and therefore have to import them. This dependency creates its own problems in the balance of payments, since these countries must generate adequate foreign exchange balances through exports to meet the requirements for imported capital goods.

Accounting and the Balance of Payments

This section presents a step-by-step explanation of how a balance of payments is constructed (using the United States for illustration). The process involves the double entry accounting system. It usually takes a little thinking to grasp the accounting basis underlying the balance of payments concept; however, this set of examples is good preparation for analyzing any country's balance of payments. The ability to analyze and interpret the balance of payments of the United States and of foreign countries permits an appraisal of their balance of payments positions and an ability to anticipate potential problems. From this appraisal can arise strategies to minimize a company's exposure to loss from balance-of-payments problems.

As noted in the first section of this chapter, the double entry accounting system requires that, for every debit there must be a credit, and vice versa. If the rules of double entry accounting are adhered to, they result in equal debits and credits when the accounting is completed. The rules do not, however, mean that the items were correctly classified, which requires an understanding of the nature of the transactions. Because countries do not share a common currency in which cash can be designated when they trade, the familiar cash account is not operative in international transactions.

A substantial portion of international trade and international business is done on a short-term credit basis, much like accounts receivable and accounts payable. There are two basic reasons for this process. One is that the payments mechanism takes place between the banking systems of the countries involved in the transaction. Banks usually effect payment after verification that the parties have met their contractual obligations. Following payment to the parties, the banks then proceed to clear their accounts with each other. The clearing process usually lags the completion of the contract terms. Another reason is that arranging short-term credit through the banking system ensures each party's contractual performance, and thereby minimizes the exposure of the parties to possible loss.

The short-term capital account, therefore, takes the place of the usual cash account. But the short-term capital account is more than a cash account, because it also includes normal short-term credit activities. The balance of payments is a hybrid of a receipts and payments account and a sources and uses of funds statement. The accounting basis of the balance-of-payments system becomes readily apparent once the role and nature of the short-term capital account are fully understood.

Consider the following examples and the entries for them in parentheses in Table 6.4. The numbers of the items in the explanation correspond to the numbers in the parentheses in the table, which presents the double entry accounting for the balance of payments. Each Example number appears twice, under Debit and under Credit. Recall the principles of accounting: debit the account that receives and credit the account that gives, as explained after the illustrations.

1(a) A Brazilian company buys equipment costing $2 million from a U.S. manufacturing corporation, and requests its Brazilian bank to issue a letter of credit in favor of the U.S. manufacturing corporation. The Brazilian company deposits the $2 million in payment for the equipment with its bank in Brazil.

(b) The bank in Brazil asks its U.S. correspondent bank, Chase-Brooklyn, to issue a letter of credit in favor of the U.S. manufacturing corporation, which then presents a draft to the Chase-Brooklyn Bank for payment.

2 The U.S. government gives $7 million of foreign aid to Thailand in the form of grain.

3 A U.S. wholesale importer buys $5 million worth of cobalt from Zaire and requests its New York bank to issue a letter of credit in favor of the Zairian company. The Zairian company presents a sight draft (that is, payable on sight) on the letter of credit to a Zairian correspondent bank of the New York bank. The draft is paid.

4 A U.S. wholesale importer pays $150,000 freight charges on the cobalt shipment from Zaire to the United States to a Liberian-registered shipping company by check drawn on the importer's New York bank.

5 Marine insurance of $10,000 is paid by check drawn on a New York bank to Lloyd's of London for insurance coverage of transport risks on the cobalt shipment from Zaire to the United States.

6 A Japanese bank transfers $1 million of deposits held in New York to its head office in Tokyo and receives an equivalent amount of yen deposit in exchange from the Central Bank of Japan.

7 A total of $2 million in travelers checks is cashed by U.S. tourists while vacationing in Spain, and the Spanish banks use the $2 million to increase their dollar balances with their New York correspondents.

8 The IBN Corporation invests $10 million in a plant shipped to its Mexican affiliate.

9 The YTT Corporation transfers $3 million worth of equipment to West Germany to expand its subsidiary manufacturing facilities.

10 U.S. citizens send a $1-million gift to the Cambodian relief fund in Thailand. The $1 million is deposited with a U.S. bank in New York,

Table 6.4 Balance-of-Payments Transactions—Double Entry Accountin (millions of dollars)

Transaction	Debit (−) ($)	Example in Text	C (+
A. Goods and services			
1. Merchandise	5.0	(3)	
2. Shipping	0.15	(4)	
3. Tourist expenditures	2.0	(7)	
4. Banking and insurance	0.01	(5)	
5. Dividends and interest			
Total, 1–5	7.16		
B. Unilateral transfers			
6. Private remittances	1.0	(10)	
7. Government transfers	7.0	(2)	
Total, 1–7	15.16		
C. Capital account			
8a. Long-term foreign investment	10.0	(8)	
	3.0	(9)	
	0.06	(12)	
	3.5	(14)	
Total, 1–8a	16.56		
8b. Allocation of SDRs			
8c. Short-term capital movements	2.0	(1b)	
U.S., private	2.5	(13)	
	1.5	(15)	
8d. Short-term capital movements Foreign, private	1.0	(6)	
D. Balancing items			
9. Short-term capital movements Foreign, official	20.0	(1	
10. Gold and SDR movements	4.5	(1	
	15.0	(1	
Total, 1–10	78.22		

termed short-term capital movement, foreign, private. The Japanese Central Bank will reduce the U.S. Federal Reserve Bank's official balances in Tokyo by a corresponding amount—a credit term.

Tourists' expenditures overseas, such as Example 7, are normally made to procure goods and services in foreign countries. Buying in a foreign country is accounted for in the same way as a foreign country shipping to the United States, or as an import transaction, which is a debit item (see the schematic balance of payments in Table 6.1).

The shipment in Example 8 of $10 million worth of plant to Mexico is an export—a credit; the purpose is for investment—a debit. Example 9 is identical to the Example 8 transaction.

The gifts of U.S. citizens in Example 10 are a private, unilateral transfer—a debit. Payment of the gift was made in Thailand by drawing down United States local short-term capital in Thailand—a credit.

In Example 11, the Canadian government drew down its official dollar balances in New York, thereby reducing Canadian claims on the United States—a debit; the gold account is credited with the sale as the account that gives.

Jack Wainwright's purchase in Example 12, of 2,000 shares of stock at $30, is considered a long-term capital investment (foreign) and, as that is the account which receives, that account is debited; he paid for it by check—a short-term capital movement—so that account is credited.

The $2.5 million dividend in Example 13 increased the U.S. short-term capital movements assets account—a debit, with a credit to the dividends account.

The $3.5-million loan in Example 14 to the Liberian affiliate is a long-term loan; the long-term foreign investment capital account is therefore debited, since it receives, and a credit is made to the account termed short-term capital movements, foreign, private, since U.S. claims against foreign countries are reduced.

The United States' private short-term capital movements assets increased in Example 15 with the deposit of $1.5 million in an Italian bank—a debit—and the capital account is credited since the loan was a long-term loan.

The IMF account increased in Example 16 with the allocation of $15 million from the United States—a debit—and the capital account is credited under the allocation of SDRs account.

In 17, the transfer of the official reserve holdings of the Bank of England to London banks reduces the short-term foreign capital (short-term capital movements, foreign, official) held in U.S. banks—a credit item—and a debit balancing item under short-term capital movements is entered to complete the transaction.

Summary Indicators

In an attempt to gain perspective on where the problems were occurring in the balance of payments and to manage the international status of the dollar, various researchers in the United States developed alternative measurement concepts to the balance of payments concept for use as "summary indicators" of the U.S. balance-of-payments position, as shown in Tables 6.5 and 6.6. The summary concepts are (1) the balance on basic transactions, (2) the balance on liquidity basis, and (3) the balance on official reserve transactions. The three balances are detailed in Table 6.5 and will be outlined in the following sections. Table 6.6 summarizes the data from Table 6.4 in the form of these summary indicators.

Table 6.5   Three Kinds of Summary Groupings of U.S. International Transactions

1. Using Concept of "Balance on Current Account and Long-Term Capital"

Goods and services
Remittances, pensions, and other transfers
U.S. government grants, capital flows, nonscheduled repayment of U.S. government
  nonliquid liabilities to other than foreign official reserve agencies
Long-term private capital flows, U.S. and foreign
  Direct investments abroad and in the United States
  Foreign securities and U.S. securities other than Treasury issues
  Other (bank and nonbank)

Balance on current account and long-term capital (basic transactions)

2. Using Concept of "Net Liquidity"

Balance on current account and long-term capital
Nonliquid short-term private capital flows, U.S. and foreign
  Claims reported by U.S. banks and nonbanks
  Liabilities reported by U.S. nonbanks
Allocation of Special Drawing Rights (SDRs)
Errors and omissions, net

Net liquidity balance

3. Using Concept of "Official Reserve Transactions"

Net liquidity balance
Liquid private capital flows, net
  Liquid claims reported by U.S. banks and nonbanks
  Liquid liabilities to foreign commercial banks, international and regional organiza-
  tions, and other foreigners

Official reserve transactions balance

4. Compensating Items

Nonliquid liabilities to foreign official agencies reported to U.S. government and U.S.
  banks
Liquid liabilities to foreign official agencies
U.S. official reserve assets, net
  Gold, SDRs, convertible currencies, and gold reserve position in IMF

Source: Adapted from U.S. Department of Commerce, Office of Business Economics, *Survey of Current Business*, Vol. 51 (June 1971), p. 30.

Table 6.6   Summary Balances of the Balance of Payments (Millions of dollars)

		Transactions Net Balance	Summary Balance
1.	Merchandise	+14.0	
2–5.	Services	+3.34	
	A. Balance on goods and services		+17.34
6–7.	Unilateral transfers	−8.00	
	B. Balance on current accounts		+9.34
8a.	Long-term capital: private	−15.06	
	C. Balance on current account and long-term capital (basic transactions)		−5.72
8b.	Allocation of SDRs	+15.0	
	D. Net liquidity balance		+9.28
8c.	Short-term capital: U.S. private	−5.0	
8d.	Short-term capital: foreign private	+14.22	
	E. Official reserve transactions balance		+18.5
9.	Short-term capital: foreign official	−23.5	
10.	Change in gold stock and SDRs		+5.0

Source: From Table 6.4.

Balance on Basic Transactions

The basic balance in Table 6.5, Section 1, and Table 6.6, Section C, is used by many countries to give a broad indication of a country's international payments position.[5] The basic balance groups the current transactions and long-term capital movements above the line into a group called the basic transactions. In Table 6.5, the items that are not in Section 1 are not part of the basic balance and are placed below the line. In Table 6.6, items below Section C are not part of the basic balance. Below-the-line items represent the compensating items that are used to finance the basic items. The compensating items under the balance on basic transactions include: all short-term capital movements, errors and omissions, and gold movements.

The inclusion of all short-term capital movements as compensating transactions has been criticized because some short-term capital movements are connected with merchandise trade, are used to finance services, and are used for investment transactions—both direct and portfolio investments.[6] The exclusion of errors and omissions from the basic transactions has also been criticized on the grounds that some portion of the errors and omissions is connected with current account activities.

The balance on basic transactions is nevertheless a useful indicator of the balance-of-payments position of both industrial and developing countries. In the case of the United States, the balance on basic transactions shows: (1) the dollars made available to foreign countries by the United States through purchases of goods and services, and investments abroad, and (2) the uses to which dollars are put by foreign countries in making similar purchases from the United States.

Balance on Net Liquidity Basis

In the balance on liquidity basis (Table 6.5, Section 2, and Table 6.6, Section D) U.S. private short-term capital movement, foreign commercial credits, and errors and omissions are moved from their position below the line in the balance on basic transactions to above the line. The transfer of these items above the line satisfies some of the criticism of the balance on basic transactions indicator.

The balance on liquidity basis treats all foreign private funds movements to the United States as "settlement" items intended to finance the basic transactions' above-the-line items. The concept takes into account that, when foreign private short-term capital flows into the United States, foreigners' claims on the United States (or, alternatively, the United States' liabilities to foreigners) increase, which has an adverse effect on the balance of payments.[7] This concept, therefore, treats all foreign private short-term capital movements as noninvestment.

The balance on liquidity basis may be viewed as a short-term measure of the extent to which a country is dependent on foreign short-term capital inflow to meet the shortfall in its balance of payments. A negative figure for foreign private capital movement indicates that foreigners' claims are being reduced as short-term capital flows outward. This outward flow improves the balance of payments position. The concept of liquidity balance can be applied to any country's balance of payments as an indicator of the country's international liquidity.

Balance on Official Reserve Transactions

The balance on official reserve transactions (Table 6.5, Section 3 and Table 6.6, Section E) makes a distinction between the claims held by foreign *official* monetary institutions and those held by all other foreigners. The concept considers U.S. gold reserves to be exposed only to official monetary authorities who may have a future claim against U.S. gold stock. Accordingly, both U.S. and foreign private short-term capital (Table 6.6, 8c 8d) are placed above the line (in contrast to their below-the-line status under the liquidity balance indicator).

Discontinuance of the Summary Indicators

The United States discontinued the use of the summary balance-of-payments indicators in 1978 because they were considered insufficient measures of the balance-of-payments position. Summary indicators focus on short-term transactions, but the U.S. balance-of-payments deficit is arrived at after U.S. long-term investment has been taken into account. When the United States has a balance-of-*trade* surplus, a deficit in the balance of *payments* is largely a result of U.S. long-term investment abroad, both direct and indirect, on which the United States has not yet received income. When the investment income is remitted, it will improve the balance of payments. Furthermore, the United States is simply exchanging long-term assets for short-term liabilities. The same holds true even when the United States has a deficit balance of trade.

For the United States, moreover, the measurement of the short-term movement of funds under the three balance-of-payments summary indicators does not appear to be appropriate when the dollar is the international numeraire.[8] Awareness of the problems arising from the role of the dollar as international numeraire and the role of the United States as world banker increased sharply with the enormous increase in international liquidity that resulted from the OPEC price increases in 1973 and 1974 and subsequently.[9]

The Sectoral Approach

The limitations in the approach to the balance of payments of the three summary indicators have led to a search for alternative measures that would reflect the dollar's role as the international currency and the United States' role as world banker. One concept that has been proposed is the sectoral approach, in which the balance of payments is divided into four basic sectors: (1) the commercial accounts of the private sector, comprising trade, transportation, and tourism, and excluding investment earnings; (2) the government accounts sector; (3) private investment accounts, including investment earnings; and (4) money market accounts.

Monitoring each of the sectors to observe their behavior patterns would provide the kind of data suitable for the analysis of the sector and evaluation of the sector's performance. The performance of one sector need not be directly correlated with the performance of another sector. For example, a drop in exports might reflect only temporary demand problems in overseas markets, which could be occurring at the same time profitable opportunities were opening up elsewhere that would result in increased outflows of long-term investment capital.

SUMMARY

The trade, investments, and payments system between residents of each country for the period of time in which the international transactions took place are summarized in the balance of payments of each country. The principle underlying the balance of payments is that the international transactions of a country should balance at the end of each accounting period: the aggregate inflow of funds from the sale of goods and services to foreigners, factor receipts from foreigners, and short- and long-term capital from private and public foreign sources should equal the aggregate outflow of funds for the purchase of goods and services from foreigners, factor payments to foreigners, and short- and long-term capital from private and public domestic sources. The balance of payments is a flow concept; it measures the flow of funds into and out of the country during the accounting period.

Each transaction is entered in the balance of payments on a double entry basis. A sale of merchandise by a U.S. firm to a foreign entity is considered an export transaction, which gives rise to a credit entry under export. The contra-entry is a debit under short-term capital claims on foreigners. When payment is effected by the foreign firm, the short-term claim on foreigners account is credited (which clears that account) and the U.S. short-term liabilities to foreigners account is debited.

The total exports and imports are netted to obtain the balance of trade. When exports exceed imports, the balance of trade is positive: the country has a balance-of-trade surplus. When imports exceed exports, a balance-of-trade deficit exists. A country with a surplus in the balance of trade has excess revenues available to meet other needs, such as long-term investment abroad or a buildup in its international reserves. On the other hand, a deficit in the balance of trade requires financing of the deficit from other sources, such as borrowing from abroad or drawing-down foreign exchange reserves.

As in the case of the balance of trade, the balance of payments is said to be in surplus or favorable when the country has an excess of total receipts over total payments. Conversely, a country with total payments in excess of total receipts is said to have a deficit or unfavorable balance-of-payments position.

Countries with a surplus in their balance of payments are in a position to increase their international reserves which, in turn, strengthens the country's currency vis-à-vis other foreign currencies. Deficits in the balance of payments have the opposite effect, draining the country's international reserves and weakening the currency.

Balance-of-payments problems are usually symptomatic of problems in the economy as a whole. A country experiencing higher rates of domestic inflation than its trading partners becomes less competitive in the world market. Its export prices increase at a faster rate than those of its competitors, which tends to cause the country to sell less than it buys. The result is a deficit in the balance of trade and a possible deficit in the balance of payments. Domestic fiscal policies causing excessive government spending and domestic monetary policies that increase the money supply too rapidly usually lead to balance-of-payments problems.

Since the United States is the leading market economy in the world and the U.S. dollar has been the major international currency since the end of World War II, the U.S. balance of payments is affected by any significant changes in capital and monetary flows among the major trading countries. The United States has been experiencing difficulties with deficits in its balance of payments since the 1950s because of the dollar's role as international numeraire.

In an attempt to manage the international status of the dollar, the United States has developed several measurement concepts of the overall balance of payments: the basic balance, the liquidity balance, and the official reserve transaction balance. The limitations of these three summary indicators, however, have led to a search for alternative measures that would reflect the dollar's role as the international currency and the United States' role as world banker. One concept that has emerged is the sectoral approach, which divides the balance of payments into four basic sectors.

SUPPLEMENTARY READING

Fritz F. Machlip, *Real Adjustment, Compensatory Corrections and Foreign Financing of Imbalances in International Payments* (Princeton, N.J.: International Finance Section, Princeton University, 1965).

J. E. Meade, *The Balance of Payments* (Oxford: Oxford University Press, 1966).

W. M. Scammell, *International Monetary Policy* (London: Macmillan, St. Martin's Press, 1970).

Robert M. Stern, *The Balance of Payments* (Chicago: Aldine Publishing Co., 1973).

NOTES

1 M. Hudson, "A Financial Payments—Flow Analysis of U.S. International Transactions: 1960–1968," *The Bulletin*, New York University, Graduate School of Business Administration, Institute of Finance, Nos. 61–63 (March 1970).

2 P. Host-Madsen, "What Does It Really Mean—Balance of Payments," *Finance and Development*, Vol. 3, No. 1 (March 1966), p. 33.

3 Hans H. Helbling, "Recent and Prospective Development in International Trade and Finance," *Federal Reserve Bank of St. Louis Review*, Vol. 56, No. 5 (May 1974), pp. 15–22; Donald S. Kemp, "U.S. International Trade and Financial Developments in 1976," *Federal Reserve Bank of St. Louis Review*, Vol. 58, No. 12 (December 1976), pp. 8–14.

4 Exceptions are the three international currencies—the United States dollar, the British pound sterling, and the French franc, which are used in their respective bloc countries—and currencies of countries in common markets or free trade areas in which monetary agreements permit common use.

5 The concept of basic balance was first used by the U.S. Department of Commerce in *The United States in the World Economy* (Washington, D.C.: GPO, 1943).

6 Z. Hodjera, "Basic Balances, Short Term Capital Flows, and International Reserves of Industrial Countries," International Monetary Fund, *Staff Papers* (November 1969), pp. 582–612.

7 W. Lederer, *The Balance of Foreign Transactions: Problems of Definition and Measurement*, Special Papers in International Economics, No. 5 (Princeton, N.J.: Princeton University Press, 1963), p. 65.

8 H. W. Mayes, *Some Theoretical Problems Relating to the Eurodollar Market*, Essays in International Finance, No. 79 (Princeton, N.J.: Princeton University Press, 1970), pp. 3–6.

9 Hans H. Helbling, "International Trade and Finance under the Influence of Oil—1974 and Early 1975," *Federal Reserve Bank of St. Louis Review*, Vol. 57, No. 5 (May 1975), pp. 11–15.

7

The Foreign
Exchange Market

The foreign exchange rate plays a crucial role in international trade and international investment. Movements in the foreign exchange rate between two currencies affect the price of goods traded between the two countries. Investment funds move in and out of a country in response to movements of the country's exchange rate and expectations of its future direction. The value of assets held in a foreign currency rises and falls with the appreciation or depreciation of the foreign currency relative to the domestic currency. Firms involved in international trade or doing business abroad are subject to gains and losses from foreign exchange movements. An understanding of how the foreign exchange market works and how the foreign exchange rate is determined is a prerequisite for dealing efficiently with the foreign exchange market to effect foreign exchange transactions.

This chapter examines the market for foreign exchange and how the foreign exchange rate is determined. The next chapter outlines some techniques that the international manager or a firm's treasurer can use to minimize the firm's exposure to foreign exchange movements.

INTERNATIONAL BANKING AND THE FOREIGN EXCHANGE MARKET

When goods and services are moved across international frontiers they give rise to a foreign exchange transaction between the parties involved. Each country has its own currency, and in most cases the currency of one country is not legal tender in any other country (that is, the currency of country A cannot be used to make payments in country B). Therefore some method of processing international payments is necessary.

Commercial banks provide the facilities for payments across national boundaries. For example, what happens if a citizen of country A wants to make payments to a citizen of country B? To illustrate, suppose that Japan Airlines (a resident of Japan for exchange purposes) purchases a Boeing 737 airplane for $12 million from the Boeing Company in the United States. Japan Airlines has the yen equivalent of $12 million to pay for the airplane, but the yen is not legal tender in the United States (the Boeing Company would not be able to spend the yen in the United States). Boeing, therefore, has to convert the yen into dollars. The conversion of yen into dollars can be done in Japan or in the United States. Boeing can require Japan Airlines to pay in dollars, in which case, Japan Airlines will ask its bank in Tokyo to convert its yen into dollars and then transfer the dollars to Boeing's account with its bank in New York. Alternatively, Boeing could accept the payment in yen and ask its bank in New York to convert them to dollars.

In either case, the yen paid by Japan Airlines are converted to dollars, either in Tokyo or in New York, before Boeing deposits them in its account. The conversion process is called an exchange; that is, the Japanese yen are exchanged for U.S. dollars. The process of exchanging one currency for another is called foreign exchange, and the arena of foreign exchange is called the foreign exchange market. The airplane sale illustrates the payment mechanism in international trade. Through the process of correspondent banking, commercial banks are able to effect payments across national frontiers.

The process outlined above would be true also for a U.S. purchase of services or capital assets in a foreign country. Examples of overseas services that give rise to foreign exchange transactions include tourism, banking, and insurance. Examples of foreign capital assets purchased by a firm or citizen of a different country could be a financial asset, real property, or a business.

A significant portion of international trade is done on a credit basis, which gives rise to management of claims for foreign currency by exporters in one country or by importers in another. If the sale of the Boeing 737 to Japan Airlines were made on medium-term credit, financed by a U.S. bank, then the U.S. bank would have yen-denominated claims against Japan Airlines, or against a Japanese bank for one calendar year. In the meanwhile, the U.S. bank can sell its yen holdings in Japan to a U.S. importer of, for example, Japanese television sets. Through the sale of its yen holdings to the U.S. importer, the U.S. bank has just made a market in foreign exchange. Several thousands of these types of transactions take place every day between U.S. exporters and importers, on the one hand, and foreign importers and exporters, on the other. These activities give rise to foreign exchange claims and payments. Foreign exchange is created through the sale of goods and services abroad (exports), and foreign exchange is used up when goods and services are purchased from foreign countries (imports).

Growth and Structure of the Foreign Exchange Market

The international operations of U.S. banks grew substantially from 1970 to 1979 (see Table 7.1). Overseas branches of U.S. banks increased from 532 in 1970 to 779 in 1979, while their total assets grew from $52.6 billion to $290.0 billion during the same period. Edge Act corporations increased from 77 in 1970 to 132 in 1979, and their total assets rose from $4.6 billion to $16.3 billion during the period. The Edge Act of 1919 empowered the Federal Reserve Board to charter U.S. corporations "engaged in international or foreign banking or other international or foreign financial operations directly or through the agency, ownership, or control of local institutions in foreign countries." The provisions of the act were limited to the international and foreign activities of U.S. banks. The International Banking Act of 1978 authorized the Federal Reserve Board to extend the provisions of the Edge Act by allowing domestic branching within the United States of corporations chartered under that act. The objective of the International Banking Act of 1978 was to stimulate competition within the United States between Edge Act corporations and banks of foreign countries operating within the United States by relaxing the constraints on Edge Act corporations operating domestically.

Several factors account for the rapid overseas expansion of the U.S. banking industry since 1970: International trade grew rapidly in the 1970s. Major U.S.

Table 7.1 Growth of International Operations of U.S. Multinational Banks

	Number		Total Assets ($ billions)	
Year Ending	Overseas Branches	Edge Act Corporations	Overseas Branches[b]	Edge Act Corporations
1970	532	77	52.6	4.6
1971	577	85	55.1	5.5
1972	627	92	72.1	6.1
1973	699	103	108.8	6.9
1974	732	117	127.3	10.1
1975	762	116	145.3	9.1
1976	731[a]	117	174.5	11.1
1977	738	122	205.0	13.4
1978	761	124	232.0	14.8
1979	779	132	290.0	16.3[c]

Source: Board of Governors, Federal Reserve System, *Annual Report* (Washington, D.C.: Fed, various issues).

[a] This decrease from 1975 is due primarily to the conversion of 30 branches in Colombia into subsidiaries to conform with Colombian banking laws.

[b] These data are derived from reports of condition that were filed at the end of the year with the Comptroller of the Currency and the Federal Reserve System, and they differ in certain respects from other statistical reports on overseas branch operations. The amounts shown are net of claims on other foreign branches of the same bank.

[c] Estimated.

multinational corporations expanded their overseas operations rapidly during this period, as international trade grew and the world economy expanded. Because of the staggering cost of their postwar rebuilding efforts, many countries were unable until the 1960s to convert their currencies to pay off the claims held against them by foreigners, but the major currencies did achieve full convertibility by that time.

Meanwhile, various controls on the flow of capital from the United States to other countries made it desirable for banks to have overseas branches from which they could continue to make loans to foreign borrowers. The interest equalization tax imposed in 1962 to eliminate any yield advantage in investing abroad made it more attractive for U.S. residents to invest in the United States. The need for dollar financing to meet foreign borrowing needs, therefore, was met by U.S. commercial banks.

Another control was the Voluntary Foreign Credit Restraint program (VFCR) inaugurated in 1965, which placed a ceiling on lending to foreign borrowers by Federal Reserve member banks. This action created an impetus for United States banks to set up overseas branches from which they could continue making loans to borrowers overseas.

Many small U.S. banks joined in the rush to set up branches and offices overseas during the 1960s. A majority of the branches created by the small banks are essentially "shell branches" representing legal entities not subject to the domestic reserve requirements. Some 70 of the 125 banks that operated offshore in 1974 had only "shell" offshore branches in Nassau and the Cayman Islands, which provided the banks with tax advantages as well as immunity from domestic reserve requirements. The nine largest U.S. multinational banks owned 540 of the 738 total overseas branches of U.S. banks and 77 percent of their total overseas assets in 1979.

After 1965, the newly created Eurodollar market flourished as U.S. banks rushed to establish foreign branches to avoid the full impact of the VFCR program controls. The foreign branches of U.S. banks were able to raise funds in the Eurodollar market outside the domestic reserve requirements and the interest-rate ceilings set by Regulation Q of the Federal Reserve System. The Eurodollar market makes up more than 70 percent of the Eurocurrency markets. (These markets are discussed in Chapter 9.)

The overseas expansion of the U.S. banking industry since 1965 has produced a network of branches and subsidiaries. The banking industries of the major European nations have experienced overseas expansion over the same period, although on a smaller scale, which has produced an additional network of branches and subsidiaries around the non-Communist world. The network of bank branches and subsidiaries together with the home banks provide the facilities for the foreign exchange market.

The Mechanics of Foreign Exchange

The following example is presented to illustrate the mechanics of foreign exchange through the banking system. This example shows how a dollar deposit in a New York bank by a Japanese firm moves through the international banking network of the Eurodollar market.

The Japanese Toyota Motor Company sells $10 million worth of cars to its distributors in the United States. The $10 million is paid into the New York bank account of Toyota Motor Company. Since the Toyota company does not need the money immediately, it decides to place the money in a three-month fixed-deposit account. Toyota proceeds to obtain interest-rate quotations from several international banks in Europe and Japan for a three-month fixed deposit. Toyota chooses a French bank, and the interest rate is agreed upon. The French bank then proceeds to instruct Toyota Motor Company to pay the $10 million into the account of the French bank in a New York bank. (At the same time, the French bank will ask Toyota where the firm would like to receive the principal and interest on maturity. For the sake of illustration, Toyota indicates that it be paid to the company's account in Morgan Guaranty Bank in New York.) The $10 million is transferred to the French bank's account in New York on the instructions of Toyota.

The French bank now has $10 million in its account in New York that must be put to work to generate interest income to pay the interest agreed upon with Toyota Motor Company for the three-month deposit, since unemployed funds do not earn any interest and result in a loss of income to the owner of the funds. The French bank proceeds to lend the money to a German bank, which instructs the French bank to transfer the funds to its branch in New York. The transactions of the French bank so far include: a deposit and a loan of the $10 million. The interest rate charged on the loan is higher than the interest to be paid on the deposit, leaving a profit margin for the French bank. The German bank may proceed to lend the money to another European bank, and so on. Telephone and telex messages are used extensively in foreign exchange transactions to expedite the movement of funds from one account to another or from one country to another.

By now, the $10 million originally paid by the United States distributors to the Japanese Toyota Company has moved from the U.S. bank to a French bank and then to a German bank in New York City. The $10 million has not physically left the United States, although it has become part of the deposits of international banks.

THE FOREIGN EXCHANGE RATE

Foreign exchange rates are prices for currencies expressed in terms of other currencies. The rates normally fluctuate to reflect the demand and supply conditions for the respective currencies arising from trade and capital movements. Normal fluctuations are generally small and correct themselves in a relatively short period of time. When some underlying problem exists in a country's economy, however, the problems are reflected in the currency, the fluctuations deepen, and their duration lengthens. If fluctuation in one direction persists, the equilibrium rate of exchange will be upset.

Foreign exchange trading takes two forms: spot and forward transactions. Each type of transaction is governed by its own trading conventions.

The Spot Rate

A spot transaction in the foreign exchange market is executed for delivery of dollars, in clearinghouse funds, against payment of the foreign currency to a foreign bank account two banking days after the date of the transaction. The spot date convention of two business days for the delivery of dollars against foreign currency deposits allows time for the parties involved in the transaction to transmit instructions overseas, and for the normal processing of the contract documents. The Canadian dollar and some Far Eastern currencies are the only exceptions to this convention; they use one business day.

In the United States, foreign exchange rates are quoted as units of dollars per foreign monetary unit. The quotation shows how much one foreign monetary unit is worth in U.S. dollars. For example, a French franc recently equaled $.1991. Foreign exchange rate quotations are made on the basis of units of foreign currency per United States dollar, for example, $1.00 was quoted at French francs 5.0226. That the two quotations have a reciprocal relationship can be easily seen; to convert from one to the other, the quotation should be divided into 1. For example, to express the number of French francs in a United States dollar, simply divide $.1991 into 1, which equals 5.0226 francs.

In response to a sell-and-buy inquiry, a bank might give the following quotation for the French franc against the dollar: 5.02, 20/25. In the quotation, the "2" cents is the most important figure because the sell/buy quotations are tied to it. It equals 200 basis points and is called "the big figure." The 20 and 25 represent 20 and 25 basis points, respectively. In the above quotation the bank is stating that it is willing to sell dollars for francs at 5.0220 francs to the dollar and buy them at 5.0225 francs to the dollar.

The U.S. banks are selling fewer francs (5.0220—representing the quantity of francs purchased per dollar) per dollar than they are buying (5.0225). They therefore make a profit:

> Buy at 5.0225 francs per dollar
> Sell at 5.0220 francs per dollar
>
> .0005 francs (gain for U.S. bank)

The U.S. bank ends up with more francs per U.S. dollar for each buy/sell transaction than it had before.

Converted from francs to dollars, the figures would be

> Buy at 5.0225 francs = $.19910403 (1/5.0225)
> Sell at 5.0220 francs = $.19912386 (1/5.0220)
>
> $.00001982 (gain for U.S. bank)

The Forward Market

The forward rate is the least understood phenomenon in international money markets, and the use of the forward market by speculators has probably helped to create the confusion about the market. The forward market is extensively used to hedge against foreign exchange risks, and it is growing in importance as a means of minimizing risk in transactions involving foreign exchange.

The forward market began in Europe some five centuries ago on the plains of Lombardy as a commodity market. Wine buyers learned not to postpone their foreign exchange until the day of their wine purchase, because the rate of exchange into local currency tended to rise on the wine-trading days. The wine buyers bought their local currency weeks ahead of the fair and put the local currency funds in fixed-interest deposits. These deposits were used to buy the wine during the fair. Through this process of buying ahead, the wine buyers were able to "lock in" the more favorable rate of exchange that prevailed when demand for foreign exchange was relatively low in the weeks before the fair. Then, when demand increased for the imported wines in the buyers' home markets and they needed more cash, they soon learned to borrow from their domestic bankers and use these supplementary funds to buy the wine-market local currency (LC) in the weeks ahead of the fair.

The cost of the wine buyers' transactions can be computed in the following manner: The wine buyer borrowed money and put it in a fixed-interest deposit until it was needed on the day of the fair. The exchange rate was based on the foreign currency (FC) of the buyer's home country vis-à-vis the LC on the day the purchase was transacted. The wine buyer paid interest on the loan from his banker and received interest on his fixed-term deposit. The excess of interest paid over interest received increased the cost of the purchase transaction. This increase in cost could be illustrated by assuming that the wine buyer paid interest on the borrowed funds at the rate of 6 percent per year and received interest on the deposit at the rate of 2 percent per year. If both transactions were made for a 3-month period, then his cost was 1 percent:

$$(6\% - 2\%) \times \frac{3 \text{ months}}{12 \text{ months}} = 1\%$$

The wine buyer covered his foreign exchange *risk* for 1 percent through the process of "forward cover." This process of forward cover continued until the depression years of the 1930s, when many European countries resorted to exchange control to regulate the flow of money across their frontiers and to protect their foreign exchange reserves. The reconstruction effort by the European countries after World War II required further conservation of vital foreign exchange earnings and inadequate reserves, resulting in further controls on the free flow of foreign exchange. The "forward outright" deal consolidated the three separate transactions in the old forward cover practice. Forward prices now represent the current spot price on the day of the transaction plus the interest differential for the period of the cover.

A "forward" contract is any foreign exchange contract with a delivery date of more than 2 days from the date of the transaction. Forward contracts, by convention, have specific maturity dates, usually 30, 60, 90, or 180 days. Maturity dates beyond 180 days are rare because of the greater risks of exchange rate fluctuations as time increases: a trader must be able to find a contract to buy foreign exchange every time he executes a contract to sell foreign exchange. This "squaring" allows him to close the "open" position created in the contract to sell. Traders usually have a problem in finding contracts to square their positions with long maturities.

The active foreign exchange forward markets deal only in the currencies of the major commercial nations which have a high trading volume and enough capital transaction to create vigorous demand and supply conditions for their currencies.

The practice today in the foreign exchange market is to quote forward rates either in outright terms or in terms of premiums and/or discounts from the spot rate. Traders generally quote both the bid and offered rates when dealing with each other. Traders are expected to stand ready to deal on either side of the market on each transaction. The difference between the bid and offered rates is termed the spread. Spreads are narrow during periods of certainty and widen during periods of uncertainty.

A United States-based trader would give the following illustrative quotations for the spot rate, and 1-, 3-, and 6-month maturity rates in terms of discounts or premiums, in basis points, on the French franc:

Spot	1 month	3 months	6 months
.1991–.1993	2–3	6–5	11–10

The trader's quote for the 1-month forward rate, given as 2–3 instead of 3–2, is meant to indicate a premium. It means that the U.S. trader is willing to sell French francs with 1-month maturity at $.1993 and buy at $.1996. The ascending quote indicates that there is a premium on the French franc; that is, the French franc is appreciating with respect to the dollar in the short run (1 month). The trader will, of course, be in a position to sell the francs bought at premium at a higher price. The 3- and 6-month forward quotes are at a discount (6 to 5, instead of 5 to 6, and 11 to 10, instead of vice versa), which indicates that the franc appreciation to the dollar is expected to be short-lived and will reverse itself within 3 to 6 months. The trader will be willing to trade francs of 3-months maturity at a discount, selling at $.1985 and buying at $.1988.

The quotations can also be expressed in outright terms as follows:

Maturity		Bid		Asked
Spot		.1991		.1993
1 month	(.1991 + .0002)	.1993	(.1993 + .0003)	.1996
3 months	(.1991 − .0006)	.1985	(.1993 − .0005)	.1988
6 months	(.1991 − .0011)	.1980	(.1993 − .0010)	.1983

The premiums and discounts in the basis point quotation are obtained directly from the outright terms quoted by taking the difference between each forward rate and the spot rate.

MANAGING THE INTERNATIONAL MONETARY SYSTEM

The gold standard formed the basis of the international monetary system for much of the nineteenth century. Full convertibility existed under the gold standard as currencies were freely exchanged for gold without any constraints by monetary authorities. The gold standard was abandoned during World War I. The British pound sterling served as the sole international reserve currency until 1919, when the United States dollar became a rival reserve currency as New York's growing importance as an international financial center began to overshadow London's. In an attempt to restore the pound sterling's role as the international reserve currency. Britain returned to the gold standard from 1925 to 1931, but abandoned it again as a result of speculative pressures on the pound. A period of instability followed Britain's abandonment of the gold standard in September 1931, during which countries adopted a floating rate system.

The Depression created strains in the international economy and the international monetary system. Countries resorted to competitive devaluation, which aggravated the volatility in the international payments system. In an attempt to restore some degree of stability to the international monetary system, the United States pegged the dollar's gold price at a fixed $35 an ounce in 1934. The following year, the United States, Britain, and France established the Tripartite Monetary Agreement of 1935, in which they agreed to cooperate in maintaining stability in their respective currencies. Following Britain's example, other countries adopted exchange equalization accounts to help reduce fluctuations in their currencies. The relatively smaller swings in exchange rates in the late 1930s indicated that some degree of stability had been restored to the international monetary system.

A conference was organized in Bretton Woods, New Hampshire, in 1944 to establish an orderly international payments system after World War II. The conference produced several agreements to govern currency parities and devaluation procedures. It created the IMF as a manager for the international monetary system, and it formulated policies on subscriptions to the IMF and borrowing quotas for member countries.

The International Monetary Fund

The IMF has direct responsibility for managing the international monetary system and for supervising exchange rates between the currencies of its member countries. The IMF was established on December 27, 1945, with an initial membership of 30 countries, held its first meeting at Savannah, Georgia, in March 1946, and started operations on March 1, 1947. The IMF is made up of contributions of currencies and gold by the member countries on the basis of an agreed formula. The membership of the IMF has grown since 1945 to 139 countries. As the membership has increased, the quota system for IMF capital subscriptions by members has been adjusted accordingly. By 1980 the IMF capital subscriptions of members totaled 39.016 billion SDRs (SDRs are a special hybrid currency combination discussed later in this chapter).

The resources of the IMF have increased since its inception through the subscriptions of increased membership, increases in the quotas of member countries, and the IMF's authority to borrow from the "Group of Ten," made up of the United States, Canada, Britain, West Germany, France, Japan, Italy, Sweden, Belgium, and the Netherlands.

The IMF has three basic purposes: (1) to foster policies among its member countries that lead to the maintenance of stable exchange rates, on which a satisfactory structure of world trade can be built; (2) to provide facilities in the form of "drawing rights"[1] through which member countries can draw on the fund's resources to meet any short-term disturbance in their respective balance of payments, or if a country experiences persistent balance-of-payments disturbances over a long period of time, the IMF can sanction a change in the member's exchange rate; and (3) to promote conditions for free trade among member countries, the elimination of exchange controls and discrimination, and the development of an efficient structure of world trade.

To these ends, the activities of the IMF are directed toward (1) the establishment of a satisfactory exchange rate policy for its membership, (2) the establishment of a system of multilateral payments to facilitate multilateral trade, and (3) the provision of SDRs to members, as noted above.

Originally, the exchange rate policy of the IMF was based on a theory of "managed flexibility," or the "adjustable peg." Under this system, the exchange rate parities of member countries were defined in terms of the U.S. dollar. The exchange rate parity of the dollar, in turn, was defined in terms of a fixed gold value, of 0.88867088 grams. Individual countries were required under the system to maintain a fixed exchange rate parity with the dollar, and to meet short-term imbalances in their balance of payments through borrowings of SDRs from the fund. Changing the fixed exchange rate parity between member country currencies and the dollar could be approved by the IMF only in cases of a persistent imbalance over a long period of time that could not otherwise be corrected. Through this system of "managed flexibility," the IMF sought to maintain stable exchange rates in order to promote a workable structure of world trade.

The system of managed flexibility worked satisfactorily until the 1960s, when Britain's persistent balance-of-payments problems caused the pound sterling to be devalued in 1967. Since the pound sterling is a major world currency, its devaluation precipitated the collapse of the Bretton Woods system. The United States agreed to a small increase in the price of gold in 1968. The deutsche mark was revalued by 9 percent in 1969, following a period of major parity readjustments after the devaluation of the pound sterling. The deutsche mark was allowed to float from May to December 1971; then, on August 15, 1971, the

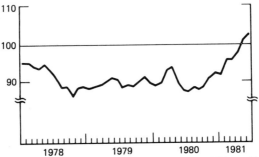

Figure 7.1 U.S. Dollar Effective Exchange Rate from 1977 to 1981. Source: IMF, Annual Report 1981.

U.S. government broke the dollar's link with gold and allowed the dollar to float, opening a new era of floating exchange rates.

At the Smithsonian Conference in Washington in December 1971, the world leaders agreed to repeg their currencies and to limit the movement of their currencies to 2¼ percent on either side of a new parity of 4½ percent spread from par value. Participants in the General Arrangements were the previously mentioned "Group of Ten." But the pound sterling was refloated in mid-1972, and by early 1973 all currencies were floating.[2] The Smithsonian attempt to maintain fixed parities had failed because fundamental imbalances between the currencies had not been corrected.

The United States dollar sustained a long downward slide during the 1970s (see Figure 7.1). From 1973 to 1975 the day-to-day fluctuations in exchange rates diminished, and between 1975 and the middle of 1977 the daily variations in exchange rates remained within a comparatively small range. But the daily variability increased substantially in the second half of 1977 and continued at high levels through 1979. This increased volatility of exchange rates may have reflected the significant deterioration in the United States balance-of-payments current account, from a positive balance in 1976 to a large negative balance in 1977 and 1978, which continued in 1979, heightening the uncertainty within the international financial community concerning the dollar's future equilibrium level.[3]

The protracted fall in the U.S. dollar's exchange value during the 1970s and the increase in daily variation in exchange rates during 1977 and 1978 created a crisis of confidence in the dollar as a suitable international reserve asset. The negative effects of the rising volatility in the exchange rates on economic activity and international investments aggravated the sense of concern among the members of the EEC. The EEC felt there was need for an alternative reserve asset to the dollar that would bring a measure of stability to the international economy.

Toward a Multiple Currency Reserve System

As noted previously, under the Bretton Woods system, the U.S. dollar became the single reserve asset in foreign exchange. All other currencies set their exchange rate parities in terms of the U.S. dollar; it became the international *numeraire*—the currency common to all other currencies. A significant portion of international transactions was, therefore, denominated in dollar terms, and the U.S. dollar became the most practical vehicle for holding international reserves.

As long as the U.S. dollar maintained a fixed gold value, it provided a stable currency value for the reserve assets held in dollars. In August 1971, however, the U.S. dollar was allowed to float, and it has continued to float except for the short period between the Smithsonian agreement in December 1971 and early 1973, when an attempt was made to return to the "managed flexibility" system. The exchange rate movements of a floating dollar are reflected in changes in the value of the reserve assets held in dollars. Depreciation of the dollar against other currencies will result in losses when the reserves are converted back into those currencies; thus a foreign exchange risk has been created by a floating dollar.

The instability of the U.S. dollar during the 1970s led to consideration of the advisability of switching from the dollar to another currency asset reserve system. But the international financial community has been unable to settle on a satisfactory alternative to the dollar as the anchor currency in the IMF system. The substitution of the German deutsche mark, the Japanese yen, or the Swiss franc as the international currency has been suggested from time to time, but these have not proved feasible. One problem is the interim need by private holders of liquid dollar assets to use their dollar holdings to finance international transactions; holders of dollar-denominated debts generally hold assets denominated in dollars to hedge their positions, and they would therefore increase their foreign exchange risk if they were to sell their dollar assets in the process of moving into another currency. Also limiting the suitability of these proposed alternative reserve assets is the absence of large-scale official diversification into these currencies.

Interest has therefore shifted to the concept of a multiple-currency reserve asset—a composite currency, or a "currency basket," made up of many currencies—to provide a stable form of international money with a capacity to spread risk. Several combinations of currencies for a basket have been proposed by the international financial community. The IMF and the EEC have formulated the currency-basket combinations that have generated the most interest.[4] Three composite currencies being used currently with varying degrees of success will be presented here: the SDR, the European Unit of Account (EUA), and the European Currency Unit (ECU), which is used by the "Supersnake" countries (see "European Joint Float" below).

The Special Drawing Right

The SDR was created in 1968 by the IMF with a fixed value of 0.88867088 grams of gold, or the equivalent of the official gold price of 1 United States dollar on that date. The IMF's purpose in creating the SDR was to create an alternative to the dollar for settlement of payment imbalances between central banks. The original composition of the SDR included not only currencies of major IMF members, but also gold, which created a degree of instability in the value of the SDR whenever the market price of gold deviated from its official (IMF) price. In 1974 gold was dropped from the SDR currency basket and the composition was limited to the 16 major trading currencies of the membership of the IMF. In the 1978 revision of the SDR currency basket, South Africa and Denmark were replaced by Saudi Arabia and Iran, to reflect the changing trade shares of these countries.

On January 1, 1981, the IMF introduced a new five-currency SDR basket which is to be used for the valuation of the SDR and the determination of the SDR interest rate. The currencies of the five members with the largest shares of exports of goods and services during the period 1975 to 1979 make up the new currency basket. The five currencies are the U.S. dollar, the deutsche mark, the French franc, the Japanese yen, and the British pound.

The currency composition of the SDR basket will be revised every 5 years beginning January 1, 1986; adjustments will be made to include the currencies of the member countries of the IMF with the largest exports of goods and services during the 5-year period ending 12 months before the effective date of the revision. The revision on January 1, 1986, for example, will cover 1980–1984.

For a currency to be replaced in the basket, the value of the exports of goods and services of the new currency over the relevant 5-year period must exceed the value of the exports of goods and services of the old currency by at least 1 percent. The amounts of the currencies in the revised valuation basket for the SDR will reflect the values of the exports of goods and services and the balances of these currencies held by other members.

The IMF each day publishes the dollar equivalent of the SDR. The valuation of the dollar equivalent of the SDR provides the international financial and commercial communities with an opportunity to use the SDR in a variety of ways in the normal course of business. A number of countries, including Saudi Arabia and Nigeria, have established an official par value for their currencies relative to the SDR. International agencies such as the Suez Canal Authority have priced their services in SDR-denominated units. Many countries are pricing their commodities in SDRs. The Chase Manhattan Bank and the London-based Hambros Bank began accepting SDR-denominated deposits in 1975.

Transactions denominated in SDRs tend to experience lower exchange risks from currency fluctuations than do many individual currencies, which are subject to short-term fluctuations. The five currencies included in the SDR currency basket stabilize the value of the SDR, since fluctuations in any one currency do not ordinarily upset the valuation of the SDR.

SDR-indexing can fix the value of a transaction. An example of the SDR deposit account offered by the Chase Manhattan Bank is presented below to show how SDR-indexing works. Using an exchange rate of 1 SDR = United States $1.19858, which was the rate on April 30, 1981, the interest income on a deposit of $1 million (SDR 834,321) for 6 months at 9.5 percent interest is equal to:

$$\text{SDR } 834{,}321 \times \frac{9.50}{100} \times \frac{180}{360} = \text{SDR } 39{,}630.23$$

The total return on the deposit (principal plus interest) at the end of the period will be

$$\text{SDR } 834{,}321 + \text{SDR } 39{,}630.23 = \text{SDR } 873{,}951.23$$

The SDR proceeds will be converted back to dollars for payment by the Chase Manhattan bank to the depositor. The conversion would be calculated on the basis of the dollar-SDR exchange rate on the date of maturity. If the exchange rate on that day is 1 SDR = United States $1.20173, the dollar conversion value would be

$$\text{SDR } 873{,}951.23 \times 1.20173 = \$1{,}050{,}253$$

We observe from this example that the intervening depreciation of the U.S. dollar did not affect the value of the deposit denominated in SDRs. The depreciation of the U.S. dollar from 1 SDR = $1.19858 to 1 SDR = $1.20173 resulted in an additional $2,752.95 in proceeds on the deposit. The SDR remains stable while the dollar fluctuates.

SDR Valuation The weight of each currency in the basket is based on the value of the country's exports of goods and services and the amount of its currency officially held by members of the IMF over the 5 years 1975–1979. The new five-currency basket is presented in Table 7.2. The initial percentage weight assigned to each currency was: U.S. dollar 46 percent, deutsche mark 19 percent French franc 13 percent, Japanese yen 13 percent, and British pound 13 per-

Table 7.2 SDR Valuation, April 30, 1981

Currency (1)	Currency Amount Under Rule 0–1 (2)	Exchange Rate[a] (3)	U.S. Dollar Equivalent (4)
U.S. dollar	0.54	1.0000	0.540000
Deutsche mark	0.46	2.2145	0.207722
French franc	0.74	5.2540	0.140845
Japanese yen	34	215.13	0.158044
British pound	0.071	2.1404	0.151968
			1.198579
		SDR value of US$1 =	0.834321
		U.S. dollar value of SDR =	1.19858

Source: IMF, *Annual Report 1981.*
[a] Middle rate between buying and selling rates at noon in the London exchange market as determined by the Bank of England, expressed in currency units per U.S. dollar except for the pound sterling, which is expressed in U.S. dollars per pound sterling.

cent. On December 31, 1980, the London noon exchange rates averaged over the 3 months ended December 31, 1980, were used to convert the initial percentage weights into units of each of the five currencies in the new basket. The currency units were computed to insure that the value of the SDR in terms of any currency on December 31, 1980, was the same as it was under the previous valuation method with the 16-currency basket.

To facilitate the daily computation of the new SDR, from January 1, 1981, the U.S. dollar exchange rate for the Japanese yen from the London rather than the Tokyo market will be used. This change makes computation of the new SDR easier since, besides fewer currencies being involved, all the exchange rates used are obtained from the London exchange market.

The U.S. dollar valuation of the SDR is shown in Table 7.2. The currency units in column 2 are divided by the dollar rate of exchange for each currency (column 3) to obtain the U.S. dollar equivalent. In the case of the pound, column 2 is multiplied by column 3 to obtain the U.S. dollar equivalent in column 4. Summing up the U.S. dollar equivalent of each of the five currencies in column 4 gives the U.S. dollar value of the SDR on April 30, 1981, at $1.19858.

The value of the SDR for any currency can be calculated the same way it is done in Table 7.2 for the U.S. dollar. The daily SDR value for a currency is computed using the daily exchange rate of the currency with the five currencies in the basket and proceeding with the valuation as shown in Table 7.2. The smaller number of currencies in the new SDR basket makes the valuation of the SDR in any currency much easier than before and should facilitate wider use of the SDR in both official and private transactions.

SDR Interest Rate   The objectives of the IMF in changing the composition of the SDR basket were to simplify the SDR, to make it more acceptable as a unit of account, to enhance the attractiveness of the SDR as an international reserve asset, and to facilitate the wider use of SDR-denominated assets and liabilities in financial markets and in international transactions.

The IMF raised the interest rate on the SDR to the full, combined, market interest rate of the SDR currencies effective May 1, 1981.[5] The IMF felt that the attractiveness of the SDR would be further enhanced by authorizing a fully market-related interest rate. This move completed the process by which the IMF, over the years, had raised the interest on the SDR by steps from its original 1½ percent per year. The interest rate had been raised from 60 to 80 percent of the combined market interest rate on January 1, 1979. The SDR interest rate and the short-term interest rates of the five countries in the SDR currency basket are shown in Figure 7.2.

The IMF made several other changes in the determination of the rate of interest on the SDR.[6] First, the reference period for establishing the combined market interest rate was reduced to a period of 15 business days preceding the last two business days of the month before the calendar quarter for which the rate of interest is determined. The previous reference period was the 6-week

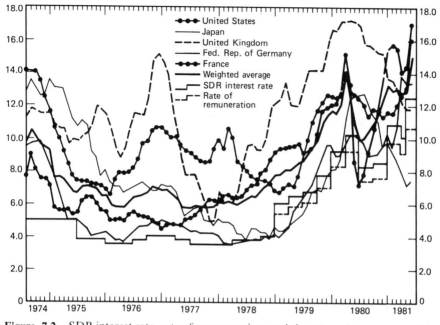

Figure 7.2 SDR interest rate, rate of remuneration, and short-term interest rates, July 1974–June 1981.[a]

Source: IMF, *Annual Report 1981*.

[a] Up to December 1980, short-term domestic interest rates are the yield on 3-month treasury bills for the United Kingdom and the United States, the rate on 3-month interbank deposits for France and West Germany, and the call money market rate (unconditional) for Japan. From January 1981, the yield on U.S. Treasury bills was converted to a coupon equivalent basis, and the discount rate on 2-month (private) bills was used for Japan. From March 1981, the basis for the interbank rates for France and West Germany was converted from a 360-day year to a 365-day year.

period ending the fifteenth day of the month before the calendar quarter for which the rate was determined. The rapid fluctuations of interest rates during the past several years have made it necessary to use a much shorter reference period with rates that are more sensitive to the current market activity.

Second, the method of deriving the combined market rate from the interest rates of the five currencies in the SDR basket was also changed. Beginning January 1, 1981, each interest rate is multiplied by the number of units of the corresponding currency in the valuation basket and by the value, in terms of SDRs, of a unit of that currency. The new method insures that the percentage share of a currency in establishing the combined market rate will follow its percentage share in the valuation basket. The percentage share of the currency will vary as the exchange value of the currency varies in relation to that of other currencies in the basket. Third, the rate of interest on the SDR will be reviewed at the end of each financial year instead of at the beginning of each calendar quarter.

The IMF has also changed its review of the level and determination of the interest rate on the SDR to an annual basis. The composition of the currency basket will be reviewed on a 5-year basis, as noted above. The discount rate on 2-month (private) bills has replaced the rate on call money as the interest rate used to represent the Japanese yen as of January 1, 1981.[7]

Abrogation of Reconstitution   The reconstitution requirement, which obligated members participating in the SDR allocation program to maintain, over a period of time, a minimum average level of SDR holdings in relation to their cumulative allocations, was abrogated effective April 30, 1981.[8] The reconstitution requirement was intended to protect the SDR from excessive use by requiring that countries retain or restore a minimum level of SDR holdings—a requirement similar to that of commercial banks requiring their borrowers to keep a minimum amount of the borrowed funds on deposit with the bank. This requirement was necessary at the inception of the SDR, since the rate of remuneration, the interest rate paid for the use of the SDR, was only 1½ percent, which made the SDR a cheap source for borrowing funds.

In January 1979 when the interest rate was raised to 80 percent of the combined market rate, the required average holding was reduced from 30 to 15 percent of net cumulative allocations. After the rise in interest rate to the full, combined market rate, the reconstitution requirement was felt to be counterproductive to IMF efforts to widen use of the SDR and was dropped.

SDR as a Unit of Account   The SDR has been gaining wider acceptance in official and private transactions as the unit of account, or as the basis for a unit of account, particularly since the reduction of the number of currencies in the SDR valuation basket. The SDR has been used in private contracts and international treaties, and by international and regional organizations such as the Nordic Investment Bank, the Arab Monetary Fund, the Economic Community of West Africa, the Asian Clearing Union, and the Islamic Development Bank.

The SDR is gaining wider acceptance among private institutions and corporations. More than 30 commercial banks in major financial centers and the Bank for International Settlements are now accepting time deposits denominated in SDRs. Demand deposit accounts denominated in SDRs are being accepted at a branch of one international bank, and it offers clearing facilities for SDR-denominated bonds. In the Eurobond market, one of the two major clearing systems has begun to accept SDR deposits in payment for the purchase of SDR-denominated issues. Cash accounts denominated in SDRs are being maintained and used in settlements within the EEC.

In January 1981 a group of London banks announced their intention of issuing and trading in CDs denominated in SDRs with uniform documentation. A secondary market for SDR-CDs was established following the banks' agreement to repurchase the CDs they had issued. It is estimated that CDs issued by the group of banks in January and February 1981 amounted to some SDR 270 million, of which SDR 150 million were issued in response to investor demand. CDs issued in fixed amounts totaled SDR 80 million (including two medium-term floating-rate CDs totaling SDR 40 million). A composite rate based on the average of interest rates quoted by five reference banks on interbank SDR deposits was used for one of the medium-term floating-rate CDs, and a rate based on the Libor rate of the component currencies was used to price the second issue.

The syndicated European credit markets have been involved in making loans denominated in SDRs. In February 1981, Sweden signed 5-year floating-rate notes denominated in SDRs for one $800-million tranche and a second tranche of $500 million. The SDR interest rate is computed on the basis of interest parity calculated on the Eurodollar deposit rate and the premium or discount on a forward sale of SDRs based on the SDR interest rate.

Ente Nazionale per L'Energia Elettrica, the electricity authority of Italy, issued SDR 100 million of floating-rate notes with an interest rate based on 6-month Eurodeposit rates for the five currencies in the SDR basket. The notes mature in 5 years. An 8-year SDR-denominated loan for SDR 83 million was arranged by the Ivory Coast. The rate of interest is based on an average of interbank rates on SDR-denominated 6-month deposits. The Nordic Investment Bank also launched an SDR-denominated bond issue for SDR 20 million in February 1981. A total of nine bond issues denominated in SDRs, totaling SDR 233 million, have been made since 1974.

SDRs and International Liquidity   The IMF provides liquidity in the international monetary system through the allocation of SDRs and the growth of reserve positions in the fund. The first type of liquidity is known as "unconditional," and the second type is called "conditioned" liquidity. The IMF provides conditional liquidity through its various lending programs and facilities. The fund directly provides reserve assets through the allocation of SDRs.

On January 1, 1981, the final allocation of SDR 4.05 billion was made in the third basic period (which ended on December 31, 1981) bringing the total SDRs in existence to more than SDR 21.43 billion, or the equivalent of about $27 billion. Table 7.3 shows the allocations of SDRs from 1970 to 1980.

The IMF has expanded the ways in which the SDR can be used to include the use of SDRs in donations as grants, purchases and sales of SDRs in both spot and forward markets, loans, swap arrangements, and pledges of SDRs. The parties are free to set the terms and conditions of individual operations. The IMF requires that the official "spot" valuation of the SDR be observed in most cases. The new valuation basket for the SDR has greatly simplified the calculation of the value of the SDR, which should facilitate its use in both official and private transactions.

Nine institutions have been designated as "other holders" of SDRs by the IMF. These institutions are authorized to acquire, hold, and use SDRs on uniform terms and conditions. The nine new holders are the Andean Reserve Fund, Bogota; the Arab Monetary Fund, Abu Dhabi; the East Caribbean Currency Authority, St. Kitts; the International Bank for Reconstruction and Development (the World Bank), and the International Development Association (IDA), Washington, D.C.; the International Fund for Agricultural Develop-

Table 7.3   Use of SDRs 1970–1980 (in millions of SDRs)

	1970–1972	1973–1975	1976	1977	1978	1979	1980
Transfers by participants to participants and other holders:							
In resignation	884	681	220	267	852	1,311	1,316
By agreement	989	1,275	353	699	1,827	318	347
To the Fund:							
Repurchases	1,088	101	446	837	347	492	1,275
Charges	149	356	629	807	747	584	519
Quota payments	—	—	—	—	220	1	5,088
Other	15	42	22	24	41	59	83
Subtotal	3,124	2,454	1,670	2,633	4,034	2,766	8,629
Transfers by the fund to participants and other holders:							
Purchases	292	46	430	428	1,025	1,266	1,556
Reconstitution	104	488	531	583	120	—	6
Remuneration	35	37	24	122	136	140	220
Other	192	5	3	13	50	67	480
Subtotal	623	576	989	1,145	1,332	1,472	2,262
Total transfers	3,747	3,031	2,659	3,779	5,365	4,238	10,891
SDR holdings at end of period							
Participants	8,686	8,764	8,656	8,133	8,110	12,479	11,803
Other holders	—	—	—	—	—	—	6
Fund's general resources account	629	551	659	1,182	1,205	869	5,572
Total[a]	9,315	9,315	9,315	9,315	9,315	13,348	17,381

Source: IMF, Treasurer's Department.
[a] Total holdings correspond to the total of net cumulative allocations.

ment, Rome; the Nordic Investment Bank, Helsinki; the Swiss National Bank, Zurich; and the Bank for International Settlements (BIS), Basel.

The European Unit of Account

The EUA was designed to provide a stable means of reference for the currencies of the countries in the EEC. The EUA is a basket of currencies intended to provide a standard of value. The composition of the basket of currencies making up the EUA has changed over time to reflect the changing economic relationships among its European member countries.

The original composition of the EUA was made up of the 17 currencies of the member countries of the European Payments Union. The composition of the EUA was changed in August 1972 to 9 currencies of the members of the EEC. In March 1979, the EUA was redefined again to associate it with the newly implemented European Monetary System (EMS), with the value of the EUA expressed in terms of the European Currency Unit (ECU) discussed below. (The currencies of member countries of the EMS qualify as reference currencies for the EUA.)

The EUA is now determined by the par values of the currencies of the eight member countries of the EMS; the deutsche mark, the French franc, the Dutch gulden, the Italian lira, the Belgian and Luxembourg francs, the Danish krone, and the Irish pound. The value of the EUA changes only when the majority of qualifying reference currencies are either revalued or devalued and the par values of all the qualifying reference currencies change.

Securities denominated in EUAs experience little or no exchange rate fluctuation; thus the risk of loss from exchange rate fluctuation has been virtually eliminated. Borrowers and lenders are attracted by the stability provided by the EUA. Bonds denominated in EUAs do not require the approval of any regulatory authority for registration and do not experience any bureaucratic delays for new issues. The yields on bond issues denominated in EUAs have been higher than on comparable issues denominated in the individual currencies.

The European Currency Unit

The ECU is made up of fixed proportions of the currencies of the EEC member countries. The relative proportions of the currencies were determined on the basis of the countries' importance in EEC trade. The ECU was created in 1970 for members of the "Snake" (eight Western European nations which formed a currency union in 1979, as detailed later in this chapter under The European Joint Float) to serve as: (1) the benchmark against which parities are set, (2) a measure of the overall strength or weakness of currencies against the average, (3) the unit of account for intervention and credit between members, and (4) a means of settlement between the monetary authorities of the EEC countries. The ECU may develop into the future international reserve currency asset.

The ECU was created on the same basis as the EUA, and the currencies in the ECU basket carry the same weight distribution as in the EUA currency basket. The rate of exchange of 1 ECU for any currency is obtained by computing the weighted average of the currencies in the ECU basket. To calculate the weighted average, the rate of exchange of the currency whose ECU value is being determined is multiplied by the weight of each currency in the basket, and the products totaled. The computation of ECU exchange parities is illustrated in Table 7.4. The data show that on December 1, 1978, the ECU was worth DM 2.516. Each day's ECU parities for the EEC member countries are published in the financial press.

Table 7.4 How the ECU is Calculated (Components of One ECU and Conversion Value of Two of Its Components on December 1, 1978)

Component Currency	Amount per One ECU	Value per DM Constituent Currency Unit	Cost of One ECU	Value per £ Constituent Currency Unit	Cost of One ECU
Deutsche mark	0.828	1.000	DM0.828	0.267	£0.2211
British pound	0.0885	3.75	0.332	1.000	0.885
French franc	1.15	0.4352	0.500	0.116	0.1334
Italian lira	109.00	0.002269	0.247	0.000605	0.0659
Dutch gulden	0.286	0.9200	0.263	0.245	0.0701
Belgian franc	3.66	0.06318	0.231	0.01685	0.0617
Danish krone	0.217	0.3591	0.078	0.09576	0.0208
Irish pound	0.00759	3.75	0.028	1.000	0.0076
Luxembourg franc	0.14	0.0632	0.009	0.01685	0.0024
			DM 2.516		£0.6715

Source: "What the EMS Involves," *Euromoney* (January 1979), pp. 46–51.

The weights applied to each currency in the basket are subject to revision every 5 years or when the trade-weight of any currency changes by more than 25 percent. Revisions to the parity values of the constituent currencies of the ECU must be acceptable to all parties.

Unfortunately, a multicurrency system like the ECU of the Supersnake is faced with the same inherent problems as those encountered in using a given currency as an alternative to the dollar as an international reserve asset. In addition, shifts in the composition of a multicurrency reserve asset would destabilize exchange rates as its holders (central banks and private individuals) restructured their portfolios of reserve assets to reflect any change in its composition. The need to restructure portfolios with each shift in the composition of currencies in a multicurrency reserve asset would increase the transaction costs of managing both official and private portfolios.

The European Joint Float

The Smithsonian Agreement in 1971 permitted currencies to float up to 2¼ percentage points either way from their par value before a need for corrective action arose. The total band, then, allowed a spread of 4½ percent from par value—a range of 9 percent between any two currencies. The member countries of the EEC, however, decided to maintain a narrower margin. The idea of a narrower margin had been proposed in 1971 to reduce the exchange-rate fluctuations between EEC currencies and to stabilize their exchange rate relationships.

The Snake

The first European joint float by members of the EEC began on April 24, 1972, and was called the "European System of Narrower Exchange Rate Margins,"

and local currency accounts. Table 7.6 lists the
ntries that have regulations controlling foreign
rst three categories; the fourth category—local
n foreign countries—is not included because it is
ain permission from the authorities in these coun-

hange Transactions

ions undertaken in normal trade for export or import
assified as commercial foreign exchange transactions.
uired for commercial transactions, and the procedures
s vary among countries, depending on the need for
exchange. In most countries with exchange control, the
ued routinely. Documentation in support of the applica-
d. The foreign exchange control regulations usually re-
hange transactions take place through a domestic bank in
English firms, for example, must carry out their foreign
ns with English banks).

Exchange Transactions

change is needed for purely financial transactions—to pay
est, to repay a foreign loan, or to purchase foreign securities—
al must be obtained to purchase the foreign exchange. The
ocess requires substantiation of the intended purpose and
ved.
erlands and Belgium, separate and parallel exchange rate markets
us types of purely financial transactions. In Belgium permits for
ial transactions can be obtained on a fairly routine basis.

Exchange Control Practices in the Major Western European Countries

hange transactions with domestic banks		Foreign Currency Accounts with Domestic Banks
ial	Financial	
k	Belgium	Belgium
d	Denmark	Denmark
e	Ireland	Ireland
	Finland	Finland
vay	France	France
den	Italy	Italy
ted Kingdom	Norway	Norway
	Sweden	Sweden
	United Kingdom	United Kingdom

or the "Snake." Each Snake currency would maintain a total margin of 2¼ percentage points (1⅛ on either side) from its par value and the whole group could float within the 4½ percent currency-to-currency margin of the Smithsonian Agreement; within these limits, the Snake was said to be "in the tunnel."

The European joint float started with the seven EEC members: France, Germany, Italy, and the Benelux countries. Four prospective EEC members—Denmark, Ireland, Norway, and Britain—joined the Snake in May 1972 (Norway subsequently did not join the EEC).

In June 1972 the United Kingdom and Ireland left the Snake, because of pressure on the pound sterling. They were followed by Italy 8 months later, as the lira also came under pressure. The unstable exchange rate system that had prevailed since the Smithsonian Agreement in December 1971 continued, and the Smithsonian system collapsed in March 1973. The Snake continued without the tunnel, and Sweden joined the European joint float. In January 1974 France left the Snake only to rejoin some 18 months later, in July 1975, and leave once again in March 1976. With the departure of Sweden in 1977, the membership of the Snake was reduced to Denmark, Germany, Norway, and the Benelux countries.

The Supersnake

The Supersnake was born on January 1, 1979, when eight countries declared their European Currency Unit (ECU) parities.[9] The five former members of the European joint float (Germany, Denmark, and the Benelux countries) were joined by France, Italy, and Ireland to form the Supersnake. The old Snake parities of the five former members were used for their new parities. France, Italy, and Ireland used the closing market rates for December 29, 1980, for their new parities for the Supersnake. The members of the Supersnake agreed to maintain margins of 2¼ percent on either side of their par values, which allowed a maximum range of 4½ percent between any two currencies in the new joint float. An exception was Italy, which maintained a 6-percent spread on either side of par, for a maximum range of 12 percent from the other currencies of the Supersnake. Currencies in the Supersnake float jointly as a group against other currencies and, therefore, preserve some degree of stability in relation to each other.[10]

Threshold of Divergence

The members of the European joint float have devised various rules to cope with problems of instability that may arise among the currencies of the Supersnake.[11] One such problem involves a change in the market rate of a currency pulling it away from its parity value with the other currencies in the joint float. Such movements can occur when a country with a strong currency pursues conservative fiscal policies, for example, causing severe strains among the relatively weaker currencies.

The monetary authorities of the Supersnake members are obliged to intervene when any of the currencies reaches its ceiling or floor, in order to prevent movement outside the 4½-percent spread. Intervention by the authorities takes the form, first, of a sale of the strong currency by the weak currency, and a purchase of the weak currency by the strong currency, using resources from the countries' respective reserves. The next step is a requirement that the nation with the weak currency take steps to deflate demand in its domestic economy through monetary and fiscal policies such as increasing interest rates and reducing deficit financing by the government. The strong-currency country, conversely, is required to take appropriate countermeasures to reflate domestic demand and ease monetary policy through lower interest rates and easier credit policies.

As noted previously, the currencies of the European joint float are permitted to deviate by 2¼ percent on either side of their ECU parity. When the market value of a currency rises above or falls below 1.6875 percent (or, 75 percent of 2¼ percent) of its ECU parity, it has passed the "threshold of divergence." Table 7.5 presents the EMS currency unit rates for the current seven members on October 30, 1980. The par value of each currency is given in Column 1; their market value on October 30, 1980, is given in Column 2. The "threshold of divergence" or divergence limit percentage is given in the last column.

As an illustration, the German deutsche mark has reached its threshold in Table 7.4. The mark reached its threshold of divergence on October 30, 1980, as shown. It reached its lowest limit against the French franc permitted within the EMS, a 6-month low against the dollar, and a 4-year low against the pound sterling. Thus support from several central banks was required to assist the mark to keep within the limits agreed by the EMS. In accordance with the requirements of the EMS rules, the German Bundesbank initially sold $19.15 million in an effort to lower the dollar/mark exchange rate from DM 1.8942 to DM 1.8866. Estimates of total dollar sales in the open market by the Bundesbank prior to the fixing of the mark rate against the ECU range between $50 million and $90 million.[12]

Table 7.5   EMS European Currency Units (ECU) Rates, October 30, 1980[a]

	ECU Central Rates	Currency Amounts Against ECU October 30	Change from Central Rate (%)	Change Adjusted for Divergence (%)	Divergence Limit (± %)
Belgian franc	39.7897	41.1210	+3.35%	+1.10%	1.53%
Danish krone	7.72336	7.90465	+2.35	+0.01	1.64
German deutsche mark	2.48208	2.56544	+3.36	+1.02	1.125
French franc	5.84700	5.91319	+1.13	−1.21	1.3557
Dutch gulden	2.74362	2.77281	+1.06	−1.28	1.512
Irish pound	0.668201	0.683672	+2.32	−0.02	1.668
Italian lira	1157.79	1214.32	+4.88	+2.68	4.08

Source: Financial Times (October 30, 1980).

[a] Changes are for ECU; therefore, a positive change denotes a weak currency. Adjustments calculated by *Financial Times*.

EXCHANGE

A

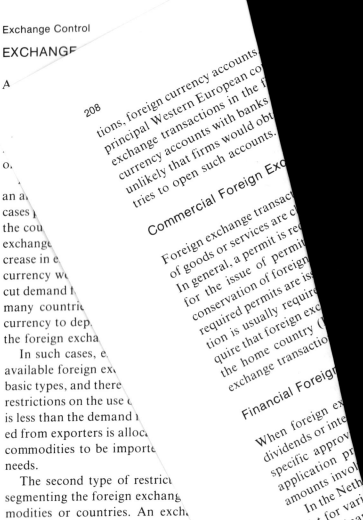

tions, foreign currency accounts
principal Western European co
exchange transactions in the f
currency accounts with banks
unlikely that firms would obt
tries to open such accounts.

Commercial Foreign Exc

Foreign exchange transac
of goods or services are c
In general, a permit is re
for the issue of permi
conservation of foreign
required permits are is
tion is usually requir
quire that foreign exc
the home country (
exchange transactio

Financial Foreig

When foreign ex
dividends or inte
specific approv
application pr
amounts invol
In the Neth
exist for vari
purely finan

o.

an a
cases
the cou
exchange
crease in e
currency w
cut demand
many countri
currency to dep
the foreign excha

In such cases, e
available foreign ex
basic types, and there
restrictions on the use
is less than the demand
ed from exporters is alloc
commodities to be import
needs.

The second type of restric
segmenting the foreign exchang
modities or countries. An exch
group of submarkets, which is ex
different exchange rates effectively s
of one currency relative to another.

A hybrid of the two types of restrict
some transactions are permitted at mark
actions, which may be restricted in quan
fixed-exchange rate basis.

U.S. firms involved in exporting, import
affected by the exchange control practices of
they do business. Thus, a review of the rules
exchange control practices of the major Europea
presented below to show the main features of the

The United States, Canada, West Germany, an
any exchange control restrictions at all. The other
nations do. The regulations governing exchange contr
commercial foreign exchange transactions, financial fo

Foreign Currency Accounts

Companies are required to obtain a permit when they want to open bank accounts in a foreign currency. This process enables the exchange control authorities to monitor such bank accounts. In some cases, firms are required to submit periodic reports on their foreign currency transactions.

The application process for foreign currency transactions is fairly routine in Belgium and Sweden. In the other countries, permits are granted on a case-by-case basis.

Local Currency Accounts

As noted previously, countries under exchange control generally do not allow a firm to open a local bank account in the firm's domestic currency (for instance, a British firm would not be allowed to open a pound sterling account with a French bank in France) except in very rare circumstances. This restriction is necessary if the exchange control is to work effectively.

SUMMARY

Since foreign exchange rates are prices for currencies expressed in terms of other currencies, movements in the foreign exchange rate between two currencies affect the prices of goods traded between countries. Moreover, investment funds move in and out of a country in response to movements of the country's exchange rate and expectations about its future direction. The foreign exchange market is made up of a network of the domestic banks of the major trading countries, their overseas branches, and correspondent banks in the other countries.

Foreign exchange trading involves two types of transactions: A spot transaction in the foreign exchange market is executed for delivery of dollars, in clearinghouse funds, against payment of the foreign currency to a foreign bank account two banking days after the date of the transaction. Foreign exchange rates are quoted, in the United States, as units of dollars per foreign monetary unit. A forward contract involves any foreign exchange contract with a delivery date of more than two days from the date of the transaction. Forward contracts, by convention, have specific maturity dates, usually 30, 60, 90, or 180 days. Forward rates are quoted either in outright terms, or in terms of premiums and/or discounts from the spot rate. The premiums and discounts in the basis point quotation are obtained by calculating the difference between each forward rate and the spot rate.

The IMF has direct responsibility for managing the international payments system and for supervising exchange rates between currencies of its member countries. Originally, the exchange rate policy of the IMF was based on a system of managed flexibility, or the adjustable peg. Under this system the exchange rate parities of member countries were defined in terms of gold—or the U.S. dollar with a fixed gold value. Individual member countries were required under the system to maintain a fixed exchange rate parity with the dollar and to meet short-term imbalances in their balance of payments through borrowings from the IMF. This system of managed flexibility worked satisfactorily until the 1970s, when persistent balance-of-payments problems resulted in devaluation of the U.S. dollar, and a system of floating rates was subsequently adopted.

The instability of the U.S. dollar during the 1970s has prompted consideration of an alternative currency asset reserve system, but so far the international financial community has been unable to identify any single currency that could satisfactorily replace the dollar. Attention has therefore shifted to the concept of a multiple-currency reserve asset—a composite currency or currency basket—to provide a stable form of international money with a capacity to spread risks.

SUPPLEMENTARY READING

Raymond G. F. Coninx, *Foreign Exchange Today* (New York: John Wiley & Sons, rev. ed., 1971).

Norman Crump, *The ABC of Foreign Exchange* (New York: St. Martins Press, 1963.

Paul Einzig, *A Textbook on Foreign Exchange* (London: St. Martins Press, 2nd ed., 1970).

Rolf M. Freuhertz, "Forecasting Foreign Exchange Rates in Inflationary Economies," *Financial Executive*, Vol. 38, No. 2 (February 1969), pp. 57–60.

Alan R. Holmes and Francis H. Schott, *The New York Foreign Exchange Market* (New York: Federal Reserve Bank of New York, 1965).

NOTES

1 H. O. Ruding, "The IMF and International Credit," *The Banker*, Vol. 128, No. 628 (June 1978), pp. 27–31.

2 Leroy L. Laney, "More Flexible Exchange Rates: Have They Insulated National Monetary Policies?" *Voice*, Federal Reserve Bank of Dallas publication (February 1980), pp. 6–18.

3 Douglas R. Mudd and Geoffrey E. Wood, "Oil Imports and the Fall of the Dollar," *Federal Reserve Bank of St. Louis Review*, Vol. 61, No. 8 (August 1979), pp. 2–6.

4 Karl Otto Pohl, "The Multiple-Currency Reserve System," *Euromoney* (October 1980), pp. 44–48.

5 IMF Executive Board Decision No. 6832 (81/65) S, adopted April 22, 1981.

6 IMF Executive Board Decision No. 6632 (80/145) G/S, adopted September 17, 1980.

7 IMF Executive Board Decision No. 6708 (80/189) S, adopted December 19, 1980.

8 IMF Executive Board Decision No. 6832 (81/65) S, adopted April 22, 1981.

9 "What the EMS Involves," *Euromoney* (January 1979), pp. 46–51.

10 "Will EMS be a Triumph or a Disaster?" *Euromoney* (January 1979), pp. 32–36.

11 "The EMS at Work," *Euromoney* (January 1979), pp. 52–55.

12 Cornelis de Pee, "The EMS: More than an Even Chance of Survival," *Euromoney* (October 1980), pp. 287–289.

8

Managing Foreign Exchange Exposure

The rate of exchange between the currencies of the various countries constantly fluctuates as a result of the effects of changing economic forces. In general, any United States merchant or corporation is exposed to the possibility of gains or losses from fluctuations in the foreign exchange rate whenever it is involved in commercial transactions that are denominated in a foreign currency. For multinational or transnational corporations,[1] the value of the net assets or liabilities of the firm that are held in a foreign country is affected by foreign exchange exposure when the value is translated into the currency of the parent company. The income stream of a foreign subsidiary or affiliate is also subject to foreign exchange exposure when translated back into the currency of the parent company. Foreign exchange exposure may be defined, in an economic sense, as the amount of gain or loss in value to which a transaction or investment abroad is exposed as a result of fluctuations in the foreign exchange rate.

An understanding of the various kinds of foreign exchange exposure should aid the firm in controlling its exposure to movements of the foreign exchange rate. The firm can use some of the techniques that have been developed to manage its foreign exchange risk and to minimize losses that may arise from foreign exchange rate movements.[2,3] The three major types of foreign exchange exposure are: (1) transaction exposure, (2) economic exposure, and (3) translation exposure.

TRANSACTION EXPOSURE

In most business transactions, a certain period of time elapses between signing a contract and the settlement date. In an international transaction, changes in the foreign exchange rate during this interval can increase (or decrease) the contract value to one of the parties to the contract, depending on the currency of denomination of the contract. For example, if the contract terms are denominated in dollars, a change in the dollar's foreign exchange rate would not affect the value of the contract to a U.S. party. But it could expose the foreign signer to a loss or gain on the transaction, depending on whether the dollar's value in relation to the foreign currency had increased or decreased by the date of settlement. The effect of the foreign exchange movement on the foreign-currency equivalent of a dollar-denominated contract value is called transaction exposure.

On the other hand, if the contract were drawn up in the foreign currency, the dollar equivalent of the value of the contract would increase or decrease with changes in the foreign exchange rate, resulting in a loss or a gain to the U.S. firm at the date of settlement. To the U.S. firm, transaction exposure arises when it enters into a transaction that is drawn up in a foreign currency and there is an interval of time between the date on which the contract is signed (contract date) and the date on which settlement will be made (settlement date).

Transaction exposure arises in international trade activities and in international borrowing and lending. International trade transactions generally carry transaction exposure because they involve a time lapse to cover the distances required for completion of the transaction. Export shipments, for example, are usually negotiated for payment either on the arrival of the goods or at some time after the goods arrive in the importer's country. In this interim, exchange rates can change. The following examples of foreign exchange risk in export and import transactions will illustrate the concept of transaction exposure.

Foreign Exchange Risks in Export Transactions

When a U.S. company makes an export sale, the terms can be fixed in either U.S. dollars or the buyer's currency. If the export sales contract is drawn up in U.S. dollars, then the U.S. exporter does not have any foreign exchange exposure. Instead, the foreign importer bears the foreign exchange risk from fluctuations in the dollar exchange rate: the importer has to pay in dollars, and if the U.S. dollar has appreciated relative to the importer's currency by the date of settlement, the importer will have to pay more of the foreign currency per dollar.

Example 8.1: A U.S. exporter sells $1 million worth of goods to an English importer in May. The export sales contract is drawn up in dollars at the May spot rate of £1 = $1.90. Payment is to be made 6 months after the date of the contract, when the goods arrive in the United Kingdom. At the end of the 6 months, the dollar has appreciated by 10.5 percent to £1 = $1.70; thus

$$
\begin{array}{llll}
\text{May at } \pounds 1 & = \$1.90, & \$1,000,000 & = \pounds 526,316 \\
\text{November at } \pounds 1 & = \$1.70, & \$1,000,000 & = \underline{\pounds 588,235} \\
\end{array}
$$

Increase in amount of pound
sterling required $\qquad = \pounds\ 61,919$

From the example, the pound sterling equivalent of $1 million in May was £526,316. By November the dollar had appreciated in relation to the pound (or the pound had depreciated in relation to the dollar), and the pound equivalent of $1 million was now £588,235. The English importer will have to pay £61,919 more because of the exchange rate changes, resulting in a foreign exchange loss on the transaction.

The reverse would have occurred if the export sales contract had been denominated in pounds sterling instead of dollars. In that case, the U.S. exporter would be exposed to possible foreign exchange gain or loss.

Example 8.2: Assume that the export sales contract for $1 million of exports to the English importer (in Example 8.1) was denominated in pounds sterling. With the spot rate in May at £1 = $1.90, the $1 million is equivalent to £526,316. Accordingly the English importer would pay £526,316 in November to the U.S. exporter. Because the dollar appreciated by 10.5 percent in the interim, making the spot rate in November £1 = $1.70, then

$$\text{May at £1} \quad = \$1.90, \quad £526,316 = \$1,000,000$$
$$\text{November at £1} = \$1.70, \quad £526,316 = \underline{\$\ \ 894,737}$$

$$\begin{array}{ll} \text{Dollar loss incurred by} \\ \text{U.S. importer} & \$\ \ 105,263 \end{array}$$

The £526,316 would be worth only $894,737, resulting in an exchange loss of $105,263 for the United States exporter.

The general rule when selling to countries whose currencies are weak and expected to depreciate, for export sales contracts involving future payments, is to require payment in dollars or other strong currency.

In cases where the currency of the foreign importer is strong and is expected to appreciate relative to the U.S. dollar, the exporter would prefer to invoice the sale in the foreign currency. If the foreign currency does in fact appreciate relative to the dollar, the exporter will realize a transaction gain. If the sales contract stipulates a dollar payment, the exporter will not be affected since the firm will receive the $1 million; the importer would gain because less foreign exchange would be required to purchase $1 million.

Example 8.3: An export sales contract for $1 million is made between a United States exporter and an English importer with payment to be made in pounds sterling at the end of 6 months. The sales contract is signed in May when the spot rate is £1 = $1.90. The pound appreciates against the dollar, and in November the spot rate is £1 = $2.10. Thus

$$\text{May at £1} \quad = \$1.90, \quad £526,316 = \$1,000,000$$
$$\text{November at £1} = \$2.10, \quad £526,316 = \underline{\$1,105,264}$$

$$\text{Gain by U.S. exporter} \qquad \$\ \ 105,264$$

By invoicing the sales contract in pounds sterling when that currency is expected to appreciate, the U.S. exporter will receive £526,316 in November (which was the equivalent of $1 million in May at the exchange rate of £1 = $1.90).

When the United States exporter converts the £526,313 payment in November to dollars at the higher exchange rate of £1 = $2.10, the dollar equivalent at the new exchange rate is $1,105,264, which results in a transaction gain to the exporter of $105,264.

If, on the other hand, the export sale had been invoiced in dollars, the English importer would have required fewer pounds to buy the $1 million to pay the U.S. exporter (at the November exchange rate of £1 = $2.10, the English importer would need £476,190 to buy $1 million, thereby saving £50,126).

The general rule is to invoice export sales in the importer's currency when it is strong and expected to appreciate between the date of the export sales contract and the date of payment. The intervening appreciation of the foreign currency will result in a foreign exchange transaction gain for the U.S. exporter.

Foreign Exchange Risks in Import Transactions

A U.S. importer can pay for its imports in either U.S. dollars, the foreign exporter's currency, a third currency, or a combination of the three. If the importer contracts to make payment in dollars, the payment is fixed in dollar terms and is unaffected by a difference in the exchange rate on the date of payment. In other words, the importer is generally protected from foreign exchange risks when the purchase contract calls for payment in dollars. But there are exceptions to this rule, for example, if the importer buys for inventory and the exporter's currency either depreciates against the dollar or is devalued subsequent to the purchase. The effect of the depreciation (or devaluation) of the exporter's currency is to reduce the dollar value of the goods. New imports would be cheaper than the goods imported prior to the change in the exchange rate. With the lower cost, the new imports could be sold at lower prices. Furthermore, the importer might be faced with actual losses—not just paper losses—if the firm has to sell the inventory at the lower price of the new imports, as other importers proceed to sell at the prevailing lower price. This situation could result in reduced profit margins, or a loss, when the inventory is sold. The importer may protect against this kind of risk by the use of a "hedge." The hedge allows the importer to sell the exporter's currency in the forward market for an amount equivalent to the value of the inventory of imported goods. (Hedging strategies are discussed later in this chapter.)

Payment in Foreign Currency

When the purchase contract is drawn up for payment in the exporter's currency or in a third currency, the U.S. importer is exposed to the risk of foreign exchange fluctuation between the date the purchase contract is signed and the date of payment. The importer's liability under the import contract will increase if the foreign currency appreciates against the United States dollar. In this case, the importer would have to pay out more dollars than were needed at the time the contract was signed. The effect of appreciation of a foreign currency on an importer's liability is illustrated in the following example.

Example 8.4:   An import purchase contract for $1 million is made between a U.S. importer and an English exporter, with payment to be made in the exporter's currency (the pound sterling) at the end of 6 months. The purchase contract is signed in May, when the spot rate is £1 = $1.90. Between May and November, the pound appreciates by 10.5 percent against the dollar, reaching £1 = $2.10 in November

$$
\begin{array}{llll}
\text{May at £1} & = \$1.90, & £526{,}316 & = \$1{,}000{,}000 \\
\text{November at £1} & = \$2.10, & £526{,}316 & = \underline{\$1{,}105{,}264} \\
& \text{Dollar amount increase needed} & & \$\ \ \ 105{,}264
\end{array}
$$

The appreciation of the pound sterling by 10.5 percent against the dollar resulted in an increase of $105,264 the U.S. importer would have to pay, which represents an increase in the cost of the imported goods. The importer would either pass the increase in cost along to the consumer by raising the price of the commodity or absorb the higher cost by taking a lower profit margin.

Forward Cover for Import Risk

The importer can use a hedging strategy for protection against currency fluctuation that might result in increased liability or foreign exchange losses. In Example 8.4, the importer contracted to buy $1 million (in pounds) of goods and to make payment 6 months later. The pound was strong and expected to rise relative to the dollar, which would increase the amount of dollars needed to make payment at the due date. The importer could use forward cover to limit the amount needed to meet the obligation when due by buying the amount of foreign exchange needed now for future delivery on the due date. If no specific date is set, future delivery can be arranged for the month the payment is due. The forward rate will include a premium for a strong currency to reflect the appreciation expected. The importer would have to buy the forward contract at the higher rate, which includes the premium, and would thus incur a cost to cover the open currency position. The forward cover is illustrated by the following example:

Example 8.5:   A U.S. importer buys $1 million of goods from an English exporter on May 31. When the purchase contract is signed, it is drawn up in pounds sterling at the spot rate of £1 = $1.90. Payment is to be made 6 months after the date of the contract, when the goods arrive in the United States. The pound sterling is appreciating against the dollar and is expected to appreciate further in the period between the date the purchase contract is signed and the payment date. The 6-month forward exchange rate for the pound sterling is selling at a premium of 500 basis points on May 31. (Basis points are explained in Chapter 6.) To protect against this exposure, the importer buys sterling in the amount of £526,316 forward 6 months from a bank at a premium of 500 basis points.

May 31	£1 = $1.90.	£526,316 = $1,000,000
May 31	Forward rate £1 = $1.95	£526,316 = $1,026,316
	Premium cost for forward cover	$ 26,316

The importer will deliver $1,026,316 to the bank in exchange for £526,316. At the end of the 6 months, on November 30, the pound has increased in value by 10.5 percent and is worth $2.10

November 30 £1 = $2.10 £526,316 = $1,105,264	
Forward contract purchased	
from bank	= $1,026,316
Savings by importer	$ 78,948

By buying the forward cover, the importer's exposure is reduced by $78,948, which the importer would have had to meet out of pocket if the transaction had not been covered. In Example 8.4, the transaction was not covered and the importer had to pay the increase of $105,264, which is equal to the total of the forward premium of $26,316 and the savings of $78,948.

The importer in Example 8.5 limited the cost to the forward premium, and since the revaluation was greater than the forward premium, the importer's exposure was limited to $1,026,316. The importer was protected from sterling appreciation above this amount.

What would have happened if sterling had not appreciated beyond £1 = $1.90 as expected by November 30, when payment was due? The premium of $26,316 paid by the importer for forward cover would have been realized as a loss to the importer.

ECONOMIC EXPOSURE

Multinational corporations have branches, subsidiaries, and affiliates (which we will lump together as "entities" for the sake of convenience) in foreign countries. The corporations invest in these entities to generate an income stream that will augment the dollar income of the parent company. The business activities of the foreign entities produce income streams in their local currencies, which must be converted to dollars when remitted to the parent company. The return on the parent company's investment in a foreign entity is measured by the present value of the after-tax cash flows that the foreign investment is expected to generate during its lifetime.

Fluctuations in the exchange rate between the dollar and the currency of the foreign country in which the entity is located affect the dollar value of both the income stream and the parent company's investment in the foreign entity. The effect of changes in the foreign exchange rate on the dollar value of the income stream generated by an investment in a foreign country, as well as the value of the investment itself, is called economic exposure. Economic exposure refers to changes in the value of future income streams as a result of changes in exchange rates, and the attendant changes in the value of the parent company's common stockholders' wealth.

The effect of foreign exchange rate changes on the value of the firm's expected cash flows and the wealth of the firm's shareholders, as measured by the economic exposure, will depend on the magnitude of the change in the foreign exchange rate (or the amount of devaluation or revaluation), changes in the operations of the subsidiary resulting from the change in the exchange rate, and the price elasticity of demand for the entity's product.[4]

Case 1   Local production and local sales

If the foreign entity uses only local inputs in its operations and sells only in the local market, a deterioration of the local currency in relation to the dollar will not affect the entity's operations—its cost of production or its selling price. Rather, the resultant economic loss would be a decrease in the entity's cash flow as measured in dollars. The following example will illustrate this point:

Example 8:6:   The Nacional Empresa, located in Mexico, is a wholly owned subsidiary of a United States multinational corporation. The Mexican firm uses local labor and materials to produce its output, which is sold in Mexico. The sales and cost information of Nacional Empresa is given in pesos in the *pro forma* income statement in Table 8.1. The foreign exchange rate of the Mexican peso for the dollar was 16 pesos = $1 at the beginning of the year. The peso was devalued to 23 pesos = $1 during the year. The effect of the peso devalua-

Table 8.1   *Pro Forma* Income Statement of Nacional Empresa for the Year Ending December 31 (Thousands of pesos)

Income		
Sales (10,000 units of output @ Peso 200/unit) =	Peso	2,000
Less Direct costs (10,000 units @ Peso 130/unit) =		1,300
Other costs		278
Depreciation		80
Pretax profits		342
Less Income tax expense		171
Profit after taxes	Peso	171
Cash Flow Due U.S. Parent Firm		
Profit after taxes	Peso	171
Plus Depreciation		80
Total cash flow from operations due U.S. parent firm	Peso	251

tion on the cash flow from the subsidiary (251,000 pesos) when measured in dollars is

Predevaluation (16 pesos = $1) 251,000 pesos = $15,688
Postdevaluation (23 pesos = $1) 251,000 pesos =   10,913

Economic loss from devaluation as
measured in dollars   = $ 4,775

The fall in the cash flow of Nacional Empresa caused by the devaluation of the Mexican peso will affect all future cash flows from this investment over its economic life. If we assume that the net cash flow each year from Nacional Empresa will be the same as in the sample year's income statement, then the present value of the future cash flows from the subsidiary would be reduced commensurately.

The effect of the reduced cash flows on the United States parent firm's shareholders' wealth position over the life of the investment can be illustrated by extending the above example. Let us assume that the project has an economic life of 5 years, and that the operations of Nacional Empresa will generate the same after-tax cash flow in pesos as shown in the *pro forma* income statement in Table 8.1. If the United States parent had a required rate of return on its investment of 20 percent, then the present value (PV) of the future cash flows before and after the devaluation of the peso would be as shown in Table 8.2. The net cash flow (NCF) changes as follows:

PV of expected NCF before devaluation = $46,905
PV of expected NCF after devaluation =   32,631
Change in the PV of expected NCF = $14,274

The $14,274 represents the discount to the PV of the expected NCFs that Nacional Empresa would generate from operations over the 5-year life of the project. This is a loss to the shareholders of the parent company, which in turn diminishes their return on equity.

The peso devaluation affected the parent company also by changing the value of its investment in the project. In the example below, let us assume that the parent company investment in the project was $40 thousand. The devaluation affected the economic viability of the investment in Nacional Empresa as follows:

	PV of Expected NCFs	Project Investment	Net PV
Before devaluation	$46,905	$40,000	+$6,905
After devaluation	32,631	40,000	−$7,369

Before devaluation, the project would have returned $6,905 above the 20-percent return required by the parent company on its $40-thousand investment. After devaluation, the net PV shows a loss of $7,369. The project's NCFs after

Table 8.2 Impact of Peso Devaluation on Parent Company's Cash Flows

Year of Invest- ment	Net Cash Flow (Pesos)	Predevaluation Exchange Rate: Peso 16 = $1			Postdevaluation Exchange Rate: Peso 23 = $1		
		NCF[a]	PV[a] Factor (20%)	PV[b] of Cash Flow	NCF[a]	PV[b] Factor (20%)	PV[b] of Cash Flow
1	Peso 251,000	$15,688	× .833 =	$13,068	$10,913	× .833	= $ 9,091
2	251,000	15,688	.694	10,887	10,913	.694	7,574
3	251,000	15,688	.579	9,083	10,913	.579	6,319
4	251,000	15,688	.482	7,561	10,913	.482	5,260
5	251,000	15,668	.402	6,306	10,913	.402	4,387
Total	Peso 1,225,000	$78,440		$46,905	$54,565		$32,631

[a]Net cash flow.
[b]Present value.

devaluation would return less than the 20 percent required by the parent company. Specifically, the project would return slightly under 12 percent after devaluation. The difference of approximately 8 percentage points represents an opportunity loss to the parent company and its shareholders.

Case 2   Local production with imported components

Another type of economic exposure arises when the local subsidiary imports part of the materials or components needed for local manufacture—a common practice of foreign entities to minimize the investment needed in the local operations. U.S. multinationals use this approach to distribute their production process among many countries.

When a local subsidiary imports some of the components used in the production of its product, its cost of production will increase when the local currency is devalued. The effect of the devaluation on the cost of production of the local subsidiary can be illustrated by the following example:

Example 8.7:   Assume that 37 percent of the direct cost of Nacional Empresa represents the cost of components imported from the United States for use in the production of the product for sale in Mexico. Assume that 10,000 units of the component are imported each year at a cost of $3 per unit, making the total import bill $30,000. At the predevaluation exchange rate of 16 pesos = $1, the local currency cost of the components imported would be 480,000 pesos. At the devalued exchange rate of 23 pesos = $1, the local currency cost increases to 690,000 pesos. The direct cost would increase from 1,300,000 pesos to 1,510,000 pesos.

The alternative courses of action open to Nacional Empresa to deal with the increase in cost are: (1) pass on the full cost increase to the consumers in the form of a corresponding price increase, (2) increase the price by a part of the increase in cost—to the extent that the market will bear, or (3) absorb the full increase in cost by taking a lower profit margin. The alternative chosen by Nacional Empresa will depend on the price elasticity of demand for the product in Mexico and the competition in the local market.

If Nacional Empresa is the only producer in the local market (that is, if it has a monopoly), as is often the case in a developing country, it is in a position to pass on the full increase in cost resulting from the devaluation. However, if there are other local producers who do not use imported components in their products, the peso devaluation will not affect their cost of production, and they will not be under any pressure to raise prices. In this case, Nacional Empresa might have to absorb some or all of the cost increase to remain competitive.

The effect of the cost increase on the cash flow of Nacional Empresa is summarized in Table 8.3. In the case where the subsidiary can raise the price by the full amount of the increased cost with no reduction in sales, the cash flow due the United States parent company remains the same in the local currency as before devaluation, and conversion loss to the United States parent would be the same as before.

**Table 8.3 Nacional Empresa Comparative Income Statement
Reflecting Cost Increase[a] with and without
Compensating Price Increase (Pesos)**

	Price Increase = Cost Increase	Price Remains the Same
Sales	Peso 2,210,000	Peso 2,000,000
Direct cost	1,510,000	1,510,000
Other costs	278,000	278,000
Depreciation	80,000	80,000
Earnings before taxes	342,000	132,000
Taxes (50%)	171,000	66,000
Earnings after taxes	171,000	66,000
Plus depreciation	80,000	80,000
Cash flow due U.S. parent company	251,000	146,000

[a] Cost increases by 210,000 pesos (see text).

In the second case, the subsidiary cannot pass the increased cost to the consumers because other local producers do not use imported components and are not raising their prices. The cash flow to the United States parent from Nacional Empresa's operations falls by half of the cost increase, or by 105,000 pesos. The conversion loss for the two alternatives after devaluation is

Price increase to match cost increase (peso 251,000) $10,913
No price increase to match cost increase (peso 146,000)   6,248
Difference $ 4,565

The preceding analysis shows that the U.S. parent would lose an additional $4,565 when it cannot pass on any of the cost increase caused by the devaluation. In this case the total loss from the devaluation would be $4,775 (see Example 8.6) + $4,565 = $9,340 in cash flows from the subsidiary. This figure represents the "worst case" situation for the United States parent company. In fact, Nacional Empresa might be able to increase its price by some part of the increase in cost. The ability to pass on any part of the increase in cost to the consumer through price increases will reduce the dollar loss in cash flows to the U.S. parent company.

Effects of Devaluation on Revenues from Export Sales

Devaluation of the peso reduces the number of units of foreign currency that the peso can buy. Export goods priced in pesos would become cheaper to foreigners because less of their currencies would be required to buy the same amount of exports priced in the devalued peso. Export revenues in pesos would be unchanged after devaluation (if the peso price and the volume of export remain the same). Export revenues measured in foreign currency units would fall, however, since each unit of foreign currency could buy more pesos.

Many countries, as a matter of commercial policy, require local affiliates of foreign companies to export a certain portion of their local production in order to earn foreign exchange. When local entities import components that use up available foreign exchange, the host country usually requires that some of the output be exported to replenish the foreign exchange.

The peso cost of imported components increases after devaluation of the peso: more pesos are required to buy the same quantity of imported components, which raises the local cost of manufacturing. If the increased local cost can be passed on in the form of higher prices for the product, then the higher peso price of exports would compensate for the increase in the cost of the imported components. If the lower price of the product in foreign markets increases sales, the increased volume may help offset lower margins.

Recall from Chapter 2 that the price elasticity of demand measures how much demand will rise or fall with each decrease or increase in the price of the product. The elasticity of demand is computed by dividing the percentage change in quantity by the percentage change in price. If this ratio equals one, both quantity and price change by the same amount. On the other hand, if the ratio is less than one, the percentage fall in quantity is less than the percentage increase in price, which would result in an increase in revenue from the product. When the elasticity is less than one, the demand is considered to be inelastic— that is, demand will be less than the change in price. Products with inelastic demand are usually necessities or products made from scarce resources.

Therefore, if the foreign price elasticity of demand for a product is less than one, then the exporting entity could conceivably increase the price of its product by more than the increase in cost to compensate for the devaluation effect on foreign exchange earnings. The extent to which it can raise its price for this purpose depends on the foreign price elasticity of demand for the product.

Balance Sheet Hedge

Multinational and transnational corporations are required to consolidate the financial statements of their foreign subsidiaries and affiliates with their own financial statements in their periodic reporting of the corporation's worldwide activities. The financial statements of the foreign entities are usually kept in their local currencies and must be translated at the prevailing exchange rate before they are consolidated with the parent's accounts. The exchange rate between the two currencies normally fluctuates over time, which affects the translated values of the foreign entity's income, assets, and liabilities and can produce gain or loss to the parent company.

The objective of the U.S. multinational or transnational corporation is to maximize the dollar equivalent of foreign earnings and reduce the company's exposure to foreign exchange risks. To achieve this objective the corporation's strategy is to increase its gains while reducing losses in foreign exchange translations.[5] In exposure management, the corporation can use several techniques to protect itself against foreign exchange risks. These techniques, generally referred to as hedging strategies, include the simple balance sheet hedge—that is, the appropriate increasing or decreasing of the exposed assets and liabilities in a foreign subsidiary.

The choice of strategy for asset and liability management depends on whether the local currency of the subsidiary is weak or strong. The general strategy for managing the assets and liabilities of a subsidiary operating in a local currency that is weak, and therefore subject to future depreciation and possible devaluation, is to maintain the lowest level of assets denominated in the weak foreign currency that is consistent with the subsidiary's operational needs. At the same time, local currency liabilities should be increased. The opposite strategy should be used in managing the assets and liabilities of subsidiaries operating in a strong local currency: the assets should be increased while the liabilities should be reduced.

Strategy for Weak Currencies

Weak currencies are usually associated with countries experiencing higher rates of inflation than their foreign trading partners. The higher rates of inflation are reflected in higher export prices, which tend to reduce foreign demand for the country's exports, and, as the prices of imports fall below domestic prices, import goods become cheaper. The cash inflows from export sales fall while cash outflows for the purchase of the cheaper imports increase, which leads to depreciation of the country's currency and possible devaluation. Weak currencies are therefore considered devaluation-prone.[6] If the local currency is devalued, the translated value of the subsidiary's assets into the parent company's currency will fall, resulting in loss of value, while the translated value of the subsidiary's local currency liabilities will increase. Therefore, the objective of management strategy in a devaluation-prone currency should be to reduce the company's asset exposure and increase its liability exposure in the local currency.

Maintaining the lowest possible level of current asssets consistent with sound financial management will leave minimal net assets or even no net assets exposed. To achieve this minimal-asset level, the balance-sheet items of current assets—cash, accounts receivable, and inventory—should be kept at the minimum level required for efficient operations.

All cash inflows not needed to meet local expenses within a given period should be transferred either to the parent company or to another strong currency account. Management should match inflows and outflows of cash as closely as possible, and any excess should be moved out of the weak-currency country by accelerating remittance to the parent company.

The subsidiary's local accounts receivable balance that is denominated in the weak currency must be maintained at the lowest level commensurate with sales by shortening the collection period.

Management should also keep inventory to the minimum necessary for production and sales. If the subsidiary is in an inflationary environment, management would want to consider its inventory valuation method in order to make sure that the method minimizes exposure to the effects of the inflation.

Consideration should be given to the possibility of prepayment of all expenses in relatively stronger currencies. When the cost of financing the prepayment exceeds the expected devaluation loss, those expenses should not be prepaid, since the net loss to the company would be greater.

At the time of a devaluation of the subsidiary's local currency relative to the parent company's currency, it would be advantageous for the parent company to repay debts in the local currency, since fewer units of the parent's currency will be needed to repay the local currency debts. In borrowing to repay debts, management should compare the costs of the alternatives of borrowing in the subsidiary's local currency or borrowing in a stronger currency. If local borrowing costs are extremely high, as is the case in many developing countries with high inflationary rates, then the net gain from devaluation after deducting the local borrowing costs (interest charges, compensating balances, commission discounts, and taxes) may be negative; that is, the local cost of borrowing may be greater than the expected currency depreciation rate. In this case, borrowing in a hard currency would be preferable to local currency borrowing. The foreign subsidiary should make maximum use of local currency accounts payable and should increase its accounts payable by lengthening the payment period or deferring payments when possible. Companies should also defer payment of accrued income taxes and Social Security taxes.

Strategy for Strong Currencies

Countries with strong currencies are revaluation-prone. Revaluation of a subsidiary's local currency would increase the amount of the parent company's currency per unit of the local currency. Liabilities held in the revalued local currency would increase, resulting in a loss for the parent company. The value of the subsidiary's current assets would also increase when translated into the parent company's currency. Thus, the situation is the reverse of the weak, devaluation-prone currency discussed above. The strategy for managing assets and liabilities of a subsidiary operating in a revaluation-prone currency would be to keep liabilities to the absolute minimum and maintain current assets at the highest level possible for efficient utilization.

The basic strategy used by the multinational corporation with a subsidiary abroad to protect a net exposed position to foreign exchange risk is the balance sheet hedge used to restructure the balance sheet items to achieve equality of exposed assets and exposed liabilities. The balance sheet hedge is useful and appropriate when there are long lead times before a currency realignment takes place or when controls have been imposed on foreign exchange.

TRANSLATION EXPOSURE

United States companies with foreign operations normally account for the operations of their foreign branches, subsidiaries, and affiliates in their published reports on the status of their overall activities. The accounts of these foreign entities are usually denominated in the currencies of their host countries, however, and for reporting purposes have to be translated into dollars. A change in the foreign exchange rate between the currency of the local subsidiary and the U.S. dollar will cause the value of the company's assets and liabilities to change when translated into U.S. dollars. Translation exposure refers to the possible loss or gain that may result from a change in the exchange rate.

Translation exposure is essentially an accounting concept that deals with the restatement of revenues, expenses, assets, and liabilities of a foreign subsidiary from the foreign currency into U.S. dollars, or the home currency of the parent company, so that the accounts can be incorporated into the accounts kept in the home currency. Translation exposure recognizes for accounting purposes the effects of changes in the foreign exchange rate on the financial statements of the foreign subsidiary when the accounts are translated from the local currency of the subsidiary to the home currency of the parent company. Translation exposure does not deal with the actual cash flows from the operations of the foreign subsidiary. The choice of accounting convention used in the translation affects the size of the exposure. Various accounting conventions are used in different countries. The United States uses the temporal method for translation; the example below uses the monetary/nonmonetary method.

Under the monetary/nonmonetary approach, the monetary assets and liabilities are translated at the exchange rate prevailing at the date of translation. The nonmonetary, or physical, assets and liabilities are translated at *historic* rates of exchange. In this method of translation, therefore, only the monetary assets and liabilities would be exposed to gain or loss resulting from changes in the exchange rate.

The concept of translation exposure is illustrated with the aid of the sample balance sheet presented in Table 8.4. This example illustrates the effects of a revaluation on translation of local currency. The assets and liabilities of IBX (Germany) Inc. are shown in the local currency, deutsche marks, with the translated value at the prerevaluation exchange rate and at the postrevaluation exchange rate. As can be observed, only the monetary items are involved in the translation at the postrevaluation rates.

Hedging Strategies for Managing Translation Exposure

When currency realignment is imminent, the balance sheet hedge cannot be used, and the corporation has to resort to other hedging techniques to protect

Table 8.4 IBX (Germany) Inc.
Translation of Local Currency Exposure (DM thousands)

	Balance Sheet at December 31	Historic Rate (Prerevaluation)		Current Rate (Post-revaluation)	
		Exchange Rate	Translated Dollar Value	Exchange Rate	Translated Dollar Value
Cash	DM 10,000	2:1	$5,000	1.8:1	$5,556
Accounts receivable	15,000	2:1	7,500	1.8:1	8,333
Inventories	10,000	2:1	5,000	2:1	5,000
Fixed assets	50,000	2:1	25,000	2:1	25,000
Depreciation	(5,000)	2:1	(2,500)	2:1	(2,500)
Net fixed assets	45,000	2:1	22,500	2:1	22,500
	DM 80,000		40,000		41,389
Accounts payable	DM 29,500	2:1	14,750	1.8:1	16,388
Taxes payable	12,500	2:1	6,250	1.8:1	6,944
Long-term debt	8,760	2:1	4,380	1.8:1	4,867
Stockholders equity	29,240	2:1	14,620	2:1	13,291
	DM 80,000		40,000		41,490

its net exposed position in a foreign subsidiary.[7] Three options are available to the parent corporation for use in managing its exposed net asset or net liability position: (1) take no action to protect the exposed position, (2) hedge on a before-tax basis, or (3) hedge on an after-tax basis.

The hedging strategies are useful in minimizing the impact of foreign exchange rate fluctuations on the net exposed asset or net exposed liability position of the corporation. There is a cost for the use of a hedge to protect an exposed position, however, and the corporation has to make a careful decision on whether the risk of loss from foreign exchange fluctuations is worth the cost of the hedge.[8] The impact of each of the three options on the corporation's translation report (or FASB 8) income and its cash flow will be illustrated in the following examples:

Example 8.8: IBX (Germany) Inc. is a subsidiary of the IBX Corporation, a multinational corporation with headquarters in the United States. On March 31, 19X0, IBX (Germany) has DM2,000,000 of net exposed current liabilities in its balance sheet, valued at the spot exchange rate of DM2 = $1. An evaluation of the forces affecting the dollar/deutsche mark exchange rate indicates that the dollar will depreciate relative to the deutsche mark over the next year and that, on March 31, 19X1, the exchange rate will be DM1.8 = $1.

The senior vice president in charge of international operations considers the three alternative courses of action on the net exposed liability open to IBX Corporation: (1) leave the company's exposed position as it is, (2) hedge on a before-tax basis, or (3) hedge on an after-tax basis.

Case 1   No-hedge decision

In this case, the IBX Corporation decides that it will not hedge its net exposed liability of DM2,000,000. The corporation's reluctance to hedge may reflect management's reluctance to incur a cost for an event that may or may not occur. Management may also feel that, should a currency realignment take place, its magnitude is not known with any certainty.[9] This uncertainty about the extent of the foreign exchange rate movement, in management's view, limits the effectiveness of the protection provided by the hedging strategy. Management therefore decides to take its chances and not cover its exposed liability position.

Table 8.5 presents the IBX Corporation translation loss resulting from its unhedged exposed position when the exchange rate appreciates from DM2 = $1 to DM1.8 = $1. The appreciation of the deutsche mark causes the translated value of IBX Corporation's liability to increase from $1 million to $1.111 million. An FASB 8 translation loss of $111,111 results from the increase in the corporation's liability when translated into U.S. dollars at the new exchange rate.

The increased U.S. dollar liability represents a potential loss that would affect the corporation's cash flow at a future date when the IBX Corporation decides to liquidate the net liability in its subsidiary, IBX (Germany) Inc. In this case, the IBX Corporation would have to pay $1.111 million instead of the original net liability of $1 million.

How does the increased foreign liability affect the cash flow of IBX Corporation? As mentioned above, the translation loss would affect the parent company's cash flow only when the company decides to liquidate the foreign liability. The parent company has several options available to liquidate the increased liability. It can directly remit the amount of $111 thousand to its German subsidiary by drawing down its cash balance, by borrowing, or by using retained earnings.

There is no income effect since the FASB 8 translation loss of $111 thousand cannot be used by IBX Corporation to reduce its United States tax liability.

Table 8.5   FASB 8 Translation Impact on IBX (Germany) Inc. Unhedged Balance Sheet Exposure (Thousands)

March 31	Exposure	Foreign Exchange Rate	Translated Value	FASB 8 Gain/ (Loss)
19X0	DM2,000	DM2 = $1	$1,000	
19X1	DM2,000	DM1.8 = $1	$1,111	$(111)

Furthermore, the loss is not deductible for tax purposes in Germany by IBX (Germany) Inc.

Case 2   Before-tax forward hedge

The FASB 8 translation loss in this case is the same as in Case 1—the $111 thousand shown in Table 8.5 It is this reported FASB 8 translation loss that the parent company wants to cover with the purchase of a forward contract. In this case, the IBX Corporation purchases a forward contract to hedge against the possibility of a loss resulting from an anticipated appreciation of the deutsche mark against the United States dollar. Management's strategy is to minimize the possible loss that would result from its exposed liability position if the deutsche mark appreciates against the dollar. The parent company is willing to assume the cost of the hedge if it provides cover for its exposed liability position.[10] The deutsche marks would be bought at the prevailing exchange rate plus the 3-percent premium at $1.03.

The FASB 8 gain is computed in Table 8.6. It shows a gain of $111 thousand which, in this example, exactly offsets the FASB 8 translation loss shown in Table 8.5. The spot rates at March 30, 19X0, and March 31, 19X1, were used to compute both the FASB 8 translation loss and the foreign exchange gain in the forward hedge contract, resulting in an exact offset of the foreign exchange loss by the foreign exchange gain, and a net FASB 8 result of zero dollars. This case illustrates the "perfect" hedge situation. The net FASB 8 result would be zero dollars for any realignment of the two currencies March 31, 19X1, the end of the contract period.

Net Income Effect—Before Tax

The net income effect of covering the company's "short" position in deutsche marks is a decline in income of $62 thousand, as shown in the before-tax column in Table 8.7. The $62 thousand represents the net income loss after taxes. IBX Corporation made a capital gain of $111 thousand on the forward contract it purchased to cover its exposed liability position in its German subsidiary. The gain is a capital gain since the contract was over 6 months long. The forward contract gain is, therefore, subject to U.S. tax. At a tax rate of 40 percent, the company's tax liability on its $111 thousand gain is $44 thousand. In addition, IBX Corporation paid a premium on the forward contract of $30

Table 8.6   IBX Corporation: Before-Tax Forward Hedge Contract to Cover Balance Sheet Liability Exposure of Subsidiary (Thousands)

March 31	Amount Bought Forward	Foreign Exchange Rate	Trans- lated Value	FASB 8 gain/ (loss)
19X1	DM2,000	DM2 = $1	$1,000	
19X2	DM2,000	DM1.8 = $1	$1,111	$111

**Table 8.7   Income Effect of FASB 8 Impact under Various
Hedging Strategies (Thousands)**

		Hedging Strategy	
		Before	After
	None	Tax	Tax
FASB 8 balance sheet loss[a]	$(111)	$(111)	$(111)
Foreign exchange gain on contract	—	—	185
Net FASB 8 gain/(loss)	$(111)	$ 0	74
Tax expense (forward hedge contract)	—	(44)	(74)
FASB 8 gain/(loss) adjusted tax effect	$(111)	(44)	$ 0
Premium expense	—	(30)	(46)
Tax credit (premium expense)	—	12	18
Net income after tax	$(111)	(62)	(28)

[a] From Table 8.5.

thousand when it purchased DM2 million at $1.03. The tax liability of $44 thousand plus the premium expense of $30 thousand amount to $74 thousand. The premium paid on the forward contract is tax deductible, however, resulting in a tax credit of $12 thousand, which is offset against the $74 thousand for tax and premium expense, leaving a loss in net income after taxes of $62 thousand. The $62-thousand net loss is the net cost of the hedge to the parent company for the protection of the net exposed liability in its subsidiary against loss from revaluation of the local currency. While the $62 thousand is significant, it is less than the $111-thousand loss incurred in the unhedged position.

Net Cash Flow Effect—Before Tax

The IBX Corporation had a positive net cash flow before taxes of $81 thousand as shown in Table 8.8. This figure represents the gain from the forward contract of $111 thousand, less the premium of $30 thousand paid for the forward contract. We can also view the cash flow before tax as the difference between the amount of $1.03 million the company paid to the bank for the forward contract and the amount of $1.111 million the bank paid over to the company as exchange. The amount of $1.03 million represents $1.0 million (the dollar cost of DM2000 thousand at DM2 = $1) and $30 thousand (the premium paid for the purchase of the forward contract). The amount of $1.111 million represents the dollar equivalent of the DM2000 thousand at the revalued exchange rate of DM1.8 = $1. The net cash flow before tax is subject to tax at a 40-percent tax rate, which results in an after-tax net cash flow of $49 thousand.

Case 3   After-tax hedge

The IBX Corporation is interested in minimizing to the fullest extent possible the impact of the FASB 8 translation loss that would result from a possible revaluation of the deutsche mark. The company's interest is focused on the

Table 8.8   Cash Flow Effect of FASB 8 Impact under Various Hedging Strategies (Thousands)

		Hedging Strategy	
	None	Before Tax	After Tax
Purchase of deutsche marks	—	$(1,030)	(1,584)
Sale of deutsche marks	—	1,111	1,709
Net cash flow (before tax)	—	81	125
Net tax payable (40%)	—	(32)	(50)
Net cash flow (after tax)	—	$49	$75

[a] Since FASB 8 exposure is unhedged, no cash flows occur in this case until the parent company decides to liquidate the exposed liability in its German subsidiary.

after-tax effects on the company's income and on the earnings per share of the company's common stock. In order to minimize the after-tax impact on net income, IBX Corporation would have to put up more cash to buy a larger forward hedge contract. The objective is to obtain an after-tax foreign exchange gain sufficient to offset the FASB 8 translation loss in full. This means that the before-tax gain must be large enough to meet both the tax obligation and the required level of after-tax foreign exchange gain.

The larger before-tax foreign exchange gain requires a larger forward contract than in Case 2. How large should the local currency forward purchase be to result in an after-tax foreign exchange gain equal to the potential FASB 8 loss from revaluation of the deutsche mark? To take account of the tax effect, the local currency exposure in IBX (Germany) Inc. is divided by (1 minus the tax rate). Since the local currency exposure was DM2,000 thousand, to obtain the amount of forward local currency (deutsche marks, in this case), the parent company should buy: DM2,000 thousand divided by (1−.40), or DM3,333 thousand. The deutsche marks would be bought at the prevailing exchange rate plus the 3-percent premium at $1.03.

As in Case 2, this case begins with a FASB 8 translation loss in the balance sheet of $111 thousand, as computed in Table 8.5. The forward contract analysis for the after-tax hedge is presented in Table 8.9. The $3.333-million forward contract results in a higher FASB 8 before-tax gain of $185 thousand from which the tax liability of $74 thousand is deducted, leaving an after-tax FASB 8 gain of $111 thousand. The FASB 8 after-tax gain of $111 thousand exactly offsets the FASB 8 translation loss of $111 thousand. For FASB 8 reporting purposes, the gain on the forward contract is reported on a before-tax basis, which would cause the parent company to report a net FASB 8 gain as follows:

FASB 8 gain on forward contract	= $185 thousand
Less FASB 8 translation loss on balance sheet liability	= 111 thousand
FASB 8 net gain	$ 74 thousand

Table 8.9 IBX Corporation: After-Tax Forward Hedge Contract to Cover Balance Sheet Liability Exposure of Subsidiary (Thousands of dollars)

March 31	Amount Bought Forward	Foreign Exchange Rate	Trans- lated Value	FASB 8 Gain on Con- tract	Tax on Con- tract Gain (40%)	Foreign Ex- change Gain on Contract Less Tax Effect
19X0	DM3,333	DM2=$1	$1,667			
19X1	DM3,333	DM1.8=$1	$1,852	$185	$(74)	$111

(   ) indicate debit.

Net Income Effect—After Tax

The income effect of the after-tax hedge is shown in the third column of Table 8.7. The net result after tax is a loss of $28 thousand. Since the adjusted tax effect of the FASB 8 gain/(loss) is zero, the $28-thousand net loss after tax will remain at that figure, at any exchange rate value of the future spot rate. The explanation is that the net loss represents the premium expense on the forward contract less the tax credit received for the premium expense. Since the two items are not affected by changes in the future spot rate, the net loss of $28 thousand will similarly not be affected by the course of the future spot rate.

Net Cash Flow Effect—After Tax

The effect on cash flow is shown in the third column of Table 8.8. The larger amount of the after-tax forward contract increased the size of the cash flow resulting in a larger net cash flow after taxes.

OTHER PROCEDURES FOR CONTROLLING FOREIGN EXCHANGE RISK

The Long-Term Currency Swap

A swap is an arrangement between two firms to exchange cash assets in one currency for cash assets in another currency and an agreement to reexchange the assets swapped at a future date. In the long-term currency swap, two firms enter into an agreement to exchange a specific amount of currency, with a commitment to reexchange the currencies on a specific date in the future. The time span for the reexchange ranges from 5 to 15 years. The following example illustrates the basic mechanics of the international long-term currency swap

Example 8.9: In January IBX Corporation wants to remit $1 million to IBX (Germany) Inc., so it enters into a swap arrangement with the Wirtschaft Corporation of West Germany. IBX agrees to pay $1 million to the New York subsidiary of the West German firm, Wirtschaft (USA), and Wirtschaft agrees to pay DM2 million to IBX (Germany) in exchange, at the January exchange rate of DM2 = $1.

The two parent companies would also agree to swap back the amount of currencies exchanged in, say, 5 years. During the 5 years of the swap agreement, the Wirtschaft Corporation would pay a net interest rate of 5 percent semiannually. This net interest represents the difference between the current 5-year term rate of interest of 14 percent in the United States and 9 percent in West Germany. The difference is usually fixed for the term of the swap agreement, but in some cases the companies would agree to a fluctuating differential to reflect their changing respective domestic interest rates. In Table 8.10, for example, the Interest differential of DM500,000 represents the difference between 14 percent of $1 million and 9 percent of DM2,000,000.

Each company pays a flat fee, from ¼ percent to ½ percent, to the broker who arranges the transaction. In addition, both companies would cover other costs incidental to the transaction, such as legal and accounting fees, and taxes. If we assume that legal and accounting fees and taxes amount to ⅛ percent for each company, then the total outlays under the swap agreement would be $1,003,750 for IBX and DM2,507,500 for Wirtschaft as shown in Table 8.10.

At the end of the 5 years, IBX Corporation will return the DM2 million to Wirtschaft Corporation in exchange for $1 million, which restores each company to its original position.

Long-term swaps have to date been limited to a few currencies (the U.S. dollar, the Canadian dollar, the pound sterling, and the Dutch gulden), but they could take place in any currency that is freely traded. Some countries with exchange control restrictions on their currency do not permit swap arrangements; two such countries are France and Brazil. The long-term swap offers several advantages over other types of financing. It has no effect on the debt/equity ratio, its cost is low, and it provides an automatic hedge against foreign exchange translation risk.[11]

Table 8.10   Long-Term Currency Swap Cost

	IBX	Wirtschaft
Swap amount	$1,000,000	DM2,000,000
Interest differential[a] (5% per year for 5 years)	—	500,000
Broker's fees (¼%)	2,500	5,000
Legal and accounting fees, plus taxes (⅛%)	1,250	2,500
Cost	$1,003,750	DM2,507,500

[a] Difference between prevailing long-term interest rates of 14 percent (U.S.) and 9 percent (West Germany) at time swap arranged.

As an exchange of cash assets, the swap does not affect the debt/equity ratio of IBX Corporation. The commitment to deliver forward deutsche marks against U.S. dollars in 10 years can, under FASB 8, be treated as a forward contract, which is not recorded in the balance sheet as a liability, and a long-term currency swap represents off-balance-sheet financing.

In comparison with alternatives, the long-term currency swap is the cheapest form of financing. In computing the net cost of the long-term currency swap, the net interest rate differential of 5 percent in Example 8.9 is offset against the opportunity cost of the $1 million being swapped, to obtain the net before-tax real cost of financing. The comparison of the before-tax real cost of 6 available financing alternatives in Table 8.11 shows that the long-term currency swap carries the lowest cost. The parallel loan is more expensive than the swap because the former involves a forward cover. Bank borrowing of dollars at 17.1 percent is the most expensive form of financing.

The forward commitment in the long-term currency swap is treated as a perfect hedge on a before-tax basis under the monetary/nonmonetary method of accounting for foreign exchange translation exposure. This treatment requires that the foreign currency proceeds of the swap be reported as assets of the company for translation at current exchange rates under FASB 8. The long-term currency swap, therefore, is a good vehicle for financing working capital, other than for inventories, since the proceeds remain in a monetary form translatable at current rates under FASB 8. When the proceeds from the swap are used for nonmonetary purposes like inventory financing or plant and machinery investment, the swap is not treated as a perfect hedge until the investment generates working capital, which can be translated at current rates under FASB 8.

Foreign Currency Loans

The foreign currency loan has been used by companies as a method of hedging their exposed foreign commitments against the risks of foreign exchange changes in the period between the commitment date and the date the deal is closed. Foreign currency receivables and foreign currency operating leases are two kinds of assets against which the foreign currency loan can be used to cover a company's foreign exchange exposure.[12]

The procedure is simple and straightforward: A company that has an exposed foreign currency receivable commitment that would be consummated at a future date simply takes out a foreign currency loan for an equivalent amount and for the same maturity as the foreign currency receivable commitment. On the date of maturity, the amount received from the foreign currency receivable would equal the loan to be repaid, plus the interest on the loan.

The foreign currency loan method of covering foreign exchange risks is illustrated in the following example:

Example 8.10: The IBX Corporation sells DM1 million worth of goods to its German subsidiary, IBX (Germany), on June 30. IBX (Germany) agrees to

Table 8.11 Comparison of Before-Tax Real Cost of Swap and Five Financing Alternatives (Percentages)

	Long-Term Currency Swap[a]	Parallel Loans[a]	Local Deutsche Mark Borrowing	Equity Financing	Commercial Paper	Bank Borrowing
Basic borrowing cost	(5.0)	(5.0)	9.0	—	10.0	14.0
Cost of 1-year forward cover[b]	—	3.0	—	3.0	3.0	3.0
Cost of currency conversion[c]	—	—	—	0.1	0.1	0.1
Opportunity cost of cash	10.0	10.0	—	10.0	—	—
Before-tax real cost	5.0	8.0	9.0	13.1	13.1	17.1

[a] Net interest rate differential payable by Wirtschaft Corporation of Germany to the IBX Corporation (see Table 8.10).
[b] Based on current rates at time financing arranged.
[c] On an annual prorated basis for comparison.

235

pay for the goods on December 31 plus 6 percent interest, making the total amount of the commitment DM1,050,000. The dollar equivalent of this amount would change as the deutsche mark/dollar exchange rate changes. IBX Corporation would proceed to cover its exposure by taking out a foreign currency loan of DM1 million for 6 months at a 10 percent rate of interest.

The accounting effect of the foreign currency loan taken out by the IBX Corporation to hedge its foreign exchange exposure is presented in Table 8.12. The monthly foreign exchange gains and losses from June 30 through December 31 are shown to range from a loss of $5,000 at the end of the first month to a gain of $6,000 at the end of the third month. The last column shows the cumulative six-month effect to be a gain of $6,000, which results from the change in the exchange rate from DM1 = $0.5 on June 30 to DM1 = $0.4940 on December 31.

The net change in the interest portion of the commitment due to the change in the exchange rate would be: $50,000 × 0.0006 = $300. The total change in the commitment, then, is the sum of the Cumulative gain of $6,000 plus the Change in the dollar value of the interest of $300, or $6,300. The Change in the dollar value of the accounts receivable DM1,050,000 commitment on December 31 amounts to DM1,050,000 × 0.006 = $6,300, which is completely offset by the cumulative gain of $6,000 plus the change in interest of $300.

Since the foreign currency loan seems to provide a simple approach to hedging against a foreign currency commitment, the question is why isn't it in widespread use? It has one serious drawback: it cannot be used to hedge against a foreign currency commitment under the provisions of FASB 8, because this type of loan may not always meet the requirements of accounting principles, as

Table 8.12 Use of Foreign Currency Loan by IBX to Hedge against Exposure on a Future Accounts Receivable Commitment (DM1 million borrowed on June 30)

Month of Loan (End of month)	DM/Dollar Exchange Rate ($)	Dollar Equivalent of DM Loan	Accounting Gain (Loss) in Month ($)	Cumulative Accounting Gain/(Loss) ($)
—	0.5000	500,000	—	—
First	0.5000	505,000	(5,000)	(5,000)
Second	0.5040	504,000	1,000	(4,000)
Third	0.4980	498,000	6,000	2,000
Fourth	0.4950	495,000	3,000	5,000
Fifth	0.4910	491,000	4,000	9,000
Sixth	0.4940	494,000	(3,000)	6,000
Cumulative gain on DM loan				6,000
Change in dollar value of interest payable from June 30 to December 31 @ 10% per year.				300
Change in dollar value of DM1,050,000 commitment				$6,300

explained below. The loan can be useful, however, in conjunction with back-to-back forward contracts to cover the exposed commitment.

Back-to-Back Forward Contracts

The back-to-back forward contract provides an alternative approach for hedging a company's exposed commitment to foreign exchange risk.[13] In the back-to-back forward contract method, the company simultaneously enters into a purchase contract and a sales contract, in forward foreign exchange, for the same maturity, in equal amounts, at the same exchange rate. The method is presented in the following example:

Example 8.11: As in the beginning of Example 8.10, IBX enters into a forward contract to sell the future deutsche mark proceeds of the future accounts receivable commitment. At the same time, IBX enters into a purchase contract to hedge against the loan taken out in Example 8.10. Both contracts are taken out for DM1 million at a rate of DM1 = $0.4190 with forward discounts of 30 basis points. The forward contracts are executed on June 30 for delivery on December 31.

The accounting effect of the back-to-back hedge is presented in Table 8.13. The first contract provides a hedge against IBX Corporation's foreign currency commitment for the sale of the proceeds when the accounts receivable is paid. The gain or loss from this contract will not be realized until maturity, on December 31. The loan taken out represents a net liability to the corporation, and the second contract provides a hedge against this net liability. The income for the period will include the gain or loss from this contract.

The amount of the hedging contract was made to equal the loan taken out in the previous example; as a result, the gain or loss on the forward contract exactly offsets the loss or gain on the loan transaction when translated. This process defers treatment of any accounting fluctuation until the accounts receivable commitment and the loan mature on December 31. The gain of $6,000 plus the net change of $300 in the dollar equivalent is exactly equal to the dollar equivalent of IBX Corporation's accounts receivable deutsche mark commitment, giving the same results as in Table 8.12.

The back-to-back forward contract has not been in widespread use because of certain practical drawbacks. Under the provisions of Paragraph 27 of FASB 8, a forward contract must be entered into the same day the foreign currency commitment is entered into for the forward contract to qualify as a "hedge of an identified foreign currency commitment."

While such a requirement is theoretically correct and meeting it is possible, it is very difficult to carry out because of practical constraints. First, the corporate treasurer is the one with the responsibility to enter into a forward contract. However, the purchasing or marketing departments are usually responsible for making the future commitments to buy and sell goods in foreign markets. This physically separates the focus of the commitment decision. Another problem is

Table 8.13 Foreign Currency Loan with Back-to-Back Forward Contracts to Hedge against a Future Commitment

Month of Loan (End of month)	DM/$ Exchange Rate	Dollar Equivalent of Foreign Currency Loan	Accounting Gain/(Loss) for Each Month ($)	Accounting Gain/(Loss) Foreign Exchange Purchase ($)	Accounting Gain/(Loss) Foreign Exchange Sale ($)	Amortized Discount, Foreign Exchange Purchase ($)	Amortized Discount, Foreign Exchange Sale ($)	Total Accounting Gain/(Loss) for Each Month
	0.5000	500,000	—	—	—	—	—	—
First	0.5050	505,000	(5,000)	5,000	NIL	500	(500)	NIL
Second	0.5040	504,000	1,000	(1,000)	NIL	500	(500)	NIL
Third	0.4980	498,000	6,000	(6,000)	NIL	500	(500)	NIL
Fourth	0.4950	495,000	3,000	(3,000)	NIL	500	(500)	NIL
Fifth	0.4910	491,000	4,000	(4,000)	NIL	500	(500)	NIL
Sixth	0.4940	494,000	(3,000)	3,000	6,000	500	(500)	6,000

timing. The decision to hedge is usually made after the commitment has been made that gives rise to a foreign exchange exposure.

The back-to-back forward contract also has some drawbacks for the bank entering into the purchase and sale contracts. The processing of the forward contracts involves preparation and confirmation procedures that increase the bank's costs. If back-to-back activities increase significantly, the costs to the bank could become very heavy. The use of back-to-back forward contracts to hedge medium- to long-term foreign currency commitments could result in a significant increase in the number of contracts that the banking community would have to handle. Consider this simple example:

A foreign currency commitment for a 4-year lease is made, and the contract calls for quarterly payments. A 4-year foreign currency loan with quarterly repayment of principal and interest is taken out to hedge against the foreign currency exposure. In this case, there will be 16 future payments under the commitment, and twice as many contracts, 32 in all, for back-to-back forward hedging would have to be taken out to cover the transaction. The magnitude of such transactions and the cost of executing all the contracts needed to cover the payment schedule present a rather unattractive picture.

A Portfolio Approach to Managing Foreign Exchange Risk

Chapter 7 discussed the trend toward use of a currency basket or a composite currency in order to stabilize exchange rates. At the private level, the corporate treasurer can build currency portfolios to meet the needs of the corporation in much the way that a portfolio manager assembles stocks to meet different objectives.

Table 8.14 shows the interest yield and exchange rate gain for a 3-month Eurodollar deposit in six major currencies and gold. The data show that, in addition to the interest income, an investor gains through appreciation of the foreign currency in relation to the dollar. The different rates of appreciation of each currency with respect to the dollar are reflected in the relative amounts of the annual average exchange rate gains. These annual rates represent the mean values of the fluctuations of each foreign currency with respect to the dollar. The highest return would have been earned by investing in the Japanese yen (an average annual exchange rate gain of 8.6 percent) and the smallest return from the French franc (0.6 percent average annual gain).

Corporate treasurers in multinational corporations who have to deal in a variety of currencies cannot avoid the responsibility of choosing currencies that will maximize the return on corporate investment within acceptable levels of risk. The corporate treasurer is in essence the portfolio manager of the corporation's currency basket. Therefore, the corporate criteria governing the trade-off between risk and return need to be specified if the portfolio is to reflect corporate objectives.

Two strategic approaches to currency management have emerged—prediction and risk-minimization. The prediction approach to currency management

Table 8.14   Dollar Yield on 3-Month Eurodeposits: Equivalent Annual Average Rates of Return

| | | Dollar Yield | | |
	Interest	Exchange Rate Gain	Total (Interest Plus Exchange Rate Gain)	In Real Terms[a]
3-month Eurodeposits				
U.S. dollar	10.3	0.0	10.3	−1.0
German mark	5.7	3.6	9.5	−1.7
Swiss franc	2.8	7.4	10.4	−0.9
Japanese yen	6.0	8.6	15.0	3.2
British pound	12.4	7.8	21.1	8.7
French franc	11.1	0.6	11.8	0.4
Gold	—	—	39.1	24.9
SDRs[b]				
Official: actual[c]	5.7	1.6	7.4	−3.6
new[c]	5.7	2.6	8.4	−2.7
100% of formula interest,[d] set				
With 3-month lag	8.1	2.6	10.9	−0.4
With 3-week lag	8.2	2.6	11.0	−0.3
Without lag	8.4	2.6	11.3	0.0
Private Euro-SDR[e]	9.4	2.6	12.2	0.7

Source: Morgan Guaranty Trust Company of New York, *World Financial Markets*, (April 1981).

[a] Dollar yield deflated by increase in industrial countries' wholesale prices of manufactured goods.

[b] Exchange rate is that of the new official five-currency unit, except line 8: the old 16-currency formulation through December 1980.

[c] Interest rate as on creditor positions in IMF SDR account, i.e., 60% of formula through December 1978, 72% subsequently through April 1981. From May 1981 the remuneration rate will be 85% of formula.

[d] The formula is weighted 42% U.S. dollar, 19% German mark, 13% each Japanese yen, British pound, and French franc on short-term domestic market rates in the five countries.

[e] Interest rate implied by total return on SDR basket components invested in 3-month Euromarket deposits.

presumes that exchange rates are predictable. Investment returns can be maximized, it is held, through prediction of the future value of the rate of exchange of the designated currencies. The risk-minimization approach emphasizes the magnitude of risk in exposed positions and the difficulty of controlling those risks. The goal of this approach, then, is to minimize risk exposure, which in turn results in higher income and return on investment.

If exchange rates could be accurately predicted, risk could be automatically minimized. Exchange rate markets have been known to be efficient in disseminating all the information considered relevant to the determination of exchange rates, with all traders informed simultaneously. To forecast exchange rates accurately, all the necessary information must be obtained in advance. However, since all this information cannot be known with any degree of accuracy in advance, attempts to forecast exchange rates have met with varying success.

Two basic characteristics of exchange rates do help forecasters to make predictions with some degree of confidence. First, some exchange rates move together in a highly correlated manner. For example, the deutsche mark and the Dutch gulden are highly correlated with the U.S. dollar. Using this relationship, forecasters can predict with a high degree of accuracy that, if the deutsche mark rises against the U.S. dollar, the Dutch gulden will also. In general, countries whose economies are closely linked tend to have currencies that are highly correlated. The close linkage of the economies of the EEC members, for example, results in a high correlation among their currencies, and a high correlation is built into currency systems such as the Snake.

Second, some exchange rates fluctuate more than others, as shown in Table 8.14. This volatility can be factored into a currency portfolio.

Minimizing Risk through Portfolio Construction

Risk can be defined as a measure of the variability in the rate of return of an asset or a portfolio of assets. Given the probability distribution, two measures can be computed: (1) the expected value of the return, or the mean, and (2) the variability of return as measured by the variance, or the standard deviation, which is the square root of the variance. With the aid of the mean and the standard deviation, the corporate treasurer or the manager of an international asset portfolio can develop portfolio-building rules for the selection of currencies.

The corporate treasurer can assemble any combination of currencies into portfolios to reflect the corporation's desired risk exposure. An alternative to assembling portfolios every time a company wishes to protect its foreign assets against foreign exchange risk is to use the "private SDR." (The SDR is the unit of account for IMF transactions.) The value of the SDR is determined from a basket of currencies, the number in which was reduced from 16 to 5 when it was made the same as the SDR interest rate basket as of January 1, 1981. The SDR currency basket is in fact a portfolio comprising the five international currencies in which the majority of world trade and investment takes place. The portfolio composition of the SDR is presented in Table 8.15. The initial weights for the five currencies were based on the value of the exports of goods and services of each country and the amounts of their currencies officially held by members of the IMF over the 5 years from 1975 through 1979. The value of the SDR in each currency is calculated daily. The composition of the SDR currency basket will be revised every 5 years beginning January 1, 1986.

The reduction of the SDR currency basket to five currencies facilitates the use of the SDR for denomination of private assets and liabilities. Transactions denominated in SDRs automatically have the effect of portfolio diversification among the five currencies making up the SDR currency basket. The SDR offers

Table 8.15   Portfolio Composition of the SDR Currency Basket

Currency	Units of Currency	Percentage Weights as of January 2, 1981	April 23, 1981
U.S. dollar	0.54	42	44.6
Deutsche mark	0.46	19	17.7
Japanese yen	34.00	13	13.1
British pound	0.071	13	12.8
French franc	0.74	13	11.9

Source: IMF, *Annual Report 1981*; IMF and the World Bank, *Finance and Development*, Vol. 18, No. 1 (March 1981).

some investors, or borrowers, an opportunity to reduce the exchange risk arising from fluctuations in individual currencies. The variability of the overall rate of return from holding an SDR-denominated asset, as measured by the standard deviation of the total yield, is likely to be substantially less than the variability of holding an asset denominated in a single foreign currency.

Table 8.16 shows the variability of the nominal yield measured as quarter-to-quarter standard deviations on total yield from three perspectives: on a U.S. dollar basis from the perspective of a U.S. resident, on a deutsche mark basis from the perspective of a West German resident, and on the SDR basis from the universal perspective of a world resident. The variability from the SDR perspective was in all cases smaller than either single currency perspective. The standard deviation of the SDR portfolio (lines 8 through 13) was substantially smaller than the standard deviation of 100 percent investment in the individual currencies (lines 1 through 6).

The historical risk/return relationship of three portfolios of currencies (portfolio I representing the SDR, portfolio II 100 percent the British pound, and portfolio III 100 percent the Japanese yen) is shown in Table 8.17. Portfolios II and III have higher returns but more risk (standard deviation) than portfolio I.

Investors and borrowers can obtain protection from exchange rate fluctuations by assembling their own currency portfolios or by the use of covered hedges in the forward markets, but government regulations in some cases limit access to foreign capital markets. The use of SDR-denominated instruments avoids that problem and has several other advantages, such as convenience, savings in transaction costs, and the substantially lower variability in yield providing for greater stability of yield. The SDR further provides for passive management of foreign currency portfolios.

Using the Portfolio Approach

The portfolio approach is especially useful to the treasurer or the currency portfolio manager of a multinational corporation who has to work with a variety of currencies on a daily basis. The two basic decisions that must be made in using this approach are the selection of the best mix of currencies and

Table 8.16   Volatility of Total Yield Measured as Quarter-to-Quarter Standard Deviation

	Dollar Yield[a]	Variability of Nominal Yield, from Perspective of		
	Total (Interest plus Exchange Rate Gain)	U.S. Resident (US$ basis)	German Resident (DM basis)	World Resident (SDR basis)
3-month Eurodeposits				
U.S. dollar	10.3	3.7	25.3	11.3
German mark	9.5	20.1	2.4	12.6
Swiss franc	10.4	35.0	18.5	24.6
Japanese yen	15.0	31.7	35.2	25.4
British pound	21.1	18.5	21.6	14.0
French franc	11.8	17.7	10.4	10.9
Gold	39.1	155.8	139.1	147.0
SDRs[b]				
Official: actual[c]	7.4	10.6	14.7	5.1
new[c]	8.4	8.9	15.1	1.8
100% of formula interest,[d] set				
With 3-month lag	10.9	8.9	16.0	2.3
With 3-week lag	11.0	9.0	16.0	2.5
Without lag	11.3	8.8	16.2	2.5
Private Euro-SDR[e]	12.2	8.8	16.6	2.9

Source: Morgan Guaranty Trust Company of New York, *World Financial Markets* (April 1981).

[a] Dollar yield deflated by increase in industrial countries' wholesale prices of manufactured goods.

[b] Exchange rate is that of the new official five-currency unit, except line 8: the old sixteen-currency formulation through December 1980.

[c] Interest rate as on creditor positions in IMF SDR account, i.e., 60% of formula through December 1978, 72% subsequently through April 1981. From May 1981 the remuneration rate will be 85% of formula.

[d] The formula is weighted 42% U.S. dollar, 19% German mark, 13% each Japanese yen, British pound, and French franc on short-term domestic market rates in the five countries.

[e] Interest rate implied by total return on SDR basket components invested in 3-month Euromarket deposits.

the proportion of each currency in the basket in order to produce the lowest possible risk and the best possible return. A process has been demonstrated in the preceding section by which the right combinations of currencies in the basket can be narrowed down; a manager could also use a trial-and-error technique to select an optimal currency portfolio.

Table 8.17   Risk and Return from Diversifying Currency Portfolios: A Comparison of an SDR Portfolio of Five Currencies and 100 Percent Portfolios in the British Pound and the Japanese Yen

	I (%)	II (%)	III (%)
U.S. dollars	20		
Japanese yen	20		100
British pound	20	100	
Swiss franc	20		
Deutsche mark	20		
French franc	20		
Portfolio Return[a]	12.2	21.1	15.0
Standard Deviation[b]	8.8	18.5	31.7
Standard Deviation[c]	2.9	14.0	25.4

Source: Table 8.15.
[a] Total dollar yield (interest plus exchange rate gain).
[b] U.S. dollar basis.
[c] SDR basis.

The historical data on the volatility of exchange rate movements show some relative stability between currency rates, which limits some of the need for frequent revision of the portfolio. However, currency portfolio managers would be well advised to subject their portfolios to a steady review process to guard against significant change in the risk profile of the portfolio.

SUMMARY

Foreign exchange exposure may be defined, in an economic sense, as the amount of gain or loss in value to which a transaction or investment abroad is exposed as a result of fluctuations in foreign exchange rates. Any U.S. business is exposed to the possibility of gains or losses from fluctuations in the foreign exchange rate whenever it is involved in commercial transactions that are de-nominated in a foreign currency.

The effect of the foreign exchange movement on the foreign currency equivalent of a dollar-denominated contract value is called the transaction exposure. Transaction exposure arises in international trade activities and in international borrowing and lending.

Multinational corporations have branches, subsidiaries, and affiliates in foreign countries whose activities produce income streams in their local currencies which must be converted to dollars when remitted to the parent company. The effect of changes in the foreign exchange rate on the dollar value of the income stream generated by an investment in a foreign country, as well as the value of the investment itself, is called economic exposure. The effect of foreign exchange rate changes on the value of the shareholders' investment, as measured by the economic exposure, will depend on the magnitude of the change in the foreign exchange rate (or the amount of devaluation or revaluation), changes in the operations of the subsidiary resulting from the change in the exchange rate, and the price elasticity of demand for the entity's product.

Translation exposure is essentially an accounting concept that refers to the restatement of revenue, expenses, assets, and liabilities of a foreign subsidiary from the foreign currency into U.S. dollars (or other home currency of the parent company) so that the accounts can be incorporated into the accounts kept in the home currency. The accounting convention selected for translation purposes affects the size of the exposure. Under the monetary/nonmonetary approach, the monetary assets and liabilities are translated at the exchange rate prevailing at the date of translation, and the nonmonetary (or physical) assets and liabilities are translated at historic rates of exchange. In this method of translation, therefore, only the monetary assets and liabilities would be exposed to gain or loss resulting from changes in the exchange rate.

Three options are available to the parent corporation in managing its exposed net asset or net liability position: (1) take no action to protect the exposed position, (2) hedge on a before-tax basis, or (3) hedge on an after-tax basis. The use of a hedge to protect an exposed position does entail costs, however, and the corporation has to make a careful decision about whether the risk of loss from foreign exchange fluctuations is worth the cost of the hedge.

Other hedging techniques and strategies available for use in managing foreign exchange exposure include the long-term currency swap, foreign currency loans, back-to-back forward contracts, and the use of currency portfolios.

SUPPLEMENTARY READING

Chemical Bank Multinational Cash Management Group, *Foreign Exchange Exposure Management* (New York: Chemical Bank, 1972).

Richard Ensor and Boris Antl, eds., *The Management of Foreign Exchange Risk* (London: Euromoney Publications Ltd., 1978).

Newton H. Hoyt, Jr., "The Management of Currency Exchange Risk by the Singer Company," *Financial Management*, Vol. 1, No. 1 (Spring 1972), pp. 1–3.

Gail Lieberman, "A Systems Approach to Foreign Exchange Risk Management," *Financial Executive*, Vol. 46, No. 12 (December 1978), pp. 14–19.

NOTES

1 "Multinational" corporation refers to a firm in which the ownership, and generally the management, of the foreign assets are primarily in the hands of those of the same nationality as the parent company. The trend recently has been toward "transnational" enterprises, in which ownership and management of foreign assets are spread among the different nationalities performing the organization's business.

2   Alan C. Shapiro, "Hedging against Devaluations—A Management Science Approach," in C. G. Alexandrides, ed., *International Business Systems Perspectives* (Atlanta: Georgia State University, 1972).

3   Bernard A. Lietaer, "Managing Risks in Foreign Exchange," *Harvard Business Review*, Vol. 48, No. 2 (March-April 1970), pp. 127–138.

4   Alan C. Shapiro and Thomas S. Robertson, "Managing Foreign Exchange Risks: The Role of Marketing Strategy," University of Pennsylvania Working Paper (1975); and Frederick W. Meierjohann, "How a Currency Index Can Help the Hedger," *Euromoney* (October 1980), pp. 245–250.

5   Stanley C. Waldner, "Can Corporate Foreign Exchange Exposures Be Managed for Profits?" *Euromoney* (June 1979), pp. 89–100.

6   Alex O. Williams, "Balance of Payments Disequilibrium and the Prediction of Parity Changes among Currencies," The Colgate Darden Graduate School of Business Administration, University of Virginia, DSWP-79-19 (1979).

7   Boris Antl and Ralph J. Massey, "The Hedger Has to Handle a Three-Pronged Fork," *Euromoney* (January 1979), pp. 99–103.

8   Boris Antl and Albert C. Henry, "The Cost and Implications of Two Hedging Techniques," *Euromoney* (June 1979), pp. 82–87.

9   Robert B. Shulman, "Are Foreign Exchange Risks Measurable?" *Columbia Journal of World Business*, Vol. 5, No. 3 (May-June 1970), pp. 55–60.

10 Steven W. Kohlhagen, "Evidence on the Cost of Forward Cover in a Floating System," *Euromoney* (September 1975), pp. 138–141; and "The Performance of the Foreign Exchange Markets: 1971-1974," *Journal of International Business Studies*, Vol. 6, No. 2 (Fall 1975).

11 Joseph A. Wemhoff, "The Long Term Currency Swap," *The Management of Foreign Exchange Risk* (London: Euromoney Publications Ltd., 1978), pp. 80–84.

12 Johan W. Fokkema, "Back to Back Forwards," *The Management of Foreign Exchange Risk* (London, Euromoney Publications Ltd., 1978), pp. 85–87.

13 Joseph M. Burns, *Accounting Standards and International Finance* (Washington, D.C.: American Enterprise Institute, June 1976).

3

Financing International Trade and Investment

9

Offshore Banking and the International Capital Markets

International banking mobilizes capital for international investment by facilitating the movement of capital from countries with surplus savings to borrowers in capital-deficit countries. Higher yields are obtained from loans made to borrowers in capital-deficit countries than would be obtained by investing the capital in a capital-surplus country. By providing the facilities for this capital movement, international banking creates liquidity in the international capital markets and contributes to overall efficiency of worldwide markets.

The international capital markets provide facilities for qualified borrowers to obtain capital from outside their country of residence. This is called offshore borrowing. The borrowers that participate in the international capital markets are (1) industrial and commercial firms, (2) financial institutions, (3) governments and government-related agencies, and (4) international institutions.

Multinational corporations (MNCs) are the main type of industrial and commercial firm involved in offshore borrowing; other kinds of firms participate in international trade to a lesser extent. Firms in need of capital funds can borrow directly from international banking syndicates, or they can issue bonds in the international market. Corporate borrowers in the international market have to compete for available funds with banks, governments, and government agencies, as well as with international institutions. The market therefore prefers to deal with high-quality corporate borrowers who are comparable, to some degree, in creditworthiness to the other participants in the market. A large portion of the total volume of bond issues is made up of the issues of high-quality corporate borrowers.

Since 1960 international banking has grown at an exceptionally rapid pace. Between 1964 and 1978 the growth rate of international bank loans averaged around 25 percent per year. The international lending market is estimated to have passed the $2 trillion mark in 1980.[1] In 1978 outstanding debt claims in the market exceeded $1.3 trillion and in 1979 amounted to an estimated $1.7 trillion.

The largest portion of outstanding debt claims is made up of interbank lending, and a significant portion of the interbank lending takes place among the head office, branches, and subsidiaries of the same bank. This lending thus represents intra-institutional claims and liabilities. Banks make use of interbank transactions to square their positions in the foreign exchange and domestic markets. Another kind of interbank transaction is loans by banks to other banks, which redeposit the funds. This process continues from bank to bank until the funds are deployed as a loan to a nonbank borrower.

Interbank lending accounts for approximately 70 percent of the total outstanding claims in the international lending market; lending to nonbank borrowers accounts for the remaining 30 percent. In 1978, lending to the nonbank segment of the market passed the $450 billion mark. This segment of the market is estimated to have exceeded $650 billion in 1980. Expressed in 1964 dollars, this nonbank segment grew at an average rate of 20 percent between 1964 and 1978. Industrial and commercial corporations along with governments are the principal constituents of the nonbank segment of the borrowing market. This segment is the most important part of the international lending market, because it is made up of ultimate borrowers, who employ the borrowed capital for productive investment purposes.

Sterling's study of the international lending market[2] revealed that international lending by commercial banks is much more widespread than previously realized. He identified 58 countries in which commercial banks were involved in international lending. Of all the countries and sectors of the international lending market, the Eurocapital markets[3] are the dominant in size and importance.

THE EUROCAPITAL MARKETS

Two markets make up what is generally called the Eurocapital markets:[4] the Eurocurrency market and the Eurobond market. The Eurocurrency market and the Eurobond market are the most active sectors of the Eurocapital markets. A large part of the growth in international lending from 1964 to 1980 took place in the Eurocurrency market—the largest segment of the Eurocapital markets. A third market, the Euroequity market, is much less important.

The Eurocurrency Market

A U.S. firm obtains a dollar loan from the London branch of a U.S. commercial bank. Another U.S. firm obtains a dollar loan from a British bank in London.

The two U.S. firms have received what is termed a Eurocurrency bank credit. A Eurocurrency bank credit is a loan in a currency that is not native to the country in which the bank office making the loan is located. Classification as a Eurocurrency loan, then, does not depend on where the loan is made; a Eurocurrency loan can be made in any country. Whether the loan is called a Eurocurrency loan depends on the currency in which the loan is made—the currency must not be that of the country in which the lending commercial bank is situated.

Eurocurrency markets are not limited to the geographical area of Europe, but include all countries where this type of lending takes place. The Eurocurrency market currently includes foreign currency liabilities and claims of banks in the major European countries, plus the Bahamas, Bahrain, the Cayman Islands, Panama, Canada, Japan, Hong Kong, and Singapore.[5]

Commercial banks operating in the Eurocurrency markets have combined to meet the growing need for large-size loans by forming consortia and syndicates. Through these forms of organization the risk in each transaction is spread among the participants.

The Eurodollar Market

Eurodollar transactions—Eurocurrency loans denominated in dollars—make up, on the average, 75 percent of the gross volume of transactions in the Eurocurrency markets. The dominant position of the Eurodollar in the Eurocurrency market reflects the role of the U.S. dollar as the single most important currency in international trade and investment; a major portion of international trade is denominated in dollars.

The Eurodollar market originated when dollar deposits were transferred by the Soviet Union and East European countries from New York to London in the 1950s to preclude any attempt by the U.S. government to embargo or sequester their dollar balances. Faced by an ailing pound sterling and exchange controls on the movement of the pound sterling out of Britain for export trade financing, the ingenious British banking system soon devised a way of utilizing these idle dollar deposits to finance British exports. So began the Eurodollar market.

Then, large deficits in the U.S. balance of payments provided foreigners with increasing dollar claims on the U.S., payments for which were deposited with banks in the Eurocurrency market area. These deposits in turn increased the liquidity of the Eurodollar market. Interbank lending among banks in the Eurocurrency system produced geometrical increases in the size of the Eurodollar market. With no reserve requirements, the potential increase is nearly infinite, since each dollar can theoretically be lent from bank to bank almost endlessly. In practice, however, the potential increase is far from infinite.

The real impetus to the rapid growth of the Eurodollar market came in the mid-1960s, when the United States moved to restrain the outflow of dollars for portfolio and direct investment abroad; this move resulted in U.S. banks shifting to an offshore base for their international activities. Offshore lending then replaced portfolio investment as a source of capital for the European borrowers who needed dollars to augment shortfalls in savings in their respective countries.

The rapid growth of the Eurodollar market has sprung also from its lack of regulations on borrowing and lending transactions, which lends flexibility and freedom from constraints to offshore transactions.

An interest equalization tax enacted by the Kennedy administration in 1962 attempted to stem dollar outflows by taxing away the yield differential that U.S. investors were obtaining in securities of foreign borrowers. Foreigners needed credit financing from the United States, which had a capital surplus during the period, and were willing to offer high yields to investors in the United States. When the interest equalization tax removed the incentive to invest in foreign securities, the need for credit financing was met through bank loans to the foreigners. Thus the flow of capital from the United States continued unabated in a different form.

Then in 1965 the Federal Reserve Board instituted the Voluntary Foreign Credit Restraint (VFCR) program, which put ceilings on the amount of loans by member banks of the Federal Reserve System to foreigners. The Board of Governors of the Federal Reserve imposed restrictions on corporations engaged in foreign banking and financing under the Federal Reserve Act by amending Section 211.8 of Regulation K. Effective February 8, 1968, U.S. banks and financing institutions organized as Edge Act and Agreement corporations must obtain prior specific consent of the Federal Reserve Board before making equity investments in a foreign business. In 1966 and 1969, when interest rates rose significantly under inflationary pressures, these Regulation Q interest ceilings became operative, limiting the rise in interest rates. Accordingly, corporations moved their certificate of deposit (CD) funds from their U.S. commercial bank accounts to deposit accounts in London, where higher interest rates were being paid. Further controls were imposed on foreign investments by the President of the United States under Executive Order 11387 (January 1, 1968, 33 F.R. 47) prohibiting U.S. citizens owning 10 percent or more of a foreign business venture from engaging in transfer of capital abroad without prior approval of the Secretary of Commerce. All ownings from these foreign investments, and short-term financial assets abroad (including bank deposits), were required to be repatriated to the United States. Under the Commerce Department's Foreign Direct Investment Regulations, the Secretary of Commerce exempted banks and other financial institutions from the requirements.

U.S. commercial banks expanded the operations of their branches and affiliates in London, and increasingly used these facilities to book their dollar loans. The loans were financed with dollar deposits made in the branches and affiliates in London. The London branches of U.S. commercial banks were not subject to reserve requirements of the Bank of England and therefore had a competitive advantage over their British counterparts. Eurodollar operations proved very profitable for the U.S. banking affiliates, and the Eurodollar market grew rapidly.[6]

Size of the Eurocurrency Market

Table 9.1 presents data on the size of the Eurocurrency market. The data are estimates derived from information obtained by Morgan Guaranty Trust Company of New York from a number of sources. In addition, the Organization for Economic Cooperation and Development (OECD) has begun compiling statistics on the Eurocurrency markets, which are published in the monthly OECD *Financial Statistics*. The gross size of the Eurocurrency market in 1980 was $1,515 billion, up from $145 billion in 1971. This represents an eightfold growth over the 10-year period. The growth of the market is even more dramatic from a 1965 base, when its gross size was $24 billion; the gross Euromarket volume in 1980 was 51 times the 1965 level.

"Gross" size in Table 9.1 means the total volume of activity in the market, including both the claims and liabilities of the banking community. Banks borrow funds from other banks to meet their lending needs. These loans between banks are included in "gross" volume of the Euromarket. Lending between banks within the Eurocurrency market, however, effectively cancels out, since the claim of one bank represents the liability of another bank within the market. Thus, gross size includes some double-counting, which should be net-

Table 9.1   Size of the Eurocurrency Market (Billions of dollars, rounded to nearest $5 billion)

| Year | Eurocurrency Market[a] | | | Eurodollars as Percentage of Gross Liabilities in All Euro-currencies |
| | Gross ($) | Claims ($)[b] | | |
		Net	On Nonbanks[c]	
1971	145	85	35	76
1972	210	110	45	78
1973	315	160	70	74
1974	395	220	105	76
1975	485	255	130	78
1976	595	320	165	80
1977	740	390	210	76
1978	950	495	265	74
1979	1,220	615	325	72
1980	1,515	755	400	74

Source: Morgan Guaranty Trust Company of New York, *World Financial Markets* (February 1982) p. 11.

[a] The Eurocurrency market is defined as the foreign currency liabilities and claims on banks in major European countries, plus the Bahamas, Bahrain, the Cayman Islands, Panama, Canada, Japan, Hong Kong, and Singapore.

[b] Gross size of market minus volume of interbank lending.

[c] Primarily to business.

Table 9.2   Distribution of Eurocurrency Bank Credits by Type of Country (Million of dollars)

Type	1977	1978	1979	1980
Industrial countries	$17,205	$28,952	$27,248	$39,450
Developing countries	20,976	37,300	47,964	35,034
NonOPEC	13,494	26,902	35,411	23,535
OPEC	7,481	10,398	12,553	11,499
Communist countries	3,394	3,767	7,325	2,809
International institutions[a]	190	160	275	429
Total	$41,765	$70,179	$82,812	$77,722

Source: Morgan Guaranty, *op. cit.*

ted out (see the "Net" column in Table 9.1). (In the U.S. market, interbank lending, which occurs in the Federal Funds market, is not counted as part of the banking system lending process in calculating the money supply.)

Net claims grew ninefold over the 10-year period—from $85 billion in 1971 to $755 billion in 1980. (In 1965, net claims were a mere $17 million.) "Net claims" includes claims on nonbanks, claims on central banks, claims on banks outside the Eurocurrency market area, and conversion of Eurofunds into domestic currencies by banks in the market area.

Eurocurrency loans to business firms make up the major part of "claims on nonbanks." As shown, this segment increased eightfold from 1971 to 1979. The size of these outstanding obligations of business firms is indicative of the importance of the Eurocurrency market as a source of financing for business investment and working capital purposes.

The last column in Table 9.1 shows how much of the gross Eurocurrency liabilities are denominated in Eurodollars. As can be seen, most Eurocurrency loans throughout the period have been denominated in dollars. Eurodollar claims reached a high of 79 percent in 1976, but fell to 72 percent in 1979.

The distribution of Eurocurrency bank credits by type of country is shown in Table 9.2. The representation of industrialized countries is falling, while that of the developing countries is rising. NonOPEC developing countries have experienced the fastest growth in receipt of Eurocurrency bank credits, followed by the Communist countries.

The Syndicated Credit Market

Individual banks make loans for small amounts on a short-term basis, and foreign branches or affiliates of U.S. commercial banks normally make loans or provide lines of credit for subsidiaries or affiliates of U.S. multinational corporations or other U.S. companies abroad. A guarantee by a parent corporation of a loan to one of its subsidiaries or affiliates can enable a single bank to provide more financing over a longer period than would be possible without the guarantee. But normally Eurocurrency loans for large amounts and for medium-term maturities are made by syndicates.

In the 1980 medium-term Eurocredit markets, new loans approached $78 billion. The longest maturity on outstanding loans of $50 million and over is 15 years, while the average maturity is 9 years. The lowest spread (between the rate on the loan and the London interbank rate) on loans of $50 million dollars and over is ⅜ of a percent. OECD borrowing made up to 55 percent of the total medium-term Eurocredit market loans.

The majority of loans are larger than $25 million, and the average size of these loans is $113 million. These large loans are made by syndicates. Syndicated loans as large as $1.5 billion have been raised by the French Treasury. Credito (Italy) and the Electricity Council (United Kingdom) have raised $1.0 billion each in syndicated loans in recent years.

U.S. domestic banks also usually form syndicates to make large loans. Loans made by U.S. domestic syndicates are called domestic multibank floating-rate term loans. Rates on these loans are tied to the prime rate or to the cost of funds to a lender.[7]

Each bank member of a syndicate contributes to the loan. In this way the commitment of each participating bank remains relatively small, risk is spread, and each participant's exposure is minimized.

Eurocurrency syndicates began in the early 1970s for several reasons. The loan requirements of national and multinational corporations and government borrowers had grown beyond the servicing capacity of any individual bank. A syndicate could mobilize the financial resources of its member banks to provide a readily available source of funds for large borrowers. Many of the large loans were for special purposes involving some degree of risk. Syndication allowed the banks to spread the risk of these large loans among the members.

Banks like to participate in a syndicate for a number of reasons. Member banks of a syndicate develop certain types of working relationships and modes of helpful cooperation. In addition, regional banks and other smaller banks have an opportunity to participate in international banking on a scale that would otherwise not be available to them. Participation in a large syndicated loan bestows a certain amount of favorable publicity on the participating banks. For the syndicate leader, the management fees provide an attractive income.

Because a syndicate has many participants, the loan must be packaged differently from the structuring of a direct loan: the syndicate leader must satisfy the other participating banks as well as the borrower.

Syndicated loans are generally of medium-term maturity—up to 15 years. They carry a floating interest rate quoted as a spread from the London interbank offered rate (Libor). London is the center of the Eurocurrency syndicated loan market. The rate is adjusted periodically—usually every 3 or 6 months. The syndicate is managed by a lead bank which has the responsibility for negotiating the terms of the loan with the borrower. The loan terms include the maturity of the loan, the amortization schedule, allowable grace period, the applicable interest rate, the various restrictive covenants that will govern the loan, and other conditions, including repayment terms.

There are three parties to Eurocurrency syndications: the borrower, the participating banks (the lenders), and the syndicate leader. The syndicate leader

Table 9.3   Ranking of Banks Selected as Lead Manager in Eurocurrency Loan Syndicates (By amount of loans signed during first half 1980; amounts in millions)

Rank	Bank	Number of Loans	Amount ($m)
1	Chase Manhattan	46	$1,740.72
2	Bank of America	31	1,546.82
3	Bank of Montreal	22	1,104.67
4	Citicorp	25	1,100.16
5	Credit Lyonnais	41	1,053.05
6	National Westminster	21	1,046.00
7	Lloyds	26	816.53
8	Société Générale de Banque Group	18	604.05
9	Morgan Guaranty	11	602.05
10	Société Générale	19	601.28
11	Kredietbank International Group	7	579.75
12	Bank of Nova Scotia	14	577.94
13	Royal Bank of Canada	16	569.33
14	Credit Suisse First Boston	5	562.16
15	Bank Bumiputra Malaysia	3	555.00
16	Schroder Wagg	6	537.30
17	Bankers Trust	14	533.78
18	Merrill Lynch	4	529.25
19	Dresdner Bank	16	514.32
20	Canadian Imperial Bank of Commerce	11	514.31
21	Midland	18	494.51
22	Banque Nationale de Paris	15	478.90
23	Shearson Loeb Rhoades Int'l.	7	442.00
24	DG Bank	13	430.06
25	Toronto Dominion	8	423.76
26	Credit Commercial de France	10	388.32
27	Manufacturers Hanover	16	380.74
28	First National Bank of Chicago	14	376.83
29	Banque de Paris et des Pays-Bas	5	376.25
30	Banque Bruxelles Lambert	2	355.00
31	Credit Agricole	8	347.32
32	National Bank of Canada	6	338.56
33	Deutsche Bank	11	317.11
34	West-LB	12	305.01
35	Fuji Bank	9	298.94
36	American Express	12	292.67
37	Barclays	12	289.49

Table 9.3 (*continued*)

Rank	Bank	Number of Loans	Amount ($m)
38	SG Warburg	5	280.00
39	Hill Samuel	7	272.33
40	Wells Fargo	5	255.79
41	Hambros	7	240.86
42	Grindlays	11	197.56
43	Orion	8	196.24
44	Chemical Bank	9	195.77
45	Commerzbank	8	182.09
46	Gulf International Bank	9	181.66
47	Standard Chartered	8	173.47
48	Dai-Ichi Kangyo Bank	3	167.50
49	Amsterdam-Rotterdam Bank	8	165.54
50	Libra Bank	7	160.89

Source: Euromoney Syndication Service, *Euromoney* (August 1980), p. 78.

performs the functions of a conventional broker or agency for the syndicate, and works with the borrower in structuring the loan. The structuring process involves drawing up the terms of the loan contract to meet the borrower's needs and market conditions. Responsibility for ensuring that the borrower's needs and circumstances are carefully considered involves a full credit analysis of the borrower and a full appraisal of the risk factors involved in the loan transaction.

For larger loans, most syndicates increasingly use several lead banks, which serve as a management syndicate for the whole syndicate (they receive a fee for these management services). This trend has resulted in a race within the banking community to become lead managers. Table 9.3 presents the ranking of lead managers for Eurocurrency syndicated loans signed during the first half of 1980. The rankings provide a guide for corporate managers seeking a lead bank for a Eurocurrency loan. Any of the top 50 banks listed would provide adequate and satisfactory services. For small loans, a single bank may handle the request.

As a group, U.S. banks dominate the Eurocurrency lending market. Note in Table 9.3, for example, that there are 14 U.S. banks in the top 50 lead banks; Chase Manhattan and Bank of America hold the first and second places in the rankings, and Citicorp is fourth after the Bank of Montreal. Changes in the relative market share of the banking community in each of the leading countries are shown in Figure 9.1. U.S. banks' share of the growing market declined in

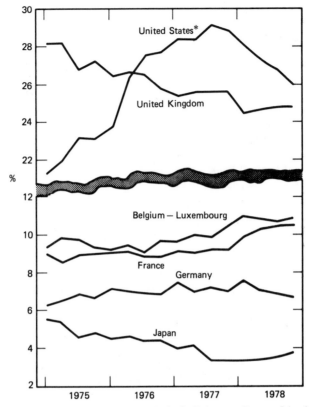

*Includes offshore branches of United States banks in the Bahamas, Cayman Islands, and Panama; after 1975 includes also branches in Hong Kong and Singapore.

Figure 9.1 Eurocurrency Lending: Market Share of Banks in the Leading Eurocurrency Market Cousntries, 1975–1978; percentage. (Source: Bank of International Settlement.)

1977 and 1978. The United Kingdom's share seems to have stabilized and may be increasing.

Is the recent decline in the United States' share of the Eurocurrency lending market a temporary phenomenon or a structural change in the market? Factors other than loan demand in the international bank credit market, such as the strength of U.S. domestic credit demand and the constraints imposed on U.S. banks' foreign lending by the Federal Reserve Board and other regulating agencies, are believed to contribute to the apparent decline of the U.S. market share. When the Eurocredit market cycle turns up again, and profitability conditions improve, the share of U.S. banks is expected also to turn upward.

Table 9.4 presents the 14 top-ranked U.S. bank lead managers in the Eurocurrency syndicated loan rankings. The 14 leading banks account for the major portion of U.S. bank lending in the Eurocurrency syndicated loan market.

Table 9.4   Rankings of U.S. Banks Selected as Lead Manager of Eurocurrency Loan Syndicates (By amount of loans signed during first half 1980; amount in millions)

Bank	Rank	Rank in Total Euro-currency Loan Syndicate Market	Loan Number	Loan Amount ($)	Percentage of U.S. Total
Chase Manhattan	1	1	46	1,740.7	21.3
Bank of America	2	2	31	1,546.8	19.0
Citicorp	3	4	25	1,100.1	13.5
Morgan Guaranty	4	9	11	602.0	7.4
Bankers Trust	5	17	14	533.7	6.5
Merrill Lynch	6	18	4	529.2	6.5
Shearson Loeb Rhoades Int'l.	7	23	7	442.0	5.4
Manufacturers Hanover	8	27	16	380.7	4.7
First Chicago	9	28	14	376.8	4.6
American Express	10	36	12	292.6	3.6
Wells Fargo	11	40	5	255.7	3.1
Chemical Bank	12	44	9	195.7	2.4
Continental Illinois	13	78	5	86.7	1.1
Crocker National	14	87	2	72.5	0.9
Total				$8,155.2	100.0

Source: Euromoney Syndication Service, *op. cit.*

International Bond Market

The international bond market is the second major sector of the international capital market. The international bond market is made up of the Eurobond market and the foreign bond market. For a bond to be classified as an international bond it must be sold almost exclusively outside the country of the borrower, in contrast to a domestic bond, which is sold largely in the country of the borrower. When a borrower issues an international bond, however, the "foreign" lenders could include foreign branches and affiliates of banks in the borrower's country.

An international bond may be issued by an international or a national syndicate of banks. When an international syndicate of banks underwrites an international bond issue, that issue is called a Eurobond issue. When an international bond is underwritten by a syndicate of banks in the same country, it is called a foreign bond. A Eurobond issue is not limited to international bonds underwritten by syndicates in the Eurocapital markets; it represents a generic name given to all international bond issues underwritten by an international syndicate of banks. The Eurobond market is the largest and the dominant market for international bonds, which is why the name is applied to all international bond issues underwritten by an international syndicate of banks.

Table 9.5 presents a recent ranking of the top 18 lead managers of the international bond market syndicates. The Deutsche Bank and Credit Suisse First Boston had had the same positions in the year-earlier period. S. G. Warburg, in third place, had been ranked eighth in the first half of 1979, while Morgan Stanley's seventh place represented a decline.

The top lead managers of international syndicates have the facilities to provide counsel and advice to companies who may be planning to issue notes or bonds in the international bond markets. These companies arrange the packaging of issues for borrowers, as well as manage the flotation of the issue.

A breakdown of recent international bond issues by type of borrower and denomination is presented in Table 9.6. Eurobond issues made up approximately 45 percent of the international bond issues from 1975 to 1979 with the exception of 1977 when the Eurobond share rose to 52 percent. Until 1976, the U.S. capital markets provided a larger source of capital for foreign companies and sovereign entities than did foreign countries. A comparison of the foreign bond issues in the United States and outside the United States shows that, since 1977, capital sources in foreign countries have been supplying more capital than the United States, thus reversing the previous long-term trend.

Table 9.5 Rankings of Lead Managers of International Bond Syndicates
(Based on total notes and bonds issued in first half 1980; amounts in millions)

Rank	Manager	Number	Amount ($)	Percentage Share
1	Deutsche Bank	16	1,586.2	18.0
2	Credit Suisse First Boston	14	1,167.2	13.2
3	S. G. Warburg	10	848.0	9.6
4	Paribas	7	788.3	8.9
5	Goldman Sachs	6	735.0	8.3
6	Dresdner Bank	7	720.2	8.1
7	Morgan Stanley	9	705.1	8.0
8	Salomon Brothers	5	600.0	6.8
9	Citicorp	5	442.2	5.0
10	Wood Gundy	6	377.2	4.2
11	Merrill Lynch	6	320.0	3.6
12	Credit Lyonnais	5	284.2	3.2
13	Commerzbank	4	276.7	3.1
14	European Banking Company	3	275.0	3.1
15	Hambros	5	268.6	3.0
16	Credit Commercial de France	3	250.9	2.8
17	West LB	4	221.6	2.5
18	Banque Nationale de Paris	4	215.0	2.4

Source: Euromoney Syndication Service, *op. cit.*

Direct issues by U.S. companies of Eurobonds remained below $1 billion until 1977, but in 1979 Eurobond issues by U.S. companies amounted to almost $3 billion. Issues by U.S. companies during full-1980 may have matched 1979 figures. The Eurobond market is used to a greater extent by the foreign affiliates of U.S. companies than by parent companies. A significant portion of the borrowings by foreign çompanies, in fact, is made up of foreign affiliates of U.S. companies.

On the other hand, U.S. companies have not been very active in the foreign bond market. From Table 9.6, one can see that total issues by U.S. companies amounted to about $200 million in 1978 and 1979 but may have reached the $300 million mark in 1980. Foreign affiliates of U.S. companies have used the foreign bond market more actively than the domestic firms, but comparatively

Table 9.6   International Bond Issues 1974–1980 (Billions of U.S. dollars or equivalent)

Type	1974	1975	1976	1977	1978	1979	1980
International bond issues	$6.9	$19.9	$32.5	$34.0	$34.2	$41.0	$41.9
Eurobond issues	2.1	8.6	14.3	17.8	14.1	18.7	23.9
Borrower							
U.S. companies	0.1	0.3	0.4	1.1	1.1	2.9	4.1
Foreign companies	0.6	2.9	5.3	7.3	4.5	7.2	9.0
State enterprises	0.5	3.1	4.1	4.7	3.3	4.5	5.8
Governments	0.5	1.7	2.2	2.9	3.6	2.4	3.1
International organizations	0.4	0.6	2.2	1.7	1.5	1.7	1.9
Denomination							
U.S. dollar	1.0	3.7	9.1	11.6	7.3	12.6	16.4
Deutsche mark	0.3	2.3	2.7	4.1	5.2	3.6	3.6
Dutch gulden	0.4	0.7	0.5	0.5	0.4	0.5	1.0
Canadian dollar	0.1	1.6	1.4	0.7	—	0.4	0.3
Other	0.4	1.3	0.6	0.9	1.2	1.3	2.5
Foreign bond issues in the United States	3.3	6.5	10.6	7.4	5.8	4.5	3.4
Foreign bond issues outside the United States	1.4	4.9	7.6	8.8	14.3	17.7	14.5
Borrower							
U.S. companies	0.1	0.1	—	—	0.2	0.2	0.3
Foreign companies	0.5	1.4	1.7	1.4	2.1	3.5	3.2
State enterprises	0.6	1.3	2.4	2.4	3.2	3.3	2.8
Governments	0.1	0.8	1.3	2.0	5.8	7.7	4.1
International organizations	0.2	1.4	2.2	2.8	3.1	3.1	4.1
Denomination							
Deutsche mark	0.3	1.1	1.3	2.2	3.7	5.3	4.8
Swiss franc	0.9	3.3	5.4	5.0	5.7	9.7	7.6
Dutch gulden	—	0.2	0.6	0.2	0.3	0.1	0.3
Japanese yen	—	—	0.2	1.3	3.8	1.8	1.1
Other	0.3	0.2	0.1	0.1	0.7	0.7	0.7

Source: Morgan Guaranty Trust Company, *World Financial Markets*, various issues.

less than they have used the Eurobond market. Foreign bond issues by other foreign companies have been correspondingly lower as well. Many foreign companies float domestic bond issues in their respective countries when they want to borrow funds instead of using the foreign bond market.

The participation of developing countries in the international bond markets has been minimal; borrowings in the international bond markets by developing countries amounted to $755 million in 1977, or only 7½ percent of total external bond issues. Their share increased to 12 percent in 1978, reaching $4,159 million, but fell back to 7½ percent in 1979, when the total bond issues of developing countries amounted to only $3,085 million. Their share of new issues in 1980 appears to have remained at the 7½-percent level.[8]

Support for greater access for developing countries to the international bond market is growing. Two recent articles, in *Financial Market Trends* and *Euromoney*, have addressed the question of the accessibility of the international bond markets to developing countries[9] According to OECD statistics, medium- and long-term Eurocredits, Eurobonds, and foreign bonds of developing countries increased from $8 billion in 1973 to $47.6 billion in 1979. Much of the financing was done through medium- and long-term syndicated bank credits. International bond issues accounted for less than 10 percent, except for the years 1976, 1977, and 1978, when their share rose to 10-20 percent.

The World Bank estimates that the annual financing needs of developing countries will increase from $64 billion in 1976 to $280 billion in 1985 and $470 billion in 1990.[10] Since the developing countries require financing to pay for capital projects that represent exports of the industrial countries, alternative sources of financing must be made available to supplement Eurocredits now being used. The World Bank believes that the international bond markets must respond to the financing needs of the developing countries. Fears based on losses experienced in past periods need not preclude investing in these countries in the future; the credit experience of the international banks that have provided the Eurocredits to developing countries should allay such fears.

The Eurobond Market

In 1971, public issues accounted for 79 percent of total Eurobond issues. This percentage has fallen somewhat in the ensuing years; in 1975, for example, public issues accounted for only 62 percent of total Eurobond issues. Conversely, the importance of private placement in Eurobond issues has been increasing over the years. From a mere 25 percent of total issues in 1971, the share of private placement has steadily increased to reach 52 percent in 1974. One factor contributing to the growth of private placement was the introduction of floating rates in some Eurobond issues.

The "tombstone" duplicated as Figure 9.2 is an announcement of a Eurobond sale. Note that IBM Canada Limited has floated a 10½-percent debenture due July 1, 1985, for $50 million (United States): the bond is denominated in U.S. dollars, not Canadian dollars, which makes it an international bond.

IBM

IBM Canada Limited

U.S. $50,000,000
10½% Debentures due July 1, 1985

WOOD GUNDY LIMITED   MORGAN GUARANTY LTD   SALOMON BROTHERS INTERNATIONAL

ALGEMENE BANK NEDERLAND N.V.   A. E. AMES & CO.
Limited   AMSTERDAM-ROTTERDAM BANK N.V.   BANCA COMMERCIALE ITALIANA

BANK OF AMERICA INTERNATIONAL
Limited   THE BANK OF BERMUDA
Limited   BANK LEU INTERNATIONAL
Ltd.   BANK OF TOKYO INTERNATIONAL
Limited

BANQUE BRUXELLES LAMBERT S.A.   BANQUE FRANCAISE DU COMMERCE EXTERIEUR   BANQUE DE L'INDOCHINE ET DE SUEZ

BANQUE NATIONALE DE PARIS   BANQUE DE PARIS ET DES PAYS-BAS   BARCLAYS INTERNATIONAL GROUP   BARING BROTHERS & CO.,
Limited   BERGEN BANK

BERLINER HANDELS- UND FRANKFURTER BANK   CAISSE DES DEPOTS ET CONSIGNATIONS   CHASE MANHATTAN
Limited   CHEMICAL BANK INTERNATIONAL
Limited

CHRISTIANIA BANK OG KREDITKASSE   CIBC LIMITED   CITICORP INTERNATIONAL GROUP   COMMERZBANK
Aktiengesellschaft   COPENHAGEN HANDELSBANK

COUNTY BANK
Limited   CREDITANSTALT-BANKVEREIN   CREDIT COMMERCIAL DE FRANCE   CREDIT LYONNAIS   CREDIT SUISSE FIRST BOSTON
Limited

DEN DANSKE BANK
af 1871 Aktieselskab   DEN NORSKE CREDITBANK   DEUTSCHE BANK
Aktiengesellschaft   DOMINION SECURITIES
Limited   DRESDNER BANK
Aktiengesellschaft

EUROPEAN BANKING COMPANY
Limited   GOLDMAN SACHS INTERNATIONAL CORP.   GREENSHIELDS
Incorporated   GROUPEMENT DES BANQUIERS PRIVÉS GENEVOIS

HAMBROS BANK
Limited   HILL SAMUEL & CO.
Limited   IBJ INTERNATIONAL
Limited   JARDINE FLEMING & COMPANY
Limited   KIDDER, PEABODY INTERNATIONAL
Limited

KLEINWORT, BENSON
Limited   KREDIETBANK N.V.   KUWAIT INTERNATIONAL INVESTMENT CO. S.A.K.   KUWAIT INVESTMENT COMPANY (S.A.K.)

LAZARD BROTHERS & CO.,
Limited   LAZARD FRERES ET CIE.   LLOYDS BANK INTERNATIONAL
Limited   MANUFACTURERS HANOVER
Limited

McLEOD YOUNG WEIR INTERNATIONAL   MERRILL LYNCH INTERNATIONAL & CO.   SAMUEL MONTAGU & CO.
Limited   MORGAN GRENFELL & CO.
Limited

MORGAN GUARANTY PACIFIC
Ltd.   MORGAN STANLEY INTERNATIONAL   NESBITT, THOMSON
Limited   ORION BANK
Limited   PKBANKEN INVESTMENTS
Ltd.   PRIVATBANKEN A/S

N. M. ROTHSCHILD & SONS
Limited   THE ROYAL BANK OF CANADA (LONDON)
Limited   SAUDI INTERNATIONAL BANK
Al-Bank Al-Saudi Al-Alami Limited   J. HENRY SCHRODER WAGG & CO.
Limited

SKANDINAVISKA ENSKILDA BANKEN   SOCIÉTÉ GÉNÉRALE   SOCIÉTÉ GÉNÉRALE DE BANQUE S.A.   STRAUSS, TURNBULL & CO.

SVENSKA HANDELSBANKEN   SWISS BANK CORPORATION (OVERSEAS)
Limited   UNION BANK OF SWITZERLAND (SECURITIES)
Limited

S. G. WARBURG & CO. LTD.   WARDLEY LIMITED   WESTDEUTSCHE LANDESBANK
GIROZENTRALE

July 2, 1980   *All of these Securities have been sold. This announcement appears as a matter of record only.*

Figure 9.2   Eurobond issue announcement. (Source: *The Financial Times*, London, July 2, 1980.)

IBM Canada Ltd., a subsidiary of IBM, is floating this issue in its own name. Notice the IBM logo at the top of the announcement, which indicates the parent company's backing for an issue of one of its subsidiaries.

The bond issue is underwritten by an international syndicate, making it a Eurobond. The syndicate leaders are Wood Gundy Limited, Morgan Guaranty Ltd, and Salomon Brothers International. They have joint responsibility for managing the issue and will share the management fee. The note at the bottom indicates that all the securities involved in the issue had been sold by the time the announcement was made, which attests to the excellent credit rating of IBM and its affiliates worldwide. This issue is a fixed-rate offer. A fixed interest rate means that the bond issue is fixed at a specified rate for the life of the bond and does not vary with Libor as floating rates do.

Floating the Issue   As shown in the IBM Canada Limited example, a Eurobond can be issued by a parent company or by one of its subsidiaries located overseas. Eurobond issues are generally underwritten by an international syndicate of banks. In the IBM Canada issue, the bond issue was denominated in United States dollars and sold in countries other than the country of the currency in which it is denominated. The anonymity of ownership of a Eurobond is preserved, since the bonds are always made in bearer form. An attractive feature is that all interest on a Eurobond is paid without withholding or any other taxes.

A corporation or one of its foreign subsidiaries can float a Eurobond issue by contacting one of the group of banks that operate as managers for Eurobond syndicates. The managing banks, in turn, have a lead bank, which acts as the lead manager for the issue. The lead bank provides advice to the borrowers on how to proceed in packaging the issue and will make all necessary arrangements.

The managing banks, or managers, initiate the process of introducing the issue to the market by inviting other banks and financial institutions, usually by telex, to participate in both underwriting and subscribing to the issue. In underwriting the issue, the managers and the participating banks form the selling group. Members of the selling group subscribe to the issue for their own account and inform their clients by telex of the availability of the issue for subscription. A brief summary of the borrower's characteristics and the terms of the issue are included in communications sent by telex to the underwriting banks. The same basic information is passed on by the underwriting banks to their clients.[11] The terms of the issue include the amount of the issue, the coupon rate, and the price. A coupon is the contractual interest rate paid to the holder of a bond over its life. It is technically called coupon because the bondholder receives a book of coupons which are exchanged for periodic interest payments. A copy of the prospectus, also known as the offering circular, is sent by mail to the underwriter at the time the telex is sent. The underwriter in turn provides copies of the prospectus to those clients who express interest in the issue.

Subscription Period   The subscription period is normally a period of between 7 and 10 days after the issue is introduced by the dispatch of the telex. During the subscription period the underwriting banks are involved in selling the issue to their clients. Issues of relatively small amounts may be subscribed fully by the manager and underwriters themselves for their own accounts. The subscription period for such issues is usually short. Very large issues may have longer subscription periods because a large number of clients may be involved.

Closing the Deal   The final terms of the issue are determined by the managers and the borrower at the end of the subscription period. When an issue is oversubscribed, several options are available to the borrower and the management group. If the borrower has a need for the amount oversubscribed, the group may decide to expand the issue to take in the oversubscription. On the other hand, if the borrower needs only the amount of the issue, the terms of the issue may be altered to make it less attractive and reduce the demand. The terms of the issue are altered by either lowering the coupon rate or raising the issue price. The opposite action may be taken when an issue is undersubscribed.

The final terms of the issue and the allocation of the issue would be referred to the underwriting team for their approval, which is communicated to the lead manager by telex. Following the approval of the final terms, the underwriting team signs the agreement to formalize the issue.

The subscribers to the issue have two weeks in which to make payment for their subscription. Payments are made into a bank account opened for this purpose. The amount collected for the issue is then transferred to the borrower's account, and the borrower authorizes the managers to distribute the bonds to the investors. The majority of Eurobonds are deposited by banks and investors in two clearinghouses—Cedel and Euro-clear—for safe custody. Some investors decide to leave their Eurobonds in the custody of their banks, which collect the coupon interest for their clients.

Alternative Methods of Structuring an Issue   In an alternative approach, the final terms of an entire issue are specified and fixed, and the final agreements formalizing the issue are signed prior to the opening of the subscription period. This approach is attractive when the market is volatile. A selling group and a separate sub-underwriting group are used when this approach is followed in structuring an issue.

The "tender bid" approach was used in floating a Eurobond issue by the European Bank (EIB) and the kingdom of Sweden. In the tender bid, a selected number of banks are invited to bid for the whole or part of the issue at a specified net price. The EIB invited 50 banks to submit bids indicating what price they were willing to pay for the issue. Information on the coupon and issue price was not made available in the telex invitations sent out on the issue. The underwriting syndicate discussed the yield basis of the issue with the borrowers during the selling period. The coupon and issue price were fixed in line with market conditions at the end of the selling period. The tender bid process made possible a smaller underwriting group and a shorter selling period, which resulted in a much reduced commission, about half the normal amount.

Collateral Features   The majority of Eurobond issues, including notes and debentures, are not secured by collateral. The secured issues are mortgage bonds. The instrument is a certificate that is drawn up in bearer form, making it transferable without the identification of the investor. Interest coupons are attached to the certificate.

Redemption Features

Call Provision   A call provision is included in most Eurobond issues with long maturities (usually greater than 5 years). A call premium of 1½ to 2 percent is payable if the bond issue is called during the first year after the non-call period (see below). The premium declines by ¼ or ½ percentage points annually after the first year in which the bond could be called. A borrower generally exercises its right to call the bond if general interest rates in the marketplace fall to a level that would dictate new borrowing instead of continuing to pay the higher coupon rate. The borrower is precluded from calling the bond until after the non-call period. The non-call period is determined as part of the terms of the issue and in light of market conditions. The length of the non-call period varies from issue to issue.

Sinking Fund   Borrowers are required to set up a sinking fund for issues with maturities longer than five years. The sinking fund is used on a set schedule to redeem a specified portion of the outstanding issue.

Purchase Fund   The purchase fund provision requires the borrower to retire a specified amount of the issue each year, unless the bond market price is above the issue price. If the borrower is unable to complete the repurchase of the yearly quota during the purchase period because the bond price is higher than the purchase price, then the borrower is required to increase the next year's purchase quota to include the shortfall in the previous year's purchase. In that situation, the purchase is effected only when the bond price falls below the issue price during the purchase period.

In a sinking fund, the borrower is required to redeem a set amount annually regardless of the price of the bond. In a purchase fund, the borrower is required to redeem a specified amount of a bond each year whenever the market price of the bond falls below the issue price.

The Eurodollar Market   The Eurodollar market is the dominant sector of the Eurobond market. Table 9.7 shows recent rankings of the top 25 lead managers of international syndicates which underwrite issues of Eurodollar notes and bonds. A number of U.S. banks and investment banking houses rank among

**Table 9.7   Ranking of Lead Managers of Eurodollar
Notes/Bonds Syndicates (Based on amount of issues
during first half of 1980)**

Rank	Manager	Number	Amount ($ millions)
1	Credit Suisse First Boston	9	805
2	Goldman Sachs	6	735
3	S. G. Warburg	6	680
4	Paribas	4	615
5	Salomon Brothers	5	600
6	Morgan Stanley	5	515
7	Deutsche Bank	3	475
8	Wood Gundy	5	325
9	Merrill Lynch	6	320
10	Dresdner Bank	1	300
11	Cointinental Illinois	2	200
12	Caisse des Depots et Consignations	2	185
13	Union Bank of Switzerland	2	180
14	Swiss Bank Corporation	2	150
15	Hambros	2	130
16	Credit Lyonnais	1	125
17	Dean Witter Reynolds	2	125
18	Dillon Read Overseas	2	115
19	Banque Nationale de Paris	2	115
20	Orion Bank	2	100
21	Nomura	2	80
22	Den norske Creditbank	1	75
23	Chase Manhattan	1	75
24	Daiwa Europe	2	55
25	Nikko Securities	2	55

Source: Euromoney (August 1980), p. 114.

the top 25 lead managers of Eurodollar syndication. Advice on how to borrow
from the Eurodollar market can be obtained from any of these firms.

Foreign Bonds

If IBM Canada (Figure 9.2) had wanted to obtain a particular foreign currency,
deutsche marks for example, to consummate a transaction in Germany, it could
have floated an international bond in Germany, indicating its desire to obtain
the proceeds of the issue in deutsche marks. This would be a foreign bond. The
foreign bond provides a useful way of varying foreign currency financing or of
obtaining a particular currency. Any firm of satisfactory creditworthiness can
participate in the foreign bond market.

The data presented in Table 9.6 show that foreign bond issues in the United States made up around 60 percent of the foreign bond issues in each of the years from 1975 to 1979, with the exception of 1977. More foreign bond issues were floated in the United States than abroad until 1977 when issues in the United States fell below issues outside the United States. This change shows a shift in the availability of capital. With the high liquidity in Europe and Japan caused by the increase in petrodollars, borrowers were able to tap the European and Japanese capital markets for funds. The Swiss franc leads in currency of denomination of foreign bond issues, followed by deutsche marks and the Japanese yen.

State enterprises, governments, and international organizations have been the major participants in the foreign bond markets; they accounted for over 80 percent of the issues in 1976–1979. U.S. companies have not been active participants in the foreign bond market. Their participation rate is much higher in the Eurobond market. Several explanations have been suggested: For one, most United States companies can get the funds they need from their domestic capital markets. The companies borrowing abroad are largely multinational corporations, with excellent credit ratings, which borrow in the Eurobond market. Subsidiaries and foreign affiliates of U.S. companies are more likely to borrow from the Eurobond market than the foreign bond market. Regulations governing lending in various countries may constrain U.S. companies from participating in the capital markets of those countries.

The terms, conditions, and procedures of the foreign bond market are similar to those of the Eurobond market, but there are differences. In the foreign bond market, the syndicate that is underwriting an issue is made up of banks from the country in whose currency the bond is denominated. Foreign bond issues are normally small-to-medium in size.

A U.S. company that wants to float a foreign bond issue should start by contacting its domestic bankers, who will provide counsel and advice about the best approach, and will recommend a syndicate leader in the country whose currency the U.S. company wants. Alternatively, the company can contact the New York office of one of the banks of the country in which it wants to float the foreign bond.

Bond Yields

Yields on international bonds denominated in United States dollars have been consistently higher than on bonds denominated in other currencies. Table 9.8 presents the historical average yields for the years 1976 through 1979. Yields on Swiss franc-denominated bonds have been the lowest in comparison to the deutsche mark and the dollar, but as of mid-1980, yields on Swiss franc-denominated bonds appeared to be approaching those on the deutsche mark-denominated bonds. Yields increased from 1976 to 1979 on all bonds and the trend continued in 1980.

International bonds issued by European companies have higher yields than international bonds issued by U.S. companies, which may be indicative of the

Table 9.8   International Bond Average Yields

Issues	1976	1977	1978	1979	1980
U.S. companies					
U.S. dollars	7.39%	7.95%	8.55%	10.13%	11.76%
Swiss franc	5.46	5.31	5.70	6.61	7.27
European companies					
U.S. dollar	8.56	8.42	9.21	10.93	12.42
Deutsche mark	7.38	6.80	6.84	7.55	8.79
Governments					
U.S. dollar	8.90	8.42	9.12	10.66	11.83

Source: Morgan Guaranty Trust Company of New York, *World Financial Markets* (July 1980).

fact that the U.S. companies that use the international bond market are mostly the big multinational companies with excellent credit ratings. Most U.S. companies still use the domestic capital markets for their bond issues. In comparison, more European companies issue international bonds, and their ratings overall may not be as high as those of U.S. multinational companies. The difference in the average yields presented in Table 9.8 between the bonds issued by U.S. multinational corporations and the European companies may therefore represent premiums for the relatively lower ratings of the European companies.

SUMMARY

The international capital markets provide facilities for qualified borrowers to obtain capital from outside their country of residence. This process is called offshore borrowing. The type of borrowers who participate in the international capital markets are (1) industrial and commercial firms, (2) financial institutions, (3) governments and government agencies, and (4) international institutions. Firms in need of capital funds can borrow directly from an international banking syndicate, or they can issue bonds in the international market.

The international lending market was estimated at over $2 trillion in 1980. The largest portion of outstanding debt claims is made up of interbank lending, which accounts for approximately 70 percent of the total outstanding claims in the international lending market, with nonbank borrowers accounting for the remaining 30 percent. In 1978, lending to the nonbank segment of the market passed $450 billion, and it was expected to exceed $650 billion in 1980.

The Eurocapital market is made up of the Eurocurrency market, the Eurobond market, and, much less important, the Euroequity market. A Eurocurrency loan can be made in any country; whether the loan is defined as a Eurocurrency loan depends on the currency in which the loan is made and the country in which the lending commercial bank is situated. Eurodollar transactions make up, on the average, 75 percent of the gross volume of transactions in the Eurocurrency market. The dominant position of the Eurodollar in the Eurocurrency market reflects the role of the U.S. dollar as the single most important currency in international trade and investment.

Eurocurrency loans for large amounts and for medium-term maturities are normally made by syndicates. The majority of loans are larger than $25 million, and the average size of these loans is $113 million. The loan terms include the maturity of the loan, the amortization schedule, the allowable grace period, the applicable interest rate, the various covenants that govern the loan, and other conditions, including repayment terms.

The international bond market is made up of the Eurobond market and the foreign bond market. For a bond to be classified as an international bond it must be sold almost exclusively outside the country of the borrower, in contrast to domestic bonds, which are sold largely in the country of the borrower. An international bond may be issued by an international or a national syndicate of banks. When an international syndicate of banks underwrites an international bond issue, that issue is called a Eurobond issue. When an international bond is underwritten by a syndicate of banks in the same country, it is called a foreign bond. The Eurobond market is the dominant market for international bonds, which is why the name is applied to all international bond issues underwritten by an international syndicate of banks.

Direct issues by U.S. companies of Eurobonds in 1979 amounted to almost $3 billion. A significant portion of the Eurobond borrowings by foreign companies is made up of foreign affiliates of U.S. companies. But U.S. companies and their foreign subsidiaries have not been very active in the foreign bond market, nor have non-U.S. companies.

The participation of developing countries in the international bond markets has been minimal ($755 million in 1977, or only 7½ percent of total external bond issues). Greater access for developing countries to the international bond markets has been urged.

A Eurobond issue can be floated by a parent company or by one of its subsidiaries located abroad, and it is generally underwritten by an international syndicate of banks. The managing banks initiate the process of introducing the issue to the market by inviting other banks and financial institutions to participate in both underwriting and subscribing to the issue. During the subscription period, the underwriting banks are involved in selling the issue to their clients. The final terms of the issue are determined by the managers and the borrowers at the end of the subscription period. The majority of Eurobond issues, including notes and debentures, are not secured by collateral. The redemption features include a call provision, a sinking fund, or a purchase fund. In a sinking fund the borrower is required to redeem a specified amount annually without regard to the price of the bond. In contrast, in a purchase fund, the borrower is required to redeem a specified amount of the bond each year whenever the market price of the bond is less than the issue price.

The terms, conditions, and procedures in the foreign bond market are similar to the Eurobond market, but have certain differences. The syndicate underwriting a foreign bond issue is made up of banks from the same country in whose currency the bond is denominated. Issues of foreign bonds are normally small-to-medium in size.

NOTES

1 J. F. Sterling, "How Big Is the International Lending Market?" *The Banker*, Vol. 130 (January 1980), pp. 77–87.

2 *Ibid.*

3 Although "Eurocapital market" specifically refers to medium- and long-term borrowing and lending, and "Eurocurrency market" refers to short-term borrowing and lending, general usage refers to "Eurocapital market" to mean both markets.

4 Sidney M. Robbins, Robert B. Stobaugh, William T. Gregor, and John C. Kirby, *How to Use International Capital Markets: A Guide to Europe and the Middle East* (New York: Financial Executives Research Foundation, 1976).

5 OECD, "Access of Developing Countries to International Financial Markets," *Financial Market Trends*, No. 13 (1980).

6 Economics Department, Citibank, *Global Financial Intermediation* (New York: Citibank, 1980).

7 Robert N. Bee, "Syndication," *Offshore Lending by U.S. Commercial Banks*, F. John Mathis, ed. (Washington, D.C.: The Bankers' Association for Foreign Trade and Robert Morris Associates, 1975).

8 Andre M. Conssement, "Why the Bond Market Should Open Up for Developing Countries," *Euromoney* (August 1980), pp. 117–127.

9 OECD, *op. cit.* and Conssement, *op. cit.*

10 World Bank, *World Development Report* (1979).

11 Orion Bank Limited, *International Capital Markets: An Investor's Guide* (London: Euromoney Publications Ltd., 1979), p. 76.

10

Export and Import Financing by Commercial Banks

As United States international trade has grown since the end of World War II, the scope and variety of financing instruments that are required to service the needs of the export and import trade have also grown. The major sources of financing for international trade are commercial banks. The traditional forms of financing by commercial banks include short-term advances against bills of lading and shipping documents, loans to overseas buyers, and loans to shippers for working capital purposes.

The methods of financing have changed over the years, however, to accommodate the growth and diversity of imports and exports. Newer instruments of financing include the extension of direct loans by United States commercial banks to foreign importers to finance United States exports, and the purchase by United States commercial banks of export credit obligations of foreign importers.

Originally, United States commercial banks granted credit only to United States businesses, but the policy was changed following the provision of guarantees by the Export-Import Bank of the United States to United States commercial banks to cover commercial and political risks involved in extending export credits to finance United States exports. The Export-Import Bank (Eximbank) is an agency of the United States government whose policies have been geared toward encouraging and supporting United States export trade. It will be described in more detail in Chapter 11, but its relationship to commercial banks' export financing needs to be mentioned here briefly.

The greater part of United States export credit is to finance exports to Third World countries where political and commercial risks are greater than in the industrialized countries. By providing export credit guarantees, the Eximbank significantly reduces the risk exposure of United States commercial banks in granting export credits, and thus facilitates trade with the Third World countries.

The Eximbank loan program also provides direct financing for export credit. Eximbank direct loans are made on a joint basis with U.S. private financial institutions. Finance companies and factoring firms participate in financing U.S. international trade to a considerably smaller extent than do commercial banks and the Eximbank.

U.S. commercial banks have built up over the years an extensive international network of contacts, considerable know-how, and correspondent relationships around the world, enabling them to provide the financial services necessary to cope with the rapidly growing international trade. Technological advances in telecommunications have contributed to the ability of banks to provide timely and efficient worldwide services. Telex (radio teleprinter), mail, cable, the telephone, and in particular, radio transmission via satellite have speeded up the transmission of data.

In addition to providing financial services, commercial banks are increasingly gaining competence and facility in providing their U.S. export and import clients with advisory services on how to do business abroad, as well as on the creditworthiness of overseas buyers or sellers—useful information indeed to United States businesses.

EXPORT FINANCING BY COMMERCIAL BANKS

Commercial banks have developed a variety of ways to finance exports. As indicated previously, much of export financing is made up of export credits that take the form of loans or advances. Such loans can be made with recourse to the exporter or without recourse.[1] The difference between these two categories is the party that has ultimate responsibility for repayment of the loan. "With recourse" means the bank has recourse to the exporter for the export credit provided. In this case, therefore, the bank is interested in the ability of the exporter to repay the loan. In the second case, "without recourse," the bank extends export credit without recourse to the exporter, and therefore, the bank has to determine the ability of the foreign *buyer* to meet the debt obligation.

Commercial Bank Financing with Recourse to the Exporter

Export credit financing of United States exports by U.S. commercial banks may be made with or without physical evidence of a negotiable instrument, such as a draft or bill of exchange, which documents the exact process of foreign collection. The common methods of financing with recourse are the export letter of credit and the open account.[2] Both methods can involve the use of an export dollar draft (or foreign currency draft) drawn by the seller on the buyer.

Export Letters of Credit

The export letter of credit is one of the oldest financing instruments in international trade. In comparison with the other methods of financing, the export letter of credit provides a high level of protection for the seller. An export letter of credit originates with the foreign buyer's bank, outside the United States, and is advised or confirmed by a U.S. commercial bank on behalf of its foreign correspondent bank for the account of its customer. It is important to recognize the dual role of the letter of credit. It is an *export* letter of credit to the U.S. seller, and at the same time it is an *import* letter of credit to the foreign buyer of the U.S. export.

A letter of credit represents an irrevocable undertaking on the part of the buyer's bank to the seller that the bank will make payments on behalf of the buyer under specified conditions. International letters of credit usually involve more than one bank. An issuing bank in the buyer's country originates the letter of credit at the request of the importer and transmits it to a correspondent bank (the advising/confirming bank) located in the seller's country. When the seller is a U.S. exporter, the advising bank will be a U.S. bank. The advising bank will then send advice of the issue of an export letter of credit to the U.S. exporter informing him that the foreign buyer's bank has issued an irrevocable letter of credit in his favor.

When the importer's bank requests its U.S. correspondent to confirm a letter of credit, both banks are under an obligation to honor the credit to the beneficiary (or U.S. exporter) if the exporter provides the necessary documentation and meets all of the other conditions. The letter of credit represents an authorization to the U.S. exporter to draw a draft on a U.S. bank. The draft, with the relevant supporting documents, would be presented directly, through a collecting bank, or by the beneficiary's representatives at the port of shipment for payment to the U.S. bank that advised, confirmed, or issued the letter of credit. The bank will proceed to make the payments after ensuring that all documents are in order. The amount paid on the draft is later collected from the foreign importer.

An export letter of credit provides many advantages for both the U.S. exporter and the foreign buyer. The banking facilities in the United States and in the buyer's country provide the channels for financing and paying for the transaction. The U.S. exporter is assured of payment by its domestic bank, which minimizes the financial risk of nonpayment or slow payment. The importer, for his part, is assured that the exporter will furnish the proper documentation to the bank in the United States before payment is made.[3] (Foreign governments find that requiring export sales to be made by letter of credit is a convenient way of enforcing exchange control.)

A letter of credit can be revocable or irrevocable. A *revocable* letter of credit permits the issuer to revoke the request to pay the receiving party at any time, if certain specified conditions are not met. It is generally advisable for the U.S. exporter to avoid revocable letters of credit, since such documents permit the issuer, which in the case of a U.S. exporter will be a foreign buyer, to revoke the terms of the letter of credit almost at will. The U.S. exporter can therefore lose the very protection from delinquency or default that a letter of credit should provide. The foreign buyer may use the revocation also to renege on the contract if circumstances change after the contract is consummated. Technically, letters of credit that are issued as *irrevocable* in effect become revocable when specified conditions are not met by the beneficiary. In effect, the nonconforming documents become a collection item losing the protection of the letter of credit.

Consider the following illustration of the export letter of credit process. The U.K. Import Trading Co. wants to buy two machines from the U.S. Export Trading Co. The U.K. Import Trading Co. wants to pay for the machines after their arrival in the United Kingdom. On the other hand, the U.S. Export Trading Co. prefers to receive payment for the merchandise at the time it is shipped from the United States. Since the transaction involves the currencies of two countries, the two parties to the transaction have to agree which of the currencies will be used in drawing up the sale documents. The advantage to the party whose currency is used for quotation in the sale documents is that foreign exchange fluctuations do not affect the amount that party has to pay or will receive. On the other hand, the buyer (or seller) who has to pay (or receive payment) in a foreign currency has to make up for any depreciation in its currency relative to the other currency. The U.S. Export Trading Co., therefore, prefers to receive payment in dollars, while the U.K. Import Trading Co. would rather have payment made in pounds.

Assume that demand is high for this particular type of machine relative to the available supply. It is a seller's market. The U.K. Import Trading Co. is anxious to get the machines and has therefore agreed to make payment in U.S. dollars.

The U.K. Import Trading Co. then arranges for its bank to provide an irrevocable letter of credit for $100,000 to cover the cost and freight (C&F) of the two machines to London from New York. The letter of credit will enable the U.S. Export Trading Co. to obtain payment at the time of shipment of the machines. The U.S. Export Trading Co., in turn, is obligated to arrange for shipment of the machines to London, with the total cost of machines and shipment not to exceed the contract price of $100,000.

If an importer does not have funds available to deposit with its bank at the time the application for issuance of a letter of credit is made, it may have to apply for a line of credit to cover the letter of credit. The U.K. Import Trading Co. does not have the $100,000 and applies for a line of credit with the request for the $100,000 letter of credit.

The U.K. Bank Ltd. approves the line of credit for the specific dollar limit and purpose for which the credit will be used. The bank requires that shipping documents convey title to the U.K. Bank Ltd. by requiring that all bills of lading be endorsed in blank or to the orders of the U.K. Bank Ltd. A bill of lading so endorsed serves as collateral for the line of credit. When the bills of lading are endorsed in blank, the bank can fill in the blanks to its order, if necessary, and can collect the machines by presenting endorsed bills of lading to the carrier. If the U.K. Import Trading Co. should fail to reimburse the U.K. Bank Ltd., the bank can take possession and sell the machines.

The export letter of credit authorizes its beneficiary, the U.S. Export Trading Co., to draw "sight" drafts (payable on sight) for the amount of $100,000 on the U.K. Bank Ltd. The U.S. Export Trading Co. is required to have complete sets (usually three) of specified documents (bills of lading) to accompany drafts presented for payment.

Export Drafts with Letters of Credit   Export drafts are frequently used with letters of credit. An export draft is drawn by the seller (in the preceding example, the U.S. Export Trading Co.) on the foreign buyer (the U.K. Import Trading Co.) with instructions for the payment of the draft. The export draft may require payment on presentation (a sight draft) or at an established future date ("time" draft). The drawer of the draft (the seller) often indicates the duration of the time draft (or draft "tenor") by specifying payment 30, 60, 90, 120, or 180 days after presentation ("after sight") of the draft or after the date of the draft ("after date").[4]

U.S. exporters generally send their export drafts through their U.S. banks for collection and specify that payment be made to the order of the bank, which is known in this case as the "remitting bank." The seller, as drawer of the draft, can receive payment directly by specifying itself as the party to whom payment is to be made. The use of a bank facilitates the collection process, however.

As a common practice, U.S. exporters draw export drafts in U.S. dollars, although drafts may be drawn in other currencies. The shipping documents needed by the foreign buyer to take delivery in the country of destination are sent with the export draft. These documents usually include bills of lading in negotiable form (that is, endorsed in blank), commercial invoices, consular invoices, and an insurance certificate or policy.

Figure 10.1 is a flowchart of the process involved in using a sight draft export letter of credit to effect payment for the two machines exported from the United States to the United Kingdom. Starting the process in the upper right-hand box, the U.K. Import Trading Co. submits an application for $100,000 credit to the U.K. Bank Ltd. in London. The bank then issues a letter of credit and sends it to the U.S. Export Trading Co. in New York. Since the credit is for dollars instead of pounds, the U.S. Export Trading Co. must draw its draft on the U.S. Bank Inc. and present it to the New York bank for payment. In this case the U.K. Import Trading Co. will be responsible for all charges, including those of the U.S. Bank Inc. This type of credit is called a "straight" credit and refers to credits payable by a bank in the country of the seller rather than a bank in the country of the buyer.

This type of payment arrangement is also known as a "foreign currency" credit. The U.K. Import Trading Co. must provide the $100,000 without regard to exchange rate fluctuations between the dollar and the pound. In other words, the U.K. Import Trading Co. is obligated to pay, to the U.K. Bank Ltd., when requested, whatever amount in pounds is necessary to buy $100,000, and

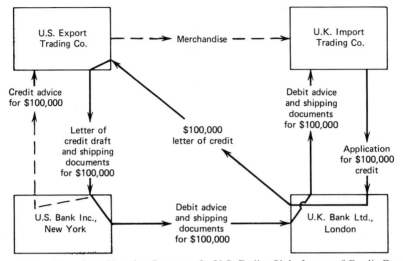

Figure 10.1 Flowchart Showing Process of a U.S. Dollar Sight Letter of Credit Covering an Export.

the company is therefore open to risks from adverse fluctuations in the foreign exchange rate.

The U.K. Bank Ltd. issued the credit and sent the original letter of credit directly to the beneficiary, the U.S. Export Trading Co. A copy was also sent to the U.S. Bank Inc. with an authorization for the account of the U.K. Bank Ltd. to be debited when the U.S. Bank Inc. made the payment. The U.S. Bank Inc. will pay the U.S. Export Trading Co. when the company presents its draft if the bank is satisfied that the shipping documents presented with the draft conform to the terms of the credit. The U.K. Bank Ltd. dollar account at the U.S. Bank Inc. will be debited for the amount of $100,000. The U.S. Bank Inc. will then retire the draft and send the documents to the U.K. Bank Ltd. together with an advice of the debit to the bank's U.S. dollar account. The U.K. Bank Ltd. will examine the documents, and if it finds the documents in order, it will then debit the U.K. Import Trading Co.'s account for the pound equivalent of $100,000. The shipping documents, properly endorsed by the U.K. Bank Ltd., will be sent together with a copy of the debit advice to the U.K. Import Trading Co. With all the appropriate documents in hand, the British importer is ready to collect the shipment when it arrives.

In the above illustration, all of the documents were in order and settlement was effected without a hitch. Occasionally, however, problems arise which must be resolved before the process can be concluded. For example, in the case above, the draft drawn up by the U.S. Export Trading Co. was retired by the U.K. Bank Ltd. when it found the documents sent by the U.S. Bank Inc. in order and made payment to the bank. If, however, the U.K. Bank Ltd. had found that the documents it had honored did not conform to the credit terms (that shipment was made from Baltimore, Maryland, for example, instead of from New York as stipulated in the contract), and, as a result, the shipment was not accepted by the U.K. Import Trading Co., the U.K. Bank would have had a problem because it would not have had recourse to the U.S. Export Trading Co. or the U.S. bank for payment. The U.K. bank would have contacted the three other parties involved (the U.K. Import Trading Co., the beneficiary, and the U.S. bank) to settle the matter.

If the U.K. Bank Ltd. had observed prior to honoring the draft that the bills of lading indicated shipment was to be from Baltimore instead of New York, the bank would have inquired whether its customer would agree to waive the discrepancy; if the U.K. Import Trading Co. had then agreed to the waiver, the U.K. Bank Ltd. would have proceeded to honor the draft, since the waiver would have corresponded to amending the letter of credit as to the port of shipment.

If, on the other hand, the U.K. Import Trading Co. had refused to waive the discrepancy, the U.K. Bank Ltd. would have communicated the situation to the U.S. Bank Inc. and awaited further instructions as to the disposition of the documents. In practice, the buyer and seller would have compromised; for example, the seller might have agreed to give the buyer a rebate in compensation for the discrepancy. The buyer would then have instructed its bank to authorize payment less the rebate. The U.K. Bank Ltd. would then have instructed the U.S. Bank Inc. to honor the draft for the reduced amount. Sometimes the seller refuses to waive the discrepancy and advises its U.S. bank to instruct the foreign bank to find another buyer and collect the funds from the new buyer.

A draft in foreign currency accepted by a U.S. bank is known as a "foreign currency acceptance." A foreign currency acceptance may be theoretically rediscounted by the Federal Reserve Bank. It cannot be readily sold, however, in the open market.

Deferred-Payment Letter of Credit   A deferred-payment letter of credit permits the advising bank to provide deferred financing when a beneficiary presents the necessary documents. The bank makes periodic payments at scheduled dates upon presentation of sight drafts. The bank can provide short-term loans against the periodic sight drafts. The deferred-payment letter of credit is an excellent vehicle for making payments under a contract that lasts several years, while obtaining protection against loss for the issuer. A 4-year contract, for example, can be tailored under a deferred-payment letter of credit for the beneficiary to present sight drafts for payment each half year.

Standby Letter of Credit   A "standby" letter of credit is also known as an "undertaking" letter of credit. A standby letter of credit is a request for credit facility by one party to be available for use by a third party when and as needed. This process is widely used by multinational companies to arrange contingency financing for their affiliates abroad. Such companies usually ask their U.S. banks to back up a line of credit through a foreign local bank where its foreign affiliate does its banking. The foreign affiliate would draw upon its standby credit for working capital or other specified purposes.[5]

U.S. regulations and good banking practice require that banks treat standby letters of credit as loans to the issuer, and these letters of credit must be included in the borrower's line of credit with the issuing bank.[5]

Bid or Performance Letter of Credit   A "bid" of "performance" letter of credit is sometimes used by U.S. corporations in place of a performance bond or a surety bond. A bid letter of credit represents a "good faith" warranty of the bidder, and usually just a small or nominal percentage of the contract price is required to establish the good faith. In some cases, however, up to 50 percent of the contract price may be required for a performance letter of credit that is intended to provide insurance for performance. When the issuer of a performance letter of credit fails to perform in accordance with the terms of the contract between the issuer and the beneficiary, the beneficiary is empowered under the credit terms to draw against the performance letter of credit upon the presentation of a statement stating the issuer's failure to perform.

Back-to-Back Letter of Credit   Back-to-back letters of credit are usually issued to middlemen or traders who act as intermediaries between a buyer and a seller. These middlemen are known by a variety of names, such as, wholesale distributors, import/export merchants, or foreign distributors. For a percentage commission, the middlemen act as facilitators between a manufacturer in the United States—who may not want to become directly involved in international trade or who may be located at a considerable distance from the port—and the foreign buyer.

In a back-to-back letter of credit, two letters of credit are issued in order to consummate the transaction. The foreign buyer requests a letter of credit in favor of the U.S. intermediary company, to be issued by the foreigner's local bank and transmitted to a U.S. correspondent, the advising bank. The intermediary company in turn may request a back-to-back letter of credit to be issued by the U.S. advising bank in favor of the U.S. manufacturer. (Alternatively, the U.S. intermediary company may request the U.S. advising bank to assign the letter of credit to the United States manufacturer.) The U.S. bank will issue a back-to-back letter of credit to the manufacturer for an amount not greater than the letter of credit it has in hand from the foreign buyer.

The back-to-back letter of credit may not be completely risk-free for the U.S. advisory bank when the bank functions as the issuing bank for the U.S. intermediary company. If, for example, the U.S. manufacturer is situated at an inland location and its policy is to ship overland to port of embarkation only, then once the consignment gets to the port of embarkation, the manufacturer could present his draft to the U.S. bank for payment. However, shipping problems could cause subsequent delay or loss of shipment, in which case the U.S. bank would be exposed to risk of loss.

Open Account Method of Trade Financing

In this method of financing export credit, no negotiable instruments (such as a draft or a bill of exchange) are used to document the credit extended by the bank. The buyer and seller arrange the terms of the transaction and the time of payment. The exporter usually sends the shipping documents directly to the buyer with a request that the buyer remit payments to the exporter's bank. Although an open account has the advantage of being very simple, it also exposes the exporter, and the bank when financing the seller, to maximum risk. No documentary evidence governs the terms of payment, and much of the transaction is handled outside the normal banking channels. Thus, an exporter should use this method only when the buyer is well known and the exporter is aware of the buyer's financial capacity.

Export Drafts with Open Accounts

Exporters dealing with established foreign customers or foreign buyers with excellent credit may not need the protection of a letter of credit. The exporter may choose to accept payment on a draft basis. In a draft used with an open account, the seller draws on the buyer unconditionally instructing the buyer to pay the amount of the draft. Because the exporter assumes the credit risk until collection is made, the exporter must make sure that credit information on the foreign importer is reliable before selling on an export draft basis.[7] Payment by draft is less costly than payment by letter of credit and thus allows the exporter to be more competitive in bidding for sales.

Payment Arrangements   The same two types of drafts are normally used with open accounts as are used with letters of credit: sight drafts and time drafts.

The draft specifies the party to whom payment is to be made. The practice in the United States is to request that payment be made to the exporter's bank, which handles the collection of the draft for the exporter. Payment for exports from the United States are usually denominated in dollars, which avoids the problem of foreign exchange. (When dealing with foreign countries in which dollars for foreign exchange may be in short supply, the exporter should usually instruct the collecting bank to accept local currency payments to cover drafts denominated in U.S. dollars—if the importer will assume all foreign exchange risks in writing.)

All shipping documents needed by the foreign buyer to take delivery of the export goods must be sent with the draft. The documents include bills of lading endorsed in blank (which makes them negotiable), insurance policy, consular invoice, commercial invoice, and all other documents pertaining to the shipment.

Letter of Instruction   Accompanying the draft is a letter addressed to the collecting bank in the importer's country and containing instructions on the procedure for delivery of the shipment to the foreign importer by the collecting bank. This letter contains instructions on (1) release of documents, (2) advice of fate (information on payment and acceptance or nonpayment and nonacceptance), (3) method of transmitting payment, and (4) payment of collection charges.

For shipment against a sight draft, the collecting bank will be instructed to release the documents to the importer on payment of the draft. For time drafts the importer has to accept the draft and confirm arrangements for payment before the collecting bank releases the documents. Collecting banks in many foreign countries prefer to hold onto the documents until the shipment arrives before the draft is presented for payment or acceptance.

The remitting bank will be advised of action taken by the collecting bank on presenting the draft for payment or acceptance and the remittance of the proceeds of the draft.

Loan Collection   An exporter in need of funds can arrange with the remitting bank for a loan against the draft drawn on the foreign importer that is in the process of collection. The three principal kinds of loans an exporter can obtain against drafts in the process of collection are (1) a loan on a cash-advance, or liquidation, basis, (2) a loan on a note basis, and (3) a loan on an acceptance basis.

1   *Cash-Advance Basis*   The exporter receives credit from the bank for the face amount of the draft, or part of the face amount of the draft, and the proceeds of the draft are used to liquidate the advance.

2   *Note Basis*   The exporter borrows from the bank on a note using the draft deposited with the bank as collateral. The proceeds of the draft are used to liquidate the note.

3   *Acceptance Basis*   Under the acceptance basis, the exporter draws a time draft on his bank, using the export draft in process of collection as collateral. The bank accepts the time draft and discounts it, effectively making a discount loan to the exporter. The proceeds of the export draft are used to liquidate the discounted time draft. Banks usually extend this facility only to companies with a great deal of export business, which provides a steady collection process and ensures that the time drafts will be paid when due.

Foreign Currency Drafts   Export transactions are sometimes denominated in foreign currencies. U.S. exporters bidding on contracts or the sale of big ticket items are sometimes required to quote their contract price in the currency of the foreign buyer. Importers in countries with foreign exchange restrictions may not have dollar foreign exchange readily available for payment of imports from the United States. In that case, an export draft is drawn in the currency of the buyer. This is called a foreign currency draft.

Recall from Chapters 7 and 8 that, when a U.S. exporter denominates a transaction in a foreign currency (as in drawing a foreign currency draft), the exporter is exposed to the risk that the exchange rate between the U.S. dollar and the foreign currency will change from the rate at the time the draft was drawn. The exchange rate could move in favor of the U.S. dollar (if the U.S. dollar strengthened relative to the foreign currency) or it could move in favor of the foreign currency, in which case the dollar becomes the weaker currency.

When the exchange rate moves in favor of the U.S. dollar, the U.S. exporter will have fewer dollars when the foreign currency is converted to dollars, which represents a loss in dollar terms to the exporter. To protect itself from possible loss from foreign exchange fluctuation, the exporter can sell the foreign currency proceeds of the foreign currency draft to the U.S. bank now, for delivery at the future date when the proceeds of the draft are due for payment to the exporter. This is called a forward exchange contract, and its cost represents a normal business expense that should be included in the price of the contract.

Exporters dealing in a currency whose exchange rate moves in favor of the foreign currency and against the dollar would get back *more* dollars than the contract price when payment is made and the foreign currency draft is converted back to dollars. Currencies such as the deutsche mark, the Japanese yen, and the Swiss franc have shown exchange rate movements in their favor against the U.S. dollars in the past two decades. Lately the dollar has regained some favorable exchange rate movements in relation to these currencies.

Exporters generally sell their foreign currency drafts to banks irrespective of whether they are dealing with a stronger or weaker currency. Some do not want to be bothered with foreign exchange activities; others profess ignorance in that area. (European exporters have developed greater aptitude than United States exporters for handling foreign exchange transactions.) The exporter's bank is in a position to provide information on the trend of the exchange rate between the dollar and the relevant foreign currencies, and on the foreign exchange market expectations. As a rule, when dealing with weaker foreign currencies that may depreciate against the dollar, the exporter should sell the foreign currency draft to the bank for delivery at the time the exporter is scheduled to receive payment.

Commercial Bank Financing without Recourse

In bank financing without recourse, the exporter is relieved of all financial obligations once the foreign buyer accepts the shipment. The exporter is paid and is free to continue business without further responsibility for the financial performance of the foreign importer or regard to the bank's collection process.

U.S. banks are increasingly resorting to this nonrecourse financing because U.S. exporters and corporations prefer it. It allows them to collect their sales revenue faster than with recourse financing while reducing their risk exposure at the same time, and allows them to reinvest the money to earn profits elsewhere.

Banks themselves find nonrecourse financing increasingly attractive. Under nonrecourse financing, banks usually charge higher interest rates than those charged for export credits with recourse, and the higher interest rates, of course, bring in more profits to the banks.

Export Credit Insurance

The risks under nonrecourse financing are insured by an Eximbank-sponsored private program which coordinates 53 U.S. insurance companies into the Foreign Credit Insurance Association (FCIA). The FCIA provides short-term and medium-term, comprehensive, political and credit risk coverage. It provides coverage for 95 percent of the foreign political risk and 90 percent of the foreign commercial risk in nonrecourse financing. Either the borrower or the commercial bank can obtain FCIA insurance coverage: the commercial bank can obtain an FCIA policy to cover a loan transaction, or the borrower can obtain an FCIA policy, which is then assigned to the bank.

FCIA coverage applies to short-term and medium-term export credit. Generally, short-term acceptances under FCIA-insured nonrecourse financing are for 180 days. (The Federal Reserve Bank has approved the eligibility of 270-day acceptances for discounting.) Banks may charge the interest to the exporter for the number of days the loan is open, or they may simply collect interest on a straight-discount basis.

For medium-term nonrecourse financing under FCIA coverage, loans are usually from 6 months to 5 years. Transactions normally involve durable capital equipment that will be in use during the period the loan is outstanding.

For large projects (amounts in excess of $1 million), the Eximbank offers a participation financing program involving the buyer, the commercial bank, and the Eximbank. The Eximbank makes a direct loan up to 50 percent of the amount at an interest rate below the prime rate. The buyer is required to participate by making a down payment, and the commercial bank makes a loan to the buyer for the balance. The commercial bank's loan can be covered by an Eximbank guarantee as well as FCIA insurance.

The U.S. suppliers may be paid directly or through a letter of credit. For amounts in excess of $1 million, disbursements may be made over a period of up to 4 years. Repayments for medium- and long-term loans may be scheduled for a period up to 10 years. Under the Eximbank participation program, the commercial bank is permitted to collect the early installment repayments to increase its liquidity, while the Eximbank collects the later installment repayments.

Export Credit Guarantees

The Eximbank also provides a guarantee program to commercial banks to cover their export credit financing. The guarantee program is another way of helping commercial banks reduce their risk exposure in export credit financing. The Eximbank programs are discussed in detail in Chapter 11.

IMPORT FINANCING BY COMMERCIAL BANKS

Import financing is similar to the export financing described previously, but with the roles reversed. The U.S. businessman is now the importer and payment has to be made to the foreign exporter. The U.S. importer has to pay for the imports either from the company's funds or with the aid of a loan from a U.S.

bank. If payment is from the importing company's funds, the company may buy a draft and request a telegraphic transfer to the foreign exporter. This method is the most direct, but the importer is not using the banks to control his exposure.

Alternatively, the importing company may request the insurance of a letter of credit and pay for it with company funds. This process uses the banking channels to control risk exposure, since the exporter will have to present all the export documents before payment is made by the foreign advising bank. As noted previously, because of the protection it provides, the letter of credit is widely used in international trade.

U.S. importers invariably use an irrevocable letter of credit that cannot be canceled or changed once it has been issued. Thus the U.S. importer must ensure that the terms and conditions of the transaction are correct and in accordance with the importer's requirements.

Credit for Import Financing

When an importer requests a letter of credit, the importer also invariably needs import credit financing. The importer completes an application form which requests the bank to issue an irrevocable letter of credit in favor of the foreign exporter, and provides the beneficiary with an irrevocable commitment from the issuing bank to pay drafts drawn by the beneficiary and negotiated in accordance with the terms of the letter of credit. The foreign exporter's draft drawn on the letter of credit is forwarded to the U.S. issuing bank for payment. The importer's account will be charged when payment is made on the draft. The export documents accompanying the draft are usually checked by the importer's bank to verify that the documents conform to the terms of the letter of credit before payment is made. The bank is not in a position to assume responsibility for anything but verifying that the documents are in accordance with the terms of the letter of credit.

The importer will have to reimburse the issuing bank for repayment of the draft on the letter of credit before the bank releases the import documents, which the importer must have in order to claim the imported goods. An importer with a good credit standing may be allowed by the bank to take possession of the imported goods in exchange for a trust receipt to the bank, and hold the goods, or the proceeds from the sale of the goods, for the disposal of the bank.

Importers should also consider the advisability of having their letter of credit provide for time drafts that serve as interim financing. Whether or not time drafts can be used depends on the nature of the product and how it is to be sold.

The following example illustrates the transactions involved in an import letter of credit—a process similar to that for the export letter of credit discussed earlier.

The U.S. Import Trading Co. wants to buy 2,000 bolts of cloth from the U.K. Export Trading Co. After some consideration, the U.K. Trading Co. (the seller) agrees to accept U.S. dollars in payment.

The U.S. Import Trading Co. wants to pay for the merchandise after its arrival in the United States. The U.K. Export Trading Co., on the other hand, prefers to have payment for the merchandise at the time it is shipped. The U.S. Import Trading Co. agrees to arrange with its bank in the United States to provide an irrevocable letter of credit for $100,000 to cover 2,000 bolts of cloth C & F to New York from London. The leter of credit will enable the U.K. Trading Co. to obtain payment at the time of shipment of the merchandise. The U.K. Export Trading Co. arranges shipment of the merchandise to New York, with the cost of the merchandise and shipment not exceeding $100,000.

The U.S. Import Trading Co. must apply to its bank in the United States for the letter of credit for $100,000. The issuance of the letter of credit may involve two transactions: opening a line of credit, if the U.S. Import Trading Co. doesn't have the necessary funds at the time the application is made, and issuing the letter of credit.

The U.S. Import Trading Co. submits an application for a line of credit and requests that a letter of credit be issued to the U.K. Export Trading Co. for the amount of $100,000. The U.S. Bank Inc. opens a line of credit for the U.S. Import Trading Co. The line of credit specifies the dollar limit, the particular purpose for which the credit will be used, and a requirement that shipping documents convey title to the U.S. Bank Inc. by having all bills of lading endorsed in blank or to the order of the bank.

The import letter of credit authorizes the beneficiary, the U.K. Export Trading Co., to draw a sight draft for $100,000 on the U.S. Bank Inc. The U.K. Export Trading Co. is required to have complete sets of the specified documents (bills of lading) to accompany its drafts when they are presented for payment.

Figure 10.2 illustrates this process of a U.S. dollar sight letter of credit covering the import of 2,000 bolts of cloth from the United Kingdom to the

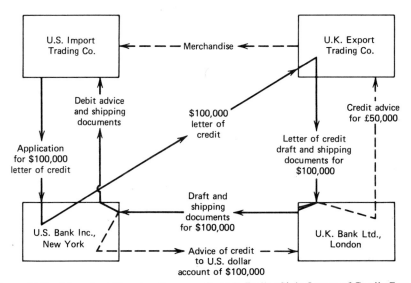

Figure 10.2 Flowchart Showing Process of a U.S. Dollar Sight Letter of Credit Covering an Import.

United States. Starting in the upper left square, the U.S. Import Trading Co. submits an application for a $100,000 letter of credit to the U.S. Bank Inc. in New York. The bank issues the letter of credit and sends it to the U.K. Export Trading Co. in London, with an advice to credit its U.S. dollar account at the U.K. Bank Ltd. for $100,000. The credit advice includes the following statement of the U.S. Bank Inc.'s commitment:

> We hereby engage with drawers and/or bona fide holders that drafts drawn under and negotiated in conformity with the terms of this credit will be duly honored on presentation.[8]

The U.K. Bank Ltd. accepts the credit advice from the U.S. Bank Inc. and negotiates the draft for $100,000 that was presented by the U.K. Export Trading Co. The draft will be negotiated at the rate of exchange at which the U.K. Bank Ltd. is currently buying dollars in exchange for pounds. The rate charged by the U.K. Bank Ltd. includes a margin for the costs of the transactions and the interest charges for the bank's funds for the period between payment to the U.K. Export Trading Co. and its receipt of credit from the U.S. Bank Inc. Assuming that the U.K. Bank Ltd.'s rate of exchange on the day the draft is presented is $2/£1, the $100,000 of the draft is expressed as £50,000. The U.K. Bank Ltd. endorses the credit and returns it to the beneficiary, the U.K. Export Trading Co., with the U.K. Bank Ltd.'s check for £50,000.

The U.K. Bank Ltd. then airmails the drafts and documents to the U.S. Bank Inc. in New York. If the U.S. Bank Inc. finds the documents in order, it credits the U.K. Bank Ltd. by airmail advice. At the same time, the U.S. Bank Inc. debits the account of the U.S. Import Trading Co. and mails the endorsed shipping documents with the debit advice to the importer. The U.S. Import Trading Co. is now in a position to collect the shipment of merchandise when it arrives.

Foreign Currency Payments

Foreigners exporting to the United States invariably prefer to have payment made in their domestic currencies. Therefore, the U.S. importer has to request its bank to issue an import letter of credit denominated in the foreign currency. The importer then has to make payment in the foreign currency and, in order to do so, has to obtain the foreign currency in the foreign exchange market at the time the payment is due. The U.S. importer can make use of a foreign currency credit for this transaction.

There are some differences between a foreign currency credit and the U.S. dollar credit described previously. In the example of the import to the United States of cloth, the foreign currency credit would be in pounds instead of in dollars. The pounds would be provided by the U.K. Bank Ltd. and the drafts would be drawn on and presented to the U.K. Bank Ltd. rather than the U.S. Bank Inc. The U.S. Import Trading Co. would be responsible for all charges, including those of the U.K. Bank Ltd. This type of credit is also known as a "straight" credit, a term used to describe credits payable through a bank in the seller's not the buyer's country. Figure 10.3 presents a flowchart of the process involved in a foreign currency credit.

The U.S. Bank Inc. issues the letter of credit and sends the original directly to the U.K. Export Trading Co. An authorization is sent at the same time to the U.K. Bank Ltd. to effect payment when the draft is presented and debit the account of the U.S. Bank Inc.

As noted, a problem in dealing with the two currencies is that their exchange rate may vary over time. If the exchange rate between the two currencies moves against the dollar when the U.S. importer must make payment, more dollars will be needed than when the purchase was arranged. The increase in the dollar liability effectively increases the cost of the imported goods. The higher costs may result in losses to the importer if the higher costs cannot be passed along in the price.

Like the exporter, the importer can limit the exchange risk by covering the exposure through the foreign exchange forward market. At the time the imported goods are ordered or when the letter of credit is issued, the importer can contract to buy foreign exchange when the import draft matures. (The importer can use a one-step procedure by making the forward contract at the time the letter of credit is issued.) The cost of the forward premium should be incorporated in the price of the imports as a normal cost of doing business.

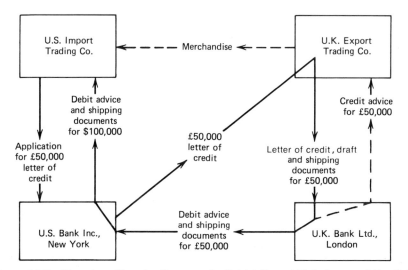

Figure 10.3 Flowchart Showing Process of a British Pound Sight Letter of Credit (or Foreign Currency Credit) Covering an Import.

SUMMARY

Commercial banks play a key role in financing international trade. They constitute an international banking network, in cooperation with commercial banks in foreign countries, that provides the channels for payments, communications, and other services in support of international trade. U.S. commercial banks cooperate with the Eximbank, its FCIA, and other private and governmental agencies to provide export credit financing and insurance to facilitate United States export trade.

Much export financing represents export credits that take the form of loans or advances to the exporter with or without recourse to the exporter. When a loan is made with recourse, the exporter retains the ultimate responsibility for the repayment of the loan. Methods of financing with recourse in common use are the export letter of credit, a dollar draft or foreign currency draft, and an open account. The export letter of credit, in particular, provides a high level of protection for exporters and importers, simplifies the export process, and ensures that payment will be received for merchandise exported.

In bank financing without recourse, the exporter is relieved of all financial obligations once the foreign buyer accepts the shipment. The guarantee and insurance programs of Eximbank have fostered a shift in U.S. commercial bank policy from recourse loans to nonrecourse loans to exporters, which frees the exporter from the burden of collection.

Import financing is similar to export financing, with the roles reversed. Foreign exchange facilities of commercial banks make it possible for exporters and importers to cover foreign exchange exposure when dealing with foreign currency drafts.

SUPPLEMENTARY READING

Gerhard W. Schneider, *Export-Import Financing: A Practical Guide* (New York: John Wiley & Sons, 1974).

F. John Mathis, Ed., *Offshore Lending by U.S. Commercial Banks* (Washington, D.C.: Bankers Association for Foreign Trade and Robert Morris Associates, 1981).

Francis A. Lees, *International Banking and Finance* (New York: John Wiley & Sons, 1974).

NOTES

1 F. John Mathis, Ed., *Offshore Lending by U.S. Commercial Banks* (Washington, D.C.: Bankers Association for Foreign Trade and Robert Morris Associates, 1981).

2 *The Financing of Exports and Imports* (New York: Morgan Guaranty Trust Co., May 1977).

3 Henry Harfield, *Bank Credits and Acceptances* (New York: Ronald Press, 5th ed., 1974).

4 Ernest D. Shaw, *Practical Aspects of Commercial Letters of Credit* (New York: Irving Trust Co., 1977), p. 14.

5 Henry Harfield, "The Sensible Use of Acceptances and Letters of Credit," *The Journal of Commercial Bank Lending* (November 1973).

6 Board of Governors, Federal Reserve System; Regulation H, S208.8(d) gives detailed explanation to Interpretive Ruling No. 7.1160 on application of lending limits to standing letters of credit.

7 Reliable credit information on the foreign buyer can be obtained from commercial banks engaged in international trade, foreign trade organizations, the U.S. Department of Commerce in Washington, D.C., and its regional offices, the consular commercial attache of the U.S. State Department, and the Export-Import Bank.

8 Shaw, *op. cit.*

11

The Export-Import Bank of the United States

The Export-Import Bank (Eximbank) of the United States, which was established to facilitate and aid in the financing of U.S. exports has been an important source of export financing since its creation. The Eximbank has developed several programs of insurance, guarantees, and financing to assist the U.S. exporter, and it provides financial services to support the wide spectrum of products and projects in U.S. foreign trade.

The Eximbank was established in 1934 by executive order as a banking corporation organized under the laws of the District of Columbia. The Export-Import Bank Act of 1945 made the bank an independent agency of the federal government. An amendment to the Act in 1947 reincorporated the bank under federal charter.

OVERVIEW OF THE EXIMBANK

The two basic policies of the Eximbank were laid down by the 1945 Act and apply to all its programs and activities. First, the bank supplements and encourages private capital; it does not compete with it. Second, its loans are made for specific purposes and they must be reasonably likely to be repaid. The Eximbank does not make grants. It charges fees and premiums for its guarantees and insurance, the fees being commensurate with the risks involved.

Administration

The Eximbank is managed by five directors, who are appointed by the President and confirmed by the Senate. The board of directors consists of the president and chairman of the bank, the first vice president and vice chairman, and three other members. The primary responsibilities of the board of directors are setting the policies of the bank and approving bank loans, guarantees, and insurance. Approval authority for guarantees and insurance transactions up to a value of $1 million is delegated by the board of directors to a loan committee.

The National Advisory Council on International Monetary and Financial Policies (NAC) reviews Eximbank policies and advises the bank on loans and guarantees of $30 million or more. The NAC also has responsibility to review any application by a potential borrower from (1) a country where property of U.S. citizens has been expropriated and the issue of adequate compensation has not yet been resolved or (2) a country that is delinquent in its debt payments to the U.S. government.

Financing Operations

The activities of the bank can be grouped into two general areas, depending on who is receiving the bank's credit: the buyer or the seller. In the bank's terminology, it has two financing "windows." The first window gives buyer credit or project financing: that is, it makes direct loans for long time periods at a fixed rate of interest, and it guarantees private loans for heavy capital equipment and capital-intensive projects. The second window provides supplier credit through medium-term commercial bank guarantees, short- and medium-term export credit insurance, and discount loans.

The first, or project financing, window is geared toward big ticket products and long-term projects—involving a repayment period of 5 years or longer. This window is used to help finance the purchase of heavy capital equipment, commercial jet aircraft, locomotives, and for other major outlays. The window's project financing supports exports of "turnkey" projects such as manufacturing, electric power, and petrochemical plants, and large mining or construction operations. Capital equipment and project financing accounted for 75 percent of the Eximbank's $33.2-billion financing outstanding at the end of 1980. About 70 percent of this financing covered U.S. exports to developing countries.

The second, supplier credit, window supports export sales of less costly items involving shorter repayment periods: short-term loans are up to 6 months, medium-term, from 6 months to 5 years. Aproximately 3,000 U.S. exporters use Eximbank supplier credit financing annually.

The two operations of the Eximbank (the buyer and seller windows) are carried out through four major programs: (1) facilitating major export transactions through direct lending and financial guarantees, (2) providing protective guarantees to commercial banks in medium-term export financing transactions, (3) rediscounting commercial banks' medium-term export loans to provide a fixed rate of interest on the transactions supported, and (4) cooperating with the FCIA to provide export credit insurance to United States exporters. These programs are explained in more detail in the latter part of this chapter.

Funding Sources

The bank's operations, loans, and guarantee and insurance programs are funded through the bank's own resources and borrowings from (1) the U.S. Treasury, (2) the Federal Financing Bank, and (3) private sources. The bank's resources of approximately $3 billion at the end of the 1979 fiscal year (October through September) were about one-third capital stock held by the U.S. Treasury and about two-thirds a reserve for contingencies and defaults. The bank can borrow up to $6 billion directly from the Treasury for its short-term needs. It can borrow from the Federal Financing Bank for long-term loans. Notes payable to the Federal Financing Bank on September 30, 1980, totaled $10.07 billion. The Eximbank's long-term loan assets amounted to $13.76 billion. The bank also has income from fees and interest, which is used first to meet its administrative expenses, then applied to its lending capability.

Operating Ceilings

Under the Export-Import Bank Act of 1945, the Eximbank is authorized to make commitments for loans, guarantees, and insurance up to $40 billion at any one time. The bank's authorization prescribes a formula for counting loans, guarantees, and insurance charged to the $40 billion limitation: loans are charged against the authorized amount on a 100-percent basis; guarantees and insurance are charged at not less than 25 percent of the Eximbank's contracted liability, up to a total of $25 billion at any one time. In effect, this method of charging commitments raises the ceiling on combined guarantees and insurance to $18.75 billion (in face amount): since only 25 percent of the combined guarantees and insurance is charged against the $25 billion limit, only $6.25 billion is counted. Deducting the $6.25 billion from the Eximbank's total authorization of $40 billion leaves $33.75 billion available for lending (which is charged at the full, 100-percent rate of face value). Adding this $33.75 billion pool to the $18.75 billion available for guarantees and insurance, the Eximbank's total effective lending capability is $58.75 billion.

The committed and uncommitted amounts authorized to the Eximbank to lend, guarantee, and insure on September 30, 1980, are presented in Table 11.1. The committed funds represented 61 percent of the authorized amount of $40 billion, which left the bank ample capacity to make new commitments under its authority. Guarantee and insurance commitments on the 25-percent basis totaled only $11.75 billion against a limit of $25 billion. The Eximbank, therefore, had plenty of flexibility in making future commitments under the 2 programs.

The annual operating and expense budget ceilings for the Eximbank are established by the U.S. Office of Management and the Budget. The year's ceilings for the loan, guarantee, and insurance programs are established by Congress in the annual Foreign Assistance and Related Programs Appropriations Act.

Table 11.1   Committed and Uncommitted Authority of Eximbank September 30, 1980 (Millions of dollars)

Category			Charge
Loans outstanding		$13,765.1	
Loans undisbursed		7,647.5	$21,412.6
Guarantees	$ 6,178.2		
Insurance	5,570.8		
	$11,749.0 (@) 25%		2,937.3
Committed			24,349.9
Uncommitted			15,650.1
Total statutory authority			$40,000.0

Source: Export-Import Bank of the United States, *1980 Annual Report* (Washington, D.C.; Eximbank, 1980).

Distribution of Eximbank Commitment and Exposure by Geographical Area

A geographical breakdown of authorizations made under the three major programs (loans, guarantees, and insurance) of the Eximbank for the 1979 fiscal year and of the bank's total commitment and exposure at the end of the 1979 fiscal year are shown in Table 11.2. The distribution of Eximbank authorizations for fiscal year 1979 shows that the major part of the bank's activities related to U.S. export trade with the developing countries of Africa, Asia, and Latin America; 81 percent of the loans, 85 percent of the guarantees, and 89 percent of medium-term insurance authorizations by the Eximbank in 1979 were for the developing countries. In the last column of Table 11.2, the worldwide exposure of the Eximbank at the end of September 1979 is shown. This represents the outstanding totals of loans, guarantees, and insurance provided by the Eximbank program. Table 11.2 presents a program breakdown of the Eximbank worldwide exposure for 1979 and 1980.

Most of the trade with the industrialized countries is financed through the normal private financial and credit channels of commercial banks in the United States and other industrialized countries, which are fully developed and can provide much of the financing and credit needs within their national boundaries. Furthermore, the financial institutions within the industrialized countries provide normal guarantees, as well as financing, for their customers. In addition, U.S. commercial banks have branches and affiliates in the developed countries, which facilitates financing of U.S. exports to those countries.

Another important reason for lack of Eximbank financing in the industrialized countries is the capability of those countries to earn foreign exchange, which allows for easy transfer of funds into and out of a country. The capacity of developing countries to earn foreign exchange is not as great as that of the

Table 11.2   Eximbank Commitment and Exposure by Geographical Area (Fiscal 1979 authorizations $ millions)[a]

Area	Loans	Guarantees	Medium-Term Insurance	Total	Exposure September 30, 1979
Africa	$ 714	$163	$ 60	$ 938	$ 3,439
Asia	1,786	248	62	2,095	9,325
Canada	10	—	2	12	374
Europe	689	139	47	875	6,035
Latin America	597	356	364	1,317	6,692
Oceania	29	2	14	45	377
Miscellaneous					(64)
Total	3,825	908	549	5,282	26,178
Discount loans				650	761
Short-term insurance	650				
Authorized				3,560	
Unshipped					1,760
Total authorizations	$4,475	$908	$549	$9,491	$28,699

1979 and 1980 Commitments and Contingent Liabilities

	At End of September 30, 1979	(Millions)	At End of September 30, 1980
Outstanding loans	$11,859.0		$13,765.1
Undisbursed loans	7,292.2		7,647.5
Guarantees contingent liability	4,961.3		6,178.2
FCIA insurance contingent liability	4,486.7		5,570.8
Total worldwide exposure	$28,699.2		$33,161.6

Source: Export-Import Bank, *op. cit.*
[a] Commitment and exposure is the extent to which the bank is committed by its fiscal-year authorizations and its total, worldwide, outstanding, cumulative exposure (past and present).

developed countries. Other factors, such as political instability, also make these countries somewhat risky for private financing.

PROGRAMS AND OPERATIONS

This section provides a guide to the programs of the Eximbank, which are grouped by (1) the value of the product or service exported and (2) the related repayment period required. Table 11.3 presents a schematic outline of the various programs. In the table, the products and services are listed under the usual financing terms and the appropriate Eximbank and FCIA programs. (The matching of products and services with financing and insurance programs in Table 11.3 should be used only as a general guide; the details of each specific transaction determine which particular program is applicable to that transaction.)

Within the three general areas of Eximbank programs, much of the bank's activity has been in the two areas of loans and export credit insurance, as shown in Table 11.3. The direct credit program has had the highest value of authorization throughout the years shown, which indicates that a fairly high percentage of Eximbank financing has been longer-term financing. A comparison of 1980 and 1976 shows that, although the number of authorizations fell, the value of the authorizations increased. This trend reflects rising exports of high-ticket goods and services and a rise in the dollar value of exports because of inflation.

The table indicates that short-term export credit insurance is the most frequent coverage bought, as would be expected. The master policies program carries the second highest amount authorized.

The rest of this chapter presents Eximbank programs under the general organization of short-term, medium-term, and long-term programs, plus special programs for small business exporters (although these programs can overlap or be combined, as will be noted).

Short-Term Programs

A part of U.S. exports to foreign buyers involves (1) short-term financing to sellers to finance the export during shipment and delivery and (2) short-term credit to sellers to finance credit sales to the foreign buyers. Short-term financing of export credit is generally made through commercial banks and other financial institutions in the United States, but financial credits to buyers in foreign countries are subject to several types of commercial and international risks. Commercial banks and other financial institutions in the United States that extend credit to finance exports, therefore, become exposed to certain risks. Naturally, the degree of risk exposure is related to the country involved in the transaction.

The Eximbank's short-term programs cover export sales up to 180 days. The Eximbank supports short-term export sales exclusively with its export credit insurance program, which is operated jointly with the FCIA.

The Foreign Credit Insurance Association

The FCIA was formed in 1961 and operates as an unincorporated, joint underwriting association under the insurance laws of New York State. The FCIA is a syndicate of 51 leading U.S. marine, property, casualty, and reinsurance companies. Under a cooperative arrangement, the FCIA manages the programs

Table 11.3 Eximbank Authorization Summary (Fiscal years 1976–1980, $ millions)

	1976			Transition Quarter			1977		
	Number	Amount	Export Value	Number	Amount	Export Value	Number	Amount	Export Value
Loans									
Direct credits[a]	150	$2,141.4	$4,895.8	17	$267.3	$599.5	52	$700.0	$1,441.5
CFF[a]	696	143.7	277.4	127	14.9	30.1	305	47.1	85.2
Discount[b]	1,226	1,203.7	678.1	242	166.0	95.3	609	473.5	199.6
Total loans	2,072	3,488.8	5,851.3	386	448.2	724.9	966	1,220.6	1,726.3
Guarantees									
Financial[a]									
Related to direct credits	60	972.9	—	5	88.5	—	13	181.0	—
Related to CFF	348	47.0	—	77	7.0	—	63	5.3	—
Unrelated to loans	2	62.6	153.5	4	61.4	188.4	15	302.7	918.6
Local cost	—	—	—	—	—	—	—	—	—
Bank	737	564.0	758.8	185	115.4	164.5	662	531.7	766.6
Other[c]	7	14.7	17.9	—	—	—	—	—	—
Total guarantees	1,154	1,661.2	930.2	271	272.3	352.9	753	1,020.7	1,685.2
Export credit insurance									
Short-term	1,046	2,185.9	2,185.9	268	459.9	459.9	968	1,961.2	1,961.2
Medium-term	940	483.0	628.0	213	83.0	111.6	597	329.5	89.1
Combined short- and medium-term	140	224.4	232.2	39	56.7	58.7	87	79.3	491.2
Master policies	31	576.6	2,168.1	11	130.9	336.3	40	988.3	2,515.2
Total insurance	2.157	3,469.9	5,214.2	531	730.5	966.5	1,692	3,358.3	5,056.7
Grand total	5,383	$8,619.9	$11,995.7	1,188	$1,451.0	$2,044.3	3,411	$5,599.6	$8,468.2

	1978		1979		1980		
Loans							
Direct credits[a]	66	$2,872.4	99	$3,724.7	137	$4,045.3	$7,735.9
CFF[a]	296	54.9	468	100.2	178	41.7	83.3
Discount[b]	527	497.3	753	650.0	875	490.8	297.0
Total loans	889	3,424.6	1,320	4,474.9	1,190	4,577.8	8,116.2
Guarantees							
Financial[a]							
Related to direct credits	4	134.3	6	201.0	15	1,318.4	—
Related to CFF	123	12.1	233	26.1	82	12.7	—
Unrelated to loans	6	96.2	7	111.7	12	572.3	1,055.9
Local cost	—	—	1	166.8	1	1.5	—
Bank	477	346.8	573	399.2	576	473.1	553.5
Other[c]	—	—	3	3.1	11	131.7	264.1
Total guarantees	610	589.4	823	907.9	697	2,509.7	1,873.5
Export credit insurance							
Short-term	927	1,961.5	1,289	2,453.0	1,682	3,018.3	3,018.3
Medium-term	704	324.1	813	347.6	870	529.6	692.6
Combined short- and medium-term	127	203.3	140	201.3	108	196.4	192.2
Master policies	33	873.5	73	1,106.5	87	1,777.4	4,215.2
Total insurance	1,791	3,362.4	2,315	4,108.4	2,747	5,521.7	8,118.3
Grand total	3,290	$7,376.4	4,458	$9,491.2	4,634	$12,609.2	$18,108.0

Source: Export-Import Bank, *Fiscal 1980 Annual Report* (Washington, D.C.).

[a] Export value for financial guarantees related to specific loans are included with the appropriate loan details.

[b] Export value for discount loans which are guaranteed or insured are included in the insurance and guarantee details.

[c] Includes lease guarantees, equipment political risk guarantees, engineering services guarantees, preshipment coverage, and contractors' guarantees.

and acts as the agent of the Eximbank in offering a variety of short-term and medium-term policies directly to U.S. exporters and commercial banks. (Medium-term policies are discussed in the section on medium-term programs.)

The policies provide coverage for political and commercial risk exposure. The Eximbank insures all political risks, and the FCIA insures the commercial credit risk with certain deductibles by the exporter to cover part of the risk. Under a reinsurance agreement which became effective October 1, 1979, the Eximbank reinsures all of the commercial losses in excess of the deductible. The total participation of the 51 insurance companies in FCIA is $15.0 million, which represents the yearly stop loss retention (amount of losses that can be sustained in a given year) of the member companies. The annual total stop loss retention by the FCIA per country is 50 percent of the yearly stop loss retention, or $7.5 million.

FCIA short-term insurance premiums average .05 percent per $100 of gross invoice value. Exporters can obtain service at any of the FCIA's 7 regional offices located in Atlanta, Chicago, Cleveland, Milwaukee, Los Angeles, Houston, and Washington. Its headquarters are in New York City.

Benefits of Export Credit Insurance

Export credit insurance provides protection for the foreign sales receivables of U.S. export companies, and therefore affords the exporter greater financial flexibility in its export operations and in entering new export markets. FCIA coverage of the commercial credit risk includes insolvency of the buyer or protracted default. The political risk coverage of the Eximbank under the FCIA export credit insurance includes war, revolution, insurrection, expropriation, and currency inconvertibility.

The benefits of export credit insurance to export companies include the following:

1 Exporters are protected against political and commercial risks over which they have no control.
2 Exporters are encouraged to make competitive offers by extending terms of payment.
3 Because risk is minimized, the exporter can broaden potential export markets.
4 Leveraging on the exporter's accounts receivable is made possible. With the assistance of the export credit insurance, the exporter is in a better position to offer credit terms comparable with those offered by its foreign competitors in overseas markets. Exporters can obtain more favorable interest rates on their financing of export credit by assigning the FCIA insurance to its commercial bank.

FCIA-Eximbank Insurance Policies

The FCIA-Eximbank insurance programs provide coverage for only a specified portion of the export sale. The exporter assumes the risk of the uninsured portion. In this way, the insurance programs spread the risk between the insurer and the insured. The FCIA and the Eximbank carry out assessments of the commercial credit and political risks for specific buyers and countries. Based on their assessments of the risk involved, the percentage of coverage may be reduced in specific cases.

The six types of policies offered in the short-term program are (1) short-term comprehensive policy, (2) short-term political-risk only policy, (3) master policy, (4) master policy for political risks only, (5) agricultural commodities policy, and (6) services policy. Five of these policies are listed in Table 11.4 with the amount of their coverage; services policies give service industries the first four types of coverage. (Although FCIA-Eximbank insurance programs are grouped by the length of coverage—short term, medium term, or long term—there are also combinations of periods, such as short and medium term.)

Short-Term Comprehensive Policy   Under the short-term comprehensive policy the exporter obtains blanket coverage for individual transactions within a discretionary limit. The approval of the FCIA is required for all sales above the discretionary limit. The blanket policy provides coverage for all or a reasonable amount of the exporter's eligible short-term sales.

This policy provides the flexibility the exporter needs to make credit decisions within the discretionary limits and take appropriate action when market conditions change.

The policy carries an annual commercial first-loss deductible provision, like medical and automobile insurance. Political losses are not subject to the deductible. The FCIA-Eximbank short-term comprehensive insurance covers 90 percent of the commercial credit risk and 100 percent of the political risk—leaving the insured exporter responsible for only 10 percent of the commercial risk.

Short-Term Political-Risk Only Policy   An exporter may have had good experience in doing business with certain foreign buyers and not feel the need to take out commercial risk coverage. A short-term policy to cover political risks only

Table 11.4   FCIA-Eximbank Short-Term Program Insurance Policies

Policy	Commercial Coverage (%)	Political Coverage (%)
Short-term comprehensive	90	100
Short-term political risk only	—	100
Master (comprehensive)	90	100
Master (political risk only)	—	100
Agricultural commodities	98	100

Source: The Export-Import Bank: Financing for American Exports—Support for American Jobs (Washington, D.C.: Eximbank, 1979).

is available for such an exporter. The political-risk only policy is not subject to the first-loss deductible provision.

Master Comprehensive Policy   The master comprehensive policy is designed for the exporting company that has marketing channels overseas in the foreign export markets. The master comprehensive policy provides a much broader coverage for sales to end-users, dealers, or distributors than does the simple comprehensive policy. The master policy allows the exporter to cover both short-term and medium-term sales. When the repayment period is extended to 5 years, the customary terms in international trade for maximum repayment apply.

A discretionary limit is assigned to the policy, which provides the exporter with the flexibility to determine the amount of insured credit to extend to individual foreign buyers. The policy has a deductible provision applicable to an annual cumulative loss factor.

The master comprehensive policy covers 90 percent of the commercial credit risk and 100 percent of the political risk. Heavy users of the master policy include the transportation equipment, construction machinery, paper and forest products, air conditioning, and chemical industries.

Master Policy—Political Risk Only   For long-established exporters with good customer relations and good dealer and distributor channels, commercial credit risk may be minimal. A special master policy has been designed for political risks only to meet the needs of this type of exporter. The premiums on this policy are lower than premiums for the comprehensive master policy, and the policy insures all of the political risk.

Agricultural Commodities Policy   The insurance program for agricultural commodity exports provides coverage for both commercial credit and political risks. It covers 98 percent of commercial risk in agricultural commodity export sales and 100 percent of political risk.

Services Policy   The services policy provides coverage for contract billings of exporters in service industries using personnel based in the United States. Exporters of services perform various types of consulting (such as engineering, architectural, management, and data processing) and other export activities such as overseas oil drilling and telecommunications design.

Comprehensive, master, and political-risk only policies similar to those described above are available for short- and medium-term coverage for these service industries.

Medium-Term Programs

The Eximbank has three programs to support medium-term export sales: (1) the FCIA medium-term export credit insurance programs, (2) the U.S. commercial bank guarantee program, and (3) the discount loan program. A combination or "switch cover" program provides a package of these programs for dealing with overseas distributors. (The Cooperative Financing Facility has been discontinued.)

Medium-Term Export Credit Insurance Policies

There are four policies under the FCIA medium-term insurance program: (1) the single-buyer policy, (2) the short- and medium-term combination policy, (3) the master policy, and (4) other specialized types of coverage, such as for preshipment and consignment sales. Medium-term policies are written on a case-by-case basis to cover a specific sale between the seller and the buyer.

These policies cover sales on repayment terms ranging from 181 days to 5 years. The products covered by the medium-term policies are relatively more expensive than those covered under the short-term policies. The products are generally capital equipment (such as printing machinery, machine tools, construction machinery, general aviation aircraft) and planning and feasibility studies.

The medium-term insurance package requires participation by the three parties involved in each transaction. First, the foreign buyer is required to make a cash payment of at least 15 percent of the contract sale price on or before delivery of the purchase to the buyer. Second, the exporter retains for its own account at least 10 percent of the financed portion of the export sale. The insurer covers the remaining amount. An example will illustrate how the risks are distributed among the buyer, the seller, and the insurer—that is, the FCIA-Eximbank:

Example: A Mexican manufacturing company buys a piece of capital equipment for $100 thousand. We assume that the Mexican manufacturer is a good commercial credit risk and will be allowed to pay the minimum down payment of 15 percent of the export sale price. Thus, the following breakdown will apply to this example:

Mexican manufacturer cash payment	
(15% of $100,000)	$ 15,000
United States exporter retains	
(10% of $85,000)	8,500
	$23,500
FCIA-Eximbank insurance coverage	76,500
Total export sale price	$100,000

In the example, the financed portion of the transaction is 85 percent, or $85,000. The U.S. exporter retains 10 percent of the financed portion (10 percent of the $85,000) or only $8,500. The FCIA-Eximbank medium-term insurance will provide coverage for 76½ percent of the export sale price, that is $76,500.

Repayment will follow a stipulated schedule which relates the terms of repayment to the amount involved in the transaction as presented in Table 11.5.

Table 11.5   Repayment Schedule for Medium-Term Transactions

Contract Value	Term (Maximum Years)
Up to $50,000	2
$50,001–100,000	3
$100,001–200,000	4
Over $200,000	5

Source: Export-Import Bank, *op. cit.*

Single-Buyer Policy   Because of the extended period of repayment, single-buyer policies are custom-designed for the individual buyer. There are two types of single-buyer policies. The first provides coverage for each individual sale transaction and would apply to a buyer who makes only a single purchase, or is not a frequent purchaser of the product or equipment, from the U.S. exporter. The second type provides coverage for repeat sales to a specific single foreign buyer.

The policies require that the buyer issue a promissory note which stipulates repayment of the financed portion of the export sale transaction in U.S. dollars payable in the United States. A repayment schedule should set up installment payments on a monthly, quarterly, or semiannual basis.

Comprehensive Short- and Medium-Term Combination Policy   Some U.S. exporters sell to dealers and distributors in foreign countries, to whom the U.S. exporter may have to offer credit terms in order to remain competitive. In some cases the overseas dealers and distributors may be affiliates of the U.S. exporter and will therefore rely on the U.S. exporter for financing. The financing required in such cases is usually for inventory and accounts receivable. The short- and medium-term combination policy is designed to meet the needs for both types of coverage to protect the exporter's financial exposure. The inventory financing aspect is covered by the short-term policy, which provides initial coverage up to 270 days for capital goods purchased, with no cash payment. The receivable financing is covered by the medium-term policy of up to 5 years, after the minimum 15-percent cash down payment has been made.

Both commercial and political risks are covered by the medium-term policy, up to 90 percent for the commercial risk and 100 percent for the political risk in normal cases. The policy also covers interest charges up to a maximum interest of 6 percent in default cases. Interest coverage is computed to either the date of payment of the claim or up to 8 months from the date of default, whichever is less.

Short- and Medium-Term Combination Policy for Political Risks Only   In cases where the U.S. exporter is dealing with an affiliate or a foreign buyer with a previous good customer-relations record, the commercial risk may be negligible or nonexistent, or the financial circumstances of the foreign dealer or distributor may be such that even without previous customer relations the commercial risk may be minimal. In such cases, the U.S. exporter may desire to obtain coverage for political risks only, which is provided by this type of policy.

Master Policy   The master policy covers both short-term and medium-term sales. It extends the repayment period of the short-term master policy by up to 5 years. Both the master policy and the combination policy are designed to protect the exporter's financial exposure to foreign dealers and distributors. The master policy also covers sales to foreign end-users as well. Whereas the combination policy is designed to insure specific financial risks in inventories and receivables of foreign dealers and distributors, the master policy has no such limitation, making it more flexible than the combination policy.

The master policy is designed to enable the exporter to minimize not only risk, but also cost, by allowing the exporter to determine in advance the amount of insured credit to extend to individual buyers within a designated limit under the policy. The master policy carries an annual cumulative commercial loss deductible.

Like the short-term policies and medium-term single-buyer policies, a master policy is available to cover political risk only.

Specialized Types of Coverage   The FCIA-Eximbank medium-term policies include coverage of special situations not covered in the preceding policies. Two such situations are (1) preshipment coverage and (2) consignment sales coverage.

1   *Preshipment Coverage Policy:* In some cases, capital equipment being exported has to be custom-made to the specifications of the overseas customer; the finished product cannot readily be sold to any other customer. In such cases, payment for the equipment is required before manufacturing starts or as manufacturing progresses. The U.S. producer usually takes out a preshipment coverage policy to protect the interest of the overseas customer who has already paid for the equipment.
2   *Consignment Sales Coverage Policy:* Some export sales are made on consignment basis with special financing packages and with the overseas customer making special arrangements to collect the consigned sale. The consignment shipment may be arranged because of some specific commercial and/or political risks, or because of the financial situation of the overseas customer. Such shipments may not be covered in any of the previous policies; the consignment sales coverage policy protects the financial interest of the United States exporter.

Commercial Bank Guarantee Program

In many situations U.S. exporters extend medium-term trade credit directly to their overseas customers in order to facilitate export sales. But with limited financing capacity, the exporters normally expect to refinance their medium-term trade credit with commercial bank financing to free some of their working capital tied up in the outstanding medium-term payables.

The Eximbank designed its commercial bank guarantee program to facilitate the purchase by commercial banks of the exporter's medium-term export credits by providing guarantees to the commercial banks. The Eximbank guarantee enables commercial banks to purchase the foreign debt obligations to U.S. exporters without recourse to the exporter. The Eximbank guarantee covers both commercial credit and political risks.

Credit Conditions   The credit conditions within the foreign buyer's country must be acceptable to both the commercial bank and the Eximbank so that the extent of their commercial credit exposure is limited. The Eximbank's credit information office, a part of the bank's division of export credits, guarantees, and insurance, maintains computerized information on the credit history of more than 50,000 foreign buyers. The bank presently offers the coverage of its commercial bank guarantees to obligations in more than 140 countries.

Risk Participation   In an effort to spread the risk and to minimize its exposure, the Eximbank has established requirements that the foreign buyer must make a cash payment of at least 15 percent of the financed portion (this minimum percentage is higher in high-risk cases). The exporter is required to set aside 10 percent of the financed portion, which may also be increased in high-risk situations.

Repayment Terms   Guidelines for repayment terms have been established by the Eximbank. The terms of repayment depend on the value of the sale. As shown in Table 11.6, terms range from 181 days to 5 years.

Guarantee Limitations   The Eximbank has limited its coverage liability in the case of default by limiting interest payments to 6 percent, or less if the underlying credit carries a lower rate. The interest accrued will be paid up to the date of payment of the claim.

Table 11.6   Repayment Terms for Commercial Bank Guarantee Program

Contract Value	Terms
Up to $50,000	181 days to 2 years
$50,000–100,000	Up to 3 years
$100,000–200,000	Up to 4 years
Over $200,000	Up to 5 years

Source: Export-Import Bank, *op. cit.*

Delegated Authority   Commercial banks that have established satisfactory records in the commercial bank export guarantee program can obtain delegated authority to commit the Eximbank without prior approval by the bank.

Bank-to-Bank Guarantees and Insurance   To assist financial institutions in the developing countries to help local importers finance their medium-term purchases of exports from the United States, the Eximbank has designed a bank-to-bank guarantee and insurance program. The program involves revolving medium-term bank lines of credit established by U.S. banks with financial institutions in developing countries.

To participate in the program, foreign banks are required to assume the risk of lending to the end-user. Unless the U.S. bank acts as an exporter of record, it is not required to assume a share of the commercial risks. (The U.S. bank assumes a standard exporter retention on commercial and political risks if it acts as the exporter of record.)

The fees charged and the coverage offered are similar to Eximbank guarantee and FCIA insurance guidelines.

Discount Loan Program

This facility is available only for loans made at fixed rates of interest. Commercial banks may not be willing to make fixed-rate loans for export credit unless they can discount such loans and reinvest their funds at current rates of interest. This situation arises during periods of high or rising interest rates, especially when a tight-money policy is being pursued. (Banks normally hold medium-term notes on loans made to exporters and foreign buyers of United States exports.) When such conditions arise, therefore, export sales may be lost for lack of export credit at competitive rates. To alleviate such problems, the Eximbank has developed a discount loan program, in which the bank discounts notes held by commercial banks by making loans against the commercial bank's purchase of a foreign obligation up to 100 percent of the financed portion of the loan. In some instances, the Eximbank may actually purchase the note. The Eximbank discounts the note on the foreign obligation with full recourse to the U.S. commercial bank, which assumes full responsibility for the commercial credit and political risks of the transaction. Commercial banks usually have FCIA-Eximbank master policy coverage for their normal operations, which covers the commercial and political risks of the transaction.

Eligibility   U.S. commercial banks, Edge Act corporations and Agreement corporations operating under Sections 25 and 25(a) of the Federal Reserve Act, and U.S. branches of foreign banks are eligible to participate in the discount loan program.

Advance Commitment   Banks must apply for advance commitment by the Eximbank to make a discount loan or to purchase their notes. They are required to certify that they would not be in a position to make the export credit without the use of the discount program. The Eximbank will then issue advance commitment to eligible banks to make loans to or buy notes from them.

Discount Rate   Loans made to commercial banks under the Eximbank discount loan program will be 1 percent below the yield a commercial bank earns on its export credit. The Eximbank has a minimum discount loan rate (MDLR), established by its board of directors for the discount loan program, which sets the lowest rate at which the Eximbank is committed to lend under the program. The MDLR will be equal to the New York Federal Reserve Bank discount rate.

Commitment Fees   Commercial banks are charged a one-time, front-end commitment fee of 2 percent, which must be paid within 120 days of the date of the Eximbank's commitment letter. The committment fee will increase the effective rate of the credit by an average of .5 percent on a typical 10-year amortization. Two variables determine the amount of the commitment fee: (1) the amount of the discount loan authorized and (2) the total term of the Eximbank's commitment.

Contract Value   The maximum contract value eligible for the discount program is $5 million. There is no minimum.

Medium-Term Direct Credit Program

In all the programs discussed so far, the Eximbank's export credit has worked through either a U.S. exporter or a U.S. commercial bank. In the next program, the bank works directly with foreign commercial banks and foreign distributors.

Foreign distributors are usually in a position to facilitate the sale of the U.S. exports of capital equipment if they can provide the foreign buyer with financing credit to pay for the purchase. The Eximbank has developed a special "switch cover" feature, which allows a U.S. exporter or commercial bank to provide the credit needed by a qualified overseas distributor to finance the purchase by end-users of capital equipment exports from the United States. The switch cover facility gives foreign distributors greater capacity to manage their inventories and enhances their ability to purchase more capital equipment from the United States. Features covered by the switch cover include commercial bank guarantees, discount loans, cooperative financing, and FCIA-insured policies. Other characteristics are the following:

1 *Eligibility:* The switch cover facility applies to capital equipment sales with a contract price of $25,000 or more.
2 *Terms:* The facility covers the cost of the capital equipment in the distributor's inventory up to 270 days if necessary before the equipment is sold to the end-user. The purchaser's promisory note will be covered by Eximbank-

FCIA risk coverage. The promissory note must be payable in U.S. dollars paid in the United States.

3 *Lien:* Private buyers not provided with a guarantee by an acceptable financial institution must take out a first lien on the capital equipment in support of the loan.

Long-Term Programs

Large export sales usually involve huge sums of money and long-term financing with repayment periods extended over many years. The nature of the projects, the risks involved, the size of the financing package, and the extended period of repayment usually preclude any single U.S. commercial bank from undertaking such financing by itself. Commercial banks generally limit their exposure to short- and medium-term export credits, but U.S. exporters of major capital equipment and projects must provide financing packages to overseas buyers that match the offerings of exporters from other industrial countries in order to remain competitive in world markets. To assist in meeting the long-term financing needs of U.S. exporters, the Eximbank provides long-term financial assistance through its direct credit program and its financial guarantee program. A combination of the two programs is usually used to support a single financing package by the bank, but loans and guarantees are increasingly being used separately to conserve the Eximbank's budget authority.

Direct Credits and Financial Guarantees

The Eximbank's direct credit program extends loans to purchasers of U.S. major projects and large product exports. These loans are normally made with private lending participants. The Eximbank's direct loan financing is made to supplement loans by commercial banks to finance foreign purchase of heavy capital equipment, technology-intensive products, industrial plants, and other major foreign projects that involve a large financial outlay and correspondingly long repayment period.

The financial guarantee program provides participating private banks with the assurance that the export credit extended to the foreign buyer under the program will be repaid. The financial guarantee is used to encourage private commercial banks to participate in the financial package.

Participation Conditions   Efforts to obtain private financing must precede all requests for direct loans from the Eximbank. Financial assistance for long-term credits are made cooperatively with commercial banks and the Private Export Funding Corporation (PEFCO). Eximbank policy is to supplement private financing to the extent that private lenders are unable or unwilling to lend because of the risks involved and the length of repayment term required. The Eximbank normally finances the longer-term maturities in a loan package and lets private financing sources cover the shorter-term maturities. The normal participation rate of the Eximbank, for both direct loans and guarantees, varies between 30 and 65 percent of the U.S. exporter's costs of a transaction. The extent of private and foreign government-supported financing determines the extent of the Eximbank's participation.

Financing Terms   The foreign buyer is required to make a cash down payment of at least 15 percent of the contract price of the U.S. purchase. Repayment of principal and interest is scheduled in semiannual installments. Repayment usually begins 6 months after either (1) the date of delivery of the product or (2) the date of project completion. The repayment installments are split among the financing parties in accordance with their cash flow needs: private financial institutions usually take the earlier repayment installments to obtain cash for new loans, while the Eximbank takes the later repayment installments.

Loan Rates   The interest rate charged varies from time to time, reflecting changes in the cost of funds and the competitive environment. At the time of writing, the bank interest rate was 10.75 percent, with a higher rate for aircraft.

Credits to Deal with Foreign Government Competition   At times U.S. exports are competing with exports from countries whose governments provide low-interest, government-supported financing to their exporters. In these situations the Eximbank will lengthen repayment terms on a case-by-case basis to enhance the competitiveness of United States exports. Nineteen credits were authorized in 1979 at rates below the Eximbank's scheduled rates, to match the terms of publicly supported foreign competition faced by U.S. exporters. In documented cases of intense foreign competition, the bank will consider providing local cost financing (financing to meet local costs in addition to import costs) as well.

Some governments combine normal export financing with foreign aid—a form of mixed credit—by charging low interest rates on government-supported foreign financing. In the past, the Eximbank has been willing to support United States exporters faced with this type of competition. For example, to support a sale of an earth satellite station to a buyer in Cyprus in December 1978 the Eximbank authorized a low-interest credit of $3.8 million at 6 percent interest to match the terms of a mixed-credit deal that the French government had made available to the Cyprus buyer. The U.S. exporter was able to make the sale with the Eximbank's low-interest export credit.

In a second case, when the governments of France, West Germany, and Japan offered the government of Tunisia a low-interest, mixed-credit financing deal, the Eximbank matched the terms of this intense government-supported foreign competition by authorizing a $100 million line of credit bearing an overall interest rate of 5.5 percent.

In order to eliminate competition based on interest rates, a schedule of minimum interest rates and maximum repayment terms (organized by the degree of economic development and financial liquidity of the importing country) has been established under the International Agreement on Officially Supported Export Credits. The schedule is presented in Table 11.7.

Table 11.7   International Agreement on Officially Supported Export Credits—Minimum Rates and Maximum Repayment Terms (In effect from November 16, 1981)

Country Classification	Minimum Interest by Maximum Repayment Period		
	2–5 Years	5–8.5 Years	8.5–10 Years or Longer
Relatively rich	11.00	11.25	NA
Intermediate	10.50	11.00	NA
Relatively poor	10.00	10.00	10.00

Source: Export-Import Bank, *op. cit.*
NA Not applicable.

Commitment Fee   The foreign buyer must pay a commitment fee of .05 percent per year on the undisbursed amount of each direct loan. The commitment fee accrues 60 days from either the date of authorization of the loan or the date the loan agreement was signed, whichever comes first.

Guarantee Fee   The Eximbank charges a guarantee fee of between .05 and 1 percent on the outstanding balance of a guaranteed loan, and a commitment fee of .0125 percent on the undisbursed amount of each guaranteed loan.

Repayment Guarantee   For long-term financing under direct credit or financial guarantee programs, the buyer is required to obtain a sponsoring financial institution in the buyer's country to provide a repayment guarantee for the buyer to the Eximbank. The usual guarantors are the central bank of the country, the finance ministry, or a government development bank. The Eximbank will accept guarantees from large commercial banks in some cases. The repayment guarantee provides a degree of assurance that the buyer will repay the loan, as required by the Eximbank's enabling legislation.

The Private Export Funding Corporation

PEFCO is a private company organized as a supplemental lending source in 1970 by United States commercial banks and industrial corporations. The objectives of PEFCO are to mobilize private capital resources at fixed rates to provide medium- and long-term export credit financing to supplement the resources provided by commercial banks and the Eximbank. The loans are unconditionally guaranteed under the Eximbank guarantee programs. A large number of export credit financing plans have involved the direct participation of PEFCO. Projects include the financing of steel mills, cement plants, aircraft sales, conventional and nuclear power plants, as well as mining projects.

Under the Eximbank direct loan program, a commercial bank undertakes the financing of a part of the loan and the Eximbank underwrites the other part.

At times, the size of the loan and the length of the repayment schedule in its share of the loan package are beyond the financing capacity of the participating commercial bank; PEFCO would normally be invited to participate in the financing package in such a situation. PEFCO sells its own debt obligations to raise funds to meet its participation activities with Eximbank guarantees.

Loan Size   The minimum size of a PEFCO loan is $1 million, and there is no maximum amount. PEFCO loans have ranged from $1 million to $116 million, with an average of $14.6 million.

Repayment Period   PEFCO normally chooses maturities between the 5-year upper limit of commercial banks and the Eximbank coverage. Repayment periods of PEFCO loans are fixed on each transaction; past loans have carried maturities up to 15 years.

Share of Individual Loans   PEFCO's participation in individual loans ranges from a low of 8 percent to a high of 45 percent. PEFCO makes loans only as part of a cooperative lending package within Eximbank financing programs. PEFCO loans have automatic Eximbank guarantees. The Eximbank's approval is required for all individual loan commitments and in determination of the terms and conditions of PEFCO's intermediate-term borrowings.

Loan-Purchase Program   PEFCO will buy from U.S. banks or other acceptable institutions export loans guaranteed by the Eximbank and other guaranteed debt obligations of foreign importers under its new loan-purchase program. The objective of the loan-purchase program is to provide primary lending institutions such as commercial banks with liquidity to finance additional export credits.

Applying for PEFCO Financing.   PEFCO's lending activity is supplemental to commercial bank export credit facilities. U.S. exporters and foreign borrowers should normally approach their regular commercial bank first, which would put together the financing package with Eximbank guarantees and PEFCO's participation.

The following minimum information must be received by PEFCO before it can indicate its interest rate on a proposed loan: (1) the amount of the loan, (2) the approximate schedule of disbursements and final availability date, (3) the repayment schedule, and (4) PEFCO's requested part of the loan.

Small Business Support Program

Small exporters have different problems from those experienced by larger firms. The Eximbank small business support program is intended to address their problems. Facilities have been designed in the program specially to assist the small new exporter to use the various Eximbank programs and to provide aid for the small exporter with a modest volume of exports. The Eximbank programs of particular interest to small exporting firms are the export credit insurance program with FCIA, the commercial bank guarantee program, and the discount loan program.

International trade is associated with multinational corporations and with bigness, so that small firms in the United States believe that there is no place for them in export trade. The small firms in the export business which have modest sales usually lack information on export markets, export opportunities, and ways of improving export sales. In addition, they often cannot obtain adequate financing. Worse, small businesses entering the export business also are usually unaware of the FCIA-Eximbank insurance program.

Small businesses in other industrialized countries, however—particularly the European countries—have had extensive trading experience with foreign importers around the world. U.S. small businesses need to seek information on exporting and on how the Eximbank can help them so that they can extend their participation in international export markets. Because of the size of their economies, export markets in developing countries can be more attractive to the small export firm than to the big multinational corporation. Moreover, developing countries are somewhat leery of doing business with huge multinational corporations for fear of domination by their massive resources. Small businesses, in contrast, do not pose any threat to these countries, and they usually welcome the interchange, with mutually beneficial results. The growing export markets of developing countries should, therefore, provide potential growth markets for small U.S. exporting businesses.

Small Business Conferences

One effort to provide the type of information on export marketing that has been unavailable to the smaller business was a series of conferences sponsored by the Interagency Committee on Small Business Export and Investment (SBEIC). This committee was formed in 1978 by Eximbank, the Small Business Administration, the U.S. Department of Commerce, and OPIC. Thousands of smaller firms were invited to 38 small business conferences, sponsored by SBEIC, on the opportunities in foreign sales for the smaller firm. With more information on foreign sales possibilities, the smaller businesses have become more interested in foreign marketing.

Small Business Advisory Service

A toll-free small business information hotline was installed by the Eximbank in February 1979. Some 5,200 inquiry calls came through during the first 9 months—on export markets, export credit financing, and on specific export transactions. The information hotline provided a much-needed information source for smaller firms that lack the resources and the time to do their own research.

Short-Term Export Credit Insurance

The Eximbank introduced a short-term export credit insurance program with the FCIA in 1978 which provided protection for export sales of smaller firms. For eligible small businesses, the Eximbank increased the coverage for commercial risks from 90 to 95 percent (with political risks covered 100 percent). Eligible small businesses retain only 5 percent of the commercial risk while paying the same rates as exporters holding regular policies with higher retentions. Smaller firms also enjoy an exemption from any commercial deductible requirements.

To be eligible for this Eximbank small business insurance and guarantee program, the firm must *not* have (1) net worth exceeding $2 million, (2) exported more than an average of $350,000 annually over the last 3 years, or (3) used Eximbank or FCIA services subsequent to January 1, 1975. The eligibility conditions, in short, restrict qualified firms to new and very small exporters.

SUMMARY

The Eximbank has developed several programs of insurance, guarantees, and financing to assist the U.S. exporter, and it provides financial services to support the wide spectrum of products and projects in U.S. foreign trade. The operations of the Eximbank can be grouped into two areas, depending on whether the bank's credit is being provided to the buyer or the seller.

The first area involves direct loans for long periods at fixed rates of interest, and financial guarantees of private-source loans for heavy capital equipment and capital-intensive projects. The second area of the bank's activities involves the provision of supplier credit through medium-term commercial bank guarantees, short- and medium-term export credit insurance, and discount loans.

The Eximbank has four major programs through which it administers buyer and seller credits. These programs (1) facilitate major export transactions through direct lending and other support activities; (2) provide protective guarantees to commercial banks in medium-term export financing transactions; (3) rediscount commercial banks' medium-term exports loans to give the banks more liquidity for further lending; and (4) cooperate with the FCIA to provide export credit insurance to U.S. exporters.

The bank's operations are funded from the bank's own resources and from (1) the U.S. Treasury, (2) the Federal Financing Bank, and (3) private financing sources. The Eximbank is authorized, under the Eximbank Bank Act, to make commitments for loans, guarantees, and insurance up to $40 billion at any one time. Loans are charged in full against the authorized amount; guarantees and insurance are charged at not less than 25 percent of the Eximbank's contracted liability against the authorized amount, with a limit of $25 billion on the total amount of guarantees and insurance that the bank can commit itself to at any one time at the fractional charge. Thus the Eximbank's total outstanding contractual commitment at any one time under the formula is $58.75 billion.

The six types of policies offered in the short-term program are (1) a short-term comprehensive policy, (2) a short-term political-risk only policy, (3) a master comprehensive policy, (4) a master policy for political risks only, (5) an agricultural commodities policy, and (6) a services policy.

The Eximbank has three programs to support medium-term export sales: (1) the FCIA medium-term export credit insurance programs, (2) the U.S. commercial bank guarantee program, and (3) the discount loan program. A combination, or switch cover, program provides a package of these programs for dealing with overseas distributors.

To assist in meeting the long-term financing needs of U.S. exporters, the Eximbank provides long-term financial assistance through its direct credit program and its financial guarantee program. The Eximbank's direct credit program extends loans, in participation with private lenders, to purchasers of major U.S. projects and large product exports. The financial guarantee program provides participating private banks with assurance that the export credit extended to the foreign buyer under the program will be repaid.

Sometimes, U.S. exports have to compete with exports from countries whose governments provide low-cost government-supported financing to their exporters. In these situations the Eximbank will make appropriate adjustments to its interest rates and repayment terms, to enhance the competitiveness of U.S. exports.

PEFCO is a private company organized in 1970 by U.S. banks and industrial corporations to mobilize private capital resources at fixed rates to provide medium- and long-term export credit financing to supplement the resources provided by commercial banks and the Eximbank. PEFCO loans are unconditionally guaranteed under the Eximbank guarantee programs.

The Eximbank's small business support program is designed to assist the new, small exporter in using the various Eximbank programs and to provide aid for the small exporter with a modest volume of exports.

12

Export Credit Financing through Foreign National and International Systems

Now that the export credit financing system of the United States has been discussed, we turn our attention to non-U.S. systems and international systems of financing export credits. Chapters 10 and 11 described the roles played by the U.S. commercial banking system and the Export-Import Bank in the financing of exports of the United States. In addition to these facilities, international agencies (such as the World Bank group, regional development banks, and the International Monetary Fund) can finance exports from the United States through loans, as discussed in this chapter.

The current practice of multinational and transnational corporations is to produce component parts of products composed of complex assemblies in different countries for assembly in still another country for regional or worldwide distribution. This approach takes advantage of differences in countries' factor endowments and technological skills to produce a product in the most efficient way. Thus we have seen the development of multinational corporations, which have production facilities in several countries and export from many countries around the world. Such corporations need to know about the foreign national export credit financing systems, as well as the international systems. Strategic planning by multinational corporations for the best location for their component-production facilities for regional or world assembly should also include careful analysis of export financing systems.

Such analysis is especially important if a portion of the components or the complete product will be exported to the developing world. As the economies of the developing countries grow, their domestic markets expand and their capacity to import increases, which provides greater opportunity for export to these markets. Although export financing is done largely through private financial institutions, as noted in Chapters 10 and 11, the risk exposure from the political instability in the majority of developing countries poses a serious drawback to private financing of exports to developing countries. Private insurance agencies that are willing to cover normal commercial risks of export credit financing are most reluctant to provide coverage for political risks. This attitude may be due to the intricacies of dealing with foreign laws and regulations. At any rate, the lack of insurance cover for political risk is a disincentive to private financial institutions to provide the necessary financing for export credit to the developing countries. To meet this need, like the United States (see Chapter 11), the governments of the other exporting countries have stepped in to provide export credit guarantees for commercial and political risks at rates that are reasonable and economical. These official systems also provide guarantees against nonpayment to commercial banks.

These government insurance and guarantee programs generally cover three basic types of commercial credit risk, as follows:

1   The buyer's failure to pay within the time stipulated in the contract, or within six months of the due date for goods that have been accepted.
2   Insolvency of the buyer.
3   Failure by the buyer to accept goods that have been shipped, as long as nonacceptance has not been caused by some action of the exporter or noncompliance with the terms of sale.

Officially supported export credit insurance covers a number of political risks, including the following:

1   Delays in payment in the exporter's currency resulting from government action or policy.
2   Imposition of new import-licensing restrictions in the buyer's country.
3   Cancellation of a valid import license of the buyer.
4   Cancellation or nonrenewal of an export license.
5   Imposition of new export licensing restrictions.
6   War, revolution, rebellion, insurrection, or similar disturbances.
7   War between the exporter's country and the buyer's country.
8   Requisition, expropriation, or confiscation of the business, or intervention in the business of the buyer or guarantors by a government authority.
9   Any other cause of loss occurring outside the exporter's country and not within the control of the exporter or the buyer.

International trade among the industrialized countries of the OECD is financed mainly through private institutions, and insurance coverage is available to protect against the commercial risks for transactions among these countries. Commercial banks and other institutions in the countries provide the necessary guarantees for bank loans to finance export credits to buyers in other industrialized countries. Although mega-ticket items and complex systems that need long-term financing may require additional public guarantees, all the necessary financing can be obtained from private banking sources for export to industrialized countries.

The commercial and political risks involved in exporting to the less-industrialized members of the OECD, to the centrally planned economies of Eastern Europe, and to the developing countries compel governments to provide insurance and guarantee programs to protect the interests of their exporters. These public programs are designed to complement private financial sources of export credit, not to compete with them, by providing insurance and bank guarantees for commercial bank financing of export credit, and by making direct loans as needed.

Commercial banks normally make short-term loans and medium-term loans up to five years, but seldom make long-term loans. To meet the need for long-term loans, official programs provide cofinancing packages with commercial banks in which the official program finances maturities beyond medium term. The official agencies normally require the commitment of private financing for the shorter maturities in the package before they will consider participation.

In almost all cases, commercial banks are involved to some extent in providing financing for export credit. All inquiries for export credit financing, therefore, should normally be initiated through the exporter's commercial bank. The banks usually have an international department or an export financing department with professional advisers to provide the exporter with all the necessary information and advice on putting together and choosing appropriate export financing packages.

The important features of the major countries' national programs and of international programs are presented in this chapter to provide information on the variety of export credit financing systems currently available.

FOREIGN NATIONAL EXPORT CREDIT FINANCING SYSTEMS

Canada

The domestic private banking system in Canada provides the bulk of the financing for the nation's export credit. As in other countries, however, although private insurance agencies can provide insurance coverage for normal commercial risks, they cannot insure against political risks. The Canadian government, in an effort to encourage financing of export credit by the banking system, therefore, has developed a system of export credit insurance and bank guarantees. The bank guarantees apply to loans made by Canadian banks to finance export credits or rediscount exporters' credits.

The Canadian export credit insurance system which insures exporters against risks of nonpayment for exports operates through a wholly owned, semiautonomous government corporation, the Economic Development Corporation (EDC). The EDC was formed in 1969 to replace the Export Credit Insurance Corporation as the provider of insurance to Canadian exporters and commercial banks against the risk of nonpayment for exports. Compared with the credit insurance agency, the EDC has wider authority and greater autonomy to provide the kind of flexibility needed to cope with the growing complexity of financing international trade. As a proprietary crown corporation, the EDC is required to underwrite only commercially sound business ventures in order to remain solvent and to operate on a self-sustaining financial basis. It does not depend on the government for budgetary support.

Export Credit Insurance and Bank Guarantees

Both Canadian export credit insurance and the bank guarantee program are administered by the EDC. It is governed by a 12-member board of directors with full responsibility for all EDC business activity. The directors represent both public and private sectors of the economy. Seven of the members of the board are senior government officials appointed by the government to represent their departments, which have responsibilities in the foreign trade area. The Department of Industry, Trade, and Commerce has two members, the chairman of the board and one member each come from the Finance and External Affairs departments, the Bank of Canada, and the Canadian International Development Agency. Five members represent private business; the president of the EDC is appointed from this group.

The operations of the EDC include projects undertaken on its own account and those undertaken on behalf of the Canadian government. Since the EDC must operate on a fiscally sound basis, it insures and finances on its own account only export business with acceptable credit risks. Export credit requests involving an unacceptable level of business risk are submitted to the government. The ministry of Industry, Trade, and Commerce may provide departmental credit if the request is considered to be in the national interest.

The EDC provides insurance coverage for export credits to suppliers and guarantees for buyer credit on financing made by commercial banks. The objective of the insurance program is to insure against the risk of nonpayment by foreign buyers when export credits are extended by suppliers or financed by banks. Insurance coverage is undertaken by the EDC for Canadian exports that are eligible for coverage of 60 percent or more of their value.

The resources of the EDC come from authorized and subscribed capital of $400 million. (All dollar amounts in this section are in Canadian dollars.) Of this amount $80 million has been subscribed. The EDC has an insurance reserve of $6 million.

The EDC has limits on its commitments for insurance liability. A ceiling of $750 million is prescribed for the export insurance it can write on its own account. An additional amount of up to $750 million can be written if specifically authorized by the government.

Types of Risk Covered   The policy of the EDC is to accept coverage only for combined commercial and noncommercial risks; coverage cannot in general be split. Comprehensive policies cover short-term export credit and provide revolving coverage for the exporter's whole year's business. The comprehensive policy provides the exporter with broad protection, while allowing the EDC to spread its risk.

Exporters who do not wish to take out a comprehensive policy on their whole year's business can select alternative coverage so long as it covers an adequate amount of risk. These exclusions to the combined-risk-only policy include sales to the United States and sales against irrevocable letters of credit. Coverage for export credit financing of medium- and long-term maturities is accepted on an individual contract basis.

Criteria for Coverage   The EDC's coinsurance policy requires the exporter to share the cost of insured risk. The exporter is required to retain a small portion of the amount insured for his own account.

The exporter is also required to assure the creditworthiness of the foreign buyer to minimize the risk exposure of the EDC. Guarantees by the Canadian government or by creditworthy institutions in the buyer's country may be required on large transactions.

Types of Coverage   The EDC offers two types of insurance coverage for export credit: the "contracts" policy and the "shipments" policy. Under the contracts policy, an exporter is covered from the time the order is booked until payment is received. This policy combines preshipment and postshipment insurance. The shipments policy provides coverage from the time the goods are *shipped* until payment is received, like most export credit policies. It is cheaper than the contracts policy because it does not cover the preshipment period.

Credit Terms   The four kinds of export transactions insured by the EDC are based on the type of product and the length of time credit is insured. Terms of coverage are specified for tangible products. Intangibles, such as services and "invisible" exports, are provided coverage as needed. ("Services" includes design, engineering, construction, technology, and marketing services to a foreign customer, and photogrammetric and geophysical surveys. "Invisible" exports include sales or licensing of patent trademarks or copyrights, advertising fees, and fees to auditors and architectural consultants.) The four classes of export transactions are:

Type of Product or Service	Terms
Consumer goods	Short term—up to 6 months
Capital goods	Medium term—up to 5 years
Heavy machinery	Long term—up to 5 years
Services—"Invisible" exports	Unspecified term

Cost of Coverage All *short-term* financing for Canadian export supplier credit is done by commercial banks as part of their regular business financing, with the EDC providing only insurance. Short-term financing costs vary with the creditworthiness of the exporter. A variable premium rate for the EDC insurance coverage is based on the credit length and the risks involved.

However, *medium-term* financing for supplier or buyer credit, which covers credit length up to 5 years, is provided by the EDC, as well as by commercial banks. The EDC rates, generally the same as the commercial rates, are based on the creditworthiness of the exporter (for supplier credit) or the foreign buyer (in the case of buyer credit). The EDC charges a variable premium for insurance cover based on the length of the credit and the risks involved in the transaction. The premiums range from a ¾ percent minimum to a maximum of 3 percent; this premium is levied on the invoiced value of the insured export.

Direct Credits and Bank Guarantees

The EDC is authorized under the Export Development Act, as revised in 1975, to make direct loans on its own account to foreign buyers for long-term export credit financing up to $4,250 million at any one time. This EDC direct lending program provides buyer credit to purchase Canadian exports of heavy capital goods and big-ticket projects. The program is designed to make Canadian exporters' credit terms competitive with those available to other countries' exporters by their respective governments. It also guarantees private loans by Canadian commercial banks to a foreign borrower.

The long-term financing provided by the EDC covers the period in excess of 5 years. Up to 5 years are usually financed by commercial banks under an EDC guarantee. A large number of long-term loans in a bank's portfolio would make the bank relatively illiquid with a correspondingly higher risk exposure.

The combination of private financing of the earlier maturities with EDC financing of the later maturities allows for maximum private participation in the financing of Canadian exports. Private participation averages 30 to 40 percent.

The board of directors of the EDC undertakes careful evaluation of the risks involved in each long-term financing transaction before financing on its own account to ensure that the transaction is commercially sound. When the EDC feels that the risks involved exceed its standards for commercially sound business, the transaction may be referred to the ministry of Industry, Trade, and Commerce for direct government financing. If it determines that the loan is in the national interest, the ministry can authorize the EDC to make the loan on behalf of the government. The risk is borne by the government in such cases. The ceiling established for government loans of this type is $850 million. Funds for financing such loans come from the general revenues of the Canadian government. Interest payments are made into the fund after the EDC costs of administration have been met.

The EDC obtains its funds for direct lending from two sources. It has the authority to borrow from the government's general revenues, on its own account, and from the capital markets. Most EDC borrowing is from government revenues but some short-term lending needs have been met by borrowing from the capital markets. These borrowings from the capital markets have been in the range of $20 million to $50 million.

France

As in Canada, most financing of export credit in France is done by private commercial banks. Almost all French exports to developed countries are financed by banks under normal commercial terms.

Public support for export credits began in 1946 when the Compagnie Francaise d'Assurance pour le Commerce Extérieur (COFACE) and the Banque Francaise du Commerce Extérieur (BFCE) were created by the French government. Insurance of export credit risks is provided by the quasi-public COFACE. Financing of export credits is conducted through the Bank of France (public at present) and the quasi-government BFCE. The Bank of France provides a special line of credit to rediscount claims with maturities over 18 months. The BFCE provides financing for export credits with maturities over 7 years and mobilizes funds for loans through bonds floated in the national and international financial markets.

New methods of financing export credits have been introduced since 1971 to reduce the burden on the Bank of France. Export credits are financed on a 100-percent basis even if COFACE insures less than 100 percent of the transaction. Credits with maturities greater than 18 months are given preferential financing, and the role of commercial banks in financing export credits has been increased.

Export Credit Insurance and Bank Guarantees

COFACE manages the official French foreign credit insurance program on behalf of the French government. COFACE was established in 1946 as a joint stock company by a group of nationalized insurance companies and banks, which makes COFACE a publicly owned corporation.

The French government supports French export trade in part through export credit insurance provided by COFACE. The insurance protects French exporters and French banks against nonpayment by foreign buyers. The insurance protection provided by COFACE enables the banks to provide 100-percent financing for export credit at preferential rates.

COFACE has a contributed capital of Fr 10 million and had an accumulated reserve of Fr 36 million at the end of 1972. For an annual fee of 2 percent of the premiums received, COFACE gets from the French Treasury an excess-of-loss cover on its short-term transactions. Insurance coverage for short-term commercial risk is provided by COFACE on its own assessment, within certain ceilings.

COFACE manages the medium- and long-term credit insurance for French exporters for the government. The director of External Economic Relations of the ministry of Economic Affairs and Finance decides whether to cover requested medium- and long-term credit, after a joint ministerial commission, the Commission des Garanties et du Credit au Commerce Extérieur, gives an advisory opinion on each application. The joint commission is made up of representatives of the ministry of Economic Affairs and Finance, the ministry of Foreign Affairs, the Credit National, the Bank of France, the operating ministry involved, COFACE, and BFCE. COFACE has much of the decision-making power in accepting medium- and long-term credit insurance within a ceiling prescribed by the director of External Economic Relations.

Coverage for commercial and political risks is provided by two classes of policies. The first covers consumer goods and light, production-line industrial goods and the second covers heavy industrial goods and large complexes.

Consumer goods include raw materials, semifinished goods, and consumer durables. The consumer goods policy covers commercial risk in all countries and political risk in selected countries. The *light capital* goods policy can cover either worldwide commercial risk with a political-risk option, or worldwide political risk with optional commercial-risk coverage.

The consumer goods and the light capital goods coverage is similar to a master policy that provides a revolving cover for the exporter's whole year's business activities for commercial risk, or, in the second option for light capital goods, for political risks.

In the case of *heavy capital goods and large complexes*, COFACE offers individual policies for political risks, with optional commercial risk coverage. Supplier credit coverage for commercial risks is limited to 80 to 85 percent of the insurable amount, with the exporter retaining 15 to 20 percent of the risk. In the case of political risk coverage, the portion covered is 90 percent. For buyer credit, COFACE covers 95 percent of both the commercial risk and the political risk of the insured amount; the buyer retains only 5 percent of the risk.

Credit Terms The credit terms depend on the type of goods financed. Short-term credit—up to 6 months—is intended for consumer goods. For light capital goods the exporter can obtain maturities of up to 3 years (up to 5 years if the transaction is a large one). The 3-year and 5-year maturities make up the medium-term credit category.

Long-term credit has different terms for coverage in developed and in developing countries. Export credits to foreign buyers for the purchase of heavy capital goods or large complexes have maturities from up to 5 years, for the most developed countries, to a maximum maturity of 10 years for buyers in the developing countries.

Conditions for Coverage COFACE requires repayment of loans in equal semi-annual installments, with no grace period allowed. The foreign buyer is required to make a down payment of 15, 20, or 25 percent of the loan, depending on the country of the buyer.

To meet the needs of foreign buyers for local-cost financing, COFACE allows credit up to a maximum of the amount of the down payment. Credit for local-cost financing carries the same terms as for export credit.

Predelivery Financing   For contracts requiring predelivery financing, COFACE has special financing packages, which provide credit facilities for advance payments to exporters. Another financing package provides for advance payments to a manufacturer when stipulated in the contract under buyer credit financing.

Costs of Export Credits   The export financing rate is based on the maturity of the financing. There is one short-term rate and two longer-term rates, as outlined below.

1 *Short-Term Rate:* The short-term rate is a three-tier rate made up of (1) a base rate, which is the basic bank rate or the prime rate, to which is added (2) a minimum bank charge of 0.4 percent, plus (3) a premium for COFACE coverage. Since the prime rate varies with the market, the total short-term rate is variable.

2 *Taux de Sortie:* The *taux de sortie* is the rate of interest applicable to medium- and long-term financing of export credit. It is a weighted average of two rates for each maturity. The *taux de sortie* has certain advantages for French export trade. The rate is independent of monetary fluctuations, which makes it fairly stable, although it is adjusted by the authorities periodically. The rate varies with the length of the maturity, but is fixed over the term of each credit. Insurance costs are added to the *taux de sortie.*

The *medium-term taux de sortie* (for credits with maturities up to 7 years) is the weighted average of:

1 The Bank of France discount rate, 9.5 percent, plus a fixed commission. This rate is weighted by a predetermined percentage.

2 A predetermined maximum rate of return for the commercial banks. This rate varies with the market, to permit the banks to earn an average return commensurate with the total financing they provide and to induce the banks to participate in the financing. Fixed commissions are added to the return.

The *long-term taux de sortie* (for credits with maturities exceeding 7 years) is a weighted average of:

1 The Bank of France discount rate, 9.5 percent, to which a fixed commission is added. The discount rate is weighted by a predetermined percentage.

2 The BFCE rate for financing, which is the same as the 7-year credit rate.

Direct Export Credit Financing

Public export credit financing is provided by the BFCE, which is a quasi-governmental banking agency. The BFCE provides direct loan financing for export credits with maturities over seven years. The bank obtains its funds by floating bonds in the French capital markets and the international Eurocurrency markets. The difference between the *taux de sortie* rate received by the BFCE and the market interest cost of the bonds is covered by the French Treasury.

West Germany

In West Germany, most export credit financing is provided by the private banking system in cooperation with the government. Export credit financing to buyers in developed countries is carried out essentially through private commercial banking channels, with private insurance covering the basic commercial risks. Two private companies offer insurance for normal credit financing of exports to developed countries: the Allgemeine Kreditversicherung A.G. and the Gerling-Konzern Speziale Kreditversicherungs A.G. (GKS).

Private insurers are somewhat reluctant to cover the political risk of export credit financing, and if they did, their premium rates would have to be so high that German exporters would be less competitive than exporters in other countries. Since 1919, therefore, the government has provided export credit insurance to help protect exporters against nonpayment for political reasons.

Financing of export credit is provided primarily by the banking system. Government assistance in this area is given through two channels: the Ausfuhrkredit GmbH (AKA) and the Kreditanstalt fur Wiederaufbau (KfW). Direct lending to developing countries is carried out by KfW with low-cost funds obtained through loans from the government. KfW also dispenses capital aid for the West German government.

Export Credit Insurance and Bank Guarantees

The West German government is authorized under the Household Law of 1962 to offer export credit insurance coverage for political and commercial risks. The objective of the public export credit insurance and guarantee program is to provide coverage for political and commercial risks in financing export credits to developing countries. The government's insurance program is administered by two private corporations: the Hermes Kreditversicherungs A.G. (Hermes) and the Deutsche Revisions and Treuhand A.G. (Treuarbeit). These companies receive applications for insurance and undertake a preliminary screening before passing them on to the West German International Committee for Export Guarantees, which reviews them and decides whether to accept them. The committee then returns the application to the companies to carry out its decision.

The committee is made up of representatives of the ministries of Economic Affairs, Finance, Foreign Affairs, and Economic Cooperation. The committee has a panel of experts for consultation and advice which is composed of representatives from the Bundesbank (the German Central Bank), KfW, AKA, and the commercial banking and export trade sectors.

The resources of the program come from annual budget appropriations by the German parliament, which at the same time establishes the year's ceiling for export credit. In 1976 the ceiling was DM60,000 million. Premium receipts are credited directly to the budget account, and all claims paid are charged to the account.

Types of Coverage The program offers joint coverage for commercial and political risk because it is felt that political risk in any of the countries of the Third World covered by the program necessarily entails commercial risk. Policies to cover risks from fluctuations in exchange rates and problems with deliveries and services in developing countries are also available to exporters within certain limits.

Two classes of policies are issued, depending on whether the foreign buyer is a private company or a government (or government agency). The first class—coverage for export credit financing to private firms abroad—is classified under "Garantie" business. In the second—export credit financing to foreign governments and bodies constituted under public law—is classified "Burgschaft" business.

Along with the two classes of coverage are three types of policies offered, based on the type of export transaction involved. The first is a one-time policy covering a single transaction. The second is for the many exporters who handle products with repeat sales, who require a revolving-type of credit to the foreign buyer. This second type of coverage provides revolving cover for an exporter's whole year's business with a given foreign buyer. The third type of coverage meets the need of the German exporter with distribution channels overseas. It covers the exporter's entire year's business with a number of buyers abroad. This third type of coverage is provided only under the Garantie (private) business classification.

Credit Terms Credit terms are based on length of coverage. *Short-term* credit covers a period of up to 6 months and generally applies to consumer goods. *Medium-term* credit covers export credit financing from 6 months to 5 years for durable goods. *Long-term* credit involves periods over 5 years. The maximum durations of credit are 8½ years for credit in the state trading countries of the Eastern bloc and 10 years for exports to developing countries.

Conditions for Coverage Several conditions are attached to the policies offered, as follows:

1 *Buyer and Guarantor Credit Standing:* The credit of the foreign buyer or guarantor must be good, in order to limit the commercial risks of the coverage. If the buyer's or guarantor's credit is doubtful, the uninsured portion of the exporter's risk may be raised.
2 *Down Payment:* A cash down payment of not less than 15 percent of the cost of the transaction must be made by the foreign buyer. Progress payments are required in coverage of certain types of transactions.
3 *Repayment:* The repayment schedule requires semiannual repayments on a regular basis. The coverage does not provide for a grace period.

4 *Local-Cost Financing:* Coverage for local-cost financing from West German commercial banks is provided on the basis of international standard practices for local standard costs. (These are interaction protocols that serve as standard bases for local-cost financing.)

5 *Creditworthiness of Buying Country:* When the country of the foreign buyer does not meet the required credit standards, maximum liability ceilings are imposed, and the exporter's portion of the uninsured risk may be increased.

Separate classifications are used to cover export credit financing to developing countries in need of aid, in the case of transactions of special importance to West Germany's export policy, and in transactions that involve risk above normal standards but are of particular interest to the West German government. These special transactions do not carry a set ceiling.

Cost of Coverage   Separate premium rates apply to transactions under each of the two classes of coverage. In general, the premium rate charged to private foreign buyers under the Garantie class of coverage is double the rate to foreign public-sector buyers under the Burgschaft coverage.

The premium for foreign private buyers (the Garantie class) depends on the term of the export credit. In the short-term period, up to 6 months, the premium is a flat 1.5 percent of the total value of the export credit financed. This rate applies also the first 6 months' coverage under the medium- and long-term coverage. For the medium-term coverage of up to 3 years, the premium changes to 1 percent per DM1,000 per month after the initial 6-month premium. Long-term coverage premium rates vary between 1.3 and 1.4 percent per year from the third year to the tenth year.

The premium charged to public-sector foreign buyers (the Burgschaft class) is a combination of rates based on the amount of export credit financed, plus a flat monthly rate, as follows:

Amount of Coverage	Premium
Up to DM3 million	1 percent
DM3 million to DM5 million	0.75 percent
Over DM5 million	0.50 percent
Plus	0.4 percent per DM1 thousand per month on all coverage

The premium paid by public-sector buyers, then, depends on the amount borrowed, plus the flat 0.4 percent monthly premium.

Direct Export Credit Financing

Direct financing of export credits by the West German government is carried out through the AKA and the KfW.

The AKA   The AKA, organized in 1952, is a consortium of all commercial banks with a subscribed capital of DM40 million. It provides supplier credit and has the refinancing of medium- and long-term loans made by German exporters to foreign buyers under 2 separate lines of credit. Line A is a totally private refinancing line of credit of the AKA consortium with no government connection or subsidy. Line B has government support and subsidy.

Loan packages by the AKA usually combine both line A and line B to take advantage of the dual benefits. Line A provides maturities up to 10 years with the exporter required to pay a lower retention than under line B, which provides a lower rate but very short maturities.

1   Line A has a DM4,000 million line of credit available. (DM800 million of this amount is used for financing of buyer credits and is referred to as line C.) The exporter is required to share the risk by retaining between 15 and 20 percent of the transaction value. The rate of interest is normally 1 percent below the market rate of interest and varies with that rate throughout the life of a loan. Loans are made for periods up to 10 years.

2   Line B has a DM3,000 million line of credit. The Bundesbank has developed a cooperative arrangement with the AKA through which AKA bills are rediscounted at a special rate of 2.1 percent above the Bundesbank's discount rate. This rate is normally substantially below the market rate, and therefore the arrangement provides low-cost financing, which is used to finance exports mainly to developing countries and state trading companies. The package of credit financing from line B and other sources cannot be granted below a 7.5-percent rate of interest.

The exporter assumes a share of the risk by retaining 30 percent of the amount of coverage. The AKA uses all repayments of the loan to pay off its outstanding loan balance first. This process increases the exporter's relative exposure.

Credits are granted under line B for periods up to four years from the date of signing of the contract. The four-year maximum period includes any period needed for the manufacture of the product, which results in a very short repayment period.

The KfW   The KfW was organized in 1948 by the German government to provide low-interest financing for the reconstruction of West Germany's post-war economy. In 1955 the KfW began redirecting its efforts toward long-term financing for exports. In the early 1960s, the KfW became the official government agency for the administration of West German capital aid programs for developing countries. The KfW also administers the export promotion fund for the government.

Japan

In cooperation with private financial institutions, the government of Japan has developed an institutional framework to provide insurance and bank guarantees for export credit financed by private banks. The objective of the government's program is to encourage and supplement private financing of Japanese exports, as well as Japanese investments overseas. Direct lending is also undertaken in the case of large transactions with longer maturities than those usually preferred by commercial banks. Through the Export-Import Bank of Japan, the Japanese government provides direct financing for export credit for maturities over 6 months at a preferential rate.

To encourage private financing of export credit, the Japanese government has set up an insurance agency, the Export Insurance Division (EID) of the Ministry of Trade and Industry (MITI), to insure commercial banks against commercial and political risks in export credits financed by these banks. Guarantees are provided also to commercial banks on loans made to foreign buyers of Japanese exports. The provision of insurance and bank guarantees for export credit has minimized the risk of loss from nonpayment for Japanese exports, which allows exporters and foreign buyers to obtain cheaper rates for export credit financing than would otherwise be possible.

Export Credit Insurance and Bank Guarantees

Officially supported export credit insurance is administered by the EID, which offered insurance first in 1930 and currently operates under the authority of the Export Insurance law of 1950. The Ministry of International Trade and Industry has access to a pool of experts in the Export Insurance Council for advice on policy questions. Members of the Export Insurance Council are appointed by the Minister of International Trade and Industry. The 12 members of the council include the Minister of International Trade and Industry and 11 other appointees from government agencies involved in foreign trade, finance, the Japanese Eximbank, and insurance.

The EID provides insurance to exporters against the risks of nonpayment for export sales. Insurance cover is also provided for refusal of commercial paper.

The EID finances its operations from its own resources—a capital fund of Y6 billion. It underwrites insurance on a commercially sound basis to remain in a solvent position. The Japanese parliament establishes annual liability ceilings for the various types of insurance coverage accepted by the EID. The ceilings established for the 1974 fiscal year were as follows, in billions of yen.

General export insurance	4,600
Export proceeds insurance	3,100
Export bill insurance	1,200
Other	1,411
Total	10,311

Types of Insurance Coverage The EID provided insurance only for supplier credit until 1970. Since then it has offered insurance cover for buyer credit financing also. The federal insurance program provides a combined coverage for political and commercial risks of nonpayment for exports. Two types of coverage are available—a preshipment policy (from the date of contract), and a postshipment policy (from the date of shipment).

A commercial paper policy provides insurance for banks to cover the risk of refusal of commercial paper. The policy covers 80 percent of the amount insured.

Exporter Retention   The EID offers a coinsurance policy in which the exporter or foreign buyer is required to retain a small portion of the risks insured under the general export insurance program; the exporter or foreign buyer retains 40 percent of the commercial risk and 10 percent of the political risk for preshipment insurance. The commercial risk retention is reduced to 20 percent for some industrial sectors in preshipment insurance. For postshipment insurance, the retention rate is 10 percent of the amount insured.

Acceptance Criteria   The creditworthiness of the buyer country is an essential criterion for the acceptance of any cover by the EID. For large projects, extensive evaluation of the creditworthiness of the buyer and the buyer's country is undertaken by the EID, the Export Insurance Council, and the ministry of Trade and Industry before acceptance of cover.

Credit Terms and Conditions   The EID is provided some flexibility in accepting cover under the Japanese official insurance and guarantee system. For example, there is no fixed maximum on credit length or minimum amount of down payment. Insurance and guarantees by the EID for postshipment export credit do not have stipulated maximum terms. The EID has flexibility in determining the maximum maturities it will accept in conformance with international practice.

1   *Short-term financing:* For export credit by suppliers covering a period up to 6 months, exporters are not required by the EID to take out a policy, although either the exporter or the bank providing the financing usually carries a policy.
2   *Long-term financing:* An exporter is required by the Japanese Eximbank and commercial banks to take out an EID insurance policy before the exporter's application for long-term export credit financing is considered for approval.

The foreign buyer is normally required to make a down payment of 20 percent of the value of the transaction. There are no fixed criteria for grace periods; in practice, however, the first installment date can be arranged to provide a grace period. Thus grace periods are effectively granted when necessary.

Local-Cost Financing   Local-cost financing is provided by the EID for export transactions in which the Japanese supplier must provide the local financing in order to assure completion of the project. The terms are guided by the OECD declaration on local-cost financing.

Cost of Coverage   A flat premium rate of 0.454 percent of the amount insured is charged on all general export insurance. For export proceeds insurance, there is an additional premium of 0.25 percent of the amount insured per year after the first year. For example, for an export credit term of 5 years, the export proceeds insurance premium rate is:

$$0.454 + 0.25(4) = 1.454 \text{ percent}$$

As can be seen, the export proceeds insurance rate is much higher than the general export insurance rate.

Direct Export Credit Financing

Official export credit financing is provided through direct credits by the Eximbank of Japan (Exim). It was established in 1950 as a government agency, and in 1975 had a capital stock of Y699.3 billion, with reserves amounting to Y2.0 billion. The capital was paid in by the government from the Industrial Investment Special Account. Exim pays no return to the government on its capital investment.

Exim has authority to borrow funds as needed from the Trust Fund Bureau, for postal savings, at an interest rate of 8 percent per year. Exim cannot borrow from, or rediscount with, the Bank of Japan. An unused facility of Exim is its authority to borrow foreign exchange from financial institutions.

A liability ceiling is imposed on Exim on the amount of loans and guarantees outstanding at any one time. The ceiling requires that the bank's total commitments outstanding at any one time must not exceed the sum of its capital and reserves plus its maximum liability limit (equivalent to 4 times its capital and reserves). The amount of the program limits of Exim for loans and guarantees outstanding as of 1974 in billions of yen was:

$$
\begin{array}{lcr}
\text{Capital} & = & 699.3 \\
\text{Reserves} & = & \underline{2.0} \\
& & 701.3 \\
& & \underline{\times 5} \\
\text{Program limit} & = & 3{,}506.5 \\
\end{array}
$$

The president, vice president, and two auditors of Exim are appointed by the Prime Minister. The president can appoint up to six executive directors of the bank. The Eximbank Act assigns responsibility to the Minister of Finance for oversight of the bank and general policy decisions. The president of Exim has the responsibility for interest-rate determination, particularly, for ensuring that it conforms to government policy objectives. Exim's budget and accounts are submitted to the parliament each year.

Exim supplements private financing of exports by providing financing for the longer maturities and guarantees to private commerical banks for financing of the shorter maturities. Exim works cooperatively with private lenders in packaging loans in accordance with its policy not to compete with private lenders in providing export credit financing. Exim usually participates in financing requirements beyond 6 months.

Since Exim financing is done on a cooperative basis with the private banking system, the application process originates with the commercial bank, where the exporter makes the initial application for export credit financing. The application is forwarded to Exim after the commercial bank has completed its own assessment of the acceptability of the transaction for financing. The commercial bank provides the financing for short- to medium-term maturities of the loan. Exim normally provides around 60 percent of the financing, with the commercial banks providing around 40 percent.

Exim now makes direct loans to foreign buyers of Japanese exports. The bank also provides guarantees for financing by commercial banks of the shorter maturities of loan packages to foreign buyers. The Japanese government's Aid program, which provides loans to developing countries, is administered by Exim.

The United Kingdom

Export credits in the United Kingdom have been financed by the clearing banks and the merchant banks at fixed interest rates since 1961. The government provides support for export credit financing through the Export Credit Guarantee Department (ECGD), a financially independent agency of the government established in 1919. Under arrangements set up between the United Kingdom government and the banks, ECGD provides insurance and guarantees for loans made by the banks to exporters; ECGD insures the banks against political and commercial risks. The United Kingdom has no specialized department or agency for direct export credit financing.

In 1970 ECGD was given authority to make direct loans and grants, and in 1972 the department was empowered to undertake investment insurance. Since 1972 ECGD has refinanced any export loans made by the clearing banks above 18 percent of their current account balances. The refinancing is done at a rate that provides an agreed-on return for the lending banks.

Export credit insurance and bank guarantees are provided by ECGD, which is under the control of the Secretary of State for Trade and cooperates with the Treasury department. ECGD operates under a liability ceiling set by the British parliament, which has been increased through subsequent legislation. ECGD is assisted in its activities by an advisory council made up of bankers and businessmen.

ECGD's insurance program provides export credit insurance against both commercial and political risks. It also provides cover for short-term external trade contracts, as well as export contracts that include goods produced in foreign countries, or the local cost of the contract. In all cases, the external activities covered by export credit insurance must provide a financial return for the United Kingdom. ECGD uses bank guarantees and refinancing facilities for clearing banks to provide postshipment export financing at competitive costs. In selective cases, preshipment financing also is available.

Types of Insurance or Guarantee Coverage

ECGD is a financially independent executive agency which does not depend on government support. It is expected to underwrite coverage for commercially sound business so that it remains viable and solvent.

Two classes of coverage are provided by ECGD: coverage under Section 1 applies to commercial business, and coverage under Section 2 applies to national-interest business. Section 1 business covers most of the insurance and guarantees provided that are considered commercially sound. Section 2 business covers those export activities that are not deemed to be commercially sound but are in the national interest. The combined statutory liability ceiling for coverage underwritten by both sections is £15,200 million.

ECGD provides for both supplier and buyer credit coverage. For suppliers, there is a comprehensive short-term policy and a specific medium- to long-term guarantee for capital goods exports. ECGD provides banks with guarantees for buyer credits financed by the banks.

Comprehensive Policy   Exporters doing repeat business with export contracts up to 6 months are required to take out a comprehensive policy on all their export business, unless they agree to an acceptable risk spread. ECGD provides cover for 90 to 95 percent of the amount insured, and the exporter retains 5 to 10 percent. Longer-term coverage is available through supplementary guarantees. ECGD coverage drops to 72 percent in cases where the foreign buyer does not accept the shipment of goods.

Capital Goods Contracts   Guarantees are provided on individual sales of capital goods up to 90 percent of the amount insured. At the option of ECGD, the amount covered by the guarantee may be increased to 100 percent of the amount insured after 1 year of satisfactory coverage.

Buyer Credit   Guarantees are provided for buyer credit to encourage exports from the United Kingdom. ECGD provides unconditional guarantees for 100 percent of the insured credit direct to banks that have made loans to foreign buyers for major capital goods purchases from the United Kingdom or for major contracts involving exports of capital goods or services.

Terms

Credit terms cover short-, medium-, and long-term maturities. The duration of the credit term is commensurate with the value of the product. Short-term maturities, up to 6 months, are provided for raw materials, semifinished goods, and consumer goods. Semicapital goods and capital goods of medium price are covered by medium-term maturities, up to 5 years, while major capital goods and projects are covered by long-term maturities, up to 10 years.

Down Payment and Repayment

Lending for export credit financing requires that the foreign buyer assume a share of the risk by making a down payment. The minimum down payment required by ECGD is 10 percent of the amount of the transaction, but most down payments are 15 to 20 percent. Repayment terms stipulate semiannual installment payments, with no grace periods.

Conditions

Comprehensive guarantees are provided for all the exporter's business within the liability limits set by ECGD. The exporter assesses the creditworthiness of the foreign buyer and decides what sales to make, guided by the general terms of the comprehensive agreement. The creditworthiness of the foreign buyer is assessed by ECGD for buyer credit contracts and supplier credit financing of specific contracts.

Local-Cost Financing

ECGD provides guarantees for loans made by banks for local-cost financing up to a 5-year maturity limit in most cases. OECD guidelines for local-cost financing are used as the basis for making loans for this purpose.

Cost of Export Credits

The cost of export credit depends on whether the credit is for predelivery financing or postdelivery financing.

Predelivery Financing   The working capital needs of the exporter for less expensive items with short production periods are usually met through the exporter's normal bank credit at prevailing market rates of interest. ECGD provides unconditional bank guarantees for predelivery financing of capital goods when the contract value exceeds £1 million or the preshipment period exceeds 1 year.

ECGD-guaranteed predelivery financing is available also under buyer credit financing plans. The contractual agreement of the foreign buyer to make progress payments is required before ECGD will approve predelivery payments to the exporter.

Postdelivery Financing   The three types of postdelivery financing are based on the period covered (over or under 2 years) and the extent of any refinancing involved, as follows:

1 *Less than Two Years:* Banks will lend 0.5 percent above their base rate for export credits carrying a 100-percent unconditional ECGD guarantee. The minimum lending rate for this purpose is 4.25 percent. (This minimum has become fairly academic since interest rates have been in the double-digit zone for nearly a decade.)

2 *Two Years or Longer:* ECGD determines the maximum rate to be charged for the specific contract. The rate for a 2-to-5-year contract in 1976 was 7 percent, and 7.5 percent for maturities over 5 years. Bank charges are added to the rate fixed by ECGD. These charges range from 0.5 percent for periods up to 5 years to 0.33 percent for periods up to 10 years. Premiums for ECGD guarantees are added to the fixed rate and the bank charges to obtain the total rate. ECGD premiums are tied to market conditions at the time the guarantee is approved; there is a best-market and worst-market rate. The rates are highest for the period up to 5 years and scale downward for the 10-year period.

3 *Refinancing:* ECGD provides liquidity to the banks by refinancing the fixed-rate loans described above when the fixed-rate loans in a bank's loan portfolio exceed 18 percent of the bank's average current account balance over the prior 12-month period. To provide incentive to the banks to make these fixed-rate loans, ECGD modified its agreement with the banks in March 1972 (amended in October 1974) to refinance the loans in excess of 18 percent of the average 12-month current account balance at a rate of return based on an average of the bank's syndicated lending rate to nationalized industries and the Treasury bill rate. The banks ar also entitled to a margin above this rate of between 0.75 percent and 1.25 percent. The allowable margin is inversely related to the market rate.

INTERNATIONAL PUBLIC LENDING INSTITUTIONS

A number of international public lending institutions provide financing for export credits and for international investment. These institutions make substantial contributions to the pool of financial resources available to U.S. businessmen to finance export credits. The major international public lending institutions are the World Bank group of institutions, the IMF facilities, and the regional public lending institutions.

Apart from providing a significant portion of the financing for export credit to the fast-growing export markets of the developing countries, these institutions provide a measure of protection to the exporter, or to the commercial bank, by ensuring that payment for exports will be received. These institutions play a crucial role in the financing of export credits in many ways. Cooperative financing arrangements have been developed among some of the international public financing institutions, national public financing agencies, and private financial institutions.

in the formation of the DFCs and work in cooperation with these local institutions to provide financing for smaller projects within their respective countries.

DFCs lend directly to public and private borrowers. Their accessibility makes them useful candidates for World Bank financing, and they are on the spot, facilitating the lending process. DFCs may be considered the local financing affiliates of the World Bank and IDA. DFCs are required to use the same criteria, standards, and terms that the bank uses in making its own loans. The DFCs assume responsibility for supervising the loans they make with World Bank funds.

The World Bank's Third Window   The "third window" refers to loans that are made on concessionary terms—terms that are less stringent than the standard terms of the bank. The fund began its lending operations in December 1975, and third-window financing was done during the two fiscal years of 1976 and 1977 on a subsidized basis through an Interest Subsidy Fund created through voluntary subscriptions from the wealthier members of the World Bank.

The subsidy operates through semiannual payments, to supplement the interest payments due the bank, of an amount equal to 4 percent a year of the outstanding principal of third-window loans, but the borrowers pay the difference in the interest between the bank's standard interest and the 4-percent subsidy paid by the fund. The total contributions received by the fund on January 15, 1976, were $130 million, which supported some $600 million in loans from the third window. The activities conducted through the World Bank's third window were transferred to the IDA in 1977.

Information to Potential Suppliers   The World Bank issues press releases and publicizes projects when loans are made. The buyer initiates action on the project for which a loan is requested with the aid of consultants, develops the required specifications, and prepares other information needed by bidders. The borrower is required to invite tenders for competitive bidding. For contracts subject to international bidding, the borrower is requested to send invitations to the local representatives of all member countries of the bank and to Switzerland. An advertisement should be placed in at least one local newspaper of general circulation in the borrower's country. For large and important contracts the borrower is required to place advertisements in well-known technical magazines and trade publications of wide international circulation.

Terms of Lending   World Bank loans have medium- and long-term maturities. The term of each loan remains fixed after it has been determined. A term is decided for each loan on the basis of the characteristics of the project, and allowing for the prospective balance of payments and external debt of the borrowing country, as appropriate. The amortization period runs the period of the estimated useful life of the project. The World Bank allows grace periods on its loans, which run from the date of contract signing until the project is operational and begins to produce economic benefits to the borrower.

The bank charges the lowest possible rate of interest that will enable it to remain financially viable, as measured by its ratio of earnings to interest requirements on funded debt, its rate of return on capital and reserves, and the adequacy of reserves. The bank charges interest only on the disbursed part of a loan, but also charges a commitment fee of 0.75 percent per year on the undisbursed balance of the loan in order to encourage borrowers to draw down the loan. The commitment charge accrues 60 days after the date of the loan.

In the case of loans made to DFCs, the World Bank arranges the amortization schedule of its loans to complement the pattern of amortization schedules of the loan portfolio of the DFC. This arrangement provides adequate flexibility for the DFC in managing its own portfolio. The bank's policy toward new DFCs is to permit the DFC to pay only a commitment fee from the date the finance company commits itself to its borrower.

Cofinancing   The World Bank has cooperated with national governments and national public institutions to provide cofinancing for numerous projects. Since 1969 the bank has collaborated with Sweden, Canada, France, the United States, West Germany, Japan, Norway, and the United Kingdom to provide financing for projects in the developing countries. The World Bank has also collaborated with the Asian Development Bank, the African Development Bank, and the Kuwait Fund to provide cofinancing for projects in their respective areas. The bank collaborated with the European Development Fund of the EEC and with the European Investment Bank to finance projects in Africa and Asia.

The Indus Basin Development Fund was set up in 1960 in a cooperative effort by the World Bank, IDA, and the governments of eight countries. It pooled a $1.2 billion fund to finance construction of the Mangla Dam on the Jhelum River and of irrigation and other works in Pakistan. Another fund, the Tarbela Development Fund, was established by the World Bank and 6 other countries to finance the Tarbela Dam and power plant on the Indus River.

The World Bank has joined with bilateral export credit agencies offering financing on commercial terms to provide funds for large revenue-earning projects. The World Bank takes the initiative in organizing and supervising the joint financing process by arranging with the export credit agency to provide a share of the financing.

The International Development Association

IDA was established in 1960 through the initiative of the United States to provide loans on "soft" terms for the poorest developing countries. The soft loans are called "credits" to distinguish them from the loans made on conventional terms by the World Bank. The objective of IDA is to provide the external financing needed by the poorest countries to purchase high-priority economic development projects primarily to build up the country's infrastructure. These countries usually do not earn sufficient foreign exchange to meet debt-service costs if the projects are financed through normal conventional lending. IDA credits provide loans on soft terms by extending the repayment term and eliminating the interest cost.

IDA credits thus provide another source of export credit financing for buyers purchasing foreign products and projects (mainly from the industrialized countries). U.S. exporters have been involved in exports financed through IDA credits or cofinanced partly by IDA credits. The role of IDA credits in the financing of export credits for the poorest countries with the worst balance-of-payments difficulties is likely to grow in the future as the cost of imported energy mounts.

IDA obtains its funds from 5 sources: members' initial subscriptions, periodic "replenishments" from its more industrialized and developed members, special contributions made by its richer members, transfers of income from the World Bank, and IDA's own accumulated net income. The usable resources of IDA, on a cumulative basis, totaled $20.8 billion as of fiscal year 1980.

Terms of Financing   Since IDA was established to provide concessionary financing to the poorest group of countries for high-priority projects, the term of IDA credits is 50 years. The credits do not bear any interest charge, and there is a grace period of 10 years from the loan contract date. The repayment schedule provides that 1 percent of the credit be repaid annually for 10 years and the remaining 90 percent be repaid at the rate of 3 percent per year over the next 30 years. IDA credits carry a basic annual service charge of 0.75 percent on the undisbursed portion of each credit; the service charge is intended to cover IDA's administrative costs.

Borrower Eligibility   Eligible borrowers from IDA are governments, or public or private entities in developing countries with per capita gross national product less than $581 (in 1977 dollars). More than 52 countries are eligible under this criterion.

Developing countries with debt-service problems may be candidates for World Bank "lending" assistance, combining World Bank conventional loans with IDA credits, which bears either a very low rate of interest or is repayable over a very long period of time.

In general, for the eligible countries, the amount of credit is determined on the basis of considerations such as population, poverty, need for external capital, economic performance, and availability of other sources of capital to the borrowing country.

Some developing countries with per capita income below $581 may not meet IDA criteria for credit because they are considered sufficiently creditworthy to borrow on conventional terms. Nigeria, for example, which is a member of OPEC and has a capital surplus, does not meet IDA criteria, since it can obtain conventional financing on its own.

Eligible Projects for IDA Credits   Projects accepted for financing with IDA credits must have high priority in the country's economic development program. Projects are appraised on the basis of their economic feasibility and potential contribution to the economy, and on the following factors: the technical, institutional, managerial, and organizational capacity of the country to carry out the project, and the procurement, commercial, and financial aspects of the project. IDA also considers the effect of social aspects of the project on the country before approving credit for financing the cost.

Local-Cost Financing   Local currency costs of a project are financed only in exceptional circumstances. The concessionary terms of IDA credits are intended to relieve the burden of debt service: the funds thus released are expected to be available to meet local currency costs. Local costs are financed for high-priority projects, such as education, when a country needs more money than it can raise through its own savings or borrowing from sources other than IDA.

Currency Used in IDA Credits   IDA credits are made in many currencies, and contractors and suppliers are normally paid in their own country's currency.

The International Finance Corporation

The opportunity to expand the volume of exports from the industrialized countries to the developing countries grows as the economies of the developing countries expand. The private sector plays a key role in the growth and development of these countries, but many developing countries have no capital markets and generate inadequate savings to finance the capital needs of new and existing enterprises.

The IFC was established as an affiliate of the World Bank in 1956 to mobilize capital to meet the financing needs of businesses in the developing countries. The IFC's objective is to assist less-developed member countries of the World Bank to further their economic development by encouraging the growth of productive private enterprise. The IFC seeks to achieve this objective by providing equity and loan capital for private enterprise in association with private investors, by encouraging the development of local capital markets, and by stimulating the international flow of private capital. The IFC also provides support for joint ventures between local and foreign businesses to develop opportunities to combine the technical and managerial expertise in industrialized countries with local market knowledge.

The activities of the IFC are similar to those of an international investment bank. The difference between them is that the IFC is an intergovernmental organization with the sole purpose of furthering economic development by providing capital to support private enterprise and by making sound investments in the economies of developing countries.

The IFC has the same membership as the World Bank and has similar articles of agreement. The total resources available to the IFC for the period 1956 to 1980 were $1.028 billion, which included:

Capital subscriptions of $447 million

A World Bank line of credit of $438 million

Participation and portfolio sales of investments of $1.095 million

Repayments and investments of $66 million

Net income of $76 million

The gross commitment of the IFC from 1956 through June 1980, net of exchange adjustments, was $3.1 billion. These commitments were made to 203 enterprises in 73 countries, and to 2 regional development corporations. Commitments for operating investments amounted to $3.045 billion; the balance of $55 million was for standby and underwriting purposes.

The geographical breakdown of the IFC's commitment was as follows: the Western Hemisphere received 39 percent, Asia received 27 percent, Africa and the Middle East received 17 percent, and Europe received 16 percent.

Investment Procedures   The IFC makes a detailed appraisal of each investment proposal before making any commitment. The preliminary information required by the IFC to make its appraisal varies with the kind of investment under consideration. Required information includes a description of the enterprise, its legal status, financial history, present and proposed operations and their environmental effect, the purposes for which the financing is required, the outlook for profits, and the amounts of financing sought. For a manufacturing enterprise, additional information is needed on the costs and availability of raw materials and other inputs, and a review is made of technical assistance and other agreements.

Investment Criteria   The IFC considers investment projects in developing countries only, because it was set up to foster economic development through the development of private industry in countries that either lack a domestic capital market or have inadequate domestic savings to finance capital formation.

Projects of interest to the IFC must have high economic priority to the developing country in which they are located. A project is considered to have high priority if it will:

Use a locally abundant natural resource

Create jobs that will produce employment opportunities for local labor

Result in exports and earn foreign exchange for the host country

Replace a product currently imported with local output

Saving foreign exchange being spent on imports has a high priority because this type of developing country does not have adequate foreign exchange balances to meet its import needs; foreign exchange earnings from exports and foreign exchange savings from import substitution help correct this problem.

To attract IFC participation, projects must be sound and profitable and must also meet the economic priority criteria—that is, the project must be profitable in a line of business that will be beneficial to the economy of the host country. The IFC will not trade benefits to the host country for profitability; both criteria must be met.

New industries that initially may need tariff protection are expected eventually to be able to compete without protection. Such industries might need some degree of technological transfer from companies in the industrialized countries. The IFC, therefore, considers the availability of sponsors who will form joint ventures a most important criterion for the success of a project. Joint ventures between companies in industrialized countries and local businesses in the developing countries can create a sound basis for business success because of the experience and competence of the businesses in the industrialized countries. The local investors contribute to the joint-venture knowledge of the national and regional market conditions as well as of labor and government relations—knowledge that complements the technological know-how of the industrial sponsor.

The ownership of projects in which IFC participates must meet two stipulations. First, participation by the chief sponsor in the capital of the enterprise must be adequate, so as to ensure a proper long-term incentive. Second, provision must be made for immediate or eventual domestic participation.

There are many exporters in the industrialized countries, particularly in the United States, that could benefit from foreign joint-venture affiliates in the developing countries to use the exporter's products as input in the local production process. United States exporters can also use a joint venture company in a developing country as a regional production center to supply neighboring countries. Such an opportunity is especially good for small- and medium-sized U.S. companies, which may have neither the capacity to produce for a large export market nor the facilities to distribute worldwide. Many consumer products imported into developing countries could readily be produced there, in part from components made by small- and medium-sized exporters in the United States.

Types of Investments   IFC financing may be used to modernize an existing plant, to acquire new machinery, or for additional working capital for a growing business. The IFC participates in a broad range of investments. Manufacturing industries that have benefited include pulp and paper products, cement, textile and fibers, iron and steel, motor vehicles and accessories, fertilizers, chemical and petrochemical products, food and food processing machinery, and general manufacturing. Other supported ventures include utilities, tourism, printing and publishing, mining, development of financing companies, and investment in money and capital markets.

IFC activities exist on all five continents, with investments highest in Latin America, followed by Asia and the Middle East, then Europe and Africa.

IFC Financing   The IFC will provide financing that will attract other financing through IFC participation. One way is the provision of early financing to form the nucleus for other funds to cluster around. Another is to provide financing at reasonable terms that would otherwise not be available. Many financing sources become available when it is known that the IFC is a participant in the venture. The IFC's participation may be seen as providing guarantees for the soundness of the venture as well as protection from risk.

The IFC will also participate in the underwriting arrangements in countries with no capital markets and will make shares available locally when the business becomes a going concern.

Investment Terms   The minimum investment that the IFC will make is $1 million, and the upper limit for an IFC investment is around $20 million. A few IFC investments above $20 million have been made; the IFC will make a larger commitment when such a commitment will attract other large investors, which will then lower the IFC's investment in the project to within the $20 million limit. The IFC provides a smaller share of the financing for new ventures and a larger share for expanding existing businesses.

The IFC does not have a fixed formula for the terms of an investment. The terms of each investment depend on the merits of the project, the local pattern of interest rates, and the general financial maturity of the country in which the investment is to be made. The IFC wants to earn a reasonable return on its investment, commensurate with the type of business and the circumstances and conditions of the country in which the investment is made. Loan amounts are generally expressed in U.S. dollars.

Repayment periods for loans are usually for 7 to 12 years, but longer maturities can be arranged for special circumstances. A grace period is allowed before repayment (on a semiannual installment basis) begins. The IFC charges a commitment fee of 1 percent a year on the undisbursed portion of a loan in order to encourage borrowers to draw down their loans.

IFC financing has no restrictions regarding the purchase of equipment or services from a particular country, and it does not require government guarantees for its loans.

The International Monetary Fund Facilities

One criterion used in the evaluation of export credit by all lenders in the national and international export credit financing systems is the requirement that the country of the buyer be creditworthy. Several factors are involved in assessing the creditworthiness of a country, including political and commercial factors. A key element of the commercial creditworthiness of a country is its ability and capacity to pay for the goods purchased abroad by its citizens. This ability is essentially the degree of liquidity in the country's balance of payments.

Countries that buy (import) more than they sell (export) may become illiquid if they do not have enough foreign exchange resources to meet the shortfall in earnings. If the country has no reserves, or if reserves are inadequate, it resorts to short-term borrowing abroad to finance the shortfall between revenues from export sales and expenditures on import purchases. A country that experiences recurrent shortfalls—deficits—in the balance of payments, would have to continue borrowing abroad to cover the shortfall year after year. Foreign lenders become increasingly reluctant to make additional loans to these countries, as the country's total outstanding debt rises to significant levels. When this point is reached, the country's ability to purchase goods abroad is constrained, and its creditworthiness is diminished as debt service becomes a problem.

The IMF, as the world's central banker, has its own credit financing system to provide liquidity for the countries that are experiencing these balance-of-payments problems. The IMF has a variety of programs designed to relieve countries experiencing illiquidity, some of which will be discussed briefly here (see Chapter 7 for a fuller discussion of the IMF). The main objectives of the IMF include the encouragement of expansion and balanced growth in international trade, the promotion of exchange stability, the elimination of exchange restrictions, and the correction of a balance-of-payments disequilibrium.

The IMF facilitates expansion and balanced growth in international trade through its credit financing facilities. Countries anticipating a shortfall in export revenue can obtain loans from IMF credit facilities to meet an expected balance-of-payments deficit. Similarly, countries with balance-of-payments problems resulting from recurrent or persistent balance-of-payments deficits can obtain loans from IMF credit financing facilities. These loans are made under programs designed to help correct a balance-of-payments disequilibrium, and they carry requirements for corrective action in varying degrees of stringency.

IMF loans are made to the central monetary authority in each member country for a specific purpose. The loans increase the liquidity in the balance of payments by providing foreign exchange for buyers in a country to purchase imported goods and services. Developing countries with balance-of-payments problems are the dominant group of users of IMF lending facilities.

The Trust Fund

The Trust Fund of the IMF provides additional balance-of-payments assistance on concessionary terms in support of the efforts of eligible developing member countries that qualify for assistance to carry out programs of balance-of-payments adjustment. By the end of January 1977, 61 member countries had qualified for fund assistance. The resources of the fund consist of gold and currencies sold, donated, or lent to it, income from investments and loans, and proceeds from repayments of loans.

The Oil Facility Subsidy Account

The Oil Facility Subsidy Account was set up to provide assistance to the IMF's most seriously affected members in meeting the interest costs for borrowing under the oil facility program[2] The account was established by the executive director of the IMF on August 1, 1975, and is funded by contributions from 24 members and Switzerland. Contributions totaling SDR 160 million are anticipated over the life of the account.[3] Contributions received as of April 30, 1981, totaled SDR 156.436 millon.[4] Payments to each eligible beneficiary from the Oil

Facility Subsidy Account are computed at a rate of 5 percent per year on the use of the 1975 oil facility by each eligible country. Participation in 1975 was restricted to the countries most seriously affected by the increased price of oil.

Thirty-nine IMF members were included in the U.N. list of most seriously affected countries. Of those countries only 18 made purchases under the 1975 oil facility and thus became the original beneficiaries of the subsidy account. Of the original 18 beneficiaries, India and the Ivory Coast did not receive a subsidy in 1981 since they had used up their purchases under the 1975 oil facility.

The 5 percent subsidy rate effectively reduced the cost to the beneficiaries of using the oil facility from 7.875 percent to 2.875 percent per year for the original beneficiaries, and from 7.74 percent to 2.74 percent per year for the additional beneficiaries for 1980–1981.

Regional Public Lending Institutions

In addition to the World Bank group and IMF facilities for financing export credit and international investment, a number of regional public lending institutions offer a source of funds to exporters and investors interested in their specific regions. These regional institutions include the European Investment Bank (EIB), the Inter-American Development Bank (IDB), the Asian Development Bank (ADB), and the African Development Bank (AFDB).

The European Investment Bank

The EIB was established in 1958 by the EEC to mobilize financing to support the development of the socioeconomic infrastructure of its member nations and to finance the industrial activity needed to facilitate economic integration of the EEC. To achieve these objectives, the EIB was assigned the following responsibilities: (1) to provide assistance in financing public projects involving two or more member nations; (2) to facilitate the adjustments necessary for location and expansion of industry in the process of economic integration; and (3) to provide development assistance for the underdeveloped regions of the EEC.

The policy of the EIB has been to cofinance projects; the EIB will provide only a portion of the financing, with private commercial banks in each country providing another portion, and the balance retained by the borrower through a down payment requirement, in order to spread the risk. The EIB cooperates with other international financial institutions, such as the World Bank, in the financing of very large projects in one or more member countries.

The interest rate charged by the EIB reflects market conditions at the time the loan is made and is fixed over the life of the loan. Loans are long-term maturities, with repayment periods of 12 to 20 years. The EIB allows a grace period of 3 to 4 years on each loan. Collateral is accepted to secure loans in place of a government guarantee, but borrowers with inadequate collateral may be required to obtain a government guarantee.

The EIB permits the borrower to receive and to repay the loan in a different currency. This facility provides some flexibility in case the borrower needs a particular currency for the transaction. The borrower can receive the proceeds of the loan in a currency selected by the EIB, including currencies of countries that are not part of the transaction; the borrower is then required to repay the loan in the same currency in which the loan was made. Or, the borrower can choose the currency of a member nation in which to receive the loan proceeds; in this case, the EIB retains the right to select the currency in which repayment is to be made.

The EIB also has the responsibility for administering the European Development Fund (EDF). The EEC established the EDF in 1959 to provide financial aid and technical assistance for the developing countries. The resources of the EDF were increased from EUA 3,457 million to EUA 5,607 million in 1979,[5] in agreements between the EEC and the 58 African, Caribbean, and Pacific (ACP) states for the period 1980–1985.

EDF funds are used for loans and grants to developing countries based on the particular situation of each country. Most EDF loans are used to finance export credits or as grants to pay for exports.

The Inter-American Development Bank

The IDB was established in 1959 to promote economic development in the Western Hemisphere and to encourage regional economic integration. The original membership comprised the United States and 20 Latin America countries.[6] The operations of IDB were financed through three independent funds: the Ordinary Capital Resources Fund, the Fund for Special Operations, and the Social Progress Trust Fund. In 1965 the IDB integrated the activities of the special operations and the social progress trust funds.

The IDB cooperates with the agencies administering the national export financing of the industrialized countries that contribute to Latin American development. Cofinancing packages are put together by the IDB and these agencies to finance export credits for exports from those countries to Latin American countries.

Ordinary Capital Resources Fund   The IDB makes loans to finance export credits on conventional terms to public and private entities of its members from its Ordinary Capital Resources Fund. The bank charges a fixed rate of interest over the life of the loan; the rate is changed periodically to reflect market conditions and the cost of funds to the bank. A commission of 1 percent is added to the interest rate for allocation to a special reserve account. The normal term of an IDB loan ranges from 10 to 20 years. Loans made by the IDB carry two stipulations: the loans must be repaid by the borrower in the currency in which the loan was made, and procurement through IDB loans is restricted to nonCommunist countries that have contributed to the Bank for Latin American Development.

In making a loan, the IDB is obliged under its articles of agreement to pay due regard to the prospects that the borrower will be in a position to meet its obligations under the loan. The bank is expected to operate on a sound basis and to make loans only where there are reasonable prospects of repayment.

Special Operations Fund   This fund is designed to provide loans on soft terms for those Latin American countries that need financing on terms that would bear less heavily on their balance of payments than loans made on the conventional basis under the Ordinary Capital Resources Fund. The terms and conditions of loans made from the Special Operations Fund are tailored to the special circumstances of each country eligible for this type of soft loan. The terms for special operations loans range from 10 to 30 years. Borrowers are permitted grace periods, as needed, from the contract date to the first installment payment. Interest rates, including a service charge on loans, begin at a minimum rate of 3 percent. The interest rate is subsidized. There are no restrictions on purchases, and borrowers can buy from any country in the nonCommunist world. Borrowers are encouraged, however, to give preference to purchases in their local economy, the United States, or other IDB members.

Social Progress Trust Fund   This trust fund (merged in 1965) made loans for infrastructure development in the Latin American countries, including such projects as low-income group housing, advanced education, water supply and sewage facilities, and agriculture.

The resources of the trust fund were provided by the United States as its contribution under the Alliance for Progress. The activities of the trust fund were combined with those of the Fund for Special Operations after the last payment into the trust fund in 1965.

The Asian Development Bank

The ADB was established in 1966 to mobilize financial resources to foster economic development in Asia. The membership of ADB is made up of countries in Asia, the United States, and other industrialized nations. One-third of the capital subscription of ADB was made up by the United States and the other industrial nations. This group also controls one-third of the voting power.

The objective of ADB is to foster economic development and regional economic cooperation. The ADB has several funds for promoting its activities. Two basic types of loans are made: regular loans on conventional terms and special loans on soft terms from a special fund for that purpose.

The African Development Bank

The objective of the AFDB is to promote economic development in its African member countries by providing financing through loans to public and private entities of its member countries. A second goal of the AFDB is to foster economic integration among its member countries by facilitating joint projects of common benefit to improve the infrastructure in member countries, promote trade, and improve regional and continental economic development.

Originally the membership of the AFDB was restricted to African countries,[7] but in May 1979, the governing council of the AFDB opened the capital of the institution to countries other than the 48 member African states. Two-thirds of the enlarged board of directors of 18 seats is reserved for Africans. Many non-African countries have expressed their interest in subscribing.

An African Reinsurance Corporation (ARC) was established in January 1977 under the auspices of AFDB, and the first meeting was held in Abidgan, Senegal, in March of that year. ARC started operations in January 1978. The membership of ARC is open to all members of the Organization of African Unity.[8] The authorized capital of ARC is $15 million. It is designed to facilitate the lending process of AFDB through its reinsurance activities.

The AFDB operates several funds within its lending activities. Its standard loans are made on conventional terms, but it also makes concessionary loans on an extended-term basis with relatively low interest rates.

SUMMARY

International trade among the industrialized countries of the OECD is financed mainly through commercial banks and other private institutions, and insurance coverage is available to protect against the commercial risks for transactions among these countries. Official guarantees are sometimes required for mega-ticket items and complete systems which need long-term financing.

Because of the political risks involved in exporting to the less industrialized members of the OECD, the centrally planned economies of Eastern Europe and the developing countries, governments have moved to protect the interests of their exporters by providing insurance and guarantee programs. The public programs are designed to complement private sources of export credit. The government agencies, therefore, usually require private financing commitments for the shorter maturities in the financing package before they consider participating in the deal. For this reason, inquiries for export credit financing should normally be initiated through the exporter's commercial bank.

In addition to national systems, a number of international public lending institutions provide financing for export credits and for international investment. The World Bank and its two affiliates, the IDA and the IFC, and IMF facilities provide various forms of financial and technical assistance for economic development. Several regional public lending institutions also offer sources of funds to exporters and investors interested in specific geographical regions.

SUPPLEMENTARY READING

Annual Reports (Washington, D.C.: The World Bank).

Development Finance Companies (Washington, D.C.: The World Bank, 1976).

13

The Decision
to Invest Abroad

Cross-border investment takes place when nationals of one country invest in any type of gainful business activity in another country. Cross-border investment goes on every day, and the growth of multinational corporations has accelerated the pace of investment in foreign countries. One can classify cross-border investment in several ways: by the duration of the investment (such as short-, medium-, or long-term) or by type of ownership (portfolio or direct). Short-term investment is generally of a temporary nature, as in the case of trade credit or a portfolio investment. A long-term investment could be either portfolio or direct investment.

The difference between a portfolio investment, in this context, and a direct investment is the degree of control by the investor over the business. In a portfolio investment, the investor has a minority ownership and is, therefore, a passive investor in the business. The purchase of foreign bonds or stocks that do not give the holder majority control is usually referred to as portfolio investment.

Direct investment, on the other hand, describes the investor's majority ownership and control of a productive foreign business. Direct investment involves the ownership of plant and machinery to produce a product or a service, and therefore involves control over the operations of a business entity in a foreign country. Direct investment thus creates the task of managing the foreign activity, which can best be undertaken by a corporate entity that has the necessary financial and manpower resources.

Companies invest in foreign businesses for a variety of specific reasons to achieve either vertical or horizontal integration. In a backward vertical integration strategy, for example, the firm integrates the source of its raw materials by investing in the foreign country that has the raw material resource. Companies may invest abroad to secure a foreign source of raw material when the domestic source runs out or becomes very expensive. In either situation securing the raw material source abroad is vitally important to the firm's production strategy. Many of the world's available natural resources are located in the developing countries, and much of the direct investment for natural resources is, therefore, made in these countries. A firm may also integrate forward either to acquire assembly facilities abroad in or near its overseas markets or because of foreign government pressure to force producers of goods that were previously imported to manufacture locally.

Most foreign *direct* investment is aimed at horizontal, rather than vertical integration. Under a horizontal strategy, the firm expands into foreign markets to sell either its existing product line or a new product line invented or adapted for the foreign market.

Several factors determine how and where a firm will integrate horizontally. These include tariff barriers on exports, transportation costs of exporting, the firm's size, the growth rate of its domestic markets, and differentiation of its products. These reasons are discussed in detail in the next sections. The balance of the chapter considers the reasons and strategies involved in foreign direct investment and analyzes the patterns and trends of U.S. corporate direct investment abroad.

STRATEGIES FOR FOREIGN DIRECT INVESTMENT

Foreign direct investment usually involves investment in plant and machinery by U.S. firms to manufacture products in a foreign country. Several factors underlie direct investment abroad,[1,2] but a particularly good understanding of the basis for a corporate decision to invest abroad for the manufacture of products can be achieved by examining the nature of the products—focusing on two questions: what types of products do U.S. firms manufacture abroad, and why don't companies make those products in the United States and export them?

To provide some answers to these two questions, the Conference Board, an association of representatives from major manufacturing, industrial, and commercial firms, commissioned a study that examined 65 investments totaling over $400 million by 56 U.S. firms to make 58 products during the 1967-to-1971 period.[3] In terms of the nature of the products, the factors that lead to foreign direct investment are the following:

1 Investment in manufacturing operations abroad often involves products that do not enter U.S. export trade and are not normally traded internationally.

2 Production abroad of products that would normally be exported may be undertaken because of:

   (a) Foreign government actions to exclude exports from abroad through quotas, tariffs, or other regulations; or

   (b) The preference of government or private customers abroad for "domestic" suppliers.

3 Firms may decide to produce certain products abroad because of economic benefits to be gained from:

   (a) The availability of lower-cost labor abroad, which is commonly associated with offshore industries;

   (b) The use of assembly or conversion points for U.S. exports that are close to major foreign markets; or

   (c) The ability to sell U.S. manufactured products *with* locally manufactured components.

4 Companies may decide to manufacture a particular product abroad for competitive reasons:

   (a) The products of foreign-owned firms operating internationally with foreign technology are dominating international markets; or

   (b) The U.S. company wants, for strategic reasons, to produce in a country where a major competitor is based.

The following sections will discuss some of these factors in more detail.

Direct Investment to Produce Products Not Generally Entering Export Trade

Certain products are uneconomical or unsuited to export to foreign markets. They are produced for the U.S. domestic market, but not traded internationally.

A key factor in a decision to invest abroad to produce certain products is the ratio of the product's weight to its value. Bulky products involve substantial transportation costs, which can increase the export price and cause the exports to lose competitive advantage over local products in foreign markets.

Three examples of products that are uneconomical to export are upholstered furniture, tufted carpeting, and corrugated containers. These products are bulky, and the weight of the product would result in heavy transportation costs if they were shipped abroad. Because of the high weight-value ratio of corrugated containers and upholstered furniture, these products are usually manufactured and distributed by region even within the U.S. domestic market.

Packaged food products, too, are normally not exported. The food products have low unit value and, in the case of baked food products, limited life. The low unit value makes these products uneconomical to export, and this type of product may experience spoilage within the customary delivery time. A food product may also need adaptation in order to find acceptability in foreign markets.

Elevators are another example. The major market for elevators in Europe is the four-passenger elevator for residential buildings. The major market in the United States, in contrast, is the large, automatic "collective" elevator. To compete in the European elevator market, the U.S. manufacturer would be best advised to acquire a foreign firm that produces the type of elevator used in the huge European residential market.

Direct Investment to Produce Products Usually Exported

Over 60 percent of foreign investment by U.S. firms involves products usually exported from the United States. What are the factors that cause a firm to establish overseas production facilities? In many cases, the exporter was faced with circumstances that either excluded or threatened to exclude U.S. exports from foreign markets. The U.S firm then made a direct investment in production facilities in those markets to maintain its market share and competitive position.

The Closed Market

Governments of foreign countries may decide they need to develop their domestic capacity to produce certain products. They proceed to take administrative action to seal off their borders to imports of those products. Such actions interrupt the activities of firms that had been exporting to these countries and had successfully developed the export markets. In such situations U.S. firms are faced with the choice of direct investment in local production facilities to service their respective overseas markets or loss of the markets altogether.

Such a situation involved the automotive industry in Mexico. U.S. automotive producers have been expanding the production capacity of their Mexican affiliates in response to a Mexican government policy announced in 1977 to encourage local production by foreign producers. The Mexican government policy, which will go into effect in 1982, will limit the value of imports by Mexican automobile producers to the value of the products they export. The Mexican facilities owned by foreign parents have essentially been assembly points importing the fabricated parts from the parents. The new plants, in contrast, will manufacture engines and other components, thus reducing the need for imports. Automobiles produced in Mexico by affiliates of U.S. producers will in turn be exported to some of the other Latin American countries.

One auto maker, for example, had in the past successfully increased the exports of its small engines to Mexico to above $3 million a year. The firm produced high-quality small engines, which were highly competitive with engines sold in the foreign markets. Worldwide exports of $30 million accounted for 20 percent of the company's total output. Although the high quality of the firm's engines gave it a competitive advantage in the Mexican market, the Mexican government wanted to develop domestic capacity to produce small engines and "informed'" the U.S. manufacturer of these plans. Initial resistance by the firm brought threats of a total ban on imports of the firm's engines. To ward off the loss of its Mexican market, then, the firm decided to make a direct investment in a production facility in Mexico.

The Protected Market

Foreign governments at times impose a tariff to protect local producers from foreign competition. Since tariffs are costs to the importer, the effect of a tariff is to raise the cost of the imported good, thereby eliminating, or at least reducing, any competitive advantage previously enjoyed by foreign competitors over local producers. The higher the tariff, the greater the price impact and loss of competitive edge in the foreign local market by the import.

Since prohibitively high tariffs have the effect of discouraging imports, they protect producers who are part of the local economy. High tarriff barriers, moreover, bolster the profitability of those firms that are in the domestic market and are more efficient. Relative to local producers, foreign producers as a rule have more efficient technology in their production operations, which gives them a competitive advantage over producers in the local foreign markets and higher rates of profitability as well.

The Common Market (EEC) provides a good example of how the imposition of tariffs has served as an inducement to U.S. firms to invest directly abroad. U.S. firms had been exporting to various European countries, but the formation of the Common Market created a customs union among countries of the market, imposing tariffs on all foreign exports to the Common Market members. The Common Market had been a lucrative one for U.S. exporters, and the tariff would have caused these firms to lose their export markets by raising the cost of their products and making them less competitive. The U.S. firms, accordingly, decided to establish local production facilities within the Common Market to maintain their market shares there. In short, the imposition of the tariff prompted foreign producers to make direct investments within the Common Market, which resulted in the transfer of technology and the creation of jobs.

In another example, a successful U.S. exporter to Japan was forced by increasingly high Japanese tariffs to accept an offer for a joint venture with Japanese partners to produce the product—specialty wine—in Japan. When the tariff on the wine reached 43 percent of the price, the U.S. firm gave in. In joining the joint venture, the U.S. firm in 1966 made a cash investment of $250,000, plus technology valued at $200,000 for a total investment of $450,000. By 1970 the company was receiving over $200,000 a year in dividends and royalties.

The Protected Market of Developing Countries

Many developing countries have historically protected certain industries in their domestic markets—particularly infant industries—by barring imports. The import ban effectively eliminates competition from abroad. An alternative protective device is to impose prohibitively high tariffs on certain imports, which essentially shuts the domestic market to such imports. The objective of the policy is to induce foreign firms to invest in local production to increase the local content in manufacturing and foster local industry.

U.S. manufacturers of automotive parts, appliance parts, and electronic components can benefit from programs in developing countries to foster local industry. The immature markets provide significant opportunities for U.S. producers to capitalize on their technological advantage.

Consider the following investment made by a U.S. firm to produce automotive parts in Argentina. The Argentine government had decided to prohibit imports of automotive components, which would certainly have affected the exports of the U.S. firm which, at the time, held over 30 percent of the local market in Argentina. The competition in Argentina was a local firm using the technology of a major British competitor of the U.S. firm. The Argentine automotive market was growing 6 percent a year, while the U.S. automotive market was growing at only a 3 percent rate. The U.S. firm decided to invest in production facilities in Argentina, in order to avoid losing a growing market to a major worldwide competitor. To this end, the U.S. firm acquired an Argentine firm that had produced automotive parts under license from the U.S. firm.

National Licensing Regulations

Licensing regulations for the sale or use of certain products may require that the product be locally manufactured. This is generally true of pharmaceuticals, for example. Regulatory authorities in many countries require that pharmaceutical products be made locally to allow for control and inspection under the licensing and testing regulations. Certain prescription drugs must be locally manufactured, tested, and licensed in the major market countries of Europe and in some other countries around the world. For this reason, pharmaceutical firms in the U.S. usually export the bulk of the raw materials in the drugs to their overseas subsidiaries and affiliates for foreign production.

The pharmaceutical industry is a major investor abroad because the rate of growth of the pharmaceutical industry abroad is much higher than in the United States. The testing requirements of many foreign regulatory authorities are less exacting than those of the United States, and, in addition, all new drugs have immediate access to the world market.

Foreign Government Preference for Local Producers

Some foreign governments require procurement from local producers. Although this practice is not widespread, it is common enough to cause some logistical problems for contracting firms that are not locally based. Certain types of contracts are more likely to be awarded to local companies than to foreign companies. For example, defense-oriented contracts and certain public works contracts are routinely given to local companies in the developed countries.

In one case, the West German affiliate of a major U.S. producer of connecting devices expanded its facilities with the help of a direct investment from the parent. The affiliate had been supplying the electronics devices to U.S. electronics companies in West Germany. The objective of the expansion was to increase its capacity in order to be in a position to serve the West German government market.

Direct Investment to Obtain Low-Cost Labor

The investments made abroad to take advantage of low-cost labor involve products that are produced to compete with goods produced in the United states. (Because of high labor costs in the United States, these products are not normally exported from the United States.) These products are found in labor-intensive industries, where production overseas with low-cost foreign labor is advantageous.

Examples of such products are apparel, electronics, and footwear. These three industries are excellent examples of the workings of the product life cycle and the comparative cost advantage concepts discussed in Chapter 2. In the mature stage of the life cycle, the products are usually standardized and mass produced by the time the firm decides to build production facilities abroad. The mass-production process simplifies the task of each labor unit, which is important because countries with an abundance of labor usually will have experienced low productivity because of low skills levels and low utilization of capital.

The low labor cost of foreign production makes the product cost-competitive and gives it a cost advantage over its counterparts produced in the United States. Direct investments in a country with abundant labor and low wages for the production of labor-intensive products is an efficient use of the country's resource, and results in an improvement in the general welfare of all countries involved.

Direct Investment for Local Supply Capability

U.S. firms exporting to overseas markets frequently experience supply problems resulting from delays in transoceanic shipment and dock strikes at ports in the United States or overseas. The long supply lines put the U.S. firms at a disadvantage in relation to their foreign competitors, which have much shorter supply lines. In the Common Market, for example, the European competitors have much shorter supply lines because their production plants are usually located in countries contiguous to their major markets.

U.S. firms, therefore, turn to local production to improve their local supply capability, especially in the industrial products market. Local supply capacity is particularly important to suppliers of industrial goods, because if they can't get the supplies when needed, they will find their orders canceled, for placement with a competing firm which has the necessary local supply capacity. Some local supply capability can be gained through the acquisition of local producers. Acquisition provides the U.S. supplier with existing production and distribution facilities; in some instances, the acquired local firm has products that the U.S. firm lacked, thereby broadening the parent firm's product line.

The Role of Transportation Costs

Transportation costs make exports more expensive, and the rise in energy costs has significantly increased the cost of transportation. Since energy costs are expected to continue to rise, many firms will make a direct investment in local production facilities to serve various regions in their foreign markets.

CHARACTERISTICS OF FIRMS THAT MAKE
FOREIGN DIRECT INVESTMENT

As noted previously, firms invest abroad to achieve horizontal or vertical integration. Studies of the characteristics of the industries in which foreign investment is comparatively heavy show that companies that make *horizontal* investments to produce the same line of goods abroad that they produce in the United States are usually oligopolies (i.e., in whose industries a few firms dominate) with product differentiation in the home market.[4]

A firm with a unique product (one in which it has a competitive advantage based not so much on price as on real or perceived superiority of product characteristics, usually identified with brand name) is in an advantageous position to invest in foreign production facilities to produce its product for the foreign domestic market. These firms are known as "differentiated oligopolies."[5] (Firms with undifferentiated products typically undertake foreign direct investment in order to produce products other than those they produce domestically.) The market characteristics of this type of firm have been examined by several researchers,[6-10] and the market characteristics of international firms were found to be associated with other characteristics, such as research and development intensity, size, and involvement in exporting.

Firms in the differentiated oligopoly category, it was discovered, owned "intangible capital" in the technology of producing the differentiated products and the marketing and management skills needed for the efficient handling of their products. These firms recoup part of their research-and-development investment costs through exporting, foreign investment, and licensing. International firms prefer foreign direct investment, to take advantage of the economies derived from multiplant operations or of underutilized entrepreneurial resources.[11] International firms are able to use internally generated funds for continued growth through direct investment for production and sales abroad without reducing profitability in the domestic market and without jeopardizing their share of the highly competitive domestic market.

The research studies have found also that U.S. firms investing abroad are generally larger and more profitable, spend more on advertising, and are more research-oriented and more diversified than the average U.S. corporation. The size of the corporation, in terms of sales and assets, constitutes an important distinction between firms that invest abroad and those that do not. The costs of investing in production facilities abroad are high; since bigger firms are considered better credit risks, they find it easier to finance the cost of the foreign investment.

THE INTERNATIONAL PRIVATE INVESTMENT POSITION
OF THE UNITED STATES

As shown in Table 13.1, U.S. private assets abroad (that is, foreign direct and portfolio investment) rose rapidly from 1970 to reach $377.2 billion by 1978—a

Table 13.1   International Private Investment Position of the United States, Selected Years, 1970–1978 ($ billions)

Type of Investment	1970	1972	1974	1976	1977	1978
U.S. private assets	$118.8	$149.7	$201.5	$282.4	$314.1	$377.2
Direct investment abroad (book value)	75.5	89.9	110.1	136.8	149.8	168.1
Portfolio investment abroad	43.3	59.8	91.4	145.6	164.3	209.1
Foreign private assets in United States	$80.7	$98.7	$117.1	$159.1	$168.7	$198.2
Direct investment in United States (book value)	13.3	14.9	25.1	30.8	34.6	40.8
Portfolio investment in United States[a]	67.4	83.8	92.0	128.3	134.1	157.4

Source: *Economic Report of the President* January 1980).
[a] Includes corporate and other bonds and corporate stocks.

threefold increase. Direct investment has always formed a substantial part of United States private assets abroad, but the proportion of direct investment in total private assets abroad has been falling since 1970. In 1970 direct investment was 63.5 percent of private assets abroad. By 1976 it had fallen to less than 50 percent, and in 1978 it stood at 44.5 percent. This proportion was nearly a third less than its 1970 level.

Conversely, portfolio investment abroad has increased substantially, rising nearly fivefold during the period. This rise reflects, in part, the efforts of the U.S. banking system to recycle a major part of the petrodollars that have flowed into the United States. ("Portfolio investment abroad" includes liabilities of foreigners to United States commercial banks for loans they made.)

The drop in the proportion of direct investment abroad in total U.S. private assets abroad does not, therefore, represent a diminution in direct investment abroad by U.S. firms. In fact, direct investment abroad more than doubled during the period—rising from $75.5 billion in 1970 to $168.1 billion in 1978. An analysis of capital expenditures abroad by U.S.-owned affiliates would show that the pace of the direct investment abroad is accelerating rather than slowing down. (The effect of foreign direct investment by U.S. companies on the receiving countries and on the U.S. domestic economy is discussed in Chapter 15).

Foreign private assets in the United States rose more slowly during the 1970-1978 period than U.S. private assets abroad; the former doubled, while the latter tripled. Again, while direct investment has always been a substantial part of U.S. private assets abroad, foreign direct investment in the United States has been a relatively small part of total foreign private assets in the United States. Most foreign private investment in the United States is in the form of portfolio investment.

The pattern of capital expenditures by majority-owned foreign affiliates of U.S. companies from 1974 to 1980 is shown in Table 13.2 and Figure 13.1. The

Table 13.2   Capital Expenditures of Majority-Owned Affiliates of U.S. Companies by Industry, 1974–1980 ($ billions)

Industry	1974	1975	1976	1977	1978	1979[a]	1980[a]
Mining and smelting	$1.1	$1.2	$0.9	$0.6	$0.6	$0.7	$1.3
Petroleum	$7.8	$8.9	$7.9	$9.3	$10.0	$12.0	$15.4
Manufacturing	$11.6	$11.3	$19.9	$12.7	$14.6	$19.2	$23.9
Food products	0.7	0.7	0.7	0.9	1.0	1.3	1.4
Paper and allied products	0.9	0.7	0.6	0.7	0.8	1.0	2.0
Chemical and allied products	2.1	2.5	2.7	2.4	2.5	3.2	3.4
Rubber products	0.4	0.4	0.3	0.3	0.3	0.3	0.3
Primary and fabricated metals	0.7	0.7	0.7	0.7	0.7	0.8	0.8
Machinery, except electrical	3.1	2.8	2.7	3.6	4.4	5.5	6.3
Electrical machinery	1.1	0.9	0.8	1.0	1.1	1.3	1.4
Transportation equipment	1.6	1.4	1.4	1.8	2.2	3.8	6.1
Other	1.1	1.3	1.1	1.3	1.6	2.1	2.3
Trade	$ 2.1	$ 2.4	$ 1.6	$ 1.8	$ 2.0	$ 2.4	$ 2.9
Other	$ 2.6	$ 3.1	$ 3.3	$ 3.1	$ 3.5	$ 4.2	$ 4.8
Total	$25.3	$26.8	$24.7	$27.5	$30.7	$38.5	$48.4

Source: Bureau of Economic Analysis, U.S. Department of Commerce, *Survey of Current Business*, Vol. 60, No. 3 (March 1980).
[a] Based on the BEA survey made in December 1979.

rate of growth in capital expenditures increased sharply in 1979, and the 1980 increase is estimated to have been as large as the 26 percent of 1979. The sharp increase in capital expenditures in 1979 was the result of three factors. First, a strong demand for automobiles and other manufactured products in the expanding economies of the foreign developed countries dictated a sharp rise in capital expenditures in order to increase plant capability for manufactured goods in those countries, particularly for automobiles. Second, rising rates of inflation in foreign countries have increased the cost of plant expansion projects, thus increasing the dollar cost of the projects; in addition, some foreign affiliates moved their spending plans forward to beat the anticipated rise in inflation. Finally, foreign curency expenditures by affiliates increased when converted into dollars as a result of the depreciation of the dollar in 1978.

Capital Expenditures Abroad by Industry

Direct investment in manufacturing activities has been increasing to such an extent that it represented approximately half of the capital expenditures of majority-owned affiliates in both 1979 and 1980. Capital spending in manufacturing is estimated to have increased by 25 percent in 1980, to reach $23.9 billion. The transportation equipment and the paper and allied products industries probably accounted for the bulk of the estimated increase.

In the transportation industry, U.S. automobile manufacturers are developing an international network for the production of fuel-efficient "world" cars.

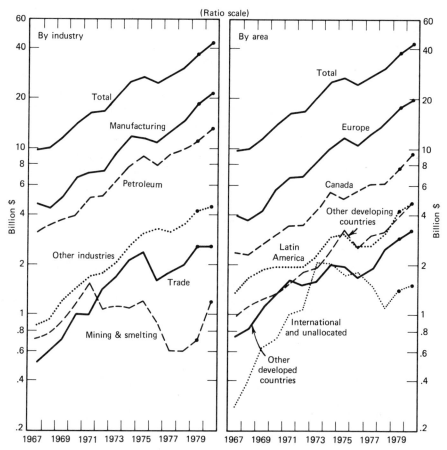

Figure 13.1 Capital expenditures by majority-owned foreign affiliates of U.S. companies (billions of dollars). Source: Bureau of Economic Analysis, *op. cit.*

Standardized components are being produced in an international plant network from a basic design, and the cars are being assembled near the major consumer markets. The world car strategy represents the first time that the U.S. automobile industry has looked beyond its domestic market for the design of its cars. The world car concept follows the basic strategy of the European and Japanese automobile producers, whose domestic markets are not large enough to absorb all their output, so they must sell in the world market.

Investment in manufacturing of paper and paper products was expected to rise in 1980 because of several factors. The natural resource for the industry is abundant in certain foreign areas, and the products are generally too bulky to export economically. In addition, U.S. manufacturers have a technological advantage over foreign competitors in making certain paper products—soft tissues, for example.

Foreign direct investment in the petroleum industry reached an estimated $15.4 billion in 1980—an increase of 29 percent from the 1979 level. Oil company affiliates intensified their efforts to find new petroleum deposits and stepped up their investments to expand production capacity following OPEC's doubling of crude oil prices in 1979.

Of the estimated $15.4 billion direct investment by petroleum affiliates, 62 percent was for investment in developed countries, particularly the United Kingdom and Canada. A planned investment of $3.7 billion by affiliates in the United Kingdom was intended to accelerate petroleum exploration and production in the North Sea area. Petroleum affiliates in Canada were expected to spend $3.4 billion on the continued development of petroleum extraction in the tar sands projects. Petroleum investment in developing countries totaled an estimated $4.9 billion in 1980 through intensified exploration of new fields to increase known reserves and through development of the fields already identified.

Capital Expenditures Abroad by Geographic Area

The data in Table 13.3 show that over 70 percent of the capital investment expenditures made each year by foreign affiliates of U.S. companies has been in the developed countries. The investments have been concentrated in Canada, the United Kingdom, and West Germany. The investment in Canada of $11.3 billion represents approximately a third of the total investment of $36 billion in

Table 13.3   Capital Expenditures by Foreign Affiliates of U.S. Companies by Area, 1974–1980 ($ billions)

Area	1974	1975	1976	1977	1978	1979[a]	1980[a]
Developed countries	$17.8	$18.8	$17.8	$20.4	$23.3	$28.9	$36.0
Canada	5.5	5.0	5.6	6.2	6.2	8.1	11.3
Europe	10.2	11.7	10.5	12.4	14.5	18.1	21.5
EEC (9)	8.8	9.9	8.8	10.7	12.6	15.6	18.5
France	1.5	1.9	1.2	1.5	1.6	1.8	2.2
Germany	2.3	2.1	1.9	2.0	2.7	3.6	4.6
United Kingdom	2.7	3.6	3.6	4.7	5.7	6.6	7.6
Other	2.4	2.3	2.2	2.5	2.6	3.5	4.1
Other European	1.4	1.8	1.6	1.7	2.0	2.6	3.0
Japan	0.8	0.8	0.6	0.8	1.1	1.3	1.4
Australia, New Zealand, and South Africa	1.2	1.2	1.0	1.1	1.4	1.4	1.8
Developing countries	$5.4	$6.4	$5.1	$5.6	$6.3	$8.1	10.4
Latin America	2.9	3.1	2.6	2.6	3.1	4.1	4.8
Other Africa	0.6	0.7	0.6	0.7	0.9	1.1	1.4
Middle East	0.8	1.3	1.1	1.4	1.1	1.1	1.8
Other Asia and Pacific	1.1	1.3	0.8	0.8	1.2	1.7	2.4
International and unallocated	2.0	1.7	1.8	1.5	1.1	1.5	1.9
Total	$25.3	$26.8	$24.7	$27.5	$30.7	$38.5	$48.4

Source: Bureau of Economic Analysis, *op. cit.*

[a] Based on the BEA survey made in December 1979.

the developed countries in 1980. The proximity of Canada to the United States makes Canada especially attractive for U.S. foreign direct investment abroad.

The estimated $10.4 billion investment expenditure in the developing countries in 1980 represents an increase of 25 percent over the 1979 level, and a 21-percent share of total estimated foreign direct investment in 1980. Latin American affiliates should have accounted for almost half of the developing countries' share of the 1980 foreign direct investment.

Several factors may account for the business investor's apparent clear preference for the developed countries. The developed countries have large industrial manufacturing complexes with strong demand for industrial goods. They also have large and affluent consumer markets, creating strong demand for many consumer goods. At the same time, competition in the developed markets, particularly in Europe, is intense. Local production greatly simplifies logistical problems by providing the supply capabilities necessary to serve customers for industrial goods and, to some extent, consumer goods. The developed market countries are also members of the OECD, which provides a certain degree of security for U.S. investors, since the United States also belongs to the OECD. The OECD countries' financial capabilities and political stability are added safeguards.

Capital Expenditures for Selected Areas by Industry

Table 13.4 presents data on capital expenditures abroad by industry for selected geographical areas, which provides a further breakdown of the pattern of direct investment by U.S. companies in their foreign affiliates.

In the manufacturing industries, 87.5 percent of foreign direct capital expenditures in 1979 and an estimated 86.0 percent in 1980 were made by affiliates in the developed countries. This emphasis on the developed countries reflects the capacity of the market in these countries to absorb the output of the manufacturing facilities. A substantial portion of manufacturing investments is in industrial goods, for which the industrially developed countries provide the markets.

In the petroleum industry, foreign direct capital expenditures rose faster in the developing countries than in the developed countries. This pattern, as noted previously, reflects the efforts of U.S. companies to explore and develop more oil fields in the developing countries.

The "Other" category of industry in Table 13.4 includes mining and smelting, trade, and other industries. Foreign direct investment in this category is directed 64 percent toward developed countries and 26 percent toward the developing countries. The mining and smelting investments in the developed countries are essentially equally divided between Canada and Australia.

Increases of 67 percent and 61 percent in foreign direct investment expenditures in transportation equipment manufacturing were made in 1979 and 1980, respectively. As part of their strategy to build an international network of component manufacturers and assembly plants for the world cars, U.S. automobile manufacturers are concentrating their foreign investments in three de-

Table 13.4 Estimated Foreign Direct Capital Expenditures by U.S. Companies for Selected Areas by Industry, 1979 and 1980

Area	1979				1980			
	Total	Petroleum	Manufac-turing	Other	Total	Petroleum	Manufac-turing	Other
	Percentage change from preceding year							
Developed countries	24	15	30	19	25	23	26	21
Developing countries	28	21	36	32	30	38	16	35
International and unallocated	38	107	—	12	25	48	—	10
All areas	25	19	31	21	26	29	25	23
	Billions of dollars							
Developed countries	$28.9	$7.8	$16.4	$4.7	$36.0	$9.6	$20.7	$5.7
Developing countries	8.1	3.6	2.8	1.7	10.4	4.9	3.3	2.3
International and unallocated	1.5	0.6	—	0.9	1.9	0.9	—	1.0
All areas	38.5	12.0	19.2	7.3	48.4	15.4	23.9	9.0

Source: Bureau of Economic Analysis, *op. cit.*

veloped countries and one developing country: Canada, West Germany, the United Kingdom, and Mexico.

SUMMARY

There are several reasons why nationals of one country select a particular type of investment in another country. Companies invest in foreign operations for a variety of reasons, all directed toward either vertical or horizontal integration. Backward vertical integration is undertaken to gain access to raw material sources, while forward integration generally involves acquisition of assembly facilities abroad. When a firm undertakes horizontal integration, it expands into foreign markets to sell its existing product lines or to market a new product line invented or adapted for the foreign market.

Direct foreign investment essentially involves investment in plant and machinery by U.S. firms to manufacture products in foreign countries. The factors that underlie a firm's decision to make a direct investment abroad include (1) a desire to market products abroad that are not normally traded internationally, (2) existence of products normally exported but affected by quotas, tariffs, or regulations imposed by foreign governments, (3) the need to produce in a foreign country where the government or private customers prefer local products, or (4) economic or competitive benefits to be gained from production abroad.

The second half of this chapter analyzed the current and expected trends in United States private investment abroad. Both foreign direct and portfolio investment by U.S. businesses and individuals is increasing, although the ratio has changed in favor of portfolio investment. The industries making major investments abroad are transportation equipment, paper and allied products manufacturing, and petroleum. The developed countries still account for the bulk of U.S. investment abroad.

SUPPLEMENTARY READING

John H. Dunning, ed., *Economic Analysis and the Multinational Enterprise* (London: George Allen and Unwin, 1974).

Charles P. Kindleberger, *American Business Abroad: Six Lectures on Direct Investment* (New Haven, Conn.: Yale University Press, 1969).

Giorgio Ragozzi, "Theories of the Determinants of Direct Investment," International Monetary Fund Staff Papers (July 1973), pp. 471–498.

NOTES

1   Thomas Horst, "Firm and Industry Determinants of the Decision to Invest Abroad: An Empirical Study," *Review of Economics and Statistics*, Vol. 54, No. 3 (August 1972), pp. 258–266.

2 Yair Aharoni, *The Foreign Investment Decision Process* (Boston: Harvard Graduate School of Business Administration, Division of Research, 1966).

3 James Greene and David Bauer, *Foreign Investment and Employment: An Examination of Foreign Investments to Make 58 Products Overseas* (New York: The Conference Board, 1975).

4 R. E. Caves, "International Corporations: The Industrial Economics of Foreign Investment," *Economica*, Vol. 38, No. 149 (February 1971), pp. 1–27.

5 Fred T. Knickerbocker, *Oligopolistic Reaction and the Multinational Enterprise* (Boston: Harvard Graduate School of Business Administration, 1973).

6 W. Gruber, D. Mehta, and H. Vernon, "The R&D Factor in International Trade and International Investment of U.S. Industries," *Journal of Political Economy*, Vol. 75 (February 1967), pp. 30–77.

7 Robert Z. Aliber, "A Theory of Direct Foreign Investment," *The International Corporation: A Symposium*, Charles P. Kindleberger, ed. (Cambridge, Mass.: MIT Press, 1970).

8 Bernard M. Wolf, "Internationalization of U.S. Manufacturing Firms: A Type of Diversification," unpublished doctoral dissertation, Yale University (1971).

9 Steppen Hymes and Robert Rowthorn, "Multinational Corporations and International Oligopoly: The Non-American Challenge," *The International Corporation: A Symposium*, op. cit.

10 Alan K. Severn and Martin M. Laurence, "Direct Investment, Research Intensity and Probability," Division of International Finance, Board of Governors of the Federal Reserve System, Discussion Paper No. 30 (May 31, 1973).

11 Richard E. Caves, "The Causes of Direct Investment: Foreign Firms' Shares in Canadian and U.K. Manufacturing Industries," Harvard Institute of Economic Research, Harvard University, Discussion Paper No. 320 (September 1973).

14

Evaluating Opportunities for Direct Foreign Investment

The preceding chapter considered some of the reasons for U.S. companies' and entrepreneurs' interest in investing abroad. Once interested, the potential investor must consider the pros and cons of the specific project. The process of deciding whether or not a project should be undertaken involves an evaluation of the project's potential cash flow. Cash outflows—the expenditures in financing the acquisition and installation of the plant and machinery, the operating costs, and the working capital requirements—must be measured against potential cash inflows, which are the proceeds generated from the sale of the product or services produced plus the sale of the asset at the end of the project's lifetime.

The expenditures to acquire the asset are made prior to the start of operations, and the operating costs are ordinarily incurred before each period's revenues from sales. In the future, similarly, sale proceeds and collections are received at different times. Therefore, the expenditures and receipts should be measured by a time profile of the cash flows. This process is known as *discounting* (see Chapter 8). Both the cash outflows and cash inflows are discounted to obtain their present value (PV), and then the present value of the cash outflow is subtracted from the present value of the cash inflow to obtain the net present value (net PV).

THE DECISION RULE

The Decision Rule is, if the net PV is positive (or, in some circumstances, zero), the project is acceptable, since it satisfies the investment objective stipulated in the required rate of return (the rate of profit the company wants to earn on the project). The required rate of return, sometimes referred to as the cost of capital, is the discount rate used to obtain the present values of the cash streams of the project.

A positive net PV indicates that the cash throw-off is sufficiently large to generate a profit greater than the investment in the asset plus the operating cost plus the profit margin required to earn the desired return on investment. When the net PV is zero, the cash throw-off is considered to be just sufficient to meet the costs and the desired level of profit. If the net PV is negative, the project's cash throw-off is not sufficient to meet the asset-acquisition and operating costs and generate an adequate profit; in this case, the recommended decision is to reject the project.

Remember that the outcome of the evaluation process is based on the assumptions made regarding the project. For example, the cash flows used in the discounting process are forecast, by whatever means, for the future periods during the operating life of the project. These forecasts involve assumptions as to costs, market expectations, and industry, economic, and social conditions. Furthermore, the discount rate, or the required rate of return, whether subjectively or objectively computed, incorporates the risk-free opportunity cost of funds plus a component for the risk assumed in undertaking the project—the premium for risk. Determination of the premium for risk involves assumptions about possible future uncertainties.

To gain a better understanding of the method of evaluating a capital asset, one must identify the approaches used to determine the costs and benefits of the project and examine the assumptions and methods of measurement of the cash flows. To elucidate this process, an example will be worked through later in the chapter, after some of the features that distinguish between the evaluation of a domestic project—a process that may be familiar—and the evaluation of a project overseas are examined.

EVALUATING FOREIGN VERSUS DOMESTIC PROJECTS

The process of evaluating a project is known as capital budgeting and, as described above, is essentially the same for a domestic project as for a foreign project. A foreign project, however, invariably involves a subsidiary or affiliate abroad that directly operates the project. We shall use "subsidiary" here for simplicity and convenience. The foreign subsidiary may be considered to be an independent unit that is financed in whole or part by the U.S. parent corporation. The investment in the project is, therefore, one step removed from the parent company, which is not always the case for a project at home. In short, the foreign project generally involves two parties—the subsidiary abroad and the parent company, which raises the question of which entity is entitled to the cash flows of the project.

Since the subsidiary operates abroad in a host country, it is subject to the laws and regulations of the host country. These regulations include income tax laws and rules about the conduct of business within the host country and limitations on remittance of profits and repatriation of capital. The laws and regulations of the host country, therefore, place constraints on the ability of the subsidiary to transfer funds from the host country to the U.S. parent company. These limitations require that two different sets of accounts be kept—one for the subsidiary and one for the parent.

Moreover, when the parent provides only part of the subsidiary's financing, the subsidiary has to obtain the additional financing it needs from local sources in the host country or from some other source. In such cases, the project's cash flows to the subsidiary will be different from the project's cash flows to the parent, even before consideration of the effects of the foreign laws and regulations.

FORCES INFLUENCING PROJECT CASH FLOWS

Various forces influence the cash flow of the project and have different effects on the subsidiary's and the parent's cash flows. These forces will be outlined here and discussed in the next sections (see also Chapter 5).

The first factor that will affect cash flows is the amount of the U.S. parent's investment in the foreign subsidiary, and what portion of the capital structure of the foreign subsidiary the parent's investment represents.

A second consideration is the impact of the cash flows between the subsidiary and the parent on the parent's overall cash flows. This impact may depend on special aspects of the subsidiary's relationship with the parent. For example, benefits to the parent's production and marketing activities arising from vertical and horizontal integration represented by the project investment must be considered. In addition, such features of the parent-subsidiary relationship as tie-in sales must be taken into account; the foreign subsidiary may be required to buy component parts or other items from the parent in order to achieve implicit royalties, quality control, or economies of scale through coordinated production between the U.S. parent and its subsidiary.

The cash flow of the project will be influenced also by the amount of the foreign subsidiary's remittances to the parent company and, as noted previously, the host country's rules and regulations constraining the ability of the subsidiary to make remittances. Differences between the host country and the United States tax rates can affect the subsidiary's remittances to the parent company.

The different inflation rates prevailing in the foreign host country and in the United States, and the impact of inflation rates on the foreign currency exchange rate between the two countries also affect a project's cash flow. Changes in the exchange rate, in turn, affect the measurement of the project's cash flows. These factors are known as inflation and exchange rate risks.

Political risks resulting from social and political instability in the host country can hurt the business environment and change the profit expectations on which the project was evaluated and the decision to invest was based. The worst-case risk would be the expropriation of the assets of the subsidiary.

EVALUATION PROCESS FOR A FOREIGN INVESTMENT PROJECT

The following example will illustrate the delineation of the cash flows between the foreign subsidiary and its U.S. parent, the measurement of the respective cash flows, and the evaluation of a project operated by a foreign subsidiary and financed by a U.S. parent company.

The Zephyr Corporation, let us say, had been exporting from the United States to Mexico for several years and had developed a sizable market for its product in that country. Mexico was a prosperous, developing country which had experienced high rates of economic growth over the past decade and showed great promise for continued high growth in the future. The Mexican market was very lucrative, with demand growing at an accelerating rate. As a result of the high demand, several European and Japanese companies had either begun local manufacturing in Mexico or had made plans to establish local manufacturing facilities in the country. The headstart on local manufacturing facilities had increased the competitive advantage of the European and Japanese companies in Mexico, through these companies' lower prices, shorter supply lines, and the tremendous pride and good-will generated for the companies by local production labeled "Made in Mexico."

The Mexican government had recently begun to restrict importation of the types of products manufactured by the Zephyr Corporation and other foreign companies. The government wanted to encourage the conservation of foreign exchange used to pay for imports. In addition, the government hoped to stimulate foreign investment in production facilities which would provide employment and accelerate economic growth.

The Zephyr Corporation wanted to continue to serve the Mexican market, which it had developed for several years, and maintain its share of the market. The company believed it might even be able to increase its market share if it established a local subsidiary.

The Zephyr Corporation decided to establish a local manufacturing company for $4.2 million. The company was to provide all the financing. Of the $4.2 million, new plant and machinery would cost $3 million, used equipment from the Zephyr Corporation was valued at $1 million, and the remaining $200 thousand would finance the working capital needs of the subsidiary.

The company expected the Mexican market to continue to grow at 10 percent per year for the next 10 years and beyond. The plant and equipment would be depreciated over 5 years. Zephyr planned to use a shorter depreciable economic life than it would normally use in the United States, because of the higher risk exposure in Mexico and the fact that operating conditions there would be less favorable. (Using a shorter depreciable lifetime for foreign projects is relatively standard practice.) The company was to use straight-line depreciation. As shown in Table 14.1, cost of sales was expected to be 40 percent of sales revenues and to remain at that level throughout the 5-year life of the project. Total costs would be 76.7 percent of sales each year. A payment of $600,000 each year would be made by the subsidiary to the parent company for manufacturing fees and accounted as a cost to the subsidiary operation. The corporate

Table 14.1 Zephyr Mexico, Ltd., Cash Flow Analysis—Capital Budgeting (Thousands)

	1979	1980	1981	1982	1983	1984
Cash inflows						
Sales		$6,000	$6,600	$7,260	$7,986	$8,785
Increase in receivables		1,000				
Cash collections		$5,000	$6,600	$7,260	$7,986	$8,785
Cash Outflows						
Cost of sales		$2,400	$2,770	$3,168	$3,625	$4,138
Selling & administrative		1,000	1,100	1,200	1,300	1,400
Supervisory fees		600	600	600	600	600
Taxes, local (40%)		560	612	677	744	819
Fixed assets						
(New)	$3,000					2,000
(Used)	1,000					
Inventory	100					100
Cash	100					100
Total outflows	$(4,200)	$4,560	$5,082	$5,645	$6,269	$4,757
Net cash flow	(4,200)	440	1,518	1,615	1,717	4,028
Cumulative net cash flow	(4,200)	(3,760)	(2,242)	(627)	1,090	5,218
PV factor of 20%	1.00	0.833	0.694	0.529	0.482	0.402
Net PV	(4,200)	367	1,053	854	828	2,057
Cumulative Net PV	$(4,200)	$(3,833)	$(2,780)	$(1,926)	$(1,098)	$989

PV Present value.
( ) Parentheses indicate negative cash flow.

income tax rate in Mexico was 40 percent, while the U.S. rate was 50 percent. The dividend withholding tax rate in Mexico on dividends paid to Zephyr was 10 percent. The U.S tax rate on subsidiary fees was 5 percent.

Analysis of the Zephyr Corporation Mexican Project

The above data on Zephyr and its Mexican subsidiary, the Zephyr Corporation in Mexico, Ltd. (Zephyr Mexico, Ltd.), were used to develop the Income and Cash Flow Statements in Tables 14.1 through 14.4.

Cash Flow Analysis

Table 14.1 presents the cash flow analysis for the capital budgeting evaluation of the project from the subsidiary's perspective. The project has a life span of 5 years from 1980 through 1984. All values have been expressed in dollars to avoid the complications of exchange rate fluctuations and simplify the process of measuring the cash flows to the subsidiary and to the U.S. parent company. (The effect of changes in exchange rates will be discussed later.)

The cash flow analysis of Zephyr Mexico is made up of two elements: the cash inflows are composed of the cash receipts from sales and collections from accounts receivable and, at the expected end of the project life, the salvage value of the plant and equipment and recovery of cash and inventory investment. The cash outflows include the operating expenses, supervisory fees, and taxes. The operating expenses are costs of sales and selling and administrative expenses, which are computed on the basis of a percentage of sales. Included in the cash outflows are the costs of the new plant and equipment purchased for the project. The cost of the used equipment transferred from the parent company to the subsidiary is the price the subsidiary would have had to pay for the equipment on the open market. The equipment has been estimated to be worth $1 million. This value would be different from the depreciated book value of the equipment in the hands of the parent company. The parent company benefits from the transfer of the equipment to its subsidiary, since it can now replace the used equipment with new equipment. Also included in the subsidiary's cash outflows are its working capital requirements of $100,000 each for inventory and cash. The asset and working capital investment are assumed to take place in 1979 prior to the commencement of operations in 1980. As shown, this investment represents a negative cash flow in 1979.

When a parent company establishes a foreign subsidiary to produce the company's product in a foreign country, in essence it transfers its technology to the subsidiary. The parent company may charge a royalty fee for the use of its technological know-how, which will recoup some of its investment in research and development of the technology. Alternatively, the parent company may levy a supervisory fee, which includes the royalty fee. The supervisory fee also covers the cost of the services of company supervisory personnel, who provide technical expertise in the production process to the foreign subsidiary.

The net cash flows are obtained by subtracting the cash outflows from the cash inflows. Except for 1979, there is a positive net cash flow in each of the years. The cumulative net cash flow is obtained by adding the net cash flows for each year to the cumulative net cash flow of the preceding year. As can be observed from Table 14.1, the cumulative net cash flow becomes positive in the fourth year of operations, 1983.

Measuring Project Income

The pro forma income statement is given in Table 14.2. A comparison of Tables 14.1 and 14.2 shows that, in Table 14.1, the cash inflow is recorded only when the cash is received; in Table 14.2, sales are recorded when the sale is made on an accrual basis. In Table 14.1, the cash outflows are also recorded only when the payment is made. In comparison, the costs in Table 14.2 are recorded on an accrual basis. The subsidiary's profit before taxes is projected to be approximately 23 percent of sales, with after-tax profits of 14 percent of sales.

Capital Budgeting Analysis for Parent Company

The capital budgeting analysis for the parent Zephyr Corporation is presented in Table 14.3. The capital budgeting analysis incorporates the identification and measurement of the cash flows of the project that accrue to the parent company. The cash inflows comprise the subsidiary's net cash flows after taxes from the project which are remitted to the parent, the sole owner of the subsidiary. The depreciation of the asset also accrues to the parent to permit

Table 14.2 Zephyr Mexico, Ltd., Pro Forma Income Statement (Thousands)

	1980	1981	1982	1983	1984
Sales	$6,000	$6,600	$7,260	$7,986	$8,785
Cost of sales	2,400	2,770	3,168	3,625	4,138
Selling & administrative	1,000	1,100	1,200	1,300	1,400
Depreciation	600	600	600	600	600
Supervisory fee	600	600	600	600	600
Total costs	$4,600	$5,070	$5,568	$6,125	$6,738
Profit before taxes	$1,400	$1,530	$1,692	$1,861	$2,047
Corporate income tax, local (40%)	560	612	677	744	819
Profit after taxes	840	918	1,015	1,117	1,228
Dividend to parents (50%)	420	459	507	558	614
Less local dividend withholding tax (10%)	42	46	51	56	61
Dividends remitted to U.S. parent	$ 378	$ 413	$ 456	$ 503	$ 553

Table 14.3 Zephyr Corporation, Capital Budgeting Analysis for Parent Company (Thousands)

	1979	1980	1981	1982	1983	1984
Project cash flows to parent						
Project net cash inflows		$ 440	$1,518	$1,615	$1,717	$4,028
Supevisory fee		600	600	600	600	600
Total cash inflows		$1,040	$2,118	$2,216	$2,317	$4,628
Cash outflows						
Capital investment outlay	$4,200					
Local dividend withholding tax paid						
by subsidiary		42	46	51	56	61
U.S. income tax[a]		49	53	59	70	77
U.S. tax on supervisory fees (5%)		30	30	30	30	30
Total cash outflows		121	129	140	156	168
Net inflow	(4,200)	919	1,989	2,076	2,161	4,460
PV factor (20%)	1.000	0.833	0.694	0.579	0.482	0.402
NPV	(4,200)	766	1,380	1,202	1,042	1,793
Cumulative NPV	($4,200)	($3,434)	($2,054)	$ 852	$ 190	$1,982

[a] See computation in Table 14.4.
PV Present value.
NPV Net present value.

recapture of the parent's investment in the project. The other item of cash inflow is the supervisory fee, as discussed before.

Cash outflows for the parent company's capital budgeting analysis include the capital investment outlay of $4.2 million made available to the Mexican subsidiary, the U.S. tax liability in Mexico, and the local dividend withholding tax paid by the subsidiary on behalf of the parent company.

Parent Company U.S. Tax Liability The United States tax liability of the parent Zephyr Corporation is presented in Table 14.4. The net U.S. tax liability is used in the capital budgeting analysis presented in Table 14.3. To compute the parent company's U.S. tax liability, first, the total income of the parent derived from the Mexican subsidiary is computed. The project income of the parent Zephyr Corporation is made up of the dividend remittance received from the subsidiary each year plus the foreign taxes paid by the Mexican subsidiary on behalf of the parent company (the foreign income tax and the dividend withholding tax). These taxes are part of the parent company's income and should be counted as such. Remembering that the U.S. tax rate of 50 percent is higher than the Mexican rate of 40 percent, to obtain the net U.S. tax liability of the parent Zephyr Corporation, the foreign taxes paid on the parent's income by the Mexican subsidiary are allowed as a credit by the U.S. Internal Revenue Service, under the provision of the double-taxation arrangement. This double-taxation protocol arrangement provides for reciprocal offsetting tax credit for foreign taxes paid on the same income, so that the same income does not get taxed twice.

Net Cash Flow and Discounting The net cash inflow is obtained by subtracting the cash outflow from the cash inflow for each year. The cash flow stream is then discounted using the required rate of return as the discount rate to obtain

Table 14.4   Zephyr Corporation, Parent Company Tax Liability Computation (Thousands)

	1980	1981	1982	1983	1984
Dividends received by parent	$420	$459	$507	$558	$614
Foreign income tax paid by subsidiary (on the basis of 50% dividend paid)	280	306	338	372	409
Dividend withholding tax paid by subsidiary	42	46	51	56	61
Total income from subsidiary	$742	$811	$896	$996	$1,094
U.S income tax (50%)	371	405	448	498	547
Foreign tax credit	322	352	389	428	470
Net U.S. tax due	$ 49	$ 53	$ 59	$ 70	$ 77

the net PV. The cumulative net PV is given in the last line of Table 14.3, which shows that the cumulative net PV becomes positive in 1982.

Decision on the Investment

After estimating the cumulative net PV, the company can decide on whether to approve the project. The Decision Rule is: Accept the project if the cumulative net PV is greater than zero.

In this case, the project will provide the company with a return greater than the desired rate of return used in discounting the cash flow. The Mexican project had a cumulative net PV of $2.2 million and therefore meets the acceptance criteria. On this basis, the project should be approved. However, approval of the project should not be based solely on the cumulative net PV criterion, since other, qualitative factors as well as marketing and operations must be considered. The objective analysis carries a great deal of weight, but should be balanced by analysis of qualitative and functional aspects.

If the cumulative net PV were zero, the project would still be acceptable under the net PV criteria, but would barely meet the return criteria. Approval would depend on the degree of confidence in the estimate of future cash flows, because if any of the assumptions on which the forecast was based proved to be erroneous, a shortfall in the cash inflows or, alternatively, an unanticipated high outflow, could occur. A shortfall in the cash inflow or excess outflow would result in a negative cumulative net PV. Therefore, when the cumulative net PV is zero, the assumptions underlying the cash flow projection should be reviewed and scrutinized before the final decision is made.

On the other hand, the project should not be rejected out of hand as long as it meets all other criteria. Recall that a cumulative net PV of zero permits the project to earn the desired return. If the company has allowed sufficient risk adjustment in the cash flow, or an adequate risk premium in the discount rate (as discussed in a later section) then the project should be accepted if the cumulative net PV is zero.

A negative cumulative net PV, however, means that the project will not generate sufficient cash flow to meet the desired rate of return. Under the Decision Rule, then, the project would not be undertaken. However, there may be other strategic or compelling reasons why the company may want to undertake the project (for example, the benefit from vertical or horizontal integration, which cannot always be accurately quantified, or a desire to enter a market that is considered to have good potential). In such cases, the company may be willing to relax the return requirement and take a lower return. The cumulative net PV should then be recomputed with a lower return discount factor, which could work out to a positive cumulative net PV that would meet the acceptance criteria. This process must be done with caution and restraint, however, since, once funds have been committed and operations begun, losses may occur if errors have been made.

Subsidiary's Remittances to Parent Company

The amount of remittance from the subsidiary to the parent and the parent's cash flows from the project depend on the amount of the parent's financing in the project. In the preceding illustration, the parent provided all the capital funds needed by the subsidiary to finance the project in Mexico. In this situation all the net cash flows of the project in the hands of the Mexican subsidiary accrue to the parent and are treated in the parent company capital budgeting evaluation.

There are several ways in which the parent company can finance the Mexican subsidiary's project, however, one of which is to provide only part of the project cost in equity and lend the balance to the subsidiary. This approach can be used when constraints on the amount of dividend remittance by the subsidiary are anticipated; host countries usually have few or no constraints on the remittance of interest and repayment of loan principal. Therefore, companies operating in countries with restrictions on dividend remittance and repatriation of equity capital generally utilize loan financing for foreign projects.

A second way of minimizing possible losses is borrowing from the local capital market or from local bankers. If all or most of the project financing can be raised locally, then the parent company's exposure to risk of loss from expropriation can be either eliminated or substantially reduced. Various combinations of local and external equity and loan packages can be developed for foreign project financing.

Project Return versus Parent's Return

The analysis of the Zephyr Corporation's Mexican project distinguished between the cash flows from the subsidiary and the cash flows of the parent. The distinction implies two separable and distinguishable activities going on that make it necessary to identify the cash flows separately. In the example, the parent company supplied all the subsidiary's capital requirements, which permitted a simple, straightforward analysis. In this case, since all funds were provided by the parent company, the required rate of return from the project for both the subsidiary and the parent corporation could be identical.

The usual practice, however, and a good one for risk protection, is for the parent to contribute only a portion of the capital, with the subsidiary borrowing the balance from local sources—sometimes from international sources. Then the required rate of return for the subsidiary may differ from the parent's since the cost of capital is different for each.

A third case arises when the parent company contributes no direct capital and lets the foreign subsidiary raise funds from the capital market of the host country or from international financial sources, with or without the parent company's guarantee. This strategy permits maximum protection against foreign risks, especially when the risk of expropriation is extremely high because of political instability. In this case, the subsidiary may very well be an affiliate and the parent company's required rate of return will definitely be different from that of the subsidiary. The cost of capital will, of course, also be different.

KINDS OF RISK IN FOREIGN PROJECT INVESTMENTS

In the preceding analysis, we assumed certainty in evaluating the cash flows of the foreign project; that is, we assumed that the future cash flows could be known, and we proceeded to forecast them. The assumption of certainty enabled us to simplify the complexities that prevail in dealing with uncertainty and risk. In the real world little is certain, especially in a project investment planned for a foreign country. All kinds of things can go wrong to prevent the success of the project.

Different Rates of Price Increases

The rate of increase in the general level of prices differs from country to country. Developing countries tend to experience higher rates of inflation in prices than the more developed countries, but no general rule can predict which countries will experience high or low rates of inflation. Since 1974, the rates of inflation in the industrialized countries have increased significantly and have moved within range of the rates experienced by many developing countries. The United States has been experiencing relatively higher rates of inflation than its chief world competitors, Japan and West Germany. These two nations and Switzerland have kept their rates of inflation much lower than those of the United States, Canada, and the United Kingdom.

U.S. businessmen doing business abroad have to consider the impact of inflation on the cash flows expected from foreign investment and on the value of assets held in foreign countries that may be experiencing high rates of inflation. High rates of inflation increase the cost of operations at a rapid pace. Of course, cash inflows from sales revenue also increase rapidly; if the cash inflows increase at the same rate as the cash outflows, the effect of inflation on the cash flows will be cancelled out. And if the cash inflows increase faster than cash outflows, the rate of profit will increase. But if costs rise faster than revenues, losses may ensue.

Inflation abroad also affects the value of assets and liabilities abroad. The burden of liabilities is reduced because repayment is made in cheaper dollars, but the book value of assets is eroded unless the assets are restated to take account of the change in the market price level. Fixed assets in particular should be reviewed periodically for restatement to allow for adjustments to the depreciation deductions. Depreciation allowance will be inadequate if depreciation is based on historical book value rather than replacement value.

Price changes abroad do not raise the same kinds of fears today as yesterday, since the United States itself is experiencing high rates of inflation and learning to cope with rapidly changing prices.

Inflation and Foreign Exchange Risks

Another effect of differing rates of inflation between countries is the change in foreign exchange rates between the currencies of the countries. As noted in Chapter 8, changes in the foreign exchange rate result in translation problems. When foreign assets and liabilities are restated under the requirements of FASB 8, resultant translation profits and losses may distort the performance picture. Also, when remittances are made, the value of the remittance may vary with changes in the exchange rate. The various strategies available to cope with foreign exchange risk are covered in Chapter 8.

Political and Social Risk

Political and social risk varies from country to country, but is more pervasive in developing countries as a whole. These countries are often undergoing rapid economic and social changes which may overtax the political and social institutions. Rapid economic changes create dislocations in the social fabric, which creates stress in the political system if it is not responding to the social and economic changes.

When political leaders are faced with a restive populace, a tried and true strategy is to redirect the discontent of the people to an external target. One tactic is the expropriation of foreign investment. Foreign investments usually become attractive targets for expropriation as countries move into a stage of development when they increasingly seek ownership and control over the various areas of economic activity and business within their national boundaries.

Therefore, although expropriations can reflect a variety of causes, the risk of expropriation increases when there is political or social instability. The loss from expropriation can range from a minimal loss of income with full compensation for the assets expropriated, to a complete loss of all income and little or no compensation for assets taken.

The U.S. government has guarantee and insurance programs to protect American business investments overseas, as described in Chapter 11. These programs significantly reduce the risk of loss from political and social dislocations and, in the worst case, expropriation. The programs carry some costs, of course, which must be borne by the business, such as premiums and (relatively low) deductibles, which are designed to spread the risk between the government and the company. Since the company retains some risk, it should still carry out a country-risk analysis in the feasibility study of a project.

The risk of expropriation is much lower today than it was, because more countries now realize the need for a good credit rating and a good international standing in order to attract foreign business.

DEALING WITH RISK IN FOREIGN INVESTMENT PROJECTS

In some situations, we have had no prior experience to guide us, and therefore do not know what outcome to expect. Such situations give rise to uncertainty.

In other situations, we may be uncertain about the outcome, but we have had prior experience of similar situations from which we can draw inferences about the probable outcome. These situations are referred to as *risky* situations, because we are in a position to measure the probability of various outcomes based on prior experience.

There are basically four approaches to dealing with risk in evaluating specific foreign project investments:(1)determining the payback period.(2)adjusting the discount rate to add a risk premium,(3) the certainty equivalent approach and (4) assigning probabilities to the cash flows. In all cases, the more prior experience can be used to reduce uncertainties to probable risks, the more worthwhile the evaluation and judgment will be. We will briefly discuss each of these methods. In addition, for the company involved in or contemplating several foreign investments, the risk of a single investment may be lessened by a portfolio approach to foreign investment.

Determining the Payback Period

The first approach, determining the payback period, determines how fast the investment can be recovered from the cash throw-offs from the project. Because of its simplicity, the payback period is widely used. It determines how fast the project would generate enough cash flows to recover the initial investment. In a risky situation, the sooner the investment can be recovered, the lower the exposure to risk.

A major drawback of the payback period approach is that it does not consider the total profitability of the project, since it does not measure the total cash flows of the project. It recognizes the project cash flows only until the investment is recovered. Thus a very profitable project that would pay back the investment over a longer period would be less desirable than a project that would recover the investment in a shorter period of time even though it was less profitable in the final analysis.

The payback period has merit, however, particularly since it minimizes risk exposure. Furthermore, the payback period is an approximation of the project's internal rate of return, when the annual cash flows of the project are constant and the project life is of sufficient duration. For example, assume that a project investment of \$1,000 will generate a cash flow of \$200 each year. The payback period is \$1,000/\$200 = 5 years. The reciprocal of the payback period is the project's internal rate of return: one-fifth, or 20 percent. The inverse relationship of the payback period to the internal rate of return, or the project return on investment, provides for some theoretical justification for the payback period.

Adjusting the Discount Rate for Risk

The second approach simply adds a premium for risk to the return that is required from the project. The premium for risk would be commensurate with the level of foreign risk that is perceived in the project. The higher the perceived level of risk, the larger the premium to be added to the required rate of return.

The implication of the higher rate of return obtained with the addition of the premium for foreign risk is that the project would have to generate a larger profit margin to compensate for the perceived higher level of risk. The rate of return is then used to discount the cash flows over time to obtain their PV in the way illustrated in Table 14.3. For the same level of cash flows, a higher discount rate will result in a lower PV for the cash inflows. If the PV of the cash inflows is too low, the net PV could become negative, and, on the basis of the Decision Rule, the project would be rejected.

One drawback of this approach is the problem of deciding the appropriate premium to add to the rate of return to reflect the perceived level of foreign risk.

Certainty Equivalent Approach

The certainty equivalent (CE) approach provides an alternative method for taking risk into account when evaluating projects with risky cash flows. In the CE approach, the cash flows are adjusted through the use of a CE factor that reflects the decision-maker's attitude toward risk ("utility function"). Three possible types of attitudes toward risk can be identified: risk-seeking, risk-indifference, and risk-aversion. A risk-seeker prefers to choose the risky outcome of a situation if given a choice between a risky and a less risky outcome with the same expected monetary returns. The risk-indifferent person exhibits indifference about a risky and a less risky outcome with the same expected monetary returns. The risk-averse person always prefers the less risky outcome to the risky outcome if the expected monetary returns are the same.

An example will illustrate the CE approach. The decision-maker is involved in a lottery-type situation in which he has a choice between a certain amount of money and the expected value of an uncertain amount of money. The decision-maker is required to indicate what certain amount, if offered, would make him indifferent to the two outcomes.

Alternative 1: An opportunity to receive a certain $30,000.

Alternative 2: A 50:50 chance of receiving $100,000 or nothing based on the outcome of a flip of a coin, with an expected value of $50,000 $(.5 \times \$100,000 + .5 \times \$0)$.

The certain amount of $30,000 is said to be the certainty equivalent of a risky $50,000 if the decision-maker indicates indifference between the two alternatives. The decision-maker therefore obtains the same "utility" from each alternative.

The CE of each period's cash flows for a project can be generated in a way similar to the preceding example. A CE adjustment factor, α, can be obtained as follows:

$$\alpha = \frac{\text{Certain cash flow}}{\text{Risky cash flow}} = \frac{30,000}{50,000} = .6$$

The CE adjustment factor ranges from 1 to zero. It is close to 1 for the present and falls the farther away the time for receipt of the cash flow is.

Since the CE cash flows have been adjusted for risk, the discount rate used for discounting the cash flows cannot contain a factor for risk; the risk-free discount rate should be used instead.

A step-by-step procedure for the CE approach can now be outlined.

1. Obtain the CE cash flows for each period for the project.
2. Substitute the risk-free rate of interest, r_f, for the risky discount rate.
3. Discount the CE cash flows with the risk-free discount rate in the usual way.
4. Subtract the PV of the cash outflows from the PV of the cash inflows to obtain the NPV.

Assigning Probabilities to the Cash Flows

The fourth approach is to estimate the probable foreign-project cash flows under various circumstances, such as business cycles, balance-of-payments changes, political instability, and social dislocations. The next step is to assess the probability of each event. The cash flows are then multiplied by the probabilities to obtain the probable cash flows, which are then discounted by a risk-free discount rate to obtain the PV and the net PV for each alternative. The probability approach is believed to be much more reliable than the technique of adjusting the discount rate.

In the probability approach, the firm's business activities are assumed to be influenced primarily by the general state of the economy in which it operates. The relationship between the future performance of the firm and the economy is expressed in expectational terms; that is, net cash flows from the company's investments are stated as a function of the expected state of the economy.

The uncertainty in the future net cash flows of an asset can be described by a probability distribution. The first step is to analyze the historical net cash flows of the asset to establish a pattern of net cash flows that can be transformed into frequencies and expressed as probabilities by dividing the frequency for each net cash flow outcome by the total of the frequencies. The probabilities thus obtained represent the historical return probabilities, which must next be adjusted to reflect for the expected state of the economy: boom, normality, or recession. With this approach, probabilities that reflect the likelihood of each state's occurring are assigned. These are then used as weights to adjust the company's expected cash flows. For example, based on prior experience, the Zeta Corporation might expect to generate the following net cash flows depending on the state of the economy in Country A:

State of A's economy (S_A)	Probability of this state of the economy occurring (P_A)	Zeta Corporation's net cash flows if state occurs ($\tilde{C}_A$) ($000)
Boom	.3	55
Normal	.5	30
Recession	.2	(10)

Table 14.5 Computation of the Expected Net Cash Flows and Standard Deviation for Zeta Corporation in Country A (Thousands)

S_A	P_A	$\tilde{C}_A$	$P_A\tilde{C}_A$	$(\tilde{C}_A - \overline{C}_A)$	$(\tilde{C}_A - \overline{C}_A)^2$	$P_A(\tilde{C}_A - \overline{C}_A)^2$
Boom (S_1)	.3	$55	$16.5	$25.5	$650.25	$195.08
Normal (S_2)	.5	30	15	.5	0.25	0.125
Recession (S_3)	.2	(10)	(2)	(39.5)	1,550.25	312.05
		$\overline{C}_A = \$29.5$			$\sigma_A^2 =$	$507.25
		$\sigma_A = \sqrt{507.25} = \$22.48$				

The mean and standard deviation of the Zeta Corporation's expected cash flows are presented in Table 14.5. The mean and standard deviation are two measures used to describe the net cash flow and risk relationship of a probability distribution.

The mean, the expected net cash flow ($\overline{C}_A$ in Table 14.5), is obtained by summing up the products of the probabilities of occurrence of each state (S_i) and the possible net cash flows (C_i). The mean as the probability-weighted average of possible net cash flows computed in Table 14.5 can be written as follows:

Expected net cash flow = (probability of S_1) (possible cash flow for S_1)
+ (probability of S_2) (possible cash flow for S_2)
+ (probability of S_3) (possible cash flow for S_3)

In Table 14.5 the mean, the expected net cash flow from the proposed investment, is 29.5. The standard deviation provides a measure of the "dispersion" of the possible net cash flows around the mean and thus the riskiness of the investment. First, the deviations from the mean are computed by subtracting the mean from each outcome ($\tilde{C}_A - \overline{C}_A$) in Table 14.5); then those figures are squared. The squared deviations are multiplied by their corresponding probabilities and the products summed to obtain the "variance." The standard deviation (σ_A in Table 14.5) is written as follows:

Standard deviation =

$$\left[\left(\begin{array}{c} \text{possible net cash} \\ \text{flow for } S_1 \end{array} - \begin{array}{c} \text{expected net} \\ \text{cash flow} \end{array} \right)^2 \left(\begin{array}{c} \text{probability} \\ \text{of } S_1 \end{array} \right) + \right.$$

$$\left(\begin{array}{c} \text{possible net cash} \\ \text{flow for } S_2 \end{array} - \begin{array}{c} \text{expected net} \\ \text{cash flow} \end{array} \right)^2 \left(\begin{array}{c} \text{probability} \\ \text{of } S_2 \end{array} \right) +$$

$$\left. \left(\begin{array}{c} \text{possible net cash} \\ \text{flow for } S_3 \end{array} - \begin{array}{c} \text{expected net} \\ \text{cash flow} \end{array} \right)^2 \left(\begin{array}{c} \text{probability} \\ \text{of } S_3 \end{array} \right) \right]^{1/2}$$

In Table 14.5 the standard deviation is $22,480. This figure is used to compare riskiness between project cash flows.

As another example, the net cash flows of the Zeta Corporation in Country B are given below for the various states of the economy:

State of B's economy (S_B)	Probability of this state of the economy occurring (P_B)	Zeta Corporation's net cash flows if state occurs ($\tilde{C}_B$) ($000)
Boom	.3	45
Normal	.5	40
Recession	.2	0

Table 14.6 presents the mean and standard deviation for this example.

The mean value can be obtained for the cash flows of each period as in Tables 14.5 and 14.6. The expected cash flows for the various periods can then be discounted in the same way that the certainty cash flows were discounted in Table 14.1. However, since the cash flows have been adjusted for risk, the risk component of the discount rate must now be eliminated. The expected values of the cash flows would therefore be discounted by the risk-free rate.

The mean and standard deviation can be used to compute additional statistical measures of risk, for example, the coefficient of variation, CV, which gives an index of the risk/return relationship. The coefficient of variation is useful because it measures the amount of risk assumed for each dollar (unit) of net cash flow (or for each dollar of return, if return is being measured). It standardizes the risk per unit of cash flow and thus makes possible a direct comparison of the risk assumed for each dollar of net cash flow generated by the project. The CV equals the standard deviation divided by the expected net cash flow:

$$CV_i = \frac{\sigma_i}{\overline{C}_i}$$

Coefficients of variation for the two projects (Country A and Country B) are given in Table 14.7. In this example, Project A has a CV of 0.76 versus the CV of 0.50 for Project B, which indicates that the risk assumed for each dollar of net cash flow is greater in Project A than in project B. If a choice had to be made between the two projects on the basis of their relative risk per dollar of cash flow, Project B would be preferred. The standard deviation of Project A, σ_A, is $22,480, which is 1.33 times the standard deviation of Project B, while the expected net cash flow of Project A is 11.9 percent less than the net cash flow of Project B—a clear indication that there is relatively more risk in Project A.

The Portfolio Approach and Risk Reduction

In the preceding discussion we dealt with alternative ways of measuring risk and comparing the riskiness of various investments, but so far we have not dealt

Table 14.6 Computation of the Expected Net Cash Flows and Standard Deviation for Zeta Corporation in Country B (Thousands)

S_B	P_B	$\tilde{C}_B$	$P_B\tilde{C}_B$	$(\tilde{C}_B - \overline{C}_B)$	$(\tilde{C}_B - \overline{C}_B)^2$	$P_B(\tilde{C}_B - \overline{C}_B)^2$
Boom (S_1)	.3	$45	$13.5	$11.5	$132.25	$39.68
Normal (S_2)	.5	40	20	6.5	42.25	21.13
Recession (S_3)	.2	0	0	(33.5)	1,122.25	224.45
			$\overline{C}_B = \$33.5$			$\sigma_B^2 = \$285.26$
			$\sigma = \sqrt{285.26} = \$16.89$			

Table 14.7 Computation of the Coefficient of Variation

	Expected Net Cash Flow $(\bar{C})$ ($000)	Standard Deviations of Net Cash Flow (σ) ($000)	Coefficient of Variation (CV)
Project A	29.5	22.48	0.76
Project B	33.5	16.89	0.50

with how to reduce risk. One approach to risk reduction that is being used with greater frequency by companies considering opportunities for direct investment abroad is the diversification of investments among a "portfolio" of projects that have low or negatively correlated cash flows. The basis for this international diversification is that the general states of economy in different countries do not move in lock step. Correlations between the economic states of countries range from high (e.g., in the case of the United States and Canada) to weak or no correlation (as in the case of the United States and some developing countries).

When projects with low or negatively correlated cash flows make up the portfolio, the pattern of their net cash flows are opposite, and the combined cash flow will be relatively stable while generating a desired level of return. By reducing variability and providing relative stability, the portfolio approach helps reduce risk. The total risk of the portfolio is less than that of the individual projects. A combination of perfectly negatively correlated cash flows will virtually eliminate all the variability in the combined cash flow, but, as the correlations increase, the variability and the risk increase.

The example of the Zeta Corporation's investment analysis of projects in Country A and Country B can be used to explain what happens when cash flows are combined. Table 14.8 presents a calculation of the "covariance" (simultaneous movement) of the cash flows of these two projects.

The expected cash flow of the portfolio is

$$\bar{C}_p = 0.5\bar{C}_A + 0.5\bar{C}_B = 0.5\,(\$29,500) + 0.5\,(\$33,500)$$
$$= \$31,500$$

The standard deviation is computed with the following formula:

$$\sigma_p = [(W_A^2\sigma_A^2 + W_B^2\sigma_B^2 + 2W_A W_B(\text{Cov}_{AB})]^{1/2}$$

which can be restated as:

Table 14.8 Calculation of Covariance of Cash Flows of Country A with Cash Flows of Country B ($ Thousands)

P_s	$(\tilde{C}_A - \bar{C}_A)$	$(\tilde{C}_B - \bar{C}_B)$	$\dfrac{(\tilde{C}_A - \bar{C}_A)}{(\tilde{C}_B - \bar{C}_B)}$	$\dfrac{P_s(\tilde{C}_A - \bar{C}_A)}{(\tilde{C}_B - \bar{C}_B)}$
.3	25.5	11.5	293.25	87.96
.5	0.5	6.5	3.25	1.63
.2	(39.5)	(33.5)	1,323.25	264.65
			Cov $(C_A C_B)$ =	354.24

Standard deviation
of the portfolio $=$

$$\left[\left(\begin{array}{c} \text{square of} \\ \text{proportion} \\ \text{of A in} \\ \text{portfolio} \end{array} \right) \left(\begin{array}{c} \text{variance of} \\ \text{net cash flows} \\ \text{of project A} \end{array} \right) + \left(\begin{array}{c} \text{square of} \\ \text{proportion} \\ \text{of B in} \\ \text{portfolio} \end{array} \right) \left(\begin{array}{c} \text{variance of} \\ \text{net cash flows} \\ \text{of project B} \end{array} \right) \right.$$

$$\left. +2 \left(\begin{array}{c} \text{proportion} \\ \text{of A in} \\ \text{portfolio} \end{array} \right) \left(\begin{array}{c} \text{proportion} \\ \text{of B in} \\ \text{portfolio} \end{array} \right) \left(\begin{array}{c} \text{covariance of net} \\ \text{cash flow A and} \\ \text{net cash flow B} \end{array} \right) \right]^{1/2}$$

$$= [(0.25)(545.85) + (0.25)(283.26)$$

$$+2(0.25)(354.24)]^{1/2}$$

$$= [136.46 + 70.81 + 177.12]^{1/2}$$

$$= [384.39]^{1/2} = \$19.6 \text{ (convert to thousands)}$$

Recall that the standard deviation for Project A was $22,480, and for Project B $16,890. The straight average standard deviation for these two projects would thus be $19,690. But the portfolio standard deviation is only $19,600—a $90 reduction from the straight average. Portfolio diversification, therefore, reduces risk by reducing the variability in the combined net cash flows. The reduction in portfolio risk comes from three factors: (1) the correlation between the project net cash flows (the lower the correlation—less than 1—the greater the reduction in risk); (2) the number of projects in the portfolio; and (3) the proportion or weight of the individual projects in the portfolio in relation to the correlations among the various projects.

The extent to which the portfolio standard deviation is below a straight average of the standard deviations of Projects A and B is directly proportional to how much below 1 the correlation coefficient between the projects is. The correlation coefficient, ρ_{AB}, is

$$\rho_{AB} = \frac{\text{covariance of net cash flows of Projects A and B}}{(\text{standard deviation of Project A}) \times (\text{standard deviation of Project B})}$$

$$= \frac{\text{Cov}(\overline{C}_A, \overline{C}_B)}{\sigma_A \sigma_B}$$

$$= \frac{354.24}{22.48 \times 16.89} = \frac{354.24}{379.91} = 0.93$$

The correlation between the cash flows of Projects A and B is 0.93, which is only slightly below the straight average of the standard deviations of the individual project cash flows because of the cash flows' high correlation. Lower correlations would have the effect of reducing the portfolio standard deviations further below the straight average of the standard deviations.

The preceding analysis indicates that managers can reduce risk in their companies' international projects through portfolio diversification. The extent by which the risk is reduced in a portfolio is directly proportional to the correlation coefficient among the project net cash flows.

Furthermore, risk reduction through portfolio diversification permits the assumption of projects with greater variability in their individual net cash flows. Since returns are normally higher for higher risks, the firm can earn higher returns by undertaking projects with higher risks and reducing the risk exposure through portfolio diversification.

SUMMARY

The process of objective evaluation of the cash flows of a foreign project is part of the general planning process connected with direct foreign investment. The evaluation of a foreign project starts with the forecast of the cash flows from the project. The cash outflows to be measured include outlays for acquisition and installation of equipment as well as provision for working capital requirements for the initial operations. Outlays for operating costs are incurred during each period of the life of the project. They constitute a continuing stream of outflows. Cash inflows are generated from sale of the products or services of the project and recoverable assets at the end of the project's life. These cash flows are measured for each period to obtain the net cash flow for each period and the cumulative net cash flow. The net cash flows are then discounted by the company's desired rate of return (or cost of capital) to obtain the net PV, which is then totaled to obtain the cumulative net PV.

The project cash flows of the subsidiary must be distinguished from the cash flows to the parent company from the remittance of dividends or from the repayment of capital. The parent company's cash flows are measured in the period of receipt, with tax payments made by the subsidiary for the parent included in the determination of the net U.S. tax liability of the parent company.

The example of the U.S. Zephyr Corporation and its Mexican subsidiary illustrated the basic method for evaluating direct foreign investment, including the mechanics of computing the relevant cash flows and income statements. Alternative forms of capital structure of a subsidiary or affiliate, based on different capital contributions by the parent company, were examined together with their respective effects on the remittances of the foreign affiliate to the parent. The effects of inflation on project cash flows and on foreign exchange rates should be considered as relevant risks that can affect a foreign project. Political and social risks, including expropriation, were also discussed.

Three methods of factoring risk into the net PV calculations were presented. Finally, a portfolio approach to capital budgeting was briefly treated to show how such an approach provides a basis for diversification in foreign investments which can produce relative stability in cash flows and meet the desired rate of return.

SUPPLEMENTARY READING

David K. Eiteman and Arthur I. Stonehill, *Multinational Business Finance* (Reading, Mass.: Addison Wesley, 2nd ed., 1979), Chapter 8.

David Zenoff and Jack Zurick, *International Financial Management* (Englewood Cliffs, N.J.: Prentice-Hall, 1969), Chapter 5.

15

The Transnational Enterprise and World Commerce

The transnational enterprise (TNE) plays an important role in world commerce.[1] TNEs, as the term is used in this chapter, are the industrial and commercial corporations engaged in the production and distribution of nearly all the goods and services entering international trade. Moreover, the investment and location policies of these enterprises determine to a large extent the structure of world trade.

During the past two decades, the rapid growth in world commerce has provided impetus for economic and social development in both the industrialized countries and the developing countries. As world commerce has expanded, the international economic system has undergone extensive changes and many opportunities have arisen for corporations in the industrial countries to extend their commercial activities around the world—through exporting, foreign direct investment, licensing, or all three.

The world political system has also changed. One important political change has been the breakdown of the old colonial empires, which has given birth to a large number of newly independent countries whose economies provide new opportunities for exports and direct investments.

This chapter will examine the shifts in the pattern of worldwide output and trade in the last two decades, discuss the role played by the TNE in the internationalization of the production process and in the rapid expansion of this trend, and will speculate on the TNE's future role in world commerce.

SHIFTS IN THE PATTERN OF WORLD OUTPUT AND TRADE

The world economy has undergone some structural transformations since the early 1960s, which have resulted in shifts in the pattern of world output and trade. Table 15.1 presents the geographical distribution of world industrial production for the period 1963 to 1977 for the developed and developing countries. The world industrial production figures show that the shares of all the advanced industrial countries except Japan fell during the period. The shares of the 10 newly industrializing countries (NICs) increased by 72 percent from 1963 to 1977, while the shares of other developing countries increased by only 9.2 percent.

Looking at the figures for individual countries reveals that, on the one hand, the shares of the United States and West Germany in world industrial production fell by 8.3 percent and 8.6 percent, respectively, during the 14-year period ending 1977. On the other hand, Japan's share of world industrial production increased by 56.8 percent during the period. The United Kingdom experienced the largest share decline in world industrial production (35.8 percent) among the advanced industrial countries.

The NICs experienced significant increases in their respective shares of world industrial production, and the Far East NICs experienced the most rapid growth of all. South Korea experienced the fastest growth in share; its share grew fivefold. Taiwan experienced the second-highest growth (318 percent). Hong Kong's share increased by 163 percent, while Singapore's share doubled. Spain's share grew by 77 percent, followed by Greece with 74 percent, Brazil with 59 percent, Yugoslavia with 42 percent, and Mexico and Portugal, with 39 percent each.

While the NICs experienced dramatic increases in their respective shares of world industrial production, the relative size of industrial production in these countries remained small in comparison with that of the advanced industrial countries. Brazil had the largest share (2.49 percent) among the NICs, but its share was still below Canada's (3.08 percent), which was the smallest of the advanced industrial countries'. Yugoslavia, Spain, and Mexico had shares around 1.5 percent. The shares of the other NICs were less than 0.5 percent, except that of South Korea.

The rapid rise in industrial production in the NICs from 1963 to 1977 reflects to a significant degree the internationalization of the production process by the TNEs through investments made in industrial production facilities in these countries. The process of internationalization of production processes facilitates intrafirm trade by the TNEs. These enterprises spread their production processes around the world to take advantage of low-cost labor in certain countries, or the abundance of natural resources or major markets in another country, or political stability elsewhere. TNEs plan their global production strategies so that they can produce component parts in South Korea, Taiwan, or Brazil, and assemble them in Mexico for export to the United States and the rest of the world. An example is General Motors' world car, which is being produced initially in three countries—the United States, the United Kingdom, and Mexico—for distribution throughout the world. The component parts for the world car are produced elsewhere and shipped to the three countries for assembly and distribution. Many industrial products assembled in the United States have components made in other countries around the world.

Table 15.1 Geographical Distribution of World Industrial Production^a (Percentages and indexes)

	1963	1970	1973	1974	1975	1976	1977
United States	40.25%	36.90%	36.59%	36.30%	34.97%	35.42%	36.90%
Japan	5.48	9.28	9.74	9.28	8.88	9.06	9.14
West Germany	9.69	9.84	9.19	8.95	8.98	8.97	8.85
France	6.30	6.30	6.25	6.35	6.25	6.25	6.15
United Kingdom	6.46	5.26	4.78	4.61	4.67	4.29	4.16
Italy	3.44	3.49	3.29	3.43	3.28	3.41	3.33
Canada	3.01	3.01	3.08	3.16	3.17	3.08	3.08
Spain	0.88	1.18	1.37	1.48	1.47	1.43	1.56
Portugal	0.23	0.27	0.30	0.31	0.31	0.30	0.32
Greece	0.19	0.25	0.30	0.30	0.33	0.33	1.33
Yugoslavia	1.14	1.25	1.31	1.43	1.60	1.53	1.62
Brazil	1.57	1.73	2.10	2.25	2.47	2.49	NA
Mexico	1.04	1.27	1.30	1.38	1.54	1.44	1.45
Hong Kong	0.08	0.15	0.18	0.17	0.17	0.21	NA
South Korea	0.11	0.22	0.32	0.41	0.51	0.63	0.69
Taiwan	0.11	0.23	0.34	0.33	0.37	0.42	0.46
Singapore	0.05	0.06	0.08	0.08	0.09	0.09	0.10
Total	5.40	6.61	7.60	8.14	8.86	8.87	9.28^c
Other developed countries^b	10.99	9.72	9.83	9.73	10.58	9.90	9.29
Other developing countries, including:	8.98	9.59	9.65	10.05	10.36	10.75	9.80
India	1.21	1.11	1.03	1.04	1.15	1.17	1.19
Argentina	0.94	1.07	1.09	1.14	1.18	1.06	1.06
World	100.0	100.0	100.0	100.0	100.0	100.0	100.0
World (1970 = 100)	66.0	100.0	121.0	122.0	115.0	125.0	129.0

Source: Organization for Economic Cooperation and Development, *The Impact of the Newly Industrializing Countries on Production and Trade in Manufactures,* Report by the Secretary-General (Paris: OECD, 1979), p. 18.

^{a} Excluding the Eastern bloc. Figures for 1970 represent value added; those for other years are based on industrial production indexes.
^{b} All other OECD countries plus South Africa and Israel.
^{c} Total includes breakdown for Brazil and Hong Kong.
NA Not available.

This intrafirm trade gives rise to exports between the countries in which the TNE affiliates are located. As intrafirm trade increases, exports of manufactured semifinished and finished goods (manufactures) also increases. Table 15.2 presents the geographical distribution of world exports of manufacturers for the years 1963, 1973, and 1976.

The OECD countries dominated world exports of manufactures. In fact, the OECD role increased during the period, from 80.49 percent to 82.76 percent. The NICs' share of world export nearly tripled meanwhile, increasing from 2.59 percent in 1963 to 7.12 percent in 1976. The share of the other developing countries decreased from 2.70 percent in 1963 to 1.55 percent in 1976. The share of the Eastern bloc countries also decreased, from 13.35 percent in 1963 to 9.65 percent in 1976.

While the United States' share of world manufactured exports decreased 21.4 percent from 1963 to 1976, Japan's share nearly doubled during the same

Table 15.2   Geographic Distribution of World Exports of Manufactures (Percentages)

	1963	1973	1976
Canada	2.61	4.16	3.32
United States	17.24	12.58	13.55
Japan	5.98	9.92	11.38
France	6.99	7.26	7.41
West Germany	15.53	16.98	15.81
Italy	4.73	5.30	5.49
United Kingdom	11.14	7.00	6.59
Spain	0.28	0.92	1.07
Portugal	0.30	0.35	0.21
Greece	0.04	0.15	0.22
Other OECD	15.65	17.63	17.71
Total OECD	80.49	82.25	82.76
Brazil	0.05	0.35	0.41
Mexico	0.17	0.64	0.51
Yugoslavia	0.40	0.55	0.60
Hong Kong	0.76	1.05	1.15
South Korea	0.05	0.78	1.20
Taiwan	0.16	1.04	1.23
Singapore	0.38	0.46	0.52
Total NICs	2.59	6.29	7.12
Other developing countries, including:	2.70	2.34	1.55
India	0.85	0.45	0.49
Argentina	0.01	0.21	0.17
Eastern bloc	13.35	10.00	9.65
Total world	100.00	100.00	100.00

Source: OECD, *op. cit.*
NIC Newly industrializing countries.

period. The United Kingdom's share of world exports of manufactures fell a dramatic 41 percent, while West Germany, Italy, and France experienced small increases in their shares.

The change in relative participation in world exports mirrors the change in the geographical pattern of world industrial production. In the case of both the United States and the United Kingdom, the TNEs had shifted some of their industrial production activities abroad by investing and locating industrial plants in countries within the EEC and the European Free Trade Area (EFTA) to take advantage of the proximity of those countries to major markets, and in the Far East and Latin America to take advantage of those areas' low-cost labor, abundant raw materials, plus the infrastructure (transportation, communication, and other basic systems) needed for business activities. This shift in the production facilities from the United States and the United Kingdom is reflected in the relative drop in exports of manufactures of the two countries.

The Role of NICs in World Trade

As the TNEs have been instrumental in the internationalization of the production process through their investment strategies and intrafirm trade, so the newly industrializing countries have served as offshore bases for export to the developing countries. The developing countries became a natural market for the NICs because of their proximity and accessibility when the domestic markets of the OECD countries were protected by high tariff barriers. Since the multilateral free trade negotiations under the auspices of GATT (see Chapter 3) led to lower tariff barriers, and special tariff preferences for the developing countries, the markets of the OECD countries have been opened to the exports of the NICs and other developing countries.

The changing role of the NICs in world trade can be seen in the rise in the NICs' share of world exports of manufactures, presented in Table 15.3. Exports of NIC manufactures to the industrial countries represented 30 percent of total

Table 15.3   NICs' Share of World Exports of Manufactures by Area (Percentages)

Area Exported to	1963	1973	1976
Industrial countries[a]	2.6	7.0	7.9
Developing countries	4.7	7.2	8.1
OPEC	3.9	5.9	6.4
Others, including	4.9	7.6	8.6
Far Eastern NICs	3.0	7.1	9.0
Eastern Bloc	1.3	2.5	3.1

Source: OECD, op. cit.
[a] OECD minus Australia and New Zealand.
NIC = newly industrializing countries.

NIC exports in 1963 (when access to the markets of the industrial countries was restricted), while exports to developing countries were 55 percent. NIC exports doubled between 1963 and 1973, and the export share of the NIC manufactures to industrial countries more than doubled. In 1973 the export of NIC manufactures to the industrial countries represented 42 percent of total NIC exports. The increased accessibility of NIC manufactures to the markets of the industrial countries significantly reduced their dependence on the markets of the developing countries. NIC exports of manufactures to developing countries fell to 43 percent of total NIC exports in 1973. These percentages of NIC exports to the industrial and the developing countries remained fairly constant into 1976.

Technological Transfer

International transfers of technology have increased substantially in the postwar period. The major flow of technology has been among firms in the industrialized countries, but technological transfer occurs also between firms in the industrialized, market-oriented economies and firms in the developing countries has been growing in the last two decades and should continue to grow nological transfer to the developing countries and the centrally planned countries has been growing in the last two decades, and should continue to grow during the 1980s. This growth has several reasons. The developing countries have become increasingly aware of the role of technology in fostering economic development and the ability to compete in international production. The centrally planned economies will continue their effort to attain technological self-sufficiency during the 1980s, and, in the process, the flow of technology to them from the industrial market economies should accelerate.

The TNEs play a central role in the transfer of technology and the rate of technological diffusion. The greater part of the technology transferred among firms in the industrial market economies involves advanced systems of the TNEs and other large U.S. international corporations. The dominant channel of transfer is through world trade. Direct forms of transfer include licenses, patents, sale of technological know-how, and direct investment.

Firms in the industrialized countries increasingly use a combination of these channels to gain new technological expertise. This practice is frequently used for electronics products and airplanes. A foreign firm in an industrialized country will contract to purchase a piece of equipment or an airplane, for example, on terms of sale based on long-term cooperation in production. This arrangement reflects the desire of foreign countries to acquire new technology for use in their domestic economies.

Meanwhile, the politics of economic cooperation between the Western market economies and the Eastern, centralized economies that has prevailed for the past two decades has provided opportunities for trade between these two groups, and along with the trade has come the transfer of technology. In addition, the rapid expansion of trade between the industrialized economies and the developing countries, and the increased flow of foreign direct investment to the developing countries, have also provided channels for the transfer of technology needed by these countries for industrialization and development.

Principal Methods of Transferring Technology

As noted previously, the three principal methods available to the TNE for the transfer of technology abroad are exporting, direct investment, and licensing arrangements.

Most technological transfer among firms in different countries takes place through the exporting and importing activities of world trade. The rate of technological diffusion, therefore, has increased with the rapid growth of world trade in the last two decades. Technological transfers through trade range from simple products to the highly sophisticated technological systems normally traded between firms in the industrialized countries. Transactions involving the sale of advanced technological systems usually contain arrangements for cooperation in production and for transfer of technological know-how and patent rights to the foreign firm buying the system.

Direct investment in foreign subsidiaries is a channel frequently used by U.S. firms to transfer technology abroad. A U.S. parent company will provide its foreign subsidiary with the technology needed for use in its manufacturing operations. The parent will usually also have to provide technical and general management skills as well as marketing expertise to enable the subsidiary to use the technology effectively. The parent company may have to provide training facilities for the local work force as well.

The parent company provides the research base for research and development activities of its foreign subsidiaries. Creamer examined the overseas research and development undertaken by U.S. MNCs during the years 1966 to 1975 and developed a statistical profile of the pattern of their expenditures.[2] Creamer's study showed that a growing portion of the research and development undertaken in the United Kingdom and West Germany was supported by U.S. parent companies' expenditures. In Canada, the expenditures by U.S. corporations made up a significant part of the country's total research and development effort. The expenditures of firms outside the United States reached an estimated 12 percent of total research and development expenditures in 1980.[3]

U.S. firms generally use licensing arrangements to transfer technology to unaffiliated foreign firms. In the protected Japanese market, for example, restrictions on direct investments and protective tariff barriers on imports make licensing arrangements the most effective means of entry for U.S. companies.[4]

Rates of Diffusion

The rate of diffusion varies with the type of technology and is determined by the degree of difficulty of transfer. The costs of transferring the technology increase with the difficulty. The three broad types of technology are (1) general technology, (2) firm-specific technology, and (3) system-specific technology.

General technology involves information that is common to an industry or trade and represents the general state of technological knowledge in the industry or trade. The technology that forms the basis of a whole industry is complex, which makes general technology the most difficult type to transfer to another country.

Firm-specific technology refers to technology specific to a particular firm's experience, activities, and know-how, but not attributable to any specific item the firm produces. The diffusion rate of firm-specific technology is higher than that of general technology.

System-specific technology concerns the technology used in the production of a product by all manufacturers within the industry. This is the least difficult of the three types of technology to transfer, and thus it has the highest rate of technological diffusion.

The choice of a method of technology transfer depends on the type of technology involved. The transfer of a TNE's system-specific technology, for example, normally involves direct investment if the TNE also wants to take advantage of proximity to foreign markets or the availability of cheap labor. Exporting is another channel that can be used for transferring system-specific technology. Licensing arrangements and direct investment are likely to be used in diffusion of firm-specific technology.

The rapid pace of technological diffusion that has resulted from the activities of TNEs has stirred up a debate on the effects of the transfer of technology on the U.S. economy. This question will be discussed below.

The Effects of Foreign Direct Investment

Over the past 30 years, U.S. technical superiority has diminished as its production technology and managerial skills have been transplanted, principally through direct investment, to the economies of foreign potential competitors. "United States types" of goods are now abundantly produced abroad with the aid of American technology and managerial know-how, which has implications for the U.S. economic and social situation. It is useful, therefore, to examine the scope and pattern of U.S. direct investment and to discuss its implications.

Table 15.4 shows the size and pattern of U.S. direct investment abroad from 1974 to 1979. The total amount reached $192.6 billion in 1979 from $167.8 billion in 1978—an increase of $24.8 billion. From 1974 to 1979, it rose by $73.8 billion—a 62-percent increase in the 5-year period.

Investments in manufacturing made up 43.4 percent of U.S. direct investments abroad in 1979. Most of this investment was in the industrialized countries of Europe, Canada, and Australasia; manufacturing investment by U.S. firms in these countries amounted to $63.9 billion in 1979, or 76.4 percent of the total U.S. direct investment abroad in manufacturing industries.

Over the past 30 years the nature and scope of public discussion of the role and effect of foreign direct investment by U.S. MNCs have changed. This change reflects a growing awareness of the impact the rapidly growing direct

Table 15.4 U.S. Direct Investment Abroad, 1978–1979 ($ billions)

	Total		Manufacturing		Change in 1979 Total Investment	
	1978	1979	1978	1979	from 1978	from 1974
Europe	69.5	81.4	36.3	41.2	11.9	36.7
EEC	55.2	64.8	32.2	36.4	9.6	29.4
Other	14.3	16.6	9.4	12.0	2.3	7.3
Canada	37.1	41.0	17.5	19.2	3.9	12.6
Australasia	6.9	7.6	3.0	3.3	0.7	2.6
Latin America	32.7	36.8	11.7	13.2	4.2	17.3
Africa	5.1	5.6	1.0	1.2	0.5	1.9
Middle East	−2.2	−0.3	0.2	0.2	1.8	−2.6
Asia	11.7	13.5	4.3	5.2	1.8	5.7
International and unallocated	6.9	6.9	—	—	—	—
Total	$167.8	$192.6	$74.1	$83.6	$24.8	$73.8

Source: Bureau of Economic Analysis, U.S. Department of Commerce, *Survey of Current Business*, Vol. 60, No. 3 (March 1980). Minuses for the Middle East represent disinvestment as U.S. companies repatriated their capital.

investment has on the capital-exporting and capital-importing countries and on the general structure of world trade.

Direct investment was viewed as helpful to the recovery of Europe following the end of World War II, and an aid in the growth of the less developed countries. In this perspective, private direct investment provided the mechanism for transferring capital, technology, and managerial skills to foster the recovery of Europe and to accelerate worldwide economic growth.[5]

The U.S. balance-of-payments problems in the late 1950s shifted focus to the effect of the growing U.S. foreign direct investment on the deficit in the balance of payments and on the drain on U.S. gold and monetary reserves (which had declined from $24.3 billion in 1950 to $19.4 billion in 1960).

Foreign Direct Investment and Domestic Capital Formation

The central question in the public debate on the role of direct investment abroad by U.S. firms is the potential displacement of U.S. export sales from production at home by competing goods produced abroad. Two recent developments have intensified the debate on the role of foreign direct investment: First, the foreign affiliates of U.S. MNCs have been expanding their export sales faster than U.S. exporters of the same product, and second, most of the direct investment abroad is being made by large U.S. corporations that are also major exporters.[6]

Several questions were raised by these developments. For one, do the direct investments made by U.S. firms abroad divert investment and expansion from production at home, thereby preventing exports from being made from production at home? Or, does the foreign direct investment cultivate foreign markets that would otherwise have been lost to foreign competitors—in which case the investment abroad bolsters domestic investment? Another question concerns the effect on American employment of investment by U.S. firms in offshore, or "runaway," plants? Such investments are made to take advantage of lower-cost foreign labor in assembly operations in labor-intensive industries (for example, electronics products, electrical appliances, textiles, and footwear). The products are then shipped back to the U.S. market to compete with similar goods produced by American labor.[7]

In response to labor pressure against increased direct investment abroad, the Burke-Hartke Bill was introduced in Congress in 1973. The bill made four proposals with respect to foreign investment: (1) U.S. shareholders owning 10 percent or more of the voting stock of a controlled foreign corporation (i.e., a corporation which is 50 percent or more U.S.-owned) would be taxed currently on their pro rata share of the earnings of that corporation; (2) the credit for foreign taxes would be terminated; (3) the foreign income of American affiliates abroad would be defined for tax purposes as *net* of foreign taxes and based on straight line-useful life depreciation; (4) the President would be authorized to place controls on capital exports and to prohibit the use of U.S. patents abroad (whether directly or by license) in cases where the use is judged to be detrimental to U.S. employment. The intent of the Burke-Hartke Bill was to repeal the foreign tax credit and to tax profits of controlled foreign corporations on an accrual basis, thereby terminating the U.S. system of tax deferral. Changes proposed in the bill would greatly simplify the tax laws on taxing income from foreign investments.

On the other side of the investments debate are the advocates of the foreign direct investment activities of U.S. MNCs. Several studies have been undertaken of the domestic effects of foreign direct investment by U.S. corporations by testing the hypothesis that direct foreign investment displaces investment that would otherwise be made domestically, curbing domestic production and employment. Testing the hypothesis centers on an investigation of the following two questions: (1) What would have happened if direct investment abroad had not been made by the U.S. firms? and (2) What are the effects of foreign investments by U.S. firms on American exports?

Displacement of Domestic Investment   Several studies have attempted to determine whether foreign investment by U.S. firms displaces domestic investment by examining the organization of multinational industrial firms. If prevented from investing abroad, or if foreign investment opportunities were not available, would these firms make comparable investments at home?

One path of investigation is to compare the growth rate of firms with and without foreign direct investment. In a study of U.S. manufacturing firms in the *Fortune* 500, Rowthorn[8] found that roughly one-quarter of their growth over the 1957-1965 period came from overseas expansion and the remaining three-quarters came from domestic growth. Of the domestic growth, two-thirds was due to the growth of the economy and one-third to increased share in the economy. Among the largest firms, expansion of overseas operations tended to account for more growth than domestic operations did, which led Rowthorn to hypothesize that the giant firms were unable to increase their share of the domestic economy and compensated by expanding overseas. As noted in Chapter 13, international firms are generally oligopolies, and several studies have linked oligopolistic characteristics to the foreign-investing propensities of these firms. The large oligopolistic firms in all industrialized countries achieve their growth objectives though overseas expansion, which uses direct investments to penetrate the overseas markets. This process of "interpenetration" by large oligopolistic firms increases industrial concentration both worldwide and nationally by displacing the smaller domestic firms in the foreign country.

Through international investment, the giant oligopolistic companies seize opportunities for continued growth that are, in many cases, not available domestically and increase their share of the world market. The alternatives to direct investment abroad for these companies would be diversification through investment in another industry or no investment at all.

Displacement of Exports   Several studies have examined the effects of foreign direct investment by U.S. firms on U.S. exports. A study in 1968,[9] for example, investigated the export-displacement effect of foreign direct investment by comparing foreign subsidiaries of U.S. firms' and U.S. exporters' shares of foreign markets. The results of this study were inconclusive. A similar study of the effect of foreign direct investment by British firms on the United Kingdom's balance of payments[10] reported that there was no displacement effect on British exports from British foreign direct investment. In the authors' opinion, if the British companies had failed to set up production facilities in the foreign markets, the effect would simply have been to allow competing firms from other industrial nations to do so.

Studies by business research groups[11] indicate that foreign direct investment by U.S. firms has *stimulated* exports from domestic production rather than displacing them. These studies provide evidence that an increasing proportion of U.S. exports comes from U.S. international firms. A survey done by the U.S. Department of Commerce[12] for 1966 and 1970 on a sample of MNCs that accounted for over 70 percent of MNC-associated trade with the United States corroborated these findings. The Commerce department study found that there was no basis for the charge by American labor unions that foreign investment by U.S. firms displaced exports from domestic production. The survey showed that exports of U.S. international firms rose by 55 percent between 1966 and 1970, which compared favorably with the 43-percent rise for all U.S. exports.

Further corroboration came from the U.S. Tariff Commission in a 1973 study.[13] Several interesting findings were reported in the study: (1) MNCs as a group increased their net exports in the period between 1966 and 1970, while the non-MNCs showed sizable trade balance declines; (2) among all manufacturing industries, MNCs increased net exports by $3.4 billion while non-MNCs increased net imports by $3.6 billion over the same period; and (3) a comparison of the share of U.S. exports in total "United States market abroad" (exports from the United States plus foreign sales of foreign affiliates of U.S. firms) in 1966 and 1970 showed[14] only a slight drop in 1970, amounting to $3 billion. This decline came from companies in the Miscellaneous category (using the SIC code), which are generally small companies using a low level of technology and high level of unskilled labor. The Tariff Commission concluded that competing foreign firms would have pre-empted the overseas markets in the absence of United States investment.

Foreign Direct Investment and Investment in the Capital-Receiving Country

An understanding of the effect of foreign direct investment on total investment in a capital-receiving country and of the nature of the "transfer" problem should help TNEs formulate their worldwide investment strategy and minimize host-country risk. Attention is usually focused on the beneficial effects of foreign direct investment, on the assumption that foreign investment supplements inadequate domestic investment reflecting inadequate local savings.

When TNEs make a direct investment in a foreign country, the country benefits economically, technologically, and socially from the investment. The beneficial effect of foreign direct investment is greater in developing countries than in developed countries, because it provides financing, technology, and managerial skills that are not available in the local economy. Much of the attention to the effect of foreign direct investment has therefore been directed to the impact on developing countries.

Past examinations of the effect of foreign investment on the quantity of private investment in the capital-receiving country generally assumed that each dollar of foreign investment generated an equal increase in total investment there.[15] Recent studies show, however, that when foreign investments provide additional resources, not all the increased resources go toward increasing the total investment in the recipient country. Some of the increased resources provided by the foreign investment go toward increasing consumption.[16]

Foreign investment affects total investment in the recipient country in other ways as well. Some types of foreign investment are complementary to domestic investment in the recipient country and, therefore, increase total investment geometrically rather than arithmetically. A TNE can determine whether a planned foreign investment will generate a disproportionate increase in total investment by analyzing the relationship of the foreign investment to domestic investment. The impact of the foreign direct investment on domestic investment can be analyzed in terms of its direct and indirect effect.

Direct Effect   Foreign investment can either (1) complement local investment, (2) substitute for it, or (3) have no direct impact on domestic investment.

The effects of the foreign investment are said to be *complementary* if the size of the increase in the domestic investment is larger than the increase in the foreign investment. Complementary effects are seen in foreign investment which involves projects with forward or backward linkages:[17] for example, a TNE invests in a foreign plant to produce washing machines and buys the steel sheeting for the panels locally; the increased demand for steel plates may necessitate expansion of steel-plate manufacturing plant capacity and thereby disproportionately increase total investment in the recipient country.

Foreign investment is said to have *substitution* effects if total investment in the recipient country increases by less than the increase in foreign investment.[18] The foreign investment becomes, wholly or partially, a substitute for domestic investment by replacing potential domestic investment. Substitution of foreign investment for domestic investment occurs when the foreign investor has a competitive cost advantage because of superior technology, better management, or tax and import privileges—all of which lead to lower costs. For example, foreign investment in a plant to produce a new type of drilling bit which cuts down on the time it takes to drill a hole and reduces labor and production time (thereby increasing operating efficiency) will definitely siphon off demand for less efficient types of drilling bits currently on the market. As a consequence, the foreign investment will supplant domestic investment by causing investment in existing types of manufacturing plants in the capital-receiving country to dry up.

Foreign investment has no impact on domestic investment when total investment in the recipient country increases by the exact amount of the foreign-investment increase. This situation occurs usually when foreign investment is made in a plant in which all or the major part of inputs for manufacturing are imported from abroad. Foreign investment will have no impact if the amount of manufacturing input required by the new investment could be easily met from existing levels of production or from using idle plant capacity that would otherwise not be used. Development models usually assume that foreign investment does not have any impact on total domestic investment.

Indirect Effects Indirect effects of foreign investment on total investment in the recipient country can be seen in the "accelerator" model of investment. The accelerator model explains that an expenditure increase creates a need for increased capacity to produce more goods, which leads to increases in investment. Foreign investment that causes changes in the level of expenditures will generate increases in investment in addition to the changes caused directly by the foreign investment.[19] The changes in investment and consumption from the direct effect of the foreign investment influence expenditures, which in turn produces indirect effects on total investment in the recipient country.

Influence of Institutional Structure

The structure of demand and production in the institutions located in the capital-receiving country can accentuate or diminish the amount of increase in imports from an inflow of foreign investment. As an example, a foreign subsidiary that uses a large portion of imported components from its parent company as inputs for production will increase its demand for these imports significantly when the parent company makes a direct investment to expand the production capacity of the foreign subsidiary. The high level of demand for imported components will cause imports to increase above the level ordinarily expected in the transfer process. But when the inflow of direct investment stimulates local production of goods that were previously imported, imports will decline as locally produced goods replace imported goods—a kind of import-subsitution effect.

On the other hand, when a direct investment is made in a foreign subsidiary engaged in exporting activities, the increase in the exports by the foreign subsidiary will cause total exports from the capital-receiving country to rise (although exports would ordinarily be expected to fall and imports to rise following foreign direct investment). Thus, the presence of institutional factors in the capital-receiving country may cause opposite effects in the transfer process.

The Transfer Problem

Another aspect of the effects of foreign investment on the receiving country is the likelihood of changes in exports and imports—that is, the "transfer" problem. The transfer problem has to do with the adjustment process in the current account of the balance of payments of the borrowing and lending countries to an increase in the amount of capital transfer.[20] The need for this adjustment arises from changes in expenditures and prices which affect exports and imports in the capital-lending and receiving countries. The effect of the adjustment process in each country depends on whether the economy is operating at a level below full employment or at full employment.

Underemployment Effects   An inflow of foreign investment to a capital-receiving country with less than full employment will cause expenditures to increase, and some of the increase in expenditures will be spent on imports, which would cause imports to increase. The outflow of capital from a capital-lending country whose economy is below full employment will cause expenditures to fall, with a corresponding decline in imports. The reduced level of expenditures will release goods in the capital-lending country for export to the capital-receiving country to meet its rise in demand for imports caused by the inflow of capital.

Full-Employment Effects   An inflow of foreign investment into the capital-receiving country when its economy is at full employment will cause the level of prices to rise relative to the prices in the capital-lending country. The prices of exports from the capital-receiving country will also increase relatively, resulting in a decline in exports while imports increase. For the capital-lending country, the relatively smaller price increases will make its exports more competitive and cause an increase in exports, while imports decline.

FUTURE OF THE TRANSNATIONAL ENTERPRISE

The TNEs have made substantial contributions to world development. As exporters they make available to other countries goods and services that would otherwise not be available. Through direct investment, they transfer managerial, entrepreneurial, and commercial skills. TNEs also transfer technological know-how by building manufacturing plants abroad. The contributions of TNEs to economic development are most visible in the developing countries.

The world economy has undergone several shocks and cyclical influences in the decade of the 1970s, which have distorted and dislocated the world economic system. The OPEC countries have accumulated over $100 billion of capital available for investing, the industrial countries are experiencing at best a sluggish recovery from the inflation/recession, and the non-oil-producing developing countries have built up a heavy debt burden and an adverse trade balance.

Several plans have been proposed since 1976 to solve these economic problems. The majority of the proposals have been made by government leaders from Japan, Austria, West Germany and Venezuela, and by officials of multinational organizations such as the United Nations and the OECD. A proposal for dealing with world economic problems was made by the Brandt Commission in its report, "North-South Survival," in early 1980.

A new proposal by Ronald E. Müller (author of *Global Reach*) calls for a "global Marshall Plan."[21] Müller recommends a cooperative working arrangement among TNEs, the OECD, OPEC, and the lesser-developed countries.

OECD and OPEC would form a cooperative development, or growth "pool," of funds for financing projects in developing countries to help stimulate growth in the latters' economies. Cooperative financing would also be available for projects in industrialized countries with lagging economies. The TNEs would carry out the projects once financing had been provided.

The success of the plan would require the commitment of all parties involved. Müller's plan calls for the United States to take the leadership role in the organization and execution of the plan. He suggests that existing multinational agencies, such as the World Bank and the regional development banks, be used, since they already have a fully trained staff and are currently involved in financing projects worldwide. The mechanism for the plan would be the creation of a trust fund within the World Bank, similar to the bank's "Energy Trust" (see Chapter 12). To gain the confidence and cooperation of developing countries, they would be given a say in decision-making commensurate with their economic weight, in much the same way as the World Bank currently allocates voting by its members.

The plan has several interesting features. The large pool of OPEC funds would be available for investment in the trust fund. The direct participation of the governments of the participating countries would provide political stability and significantly reduce political risks for the TNEs that would undertake the projects in the developing countries.

The reduced political risks contemplated by the proposal would promote a healthy commercial climate for TNEs and encourage closer cooperation among TNEs, the international banking community, and the host governments.

The proposed trust fund would be financed through the sale of bonds by the World Bank for that specific purpose. Müller suggests that OPEC members be allocated 25 percent of the issues and the remaining 75 percent be offered to private investors. Annual financing of some $10 to $12 billion could be raised from the sale of trust bonds backed by the participants in the plan. The funds would be available for financing basic development projects that are commercially sound, although 25 percent of the fund would be set aside for the least developed countries that could not meet the "commercially sound" guideline. As can be seen, such a plan would create an interesting future for the transnational enterprise.

SUMMARY

This chapter has examined the shifts in the pattern of output and trade resulting from the internationalization of the production process. The TNE has played a key role in this process and will play an even bigger role in the future. The international economic system has undergone extensive changes during the last two decades as world commerce has expanded. The breakdown of the old colonial empires spawned a large number of new countries, whose economies have provided markets and investment opportunities for the TNEs. The internationalization of the production process has facilitated intrafirm trade, and production facilities have spread around the world to take advantage of low-cost labor, natural resources, and proximity to major markets.

Although the international transfer of technology increased substantially in the postwar period, most of it was transferred within the industrialized, market-oriented nations. Recently, however, the rate of technological transfer to the developing countries and the centrally planned economies has been growing; it should continue to increase during the 1980s as the developing countries become aware of the role of technology in development, and as the centrally planned economies strive for technological self-sufficiency.

The rapid pace of technological diffusion as a result of the activities of the TNEs has raised questions about the effects of this transfer of technology on the U.S. economy. Several studies of the effects of foreign investments by U.S. firms on exports have found, however, that products arising from U.S. foreign direct investment have not displaced exports of products manufactured in the United States.

Although foreign direct investment is generally beneficial to the economy of the investment-receiving country, recent studies show that, when foreign investment provides additional resources, not all the increased resources—as previously assumed—go toward increasing the total investment in the recipient country. Some of the increased resources go toward increasing consumption.

Foreign direct investment affects total investment in the recipient country in other ways. Some types of foreign direct investment complement local investment, while others substitute for it. The impact of the investments may be direct or indirect. Other aspects of the effect of foreign direct investment on the investment-receiving country involve the likelihood of changes in exports and imports, which is known as the "transfer" problem. Managers need to understand how foreign direct investment will affect the economy of the recipient country and take these effects into consideration when formulating investment plans in order to minimize their risk exposure.

NOTES

1   The three types of business enterprise involved in world commerce are the international, the multinational, and the transnational enterprise. The *international* enterprise is basically a domestic firm engaged in exporting activities, but the term is sometimes used generically to refer to the three types of enterprises. As defined in Chapter 8, the *multinational* enterprise has foreign subsidiaries and affiliates in one or more foreign country, but the shareholders and top management are usually nationals of the parent company's home country. A *transnational* enterprise represents an evolution of the multinational enterprise in which ownership and top management are represented by nationals of the countries in which the TNE does business worldwide. It truly represents a world corporation. In this chapter, the term "transnational" enterprise will be used for the most part, since the OECD and other international organizations use it, but occasionally the other terms will be used as well.

2 Daniel Creamer, *Overseas Research and Development by United States Multinationals, 1966–1975: Estimates of Expenditures and a Statistical Profile* (New York: The Conference Board, 1976).

2 Edwin Mansfield, "Statement to the Senate Committee Concerning International Technology Transfer and Overseas Research and Development," *Export Policy, Part 7, Oversight on United States High Technology Exports*, Hearing before the Subcommittee on International Finance of the Committee on Banking, Housing, and Urban Affairs, Jointly with the Subcommittee on Science, Technology, and Space of the Committee on Commerce, Science, and Transportation of the United States Senate (Washington, D.C.: GPO, May 16, 1978),

4 T. Ozawa, *Japan's Technological Challenge to the West, 1950–1974: Motivation and Accomplishment* (Cambridge, Mass.: MIT Press, 1974).

5 U.S. Department of State, *Expanding Private Investment for Free World Economic Growth*, report prepared under the direction of Ralph I. Strauss (1959).

6 Report to the Committee on Finance of the U.S. Senate on Implications of Multinational Firms for World Trade and Improvement and for United States Trade and Labor, by the U.S. Tariff Commission (February 1973).

7 Peggy B. Musgrave, *Direct Investment Abroad and the Multinationals: Effects on the United States Economy*, prepared for the use of the Subcommittee on Multinational Corporations of the Committee on Foreign Relations, U.S. Senate (Washington, D.C.: GPO, 1975).

8 Robert Rowthorn, *International Big Business 1957–1967—A Study of Comparative Growth* (Cambridge: Cambridge University Press, 1971).

9 G. C. Hufbauer and F. M. Adler, "*Overseas Manufacturing and the Balance of Payments*, U.S. Treasury Department, Tax Policy Research Study No. 1 (Washington, D.C.: GPO, 1968).

10 W. B. Reddaway, S. J. Porter, and C. T. Taylor, *Effects of U.K. Direct Investment Overseas* (Cambridge: Cambridge University Press, 1967 and 1968).

11 A review of these business studies is given in T. Horst, *The Impact of U.S. Investment Abroad on U.S. Foreign Trade*, working paper for the Brookings Institution (1974).

12 Betty L. Barker, "U.S. Foreign Trade Associated with U.S. Multinational Companies," *Survey of Current Business*, U.S. Department of Commerce, Vol. 52, No. 12 (December 1972), pp. 20–28.

13 *Implications of Multinational Firms for World Trade and Investment and for U.S. Trade and Labor*, report of the U.S. Tariff Commission to the Committee on Finance, U.S. Senate (February 1973), p. 173.

14 Report of Tariff Commission, *op. cit.*, p. 347.

15 Hollis B. Chenery and Alan M. Strout, "Foreign Assistance and Economic Development," *American Economic Review*, Vol. 56, No. 4 (September 1966), pp. 679–733; P. N. Rosenstein-Rodan, "International Aid for Underdeveloped Countries," *The Review of Economics and Statistics*, Vol. 43, No. 2 (May 1961), pp. 107–138.

16 Keith Griffin, "Foreign Capital, Domestic Savings and Economic Development," *Bulletin*, Oxford University, Institute of Economics and Statistics, Vol. 32 (May 1970), pp. 99–112; K. B. Griffin and J. L. Enos, "Foreign Assistance: Objectives and Consequences," *Economic Development and Cultural Change*, Vol. 18 (April 1970), pp. 313–327; Anisur Rahman, "Foreign Capital and Domestic Savings: A

Test of Haavelmo's Hypothesis with Gross Country Data," *The Review of Economics and Statistics*, Vol. 50 (February 1968), pp. 137–138; Thomas E. Weisskopf, "The Impact of Foreign Capital Inflow on Domestic Savings in Underdeveloped Countries," *Journal of International Economics*, Vol. 2 (February 1972), pp. 25–38.

17   Raymond Lubitz, "The United States Direct Investment in Canada and Canadian Capital Formation, 1950–1962," unpublished doctoral dissertation, Harvard University (1966), summarized in Chapter 4, Richard Caves and Grant Reuber, *Capital Transfers and Economic Policy: Canada 1951–1962* (Cambridge, Mass.: Harvard University Press, 1971); Samuel A. Morley, "American Corporate Investment Abroad since 1919," unpublished doctoral dissertation, University of California, Berkeley (1965).

18   K. B. Griffin and J. L. Enos, *op. cit.*; see also Raymond Lubitz, *op. cit.*, and Samuel A. Morley, *op. cit.*

19   Frances Van Loo, "The Effect of Foreign Direct Investment on Investment in Canada," *The Review of Economics and Statistics*, Vol. 59, No. 4 (November 1977), pp. 474–481.

20   Richard E. Caves and Grant L. Reuber, *op. cit.*

21   The proposal is contained in Ronald Müller, *Revitalizing America's Politics for Prosperity* (New York: Simon and Schuster, 1980).

Appendixes

Uniform Customs and Practice for Documentary Credits

(1974 Revision) International Chamber of Commerce Publication No. 290

The Rules have been drawn up by the Commission on Banking Practices and Technique of the International Chamber of Commerce in consultation with the banking associations of many countries. The ICC acts to promote business interests at international levels, to foster the greater freedom of international trade, and to harmonize and facilate business and trade practices. Paris-based, the Chamber has National Committees in 51 countries and is respresented in over 30 others. In the United States, the International Chamber of Commerce is represented by its United States Council at 1212 Avenue of the Americas, New York, N.Y., 10036 (telephone 212-582-4850), which has printed and distributed the American version of the 1974 version of the 1974 revision of Uniform Customs and Practice for Documentary Credits, ICC Publication No. 290, and which holds the copyright thereto. Copyright by the International Chamber of Commerce, 1975.

Revision has been greatly assisted by the cooperation of the United Nations Commission on International Trade Law (UNCITRAL). Banks in the Socialist countries have also contributed through an ad hoc Working Party.

In conclusion I would like to give our wholehearted thanks to the Chairman of the Banking Commission, Bernard Wheble, and the Commission members for their untiring efforts to achieve agreement on this most important text, and to the many ICC members who have given their executives time to work on the new revision.

Carl-Henrik Winqwist
Secretary General of the ICC

General provisions and definitions

a. These provisions and definitions and the following articles apply to all documentary credits and are binding upon all parties thereto unless otherwise expressly agreed.

the bank authorized to pay, accept or negotiate under a credit. The decision of such bank shall bind all parties concerned.

A bank is authorized to pay or accept under a credit by being specifically nominated in the credit.

A bank is authorized to negotiate under a credit either:

i. by being specifically nominated in the credit, or

ii. by the credit being freely negotiable by any bank.

f. A beneficiary can in no case avail himself of the contractual relationships existing between banks or between the applicant for the credit and the issuing bank.

A. Form and notification of credits

Article 1

a. Credits may be either

i. revocable, or

ii. irrevocable.

Foreword to the 1974 revision

For many years the ICC Banking Commission has contributed to the facilitation of international trade through the formulation of sets of rules governing documentary credits. The last (1962) revision of the *Uniform Customs and Practice for Documentary Credits*, published as ICC Brochure 222, was used by the banks and banking associations of virtually every country and territory in the world.

Considerable changes have since taken place in international trading and transport techniques. Terms of purchase and sale have swung from the traditional FOB and CIF towards "Delivered to Buyer's Premises", and the through, multi-modal movement of unitized cargo is increasingly competing with the traditional single-mode carriage of break-bulk cargo. Consequential changes have become necessary in documentary credit practice.

Therefore we have taken a careful and critical look at the 1962 rules, amending them as appropriate to fit the 1970's and prepare for the 1980's. The changes made particularly concern the documentary aspects of multi-modal transport and unitized cargoes, the easier production and processing of documents in "short form", and the problem of "stale" documents.

b. For the purposes of such provisions, definitions and articles the expressions "documentary credit(s)" and "credit(s)" used therein mean any arrangement, however named or described, whereby a bank (the issuing bank), acting at the request and in accordance with the instructions of a customer (the applicant for the credit),

i. is to make payment to or to the order of a third party (the beneficiary), or is to pay, accept or negotiate bills of exchange (drafts) drawn by the beneficiary, or

ii. authorizes such payments to be made or such drafts to be paid, accepted or negotiated by another bank,

against stipulated documents, provided that the terms and conditions of the credit are complied with.

c. Credits, by their nature, are separate transactions from the sales or other contracts on which they may be based and banks are in no way concerned with or bound by such contracts.

d. Credit instructions and the credits themselves must be complete and precise.

In order to guard against confusion and misunderstanding, issuing banks should discourage any attempt by the applicant for the credit to include excessive detail.

e. The bank first entitled to exercise the option available under Article 32 b. shall be

b. All credits, therefore, should clearly indicate whether they are revocable or irrevocable.

c. In the absence of such indication the credit shall be deemed to be revocable.

Article 2. A revocable credit may be amended or cancelled at any moment without prior notice to the beneficiary. However, the issuing bank is bound to reimburse a branch or other bank to which such a credit has been transmitted and made available for payment, acceptance or negotiation, for any payment, acceptance or negotiation complying with the terms and conditions of the credit and any amendments received up to the time of payment, acceptance or negotiation made by such branch or other bank prior to receipt by it of notice of amendment or of cancellation.

Article 3

a. An irrevocable credit constitutes a definite undertaking of the issuing bank, provided that the terms and conditions of the credit are complied with:

i. to pay, or that payment will be made, if the credit provides for payment, whether against a draft or not;

ii. to accept drafts if the credit provides for acceptance by the issuing bank or to be responsible for their acceptance and payment at maturity if the credit provides for the acceptance of drafts drawn on the applicant for the credit or any other drawee specified in the credit;

iii. to purchase/negotiate, without recourse to drawers and/or bona fide holders, drafts drawn by the beneficiary, at sight or at a tenor, on the applicant for the credit or on any other drawee specified in the credit, or to provide for purchase/negotiation by another bank, if the credit provides for purchase/negotiation.

b. An irrevocable credit may be advised to a beneficiary through another bank (the advising bank) without engagement on the part of that bank, but when an issuing bank authorizes or requests another bank to confirm its irrevocable credit and the latter does so, such confirmation constitutes a definite undertaking of the confirming bank in addition to the undertaking of the issuing bank, provided that the terms and conditions of the credit are complied with:

the operative credit instrument (mail confirmation) and any subsequent amendments to the credit to the beneficiary through the advising bank.

b. The issuing bank will be responsible for any consequences arising from its failure to follow the procedure set out in the preceding paragraph.

c. Unless a cable, telegram or telex states "details to follow" (or words of similar effect), or states that the mail confirmation is to be the operative credit instrument, the cable, telegram or telex will be deemed to be the operative credit instrument and the issuing bank need not send the mail confirmation to the advising bank.

Article 5. When a bank is instructed by cable, telegram or telex to issue, confirm or advise a credit similar in terms to one previously established and which has been the subject of amendments, it shall be understood that the details of the credit being issued, confirmed or advised will be transmitted to the beneficiary excluding the amendments, unless the instructions specify clearly any amendments which are to apply.

so, binds the party giving the authorization to take up the documents and reimburse the bank which has effected the payment, acceptance or negotiation.

c. If, upon receipt of the documents, the issuing bank considers that they appear on their face not to be in accordance with the terms and conditions of the credit, that bank must determine, on the basis of the documents alone, whether to claim that payment, acceptance or negotiation was not effected in accordance with the terms and conditions of the credit.

d. The issuing bank shall have a reasonable time to examine the documents and to determine as above whether to make such a claim.

e. If such claim is to be made, notice to that effect, stating the reasons therefor, must, without delay, be given by cable or other expeditious means to the bank from which the documents have been received (the remitting bank) and such notice must state that the documents are being held at the disposal of such bank or are being returned thereto.

i. to pay, if the credit is payable at its own counters, whether against a draft or not, or that payment will be made if the credit provides for payment elsewhere;

ii. to accept drafts if the credit provides for acceptance by the confirming bank, at its own counters, or to be responsible for their acceptance and payment at maturity if the credit provides for the acceptance of drafts drawn on the applicant for the credit or any other drawee specified in the credit;

iii. To purchase/negotiate, without recourse to drawers and/or bona fide holders, drafts drawn by the beneficiary, at sight or at a tenor, on the issuing bank, or on the applicant for the credit or on any other drawee specified in the credit, if the credit provides for purchase/negotiation.

c. Such undertakings can neither be amended nor cancelled without the agreement of all parties thereto. Partial acceptance of amendments is not effective without the agreement of all parties thereto.

Article 4

a. When an issuing bank instructs a bank by cable, telegram or telex to advise a credit, and intends the mail confirmation to be the operative credit instrument, the cable, telegram or telex must state that the credit will only be effective on receipt of such mail confirmation. In this event, the issuing bank must send

Article 6. If incomplete or unclear instructions are received to issue, confirm or advise a credit, the bank requested to act on such instructions may give preliminary notification of the credit to the beneficiary for information only and without responsibility; in this event the credit will be issued, confirmed or advised only when the necessary information has been received.

B. Liabilities and responsibilities

Article 7. Banks must examine all documents with reasonable care to ascertain that they appear on their face to be in accordance with the terms and conditions of the credit. Documents which appear on their face to be inconsistent with one another will be considered as not appearing on their face to be in accordance with the terms and conditions of the credit.

Article 8

a. In documentary credit operations all parties concerned deal in documents and not in goods.

b. Payment, acceptance or negotiation against documents which appear on their face to be in accordance with the terms and conditions of a credit by a bank authorized to do

f. If the issuing bank fails to hold the documents at the disposal of the remitting bank, or fails to return the documents to such bank, the issuing bank shall be precluded from claiming that the relative payment, acceptance or negotiation was not effected in accordance with the terms and conditions of the credit.

g. If the remitting bank draws the attention of the issuing bank to any irregularities in the documents or advises such bank that it has paid, accepted or negotiated under reserve or against a guarantee in respect of such irregularities, the issuing bank shall not thereby be relieved from any of its obligations under this article. Such guarantee or reserve concerns only the relations between the remitting bank and the beneficiary.

Article 9. Banks assume no liability or responsibility for the form, sufficiency, accuracy, genuineness, falsification or legal effect of any documents, or for the general and/or particular conditions stipulated in the documents or superimposed thereon; nor do they assume any liability or responsibility for the description, quantity, weight, quality, condition, packing, delivery, value or existence of the goods represented thereby, or for the good faith or acts and/or omissions, solvency, performance or standing of the consignor, the carriers or the insurers of the goods or any other person whomsoever.

Article 10. Banks assume no liability or responsibility for the consequences arising out of delay and/or loss in transit of any messages, letters or documents, or for delay, mutilation or other errors arising in the transmission of cables, telegrams or telex. Banks assume no liability or responsibility for errors in translation or interpretation of technical terms, and reserve the right to transmit credit terms without translating them.

Article 11. Banks assume no liability or responsibility for consequences arising out of the interruption of their business by Acts of God, riots, civil commotions, insurrections, wars or any other causes beyond their control or by any strikes or lockouts. Unless specifically authorized, banks will not effect payment, acceptance or negotiation after expiration under credits expiring during such interruption of business.

Article 12

a. Banks utilizing the services of another bank for the purpose of giving effect to the instructions of the applicant for the credit do so for the account and at the risk of the latter.

for under credits and if they are incorporated in the credit terms banks will accept documents as tendered.

C.1. Documents evidencing shipment or dispatch or taking in charge (shipping documents)

Article 15. Except as stated in Article 20, the date of the bill of lading, or the date of any other document evidencing shipment or dispatch or taking in charge, or the date indicated in the reception stamp or by notation on any such document, will be taken in each case to be the date of shipment or dispatch or taking in charge of the goods.

Article 16

a. If words clearly indicating payment or prepayment of freight, however named or described, appear by stamp or otherwise on documents evidencing shipment or dispatch or taking in charge they will be accepted as constituting evidence of payment of freight.

b. If the words "freight pre-payable" or "freight to be prepaid" or words of similar effect appear by stamp or otherwise on such documents they will not be accepted as constituting evidence of the payment of freight.

credit expressly states the clauses or notations which may be accepted.

C.1.1. Marine bills of lading

Article 19

a. Unless specifically authorized in the credit, bills of lading of the following nature will be rejected:

i. Bills of lading issued by forwarding agents.

ii. Bills of lading which are issued under and are subject to the conditions of a charter-party.

iii. Bills of lading covering shipment by sailing vessels.

b. However, subject to the above and unless otherwise specified in the credit, bills of lading of the following nature will be accepted:

i. "Through" bills of lading issued by shipping companies or their agents even though they cover several modes of transport.

ii. Short-form bills of lading (i.e. bills of lading issued by shipping companies or their agents which indicate some or all of the conditions of carriage by reference to a source or document other than the bill of lading).

412

b. Banks assume no liability or responsibility should the instructions they transmit not be carried out, even if they have themselves taken the initiative in the choice of such other bank.

c. The applicant for the credit shall be bound by and liable to indemnify the banks against all obligations and responsibilities imposed by foreign laws and usages.

Article 13. A paying or negotiating bank which has been authorized to claim reimbursement from a third bank nominated by the issuing bank and which has effected such payment or negotiation shall not be required to confirm to the third bank that it has done so in accordance with the terms and conditions of the credit.

C. Documents

Article 14

a. All instructions to issue, confirm or advise a credit must state precisely the documents against which payment, acceptance or negotiation is to be made.

b. Terms such as "first class", "well known", "qualified" and the like shall not be used to describe the issuers of any documents called

c. Unless otherwise specified in the credit or inconsistent with any of the documents presented under the credit, banks will accept documents stating that freight or transportation charges are payable on delivery.

d. Banks will accept shipping documents bearing reference by stamp or otherwise to costs additional to the freight charges, such as costs of, or disbursements incurred in connection with loading, unloading or similar operations, unless the conditions of the credit specifically prohibit such reference.

Article 17. Shipping documents which bear a clause on the face thereof such as "shipper's load and count" or "said by shipper to contain" or words of similar effect, will be accepted unless otherwise specified in the credit.

Article 18

a. A clean shipping document is one which bears no superimposed clause or notation which expressly declares a defective condition of the goods and/or the packaging.

b. Banks will refuse shipping documents bearing such clauses or notations unless the

iii. Bills of lading issued by shipping companies or their agents covering unitized cargoes, such as those on pallets or in containers.

Article 20

a. Unless otherwise specified in the credit, bills of lading must show that the goods are loaded on board a named vessel or shipped on a named vessel.

b. Loading on board a named vessel or shipment on a named vessel may be evidenced either by a bill of lading bearing wording indicating loading on board a named vessel or shipment on a named vessel, or by means of a notation to that effect on the bill of lading signed or initialled and dated by the carrier or his agent, and the date of this notation shall be regarded as the date of loading on board the named vessel or shipment on the named vessel.

Article 21

a. Unless transhipment is prohibited by the terms of the credit, bills of lading will be accepted which indicate that the goods will be transhipped en route, provided the entire voyage is covered by one and the same bill of lading.

b. Bills of lading incorporating printed clauses stating that the carriers have the right to tranship will be accepted notwithstanding the fact that the credit prohibits transhipment.

Article 22

a. Banks will refuse a bill of lading stating that the goods are loaded on deck, unless specifically authorized in the credit.

b. Banks will not refuse a bill of lading which contains a provision that the goods may be carried on deck, provided it does not specifically state that they are loaded on deck.

C.1.2. Combined transport documents

Article 23

a. If the credit calls for a combined transport document, i.e. one which provides for a combined transport by at least two different modes of transport, from a place at which the goods are taken in charge to a place designated for delivery, or if the credit provides for a combined transport, but in either case does not specify the form of document required and/or the issuer of such document, banks will accept such documents as tendered.

C.2. Insurance documents

Article 26

a. Insurance documents must be as specified in the credit, and must be issued and/or signed by insurance companies or their agents or by underwriters.

b. Cover notes issued by brokers will not be accepted, unless specifically authorized in the credit.

Article 27. Unless otherwise specified in the credit, or unless the insurance documents presented establish that the cover is effective at the latest from the date of shipment or dispatch or, in the case of combined transport, the date of taking the goods in charge, banks will refuse insurance documents presented which bear a date later than the date of shipment or dispatch or, in the case of combined transport, the date of taking the goods in charge, as evidenced by the shipping documents.

Article 28

a. Unless otherwise specified in the credit, the insurance document must be expressed in the same currency as the credit.

Article 31. Banks will accept an insurance document which indicates that the cover is subject to a franchise or an excess (deductible), unless it is specifically stated in the credit that the insurance must be issued irrespective of percentage.

C.3. Commercial invoices

Article 32

a. Unless otherwise specified in the credit, commercial invoices must be made out in the name of the applicant for the credit.

b. Unless otherwise specified in the credit, banks may refuse commercial invoices issued for amounts in excess of the amount permitted by the credit.

c. The description of the goods in the commercial invoice must correspond with the description in the credit. In all other documents the goods may be described in general terms not inconsistent with the description of the goods in the credit.

Article 33. When other documents are required, such as warehouse receipts, delivery orders, consular invoices, certificates of origin, of weight, of quality or of analysis etc. and when no further definition is given, banks will accept such documents as tendered.

D. Miscellaneous provisions

Quantity and amount

Article 34

a. The words "about", "circa" or similar expressions used in connection with the amount of the credit or the quantity or the unit price of the goods are to be construed as allowing a difference not to exceed 10% more or 10% less.

b. Unless a credit stipulates that the quantity of the goods specified must not be exceeded or reduced a tolerance of 3% more or 3% less will be permissible, always provided that the total amount of the drawings does not exceed the amount of the credit. This tolerance does not apply when the credit specifies quantity in terms of a stated number of packing units or individual items.

b. The minimum amount for which insurance must be effected is the CIF value of the goods concerned. However, when the CIF value of the goods cannot be determined from the documents on their face, banks will accept as such minimum amount the amount of the drawing under the credit or the amount of the relative commercial invoice, whichever is the greater.

Article 29

a. Credits should expressly state the type of insurance required and, if any, the additional risks which are to be covered. Imprecise terms such as "usual risks" or "customary risks" should not be used; however, if such imprecise terms are used, banks will accept insurance documents as tendered.

b. Failing specific instructions, banks will accept insurance cover as tendered.

Article 30. Where a credit stipulates "insurance against all risks", banks will accept an insurance document which contains any "all risks" notation or clause, and will assume no responsibility if any particular risk is not covered.

b. If the combined transport includes transport by sea the document will be accepted although it does not indicate that the goods are on board a named vessel, and although it contains a provision that the goods, if packed in a container, may be carried on deck, provided it does not specifically state that they are loaded on deck.

C.1.3. Other shipping documents, etc.

Article 24. Banks will consider a railway or inland waterway bill of lading or consignment note, counterfoil waybill, postal receipt, certificate of mailing, air mail receipt, air waybill, air consignment note or air receipt, trucking company bill of lading or any other similar document as regular when such document bears the reception stamp of the carrier or his agent, or when it bears a signature purporting to be that of the carrier or his agent.

Article 25. Where a credit calls for an attestation or certification of weight in the case of transport other than by sea, banks will accept a weight stamp or declaration of weight superimposed by the carrier on the shipping document unless the credit calls for a separate or independent certificate of weight.

Partial shipments

Article 35

a. Partial shipments are allowed, unless the credit specifically states otherwise.

b. Shipments made on the same ship and for the same voyage, even if the bills of lading evidencing shipment "on board" bear different dates and/or indicate different ports of shipment, will not be regarded as partial shipments.

Article 36. If shipment by instalments within given periods is stipulated and any instalment is not shipped within the period allowed for that instalment, the credit ceases to be available for that or any subsequent instalments, unless otherwise specified in the credit.

Expiry date

Article 37. All credits, whether revocable or irrevocable, must stipulate an expiry date for presentation of documents for payment, acceptance or negotiation, notwithstanding the stipulation of a latest date for shipment.

wording: "Presented for payment (or acceptance or negotiation as the case may be) within the expiry date extended in accordance with Article 39 of the *Uniform Customs*."

Shipment, loading or dispatch

Article 40

a. Unless the terms of the credit indicate otherwise, the words "departure", "dispatch", "loading" or "sailing" used in stipulating the latest date for shipment of the goods will be understood to be synonymous with "shipment".

b. Expressions such as "prompt", "immediately", "as soon as possible" and the like should not be used. If they are used, banks will interpret them as a request for shipment within thirty days from the date on the advice of the credit to the beneficiary by the issuing bank or by an advising bank, as the case may be.

c. The expression "on or about" and similar expressions will be interpreted as a request for shipment during the period from five days before to five days after the specified date, both end days included.

Article 44. The terms "beginning", "middle", or "end" of a month shall be construed respectively as from the 1st to the 10th, the 11th to the 20th, and the 21st to the last day of each month, inclusive.

Article 45. When a bank issuing a credit instructs that the credit be confirmed or advised as available "for one month", "for six months" or the like, but does not specify the date from which the time is to run, the confirming or advising bank will confirm or advise the credit as expiring at the end of such indicated period from the date of its confirmation or advice.

E. Transfer

Article 46

a. A transferable credit is a credit under which the beneficiary has the right to give instructions to the bank called upon to effect payment or acceptance or to any bank entitled to effect negotiation to make the credit available in whole or in part to one or more third parties (second beneficiaries).

Article 38. The words "to", "until", "till" and words of similar import applying to the stipulated expiry date for presentation of documents for payment, acceptance or negotiation, or to the stipulated latest date for shipment, will be understood to include the date mentioned.

Article 39

a. When the stipulated expiry date falls on a day on which banks are closed for reasons other than those mentioned in Article 11, the expiry date will be extended until the first following business day.

b. The latest date for shipment shall not be extended by reason of the extension of the expiry date in accordance with this Article. Where the credit stipulates a latest date for shipment, shipping documents dated later than such stipulated date will not be accepted. If no latest date for shipment is stipulated in the credit, shipping documents dated later than the expiry date stipulated in the credit or amendments thereto will not be accepted. Documents other than the shipping documents may, however, be dated up to and including the extended expiry date.

c. Banks paying, accepting or negotiating on such extended expiry date must add to the documents their certification in the following

Presentation

Article 41. Notwithstanding the requirement of Article 37 that every credit must stipulate an expiry date for presentation of documents, credits must also stipulate a specified period of time after the date of issuance of the bills of lading or other shipping documents during which presentation of documents for payment, acceptance or negotiation must be made. If no such period of time is stipulated in the credit, banks will refuse documents presented to them later than 21 days after the date of issuance of the bills of lading or other shipping documents.

Article 42. Banks are under no obligation to accept presentation of documents outside their banking hours.

Date terms

Article 43. The terms "first half", "second half" of a month shall be construed respectively as from the 1st to the 15th, and the 16th to the last day of each month, inclusive.

b. The bank requested to effect the transfer, whether it has confirmed the credit or not, shall be under no obligation to effect such transfer except to the extent and in the manner expressly consented to by such bank, and until such bank's charges in respect of transfer are paid.

c. Bank charges in respect of transfers are payable by the first beneficiary unless otherwise specified.

d. A credit can be transferred only if it is expressly designated as "transferable" by the issuing bank. Terms such as "divisible", "fractionable", "assignable" and "transmissible" add nothing to the meaning of the term "transferable" and shall not be used.

e. A transferable credit can be transferred once only. Fractions of a transferable credit (not exceeding in the aggregate the amount of the credit) can be transferred separately, provided partial shipments are not prohibited, and the aggregate of such transfers will be considered as constituting only one transfer of the credit. The credit can be transferred only on the terms and conditions specified in the original credit, with the exception of the amount of the credit, of any unit prices stated therein, and of the period of validity or period for shipment, any or all of which may be reduced or curtailed.

Additionally, the name of the first beneficiary can be substituted for that of the applicant for the credit, but if the name of the applicant for the credit is specifically required by the original credit to appear in any document other than the invoice, such requirement must be fulfilled.

f. The first beneficiary has the right to substitute his own invoices for those of the second beneficiary, for amounts not in excess of the original amount stipulated in the credit and for the original unit prices if stipulated in the credit, and upon such substitution of invoices the first beneficiary can draw under the credit for the difference, if any, between his invoices and the second beneficiary's invoices. When a credit has been transferred and the first beneficiary is to supply his own invoices in exchange for the second beneficiary's invoices but fails to do so on first demand, the paying, accepting or negotiating bank has the right to deliver to the issuing bank the documents received under the credit, including the second beneficiary's invoices, without further responsibility to the first beneficiary.

g. The first beneficiary of a transferable credit can transfer the credit to a second beneficiary in the same country or in another country unless the credit specifically states otherwise. The first beneficiary shall have the right to request that payment or negotiation be effected to the second beneficiary at the place to which the credit has been transferred, up to and including the expiry date of the original credit, and without prejudice to the first beneficiary's right subsequently to substitute his own invoices for those of the second beneficiary and to claim any difference due to him.

Article 47. The fact that a credit is not stated to be transferable shall not affect the beneficiary's rights to assign the proceeds of such credit in accordance with the provisions of the applicable law.

Uniform Rules for the Collection of Commercial Paper

International Chamber of Commerce Brochure No. 254

General provisions and definitions

a. These provisions and definitions and the following articles apply to all collections of commercial paper and are binding upon all parties thereto unless otherwise expressly agreed or unless contrary to the provisions of a national, state or local law and/or regulation which cannot be departed from.

b. For the purpose of such provisions, definitions and articles:

(i) "Commercial paper" consists of clean remittances and documentary remittances.

"Clean remittances" means items consisting of one or more bills of exchange, whether already accepted or not, promissory notes, cheques, receipts, or other similar documents for obtaining the payment of money (there being neither invoices, shipping documents, documents of title, or other similar documents, nor any other documents whatsoever attached to the said items).

"Documentary remittances" means all other commercial paper, with documents attached to be delivered against payment, acceptance, trust receipt or other letter of commitment, free or on other terms and conditions.

(ii) The "parties thereto" are the principal who entrusts the operation of collection to his bank (the customer), the said bank (the remitting bank), and the correspondent commissioned by the remitting bank to see to the acceptance or collection of the commercial paper (the collecting bank).

(iii) The "drawee" is the party specified in the remittance letter as the one to whom the commercial paper is to be presented.

c. All commercial paper sent for collection must be accompanied by a remittance letter giving complete and precise instructions. Banks are only permitted to act upon the instructions given in such remittance letter.

If the collecting bank cannot, for any reason, comply with the instructions given in the remittance letter received by it, it must advise the remitting bank immediately.

Presentation

Article 1.–Commercial paper is to be presented to the drawee in the form in which it is received from the customer, except that the collecting bank is to affix any necessary stamps, at customer's expense unless otherwise instructed.

Remitting and collecting banks have no obligation to examine the commercial paper or the accompanying documents if any, and they assume no responsibility for the form and/or regularity thereof.

Article 2.–Commercial paper should bear the complete address of the drawee or of the domicile at which the collecting bank is to make the presentation. If the address is incomplete or incorrect, the collecting bank may, without obligation and responsibility on its part, endeavour to ascertain the proper address.

Article 3.–In the case of commercial paper payable at sight the collecting bank must make presentation for payment without delay.

In the case of commercial paper payable at a usance other than sight the collecting bank must, where acceptance is called for, make presentation for acceptance without delay, and must, in every instance, make presentation for payment not later than the appropriate maturity date.

Article 4.–In respect of a documentary remittance accompanied by a bill of exchange payable at a future date, the remittance letter should state whether the documents are to be released to the drawee against acceptance (D/A) or against payment (D/P). In the absence of instructions, the documents will be released only against payment.

419

Payment

Article 5.—In the case of commercial paper expressed to be payable in the currency of the country of payment (local currency) the collecting bank will only release the commercial paper to the drawee against payment in local currency which can immediately be disposed of in accordance with the instructions given in the remittance letter.

Article 6.—In the case of commercial paper expressed to be payable in a currency other than that of the country of payment (foreign currency) the collecting bank will only release the commercial paper to the drawee against payment in the relative foreign currency which can immediately be remitted in accordance with the instructions given in the remittance letter.

Article 7.—In respect of clean remittances partial payments may be accepted if and to the extent to which and on the conditions on which partial payments are authorized by the law in force in the place of payment. The clean remittance will only be released to the drawee

the event of non-acceptance or non-payment.

In the absence of such specific instructions the banks concerned with the collection are not responsible for any failure to have the commercial paper protested (or subjected to legal process in lieu thereof) for non-payment or non-acceptance.

The collecting bank is not responsible for the regularity of the form of the protest (or other legal process).

Case-of-need (customer's representative) and protection of goods

Article 10.—If the customer nominates a representative to act as case-of-need in the event of non-acceptance and/or non-payment the remittance letter should clearly and fully indicate the powers of such case-of-need.

Whether a case-of-need is nominated or not, in the absence of specific instructions the collecting bank has no obligation to take any action in respect of the goods represented by a documentary remittance.

without collecting charges and/or expenses. In such a case collection charges and/or expenses will be for account of the customer.

Article 15.—In all cases where in the express terms of a collection, or under these Rules, disbursements and/or expenses and/or collection charges are to be borne by the customer, the collecting bank is entitled to recover its outlay in respect of disbursements and expenses and its charges from the remitting bank and the remitting bank has the right to recover from the customer any amount so paid out by it, together with its own disbursements, expenses and charges.

Liabilities and responsibilities

Article 16.—Banks utilizing the services of another bank for the purpose of giving effect to the instructions of the customer do so for the account of and at the risk of the latter.

Banks are free to utilize as collecting bank any of their correspondent banks in the country of payment or acceptance.

If the customer nominates the collecting

when full payment thereof has been received.

In respect of documentary remittances partial payments will only be accepted if specifically authorized in the remittance letter, but unless otherwise instructed the collecting bank will only release the documents to the drawee after full payment has been received.

In all cases where partial payments are acceptable, either by reason of a specific authorization or in accordance with the provisions of this Article, such partial payments will be received and dealt with in accordance with the provisions of Articles 5 and 6.

Acceptance

Article 8.—The collecting bank is responsible for seeing that the form of the acceptance appears to be complete and correct, but is not responsible for the genuineness of any signature or for the authority of any signatory to sign the acceptance.

Protest

Article 9.—The remittance letter should give specific instructions regarding legal process in

Advice of fate, etc.

Article 11.—The collecting bank is to send advice of payment or advice of acceptance, with appropriate detail, to the remitting bank without delay.

Article 12.—The collecting bank is to send advice of non-payment or advice of non-acceptance, with appropriate detail, to the remitting bank without delay.

Article 13.—In the absence of specific instructions the collecting bank is to send all advices or information to the remitting bank by quickest mail.

If, however, the collecting bank considers the matter to be urgent, it may advise by other quicker methods at the customer's expense.

Charges and expenses

Article 14.—If the remittance letter includes an instruction that collection charges and/or expenses are to be for account of the drawee and the drawee refuses to pay them, the collecting bank, unless expressly instructed to the contrary, may deliver the commercial paper against payment or acceptance as the case may be

bank, the remitting bank nevertheless has the right to direct the commercial paper to such nominated collecting bank through a correspondent bank of its own choice.

Article 17.—Banks concerned with a collection of commercial paper assume no liability or responsibility for the consequences arising out of delay and/or loss in transit of any messages, letters or documents, or for delay, mutilation or other errors arising in the transmission of cables, telegrams or telex, or for errors in translation or interpretation of technical terms.

Article 18.—Banks concerned with a collection of commercial paper assume no liability or responsibility for consequences arising out of the interruption of their business by strikes, lock-outs, riots, civil commotions, insurrections, wars, acts of God or any other causes beyond their control.

Article 19.—In the event of goods being despatched direct to the address of a bank for delivery to a drawee against payment or acceptance or upon other terms without prior agreement on the part of that bank, the bank has no obligation to take delivery of the goods, which remain at the risk and responsibility of the party despatching the goods.

Revised American Foreign Trade Definitions – 1941

Adopted July 30, 1941 by a Joint Committee representing the Chamber of Commerce of the United States of America, the National Council of American Importers, Inc., and the National Foreign Trade Council, Inc.

Foreword

Since the issuance of *American Foreign Trade Definitions* in 1919, many changes in practice have occurred. The 1919 Definitions did much to clarify and simplify foreign trade practice, and received wide recognition and use by buyers and sellers throughout the world. At the Twenty-Seventh National Foreign Trade Convention, 1940, further revision and clarification of these Definitions were urged as necessary to assist the foreign trader in the handling of his transactions.

The following *Revised American Foreign Trade Definitions–1941* are recommended for general use by both exporters and importers. These revised Definitions have no status at law unless there is specific legislation providing for them, or unless they are confirmed by court decisions. Hence, it is suggested that sellers and buyers agree to their acceptance as part of the contract of sale. These revised Definitions will then become legally binding upon all parties.

In view of changes in practice and procedure since 1919, certain new responsibilities for sellers and buyers are included in these revised

Interest), C.I.F. Landed (Cost, Insurance, Freight, Landed), and others. None of these should be used unless there has first been a definite understanding as to the exact meaning thereof. It is unwise to attempt to interpret other terms in the light of the terms given herein. Hence, whenever possible, one of the terms defined herein should be used.

3. It is unwise to use abbreviations in quotations or in contracts which might be subject to misunderstanding.

4. When making quotations, the familiar terms "hundredweight" or "ton," should be avoided. A hundredweight can be 100 pounds of the short ton, or 112 pounds of the long ton. A ton can be a short ton of 2,000 pounds, or a metric ton of 2,204.6 pounds, or a long ton of 2,240 pounds. Hence, the type of hundredweight or ton should be clearly stated in quotations and in sales confirmations. Also, all terms referring to quantity, weight, volume, length, or surface should be clearly defined and agreed upon.

5. If inspection, or certificate of inspection, is required, it should be agreed, in advance, whether the cost thereof is for account of seller or buyer.

6. Unless otherwise agreed upon, all expenses are for the account of seller up to the point at which the buyer must handle the subsequent movement of goods.

Buyer must

(1) take delivery of the goods as soon as they have been placed at his disposal at the agreed place on the date or within the period fixed;

(2) pay export taxes, or other fees or charges, if any, levied because of exportation;

(3) bear all costs and risks of the goods from the time when he is obligated to take delivery thereof;

(4) pay all costs and charges incurred in obtaining documents issued in the country of origin, or of shipment, or of both, which may be required for purposes of exportation or of importation at destination.

II. F.O.B. (free on board)

Note: Seller and buyer should consider not only the definitions but also the "Comments on all F.O.B. terms" at the end of this section in order to understand fully their respective responsibilities and rights under the several classes of "F.O.B." terms.

II-A. F.O.B. (named inland carrier at named inland point of departure). Under this term, the price quoted applies only at inland shipping point, and the seller arranges for loading of the goods on, or in, railway cars, trucks, lighters, barges, aircraft, or other conveyance furnished for transportation. Under this quotation:

Seller must

Definitions. Also, in many instances, the old responsibilities are more clearly defined than in the 1919 Definitions, and the changes should be beneficial to both sellers and buyers. Widespread acceptance will lead to a greater standardization of foreign trade procedure, and to the avoidance of much misunderstanding.

Adoption by exporters and importers of these revised terms will impress on all parties concerned their respective responsibilities and rights.

General notes of caution

1. As foreign trade definitions have been issued by organizations in various parts of the world, and as the courts of countries have interpreted these definitions in different ways, it is important that sellers and buyers agree that their contracts are subject to the *Revised American Foreign Trade Definitions—1941* and that the various points listed are accepted by both parties.

2. In addition to the foreign trade terms listed herein, there are terms that are at times used, such as Free Harbor, C.I.F. & C. (Cost, Insurance, Freight, and Commission), C.I.F.C. & I. (Cost, Insurance, Freight, Commission, and

7. There are a number of elements in a contract that do not fall within the scope of these foreign trade definitions. Hence, no mention of these is made herein. Seller and buyer should agree to these separately when negotiating contracts. This particularly applies to so-called "customary" practices.

Definition of quotations

I. Ex (point of origin)

"Ex factory," "ex mill," "ex mine," "ex plantation," "ex warehouse," etc. (named point of origin). Under this term, the price quoted applies only at the point of origin, and the seller agrees to place the goods at the disposal of the buyer at the agreed place on the date or within the period fixed. Under this quotation:

Seller must
(1) bear all costs and risks of the goods until such time as the buyer is obliged to take delivery thereof;
(2) render the buyer, at the buyer's request and expense, assistance in obtaining the documents issued in the country of origin, or of shipment, or of both, which the buyer may require for purposes of exportation or of importation at destination.

(1) place goods on, or in, conveyance, or delivery or to inland carrier for loading;
(2) provide clean bill of lading or other transportation receipt, freight collect;
(3) be responsible for any loss or damage, or both, until goods have been placed in, or on, conveyance at loading point, and clean bill of lading or other transportation receipt has been furnished by the carrier;
(4) render the buyer, at the buyer's request and expense, assistance in obtaining the documents issued in the country of origin, or of shipment, or of both, which the buyer may require for purposes of exportation or of importation at destination.

Buyer must
(1) be responsible for all movement of the goods from inland point of loading, and pay all transportation costs;
(2) pay export taxes, or other fees or charges, if any, levied because of exportation;
(3) be responsible for any loss or damage, or both, incurred after loading at named inland point of departure;
(4) pay all costs and charges incurred in obtaining documents issued in the country of origin, or of shipment, or of both, which

may be required for purposes of exportation or of importation at destination.

II-B. F.O.B. (named inland carrier at named inland point of departure) freight prepaid to (named point of exportation). Under this term, the seller quotes a price including transportation charges to the named point of exportation and prepays freight to named point of exportation, without assuming responsibility for the goods after obtaining a clean bill of lading or other transportation receipt at named inland point of departure. Under this quotation:

Seller must
(1) assume the seller's obligations as under II-A (above), except that under (2) he must provide clean bill of lading or other transportation receipt, freight prepaid to named point of exportation.

Buyer must
(1) assume the same buyer's obligations as under II-A (above), except that he does not pay freight from loading point to named point of exportation.

load within the designated time:
(3) handle all subsequent movement of the goods to destination:
  (a) provide and pay for insurance;
  (b) provide and pay for ocean and other transportation;
(4) pay export taxes, or other fees or charges, if any, levied because of exportation;
(5) be responsible for any loss or damage, or both, after goods have been loaded on board the vessel;
(6) pay all costs and charges incurred in obtaining the documents, other than clean ship's receipt or bill of lading, issued in the country of origin, or of shipment, or of both, which may be required either for purposes of exportation, or of importation at destination.

II-F. F.O.B. (named inland point in country of importation). Under this term, the seller quotes a price including the cost of the merchandise and all costs of transportation to the named inland point in the country of importation.
Under this quotation:
Seller must

costs from loading point to named point of exportation;
(3) be responsible for any loss or damage, or both, until goods have arrived in, or on, inland conveyance at the named point of exportation;
(4) render the buyer, at the buyer's request and expense, assistance in obtaining the documents issued in the country of origin, or of shipment, or of both, which the buyer may require for purposes of exportation, or of importation at destination.

Buyer must
(1) be responsible for all movement of the goods from inland conveyance at named point of exportation;
(2) pay export taxes, or other fees or charges, if any, levied because of exportation;
(3) be responsible for any loss or damage, or both, incurred after goods have arrived in, or on, inland conveyance at the named point of exportation;
(4) pay all costs and charges incurred in obtaining documents issued in the country of origin, or of shipment, or of both, which may be required for purposes of exportation, or of importation at destination.

II-C. F.O.B. (named inland carrier at named inland point of departure) freight allowed to (named point). Under this term, the seller quotes a price including the transportation charges to the named point, shipping freight collect and deducting the cost of transportation, without assuming responsibility for the goods after obtaining a clean bill of lading or other transportation receipt at named inland point of departure. Under this quotation:

Seller must

(1) assume the same seller's obligations as under II-A (above), but deducts from his invoice the transportation cost to named point of exportation.

Buyer must

(1) assume the same buyer's obligation as under II-A (above), including payment of freight from inland loading point to named point, for which seller has made deduction from invoice.

II-D. F.O.B. (named inland carrier at named point of exportation). Under this term, the seller quotes a price including the costs of transportation of the goods to named point of exportation, bearing any loss or damage, or both, incurred up to that point. Under this quotation:

Seller must

(1) place goods on, or in, conveyance, or deliver to inland carrier for loading;

(2) provide clean bill of lading or other transportation receipt, paying all transportation

II-E. F.O.B. vessel (named port of shipment). Under this term, the seller quotes a price covering all expenses up to and including delivery of the goods upon the overseas vessel provided by, or for, the buyer at the named port of shipment. Under this quotation:

Seller must

(1) pay all charges incurred in placing goods actually on board the vessel designated and provided by, or for, the buyer on the date or within the period fixed;

(2) provide clean ship's receipt or on-board bill of lading;

(3) be responsible for any loss or damage, or both, until goods have been placed on board the vessel on the date or within the period fixed;

(4) render the buyer, at the buyer's request and expense, assistance in obtaining the documents issued in the country of origin, or of shipment, or of both, which the buyer may require for purposes of exportation, or of importation at destination.

Buyer must

(1) give seller adequate notice of name, sailing date, loading berth of, and delivery time to, the vessel;

(2) bear the additional costs incurred and all risks of the goods from the time when the seller has placed them at his disposal if the vessel named by him fails to arrive or to

(1) provide and pay for all transportation to the named inland point in the country of importation;

(2) pay export taxes, or other fees or charges, if any, levied because of exportation;

(3) provide and pay for marine insurance;

(4) provide and pay for war risk insurance, unless otherwise agreed upon between the seller and buyer;

(5) be responsible for any loss or damage, or both, until arrival of goods on conveyance at the named inland point in the country of importation;

(6) pay the costs of certificates of origin, consular invoices, or any other documents issued in the country of origin, or of shipment, or of both, which the buyer may require for the importation of goods into the country of destination and, where necessary, for their passage in transit through another country;

(7) pay all costs of landing, including wharfage, landing charges, and taxes, if any;

(8) pay all costs of customs entry in the country of importation;

(9) pay customs duties and all taxes applicable to imports, if any, in the country of importation.

Note: The seller under this quotation must realize that he is accepting important responsibilities, costs and risks, and should therefore be certain to obtain adequate insurance. On the other hand, the importer or buyer may desire such quotations to relieve him of the risks of the voyage and to assure him of his landed costs at inland point in country of importation. When competition is keen, or the buyer is accustomed to such quotations from other sellers, seller may quote such terms, being careful to protect himself in an appropriate manner.

Buyer must
(1) take prompt delivery of goods from conveyance upon arrival at destination;
(2) bear any costs and be responsible for all loss or damage, or both, after arrival at destination.

Comments on all F.O.B. terms

In connection with F.O.B. terms, the following points of caution are recommended:

1. The method of inland transportation, such as trucks, railroad cars, lighters, barges, or aircraft should be specified.

2. If any switching charges are involved during the inland transportation, it should be agreed, in advance, whether these charges are for account of the seller or the buyer.

3. The term "F.O.B. (named port)," without designating the exact point at which the liability of the seller terminates and the liability of the buyer begins, should be avoided. The use of this term gives rise to disputes as to the liability

ance obtained by the buyer include standard warehouse to warehouse coverage.

III. F.A.S. (free along side)

Note: Seller and buyer should consider not only the definitions but also the "comments" at the end of this section in order to understand fully their respective responsibilities and rights under "F.A.S." terms:

F.A.S. vessel (named port of shipment). Under this term, the seller quotes a price including delivery of the goods along side overseas vessel and within reach of its loading tackle. Under this quotation:

Seller must
(1) place goods along side vessel or on dock designated and provided by, or for, buyer on the date or within the period fixed; pay any heavy lift charges, where necessary, up to this point;
(2) provide clean dock or ship's receipt;
(3) be responsible for any loss or damage, or both, until goods have been delivered along side the vessel or on the dock;
(4) render the buyer, at the buyer's request and expense, assistance in obtaining the documents issued in the country of origin, or of shipment, or of both, which the buyer may require for purposes of exportation, or of importation at destination.

F.A.S. comments

1. Under F.A.S. terms, the obligation to obtain ocean freight space, and marine and war risk insurance, rests with the buyer. Despite this obligation on the part of the buyer, in many trades the seller obtains ocean freight space, and marine and war risk insurance, and provides for shipment on behalf of the buyer. In others, the buyer notifies the seller to make delivery along side a vessel designated by the buyer and the buyer provides his own marine and war risk insurance. Hence, seller and buyer must have an understanding as to whether the buyer will obtain the ocean freight space, and marine and war risk insurance, as is his obligation, or whether the seller agrees to do this for the buyer.

2. For the seller's protection, he should provide in his contract of sale that marine insurance obtained by the buyer include standard warehouse to warehouse coverage.

IV. C. & F. (cost and freight)

Note: Seller and buyer should consider not only the definitions but also the "C. & F. comments" at the end of this section and the "C. & F. and C.I.F. comments" at the end of the next section in order to understand fully their respective responsibilities and rights under "C. & F." terms.

of the seller or the buyer in the event of loss or damage arising while the goods are in port, and before delivery to or on board the ocean carrier. Misunderstandings may be avoided by naming the specific point of delivery.

4. If lighterage or trucking is required in the transfer of goods from the inland conveyance to ship's side, and there is a cost therefor, it should be understood, in advance, whether this cost is for account of seller or buyer.

5. The seller should be certain to notify the buyer of the minimum quantity required to obtain carload, truckload, or bargeload freight rate.

6. Under F.O.B. terms, excepting "F.O.B. (named inland point in country of importation)," the obligation to obtain ocean freight space, and marine and war risk insurance, rests with the buyer. Despite this obligation on the part of the buyer, in many trades the seller obtains the ocean freight space, and marine and war risk insurance, and provides for shipment on behalf of the buyer. Hence, seller and buyer must have an understanding as to whether the buyer will obtain the ocean freight space, and marine and war risk insurance, as is his obligation, or whether the seller agrees to do this for the buyer.

7. For the seller's protection, he should provide in his contract of sale that marine insur-

Buyer must
(1) give seller adequate notice of name, sailing date, loading berth of, and delivery time to, the vessel;
(2) handle all subsequent movement of the goods from along side the vessel:
   (a) arrange and pay for demurrage or storage charges, or both, in warehouse or on wharf, where necessary;
   (b) provide and pay for insurance;
   (c) provide and pay for ocean and other transportation;
(3) pay export taxes, or other fees or charges, if any, levied because of exportation;
(4) be responsible for any loss or damage, or both, while the goods are on a lighter or other conveyance along side vessel within reach of its loading tackle, or on the dock awaiting loading, or until actually loaded on board vessel, and subsequent thereto;
(5) pay all costs and charges incurred in obtaining documents, other than clean dock or ship's receipt, issued in the country of origin, or of shipment, or of both, which may be required for purposes of exportation, or of importation at destination.

C. & F. (named point of destination). Under this term, the seller quotes a price including the cost of transporation to the named point of destination. Under this quotation:
Seller must
(1) provide and pay for transportation to named point of destination;
(2) pay export taxes, or other fees or charges, if any, levied because of exportation;
(3) obtain and dispatch promptly to buyer, or his agent, clean bill of lading to named point of destination;
(4) where received-for-shipment ocean bill of lading may be tendered, be responsible for any loss or damage, or both, until the goods have been delivered into the custody of the ocean carrier;
(5) where on-board ocean bill of lading is required, be responsible for any loss or damage, or both, until the goods have been delivered on board the vessel;
(6) provide, at the buyer's request and expense, certificates of origin, consular invoices, or any other documents issued in the country of origin, or of shipment, or of both, which the buyer may require for importation of goods into country of des-

tination and, where necessary, for their passage in transit through another country.

Buyer must

(1) accept the documents when presented;

(2) receive goods upon arrival, handle and pay for all subsequent movement of the goods, including taking delivery from vessel in accordance with bill of lading clauses and terms; pay all costs of landing, including any duties, taxes, and other expenses at named point of destination;

(3) provide and pay for insurance;

(4) be responsible for loss of or damage to goods, or both, from time and place at which seller's obligations under (4) or (5) above have ceased;

(5) pay the costs of certificates of origin, consular invoices, or any other documents issued in the country of origin, or of shipment, or of both, which may be required for the importation of goods into the country of destination and, where necessary, for their passage in transit through another country.

C. & F. comments

1. For the seller's protection, he should provide in his contract of sale that marine insurance obtained by the buyer include standard warehouse to warehouse coverage.

(5) obtain and dispatch promptly to buyer, or his agent, clean bill of lading to named point of destination, and also insurance policy or negotiable insurance certificate;

(6) where received-for-shipment ocean bill of lading may be tendered, be responsible for any loss or damage, or both, until the goods have been delivered into the custody of the ocean carrier;

(7) where on-board ocean bill of lading is required, be responsible for any loss or damage, or both, until the goods have been delivered on board the vessel;

(8) provide, at the buyer's request and expense, certificates of origin, consular invoices, or any other documents issued in the country of origin, or of shipment, or of both, which the buyer may require for importation of goods into country of destination and, where necessary, for their passage in transit through another country.

Buyer must

(1) accept the documents when presented;

(2) receive the goods upon arrival, handle and pay for all subsequent movement of the goods, including taking delivery from vessel in accordance with bill of lading clauses and terms; pay all duties, taxes, and other expenses at named point of destination;

3. Although the terms C. & F. and C.I.F. are generally interpreted to provide that charges for consular invoices and certificates of origin are for the account of the buyer, and are charged separately, in many trades these charges are included by the seller in his price. Hence, seller and buyer should agree, in advance, whether these charges are part of the selling price, or will be invoiced separately.

4. The point of final destination should be definitely known in the event the vessel discharges at a port other than the actual destination of the goods.

5. When ocean freight space is difficult to obtain, or forward freight contracts cannot be made at firm rates, it is advisable that sales contracts, as an exception to regular C. & F. or C.I.F. terms, should provide that shipment within the contract period be subject to ocean freight space being available to the seller, and should also provide that changes in the cost of ocean transportation between the time of sale and the time of shipment be for account of the buyer.

6. Normally, the seller is obligated to prepay the ocean freight. In some instances, shipments are made freight collect and the amount of the freight is deducted from the invoice rendered by the seller. It is necessary to be in agreement on this, in advance, in order to avoid misunder-

2. The comments on C.I.F. terms (next section) in many cases apply to C. & F. terms as well, and should be read and understood by the C. & F. seller and buyer.

V. C.I.F. (cost, insurance, freight)

Note: Seller and buyer should consider not only the definitions but also the "comments" at the end of this section, in order to understand fully their respective responsibilities and rights under "C.I.F." terms.

C.I.F. (named point of destination). Under this term, the seller quotes a price including the cost of the goods, the marine insurance, and all transportation charges to the named point of destination. Under this quotation:
Seller must

(1) provide and pay for transportation to named point of destination;

(2) pay export taxes, or other fees or charges, if any, levied because of exportation;

(3) provide and pay for marine insurance;

(4) provide war risk insurance as obtainable in seller's market at time of shipment at buyer's expense, unless seller has agreed that buyer provide for war risk coverage (See Comment 10(c), below);

(3) pay for war risk insurance provided by the seller;

(4) be responsible for loss of or damage to goods, or both, from time and place at which seller's obligations under (6) or (7) above have ceased;

(5) pay the costs of certificates of origin, consular invoices, or any other documents issued in the country of origin, or of shipment, or of both, which may be required for importation of the goods into the country of destination and, where necessary, for their passage in transit through another country.

C. & F. and C.I.F. comments

Under C. & F. and C.I.F. contracts there are the following points on which the seller and the buyer should be in complete agreement at the time that the contract is concluded:

1. It should be agreed upon, in advance, who is to pay for miscellaneous expenses, such as weighing or inspection charges.

2. The quantity to be shipped on any one vessel should be agreed upon, in advance, with a view to the buyer's capacity to take delivery upon arrival and discharge of vessel, within the free time allowed at port of importation.

standing which arises from foreign exchange fluctuations which might affect the actual cost of transportation, and from interest charges which might accrue under letter of credit financing. Hence, the seller should always prepay the ocean freight unless he has a specific agreement with the buyer, in advance, that goods can be shipped freight collect.

7. The buyer should recognize that he does not have the right to insist on inspection of goods prior to accepting the documents. The buyer should not refuse to take delivery of goods on account of delay in the receipt of documents, provided the seller has used due diligence in their dispatch through the regular channels.

8. Sellers and buyers are advised against including in a C.I.F. contract any indefinite clause at variance with the obligations of a C.I.F. contract as specified in these Definitions. There have been numerous court decisions in the United States and other countries invalidating C.I.F. contracts because of the inclusion of indefinite clauses.

9. Interest charges should be included in cost computations and should not be charged as a separate item in C.I.F. contracts, unless otherwise agreed upon, in advance, between the sel-

ler and buyer; in which case, however, the term C.I.F. & I. (cost, insurance, freight, and interest) should be used.

10. In connection with insurance under C.I.F. sales, it is necessary that seller and buyer be definitely in accord upon the following points:

(a) The character of the marine insurance should be agreed upon in so far as being W.A. (with average) or F.P.A. (free of particular average), as well as any other special risks that are covered in specific trades, or against which the buyer may wish individual protection. Among the special risks that should be considered and agreed upon between seller and buyer are theft, pilferage, leakage, breakage, sweat, contact with other cargoes, and others peculiar to any particular trade. It is important that contingent or collect freight and customs duty should be insured to cover particular average losses, as well as total loss after arrival and entry but before delivery.

(b) The seller is obligated to exercise ordinary care and diligence in selecting an underwriter that is in good financial standing. However, the risk of obtaining settlement of insurance claims rests with the buyer.

(e) Seller and buyer should be in accord as to the insured valuation, bearing in mind that merchandise contributes in general average on certain bases of valuation which differ in various trades. It is desirable that a competent insurance broker be consulted, in order that full value be covered and trouble avoided.

VI. Ex dock

Note: Seller and buyer should consider not only the definitions but also the "comments" at the end of this section in order to understand fully their respective responsibilities and rights under "ex dock" terms.

Ex dock (named port of importation). Under this term, seller quotes a price including the cost of the goods and all additional costs necessary to place the goods on the dock at the named port of importation, duty paid, if any. Under this quotation:
Seller must
(1) provide and pay for transportation to named port of importation;
(2) pay export taxes, or other fees or charges, if any, levied because of exportation;
(3) provide and pay for marine insurance;

destination and, where necessary, for their passage in transit through another country;
(7) pay all costs of landing, including wharfage, landing charges and taxes, if any;
(8) pay all costs of customs entry in the country of importation;
(9) pay customs duties and all taxes applicable to imports, if any, in the country of importation, unless otherwise agreed upon.
Buyer must
(1) take delivery of the goods on the dock at the named port of importation within the free time allowed;
(2) bear the cost and risk of the goods if delivery is not taken within the free time allowed.

Ex dock comments

This term is used principally in United States import trade. It has various modifications, such as "ex quay," "ex pier," etc., but is seldom if ever used in American export practice. Its use in quotations for export is not recommended.

(c) War risk insurance under this term is to be obtained by the seller at the expense and risk of the buyer. It is important that the seller be in definite accord with the buyer on this point, particularly as to the cost. It is desirable that the goods be insured against both marine and war risk with the same underwriter, so that there can be no difficulty arising from the determination of the cause of the loss.

(d) Seller should make certain that in his marine or war risk insurance there be included the standard protection against strikes, riots and civil commotions.

(4) provide and pay for war risk insurance, unless otherwise agreed upon between the buyer and seller;

(5) be responsible for any loss or damage, or both, until the expiration of the free time allowed on the dock at the named port of importation;

(6) pay the costs of certificates of origin, consular invoices, legalization of bill of lading, or any other documents issued in the country of origin, or of shipment, or of both, which the buyer may require for the importation of goods into the country of

Incoterms 1953

In addition to the *Revised American Foreign Trade Definitions – 1941*, exporters occasionally may receive sales contracts which specify that the contract is subject to "Incoterms 1953." The Vienna Congress of the International Chamber of Commerce in 1953 revised various terms commonly used in international sales contracts. The definitions of these terms may be obtained from the United States Council of the International Chamber of Commerce at 1212 Avenue of the Americas, New York, N.Y. 10036.

Arbitration clause

Many exporters and importers make it a condition in their contracts that any dispute shall be settled by arbitration under the rules of the American Arbitration Association. For this purpose, the following standard arbitration clause has been suggested by the Association to be inserted in contracts:

Any controversy or claim arising out of or relating to this contract, or the breach there-

of, shall be settled by arbitration in accordance with the Rules of the American Arbitration Association, and judgment upon the award rendered by the Arbitrator(s) may be entered in any Court having jurisdiction thereof.

This procedure of submitting differences to impartial arbitration has contributed to the maintenance of good will between buyer and seller. The awards resulting from such arbitration are recognized by courts in the United States and in many other countries. The rules and procedure for such arbitration are readily available by application to the American Arbitration Association, 140 West 51st Street, New York, N.Y. 10020.

Index _____